This book provides a clear and well-informed guide to French history from the early middle ages, with the emergence of a strong state in the Ile-de-France, to the *trente glorieuses* following the Second World War and the more difficult years which followed, including the Chirac presidency. It provides the most up-to-date and comprehensive study of French history available.

Among the book's central themes are the relationship between state and society, the impact of war and such crucial questions as who possessed political power, how this power was used, and in whose interests and with what consequences. It takes account of the great figures of French history, including Philip Augustus, Henri IV, Louis XIV, the two Napoleons, Clemenceau and De Gaulle, and also the findings of modern social historians concerned with the life and death of ordinary people, the passing of generations, social structures, beliefs, and economic activity. This is a rich and entertaining guide to France for the student and general reader.

CAMBRIDGE CONCISE HISTORIES

A Concise History of France

CAMBRIDGE CONCISE HISTORIES

This is a series of illustrated 'concise histories' of selected individual countries, intended both as university and college textbooks and as general historical introductions for general readers, travellers and members of the business community.

First titles in the series:

A Concise History of Germany
MARY FULBROOK

A Concise History of Greece
RICHARD CLOGG

A Concise History of France
ROGER PRICE

A Concise History of Britain, 1707–1795
W. A. SPECK

A Concise History of Portugal
DAVID BIRMINGHAM

A Concise History of Italy
CHRISTOPHER DUGGAN

A Concise History of Bulgaria
RICHARD CRAMPTON

A Concise History of South Africa
ROBERT ROSS

A Concise History of Brazil
BORIS FAUSTO

A Concise History of Mexico
BRIAN HAMNETT

A Concise History of Australia
STUART MACINTYRE

A Concise History of Hungary
MIKLÓS MOLNÁR

A Concise History of Poland
JERZY LUKOWSKI *and* HUBERT ZAWADZKI

Other titles are in preparation

A Concise History of France

ROGER PRICE

Professor of Modern History, University of Wales, Aberystwyth

CAMBRIDGE
UNIVERSITY PRESS

PUBLISHED BY THE PRESS SYNDICATE OF THE UNIVERSITY OF CAMBRIDGE
The Pitt Building, Trumpington Street, Cambridge, United Kingdom

CAMBRIDGE UNIVERSITY PRESS
The Edinburgh Building, Cambridge CB2 2RU, UK
40 West 20th Street, New York, NY 10011–4211, USA
10 Stamford Road, Oakleigh, VIC 3166, Australia
Ruiz de Alarcón 13, 28014 Madrid, Spain
Dock House, The Waterfront, Cape Town 8001, South Africa

http://www.cambridge.org

First published 1993
Reprinted 1993, 1994, 1995, 1997, 1999, 2001

Printed in the United Kingdom at the University Press, Cambridge

A catalogue record for this book is available from the British Library

Library of Congress Cataloguing in Publication data
Price, Roger, 1944–
A concise history of France/Roger Price.
p. cm. (Cambridge concise histories.)
Includes bibliographical references and index.
ISBN 0 521 36239 3 (hardback). ISBN 0 521 36809 X (paperback)
1. France–History. I. Title. II. Series.
DC38.P75 1992
944–dc20 91-45577 CIP

ISBN 0 521 36239 3 hardback
ISBN 0 521 36809 X paperback

CONTENTS

PLATES

FIGURES

ACKNOWLEDGEMENTS

The author of a general work of this kind owes a great deal to many people, including the students taking my seminars at the University of East Anglia since 1968, colleagues past and present, and the staff of the university library. The School of Modern Languages and European History has been extremely generous in allowing study leave and providing financial assistance in support of research. I am especially grateful to William Davies of Cambridge University Press for setting me the challenge in the first place, and to the following friends who read and commented on the manuscript – Heather Price; Oliver Logan of the University of East Anglia; Malcolm Crook of Keele University and Colin Heywood and Peter Morris of the University of Nottingham. Richard Johnson at the University of East Anglia drew some of the maps with his usual efficiency and Mary Richards as copy-editor for Cambridge University Press made a number of extremely helpful suggestions. The cover illustration was suggested by Heather Price during a visit to the Musée Rodin in Paris.

My father and mother have always supported and encouraged me. I can never thank them enough. Robert and Jane Frugère have been constant friends over very many years.

My main source of inspiration remains life with Heather, Richard, Siân, Emily, and Hannah. For their constructive criticism, their patience, their love and for laughter I am profoundly grateful.

INTRODUCTION

The entity we know as France is the product of a centuries' long evolution, during which a complex of regional societies were welded together by political action, by the desire for territorial aggrandisement of a succession of monarchs, ministers and soldiers. There was nothing inevitable about the outcome. It was far from being a linear development, and we must try to avoid a teleological approach to explaining its course. The central feature was the emergence of a relatively strong state in the Ile-de-France and the expansion of its authority. Our task is to explain how and why this occurred.

The invitation to write a book covering such a broad chronological period raises both attractive and daunting prospects. It represents an opportunity to set the normally more restricted concerns of the professional historian within a broad historical context, but also creates major problems of perspective and of approach. Every history is selective, but none more so than a work covering so many centuries. The problem is what to select, how best to make sense of the chaos of events, of the succession of generations which is at the heart of history, how to define historical time and the shifting boundaries between continuity and change. A descriptive, chronologically organised political history would be possible, but would run the risk of turning into a meaningless catalogue of great men and their acts. It would also ignore the renewal of historical studies associated in particular with a series of great French historians: Marc Bloch and Lucien Febvre, founders of the so-called *Annales* school; Fernand Braudel, their successor, whose sense of place re-affirmed the geographical dimension

of history; Ernest Labrousse, who did so much to set the French
Revolution within its socio-economic context; and more recently
Georges Duby, the medievalist, Emmanuel Le Roy Ladurie, most of
whose work has focused on the early modern period, and Maurice
Agulhon, the historian of the nineteenth century, all of whom have
insisted on the regional dimension and the importance of *mentalités*.
The emergence of a modern social history since the 1920s requires even
the political historian to set great men, and the evolving institutions of
the state, within the context of a changing social system. By adopting
the perspective of the social historian, it is hoped to encourage the
reader to adopt a broader and more critical orientation. The central
theme of this book will thus be the continuing process of interaction
between state and society. The state has been defined by the historical
sociologist Theda Skocpol (in *States and Social Revolution*, 1979) as 'a
set of administrative, policing and military organisations headed, and
more or less well coordinated, by an executive authority'. The
maintenance of these administrative and coercive organisations of
course requires the extraction of resources from society – demands
which are magnified in the case of war, which has thus served as a
major stimulus to both the evolution of state institutions, and to social
and political conflict. Liberal writers at least since Locke have tended
to concentrate on the state as a morally neutral force, enforcing law
and order and defending its citizens against external threats. This
ignores the question of the social origins of legislators and law
enforcers, the ways in which they perceived their roles, and their
attitudes towards those over whom they ruled. The alternative
tradition is represented by Marx and the Italian sociologists Pareto and
Mosca who saw the state as the instrument of a ruling minority, and by
Gramsci who insisted upon the significance not only of coercive state
institutions but of the cultural predominance achieved by social élites
as means of maintaining social control and limiting the impact of the
otherwise competing value systems within a given society – an élite
being determined by legal status, the possession of wealth and
education. This is not to argue that the state somehow automatically
represents the interests of a socially dominant class. It is not even to
argue that the state is ever a unified entity. Its capacity for intervention
in society varies over time and between places. The state's engagement
in institutional, political and military competition, and efforts to

strengthen its own institutions might well lead to conflict over the appropriation of resources. Nevertheless, the recruitment of senior state officials overwhelmingly from amongst members of social élites, and the superior capacity of these to influence the representatives of the state, strongly suggests a predominating influence. Even if this is accepted, however, competition *within* the élites to influence or control state activities, remains a potent source of conflict.

The central questions posed will be about political power – why is it so important? Who possessed it? How is it used? In whose interests, and with what consequences? How do *subjects* react to the activities of *rulers,* for example to their demands for resources both to maintain themselves as landowners or entrepreneurs, or in the form of taxation to maintain the machinery of state? The likelihood of collective resistance appears to have been determined by established perceptions of rights and justice, capacity for organisation, opportunities for protest, and perceptions of the likelihood of success or the prospects of repression, and thus to have been influenced both by changes in social structures and relationships and in institutional arrangements. Why does political change occur?

It should be evident that these are questions about social systems as well as political structures and behaviour. Indeed it should be obvious that social order is maintained not simply or even primarily through state activity but by means of a wide range of social institutions, including the family and local community, through religious, educational and charitable bodies, and tenurial and workplace relationships – not according to some carefully conceived overall plan but because the processes of socialisation, and day-to-day contacts serve to legitimise and to enforce a wide range of dependencies. The sense of powerlessness so common amongst the poor and their need to be prudent suggest that the absence of overt conflict does not necessarily mean the non-existence of social and political tension. The forms of control exercised are largely determined by the attitudes created in daily life, in short by the rationale of the age, and of the group, as well as by the social structure and resources employed by both the state and social élites. Some social groups are privileged as subjects for historical study, others are marginalised. Fashions change. Thus predominantly male historians have been accused, and with reason, of gender blindness. This is not the place to argue the merits of community or

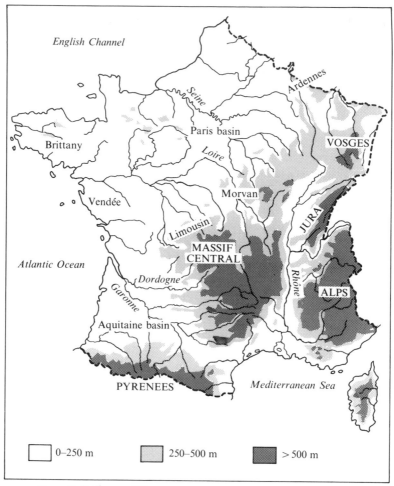

Fig 1 Relief map of France

class as opposed to gender as analytical categories, or to consider the practical difficulties of introducing gender as a concept into a history of France. Suffice it to state, what has become, and always should have been, obvious, namely that men and women have unique as well as shared experiences and that gendered perceptions affect the whole range of economic, social and political discourse and activity. The historian's objective ought to be 'to integrate any experience that was defined by gender into the wider social and economic framework' (Hufton).

Another dimension which we would ignore at our peril is the spatial – a theme which the late Fernand Braudel, reflecting the French tradition of close association between history and geography, made so much his own. The crucial importance of communications networks in limiting or facilitating the scope of both economic and political activity and the diffusion of ideas, will become obvious in the course of this work. The main purpose of this brief introduction, however, will be to set the scene by considering some of the continuities in French history.

An obvious feature of France (within its modern boundaries) is its geographical diversity. The geographer Philippe Pinchemel distinguishes five natural regions: an oceanic and temperate zone in the *north-west*, extending from the Vendee to Champagne, which is a lowland region, covered with a thick layer of fertile soil with abundant rainfall; the *north-east*, an area of plateaux, and limestone cuestas with, apart from isolated fertile areas, poor soils, and suffering from severe continental climatic conditions; the *south-west*, with its plains, hills and plateaux, is greener, more fertile and less rock strewn than the *south-east*, a region stretching from the Limousin to the plains of Provence, from Roussillon to the plains of the Saone. This he describes as a 'mosaic ... full of natural contrasts', with infertile limestone plateaux, and steep hillsides interspersed with small, discontinuous and fertile areas of plain and valley and enjoying a Mediterranean climate; and finally the *mountains* – the Massif Central, Jura, Alps and Pyrenees – inhospitable to settlement because of their thin soils and short growing season, and obstacles to the movement of men and goods. If in general terms the north belongs to the temperate climatic zone, and the south with its dry summers and high temperatures to the Mediterranean, the mountains complicate the picture, in particular pushing northern climatic traits towards the south. Furthermore, as one moves inland oceanic climatic traits give way to continental tendencies. In climatic terms, France then is characterised by important local variations, by a high degree of irregularity and seasonal anomalies in temperature and rainfall. Since time immemorial, and well into the nineteenth century – for as long as low productivity agricultural systems and isolation persisted – the menace posed by adverse climatic conditions, most notably in the north by wet summers, and in the south by drought, to staple cereal harvests, represented the threat of malnutrition or worse for the poor. At no other time was the pivotal question of control of scarce resources, of access to land and food supplies, presented with such acuity. Dearth by intensifying social tension created major political problems.

Societies subjected to climatic stress were nevertheless capable of adaptation. The development of the French landscape is indeed evidence of continuous human adaptation not only to geographical imperatives but to changing population densities and to socio-political pressures. Rural and urban landscapes are the product of a complex interaction between natural conditions and technological and demographic change, and of the complicated overlap between phases of development. The twentieth century and especially the post Second World War years with mechanisation, the use of chemical weedkillers and fertilisers and the amalgamation of farms, have seen more thoroughgoing changes than any other, but the contrasts between areas of enclosed and open field, often created in the middle ages as settlement spread especially along the river valleys and plains and lower slopes, still affect the landscape. In Picardy, the Ile-de-France, Nord and Champagne and much of eastern France in particular, wide open spaces with few trees are associated with nucleated villages and the concentration of population, although the customary practices associated with the communal grazing and collective rotation of the three-field system began to disappear from the early nineteenth century. The Mediterranean region also, although the transport revolution transformed the agriculture of its plains by giving access to mass markets for wine, remains marked by earlier structures with its concentrated habitat, and the remains of terraces cut into hillsides which signified the continuing struggle for subsistence. Only from the late nineteenth century, as population densities in the countryside declined, as autarky became unnecessary with access to reliable external supplies, did the long extension of cereal cultivation come to an end. Throughout the west, the landscape is still marked by enclosure and dispersed settlement patterns, indicating a gradual process of colonisation of the land in the middle ages. Although changes in scale have obviously occurred, the basic structure of settlement has remained remarkably permanent since the end of the middle ages. Thick hedges or granite walls mark boundaries and provide shelter for animals, whilst complex networks of often sunken lanes provide access to the fields. Lower Normandy and Brittany, Anjou, Maine

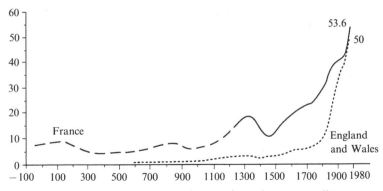

Fig 2 Graph. Comparative evolution of population (in millions).
France, and England and Wales

and the Vendee provide other distinctive types where arable farming in
the valley bottoms was combined with exploitation of forest resources
and upland pastures. Soil structures and natural resources, rather than
farming methods affected the capacity of local economies to sustain
population. Densities therefore varied considerably as did living
standards. Traditional building styles, often disguised by modern
additions, provide further reminders of past regional distinctiveness.
The railway, motor transport and decline in transport costs have led to
mass production of building materials and greater uniformity in
construction in both town and country as brick, and later concrete,
replaced worked stone or wood.

In the traditional social system prevailing until the nineteenth
century – overwhelmingly rural – the major stimulus to increased
agricultural production was population growth, and the means
employed to secure more food involved primarily the cultivation of
previously unused land, and the more frequent cropping of the existing
arable, with slow improvements in crop rotation. Overuse and the
farming of marginal land reduced productivity and increased the likelihood of harvest failure, undernourishment, the spread of disease and
the high mortality associated with a generally impoverished
environment. This largely explains the obsessive popular concern with
subsistence. In modern society the main stimulus to increasing
agricultural production is urbanisation, and the changes in diet made
possible by industrialisation and greater prosperity. Food supplies are
secure because of the possibility of importation, and productivity

increased by means primarily of technical change – fodder crops, increased specialisation and most recently motorisation, fertilisers, weedkillers, artificial insemination and selective animal and plant breeding accompanied by the amalgamation of farms. Capital has increasingly replaced land and labour as the major factor of production. Cheap bulk transport and the more rapid diffusion of information have brought new opportunities for entrepreneurs, but within far more competitive markets.

The evolution of population also had a major impact on the environment, promoting successive waves of land clearance and the cutting down of forests until the later nineteenth century, and then, through urbanisation, the extension of towns and cities into the surrounding rural areas, and the reconstruction of the cities themselves, as railway lines and broad boulevards permitted the easier penetration of goods and people, and eliminated the picturesque confusion of the late medieval to early modern structures which survived until the middle of the nineteenth century. Again the post-1945 years have seen far more extensive destruction and building than ever before. The centuries' long creation of an urban network has been of crucial significance for the overall development of French society. The urban population performs key commercial, administrative, judicial, military, religious and cultural functions. In so many respects market villages and towns of varying sizes were the essential dynamic element within society. Growing as they did on crossroads in the communications systems, their demands served to stimulate the rural production of foodstuffs and manufactures, whilst additionally they exercised growing administrative and political control over their hinterlands. Constructing a typology is difficult. Slow and expensive communications promoted the development of a network of often small market centres. Most small towns achieved only local or regional significance. The larger centres were, even before the coming of the railway, served by high capacity water or seaborne links and by the circulation of thousands of little barges or ships. Paris, benefiting from the Seine and its tributaries which brought food, fuel and timber for construction, but also major regional centres like Lyons, or ports like Marseilles, Bordeaux and Rouen played a central historical role. Their locations and activities and those of their hinterlands clearly affected the regional distribution of wealth. They exerted considerable administrative and cultural influence, served as residential centres for local élites and a complex mixture of professional and craftsmen. They also attracted large numbers of the poor and destitute in hope of work or charity. Industrialisation promoted a process of selective and accelerated growth within this essentially medieval urban network. In the process, to meet the needs of growing populations for housing, work, services, education and hygiene, and to ease the movement of goods and people, the fabric of towns underwent a drastic transformation. Here again it was population growth, improved communications and market integration which encouraged technological innovation. The structure and technology of manufacturing activity had remained fundamentally unchanged since the middle ages. The late eighteenth and nineteenth centuries saw the application of mechanical power in the factory system, to compete with traditional dispersed urban and rural workshops. This heralded an era of continued and accelerating technological innovation, with especially rapid phases of growth in the 1840s, 1890s and after 1945.

The stress upon communications is surely not misplaced. The quality of links by land and water determined not only the possibilities for trade, the structure of demand for food and manufactures, and the capacity of city populations to grow, but also the ability of governments to inform themselves, to pass on instructions, and to impose their authority. Before the nineteenth-century transport revolution, the sheer size of France and its continental structure made the problems of communication and control far more acute than in Britain, an island easily penetrated by water.

The unity initially imposed by political activity and military power was reinforced by means of an increasingly pervasive communications revolution, a process beginning in the eighteenth century with the improvement of roads and waterways and proceeding by means of the introduction of funadamentally new technologies – railway, telegraphy, telephones, and most recently information technology, with their impact reinforced through universal education and the mass media. These innovations have provided previously undreamed of facilities for the movement of people and products, means of entertainment, of education and ultimately of social control. Through them was created a more highly developed sense of belonging and eventually of nationalism in the contemporary sense. Economic, social, cultural and political integration are thus all fundamentally dependent upon the development of the means of communications and, with a genuine circularity, upon the demand for better communications inspired by changing perceptions of a society's economic, cultural and political needs.

The structure of this book is dictated by its length and by its main objective which is to provide the reader with an understanding of contemporary France. It is impossible to understand the present without considering the past, but it might be argued that the impact of the past declines with time, so the recent past will receive more detailed consideration than periods less close to our own.

Each of the chapters will focus upon a more or less lengthy period identified by the predominance of continuity over change in the evolution of economic and social structures and political problems. The long medieval and early modern period was characterised by the struggle of kings anxious to assert themselves against the claims of territorial magnates and an unruly nobility, and within the context of a population system in which growth was kept in check by low agricultural productivity, and repeated Malthusian crises, and the economy characterised by the slow penetration of rural society by capitalism and urban initiative. The Revolution and Empire were the results of the failure to establish a coherent and effective political system and resulted in the rise of a mass politics within the context of a society undergoing transition to modern capitalism. The period from 1815 to 1914 saw the acceleration of economic, social and political change, and a long battle between the proponents of political reform (of *mouvement)* and those of *résistance,* the latter supported usually by the state. This was followed by a period of economic and social stagnation and devastating war from 1914 to 1945; and then the unprecedently prosperous decades of reconstruction and economic growth, and of massive social change which followed the Second World War. Inevitably, given the delay between writing and publication, this book will be out of date as far as the present is concerned. However if it assists in the understanding of events it has not even contemplated, it can be counted a success.

PART 1

MEDIEVAL AND EARLY MODERN FRANCE

INTRODUCTION

The purpose of this section is to consider the making and evolution of the social and political systems which developed in France during the middle ages and early modern period until 1789, the development of what German historians have labelled the *Lehnstaat* or feudal monarchy, and of its successor *Ständestaat* or state of the society of orders. This was a world ruled by kings and princes with a dominant aristocratic and noble social élite, and which, in spite of its burgeoning towns, remained overwhelmingly rural and agricultural. Power depended both upon wealth and the control of scarce resources, and especially access to land, and upon status, defined as a 'social estimation of honour' by the German sociologist Max Weber, and accorded in particular to the priests, who prayed for human salvation, and to the warriors who defended society. These concepts, sanctified by the Church, legitimised social relationships and served to justify a complex of contemporary modes of social control. In the last resort, however, the ability to squeeze taxes, rents, feudal dues and tithes out of the population depended upon the use of armed force.

When might France be said to have come into existence? The process of state construction was, as we shall see, uneven and interrupted. It involved the creation, in the aftermath of the collapse of the Roman Empire and of the Frankish Kingdoms which replaced it, of political organisations capable of assuming control over broader territories, and of mobilising their economic and human resources. It took the form of a struggle between competing territorial magnates for local, regional, and finally national supremacy. In this process some political units grew in size at the expense of their competitors. To a large extent this is a history of war, but military prowess was closely linked to processes of commercialisation, improved communications and urban growth. These were developments which had positive appeal to territorial magnates. The growth of bureaucratic and military power increased their ability both to subordinate subjects and to wage external war. The development of the state thus involved both a reinforcement of the means of social control and served as a cause of conflict, the latter due to competition within élites internally and to resistance by non-élites to efforts to control and to exploit them, as well as to rivalry with external competitors. For the subject peoples there was nothing like a modern sense of nationalism. By the late middle ages, a vague sense of loyalty to a particular dynasty might have been created, and a sense, derived from the Hundred Years' War, of being different from other peoples. Even then local solidarities and the strength of custom and culture make it extremely difficult to generalise about either social or political developments. The outlook of most of the population was determined by a process of socialisation within the family and small face-to-face community. This established norms of behaviour and provided an essentially self-regulating mechanism of control, within which respect for the priest and *seigneur* was usually an unquestioning response to the desire for security and sustenance in this world and salvation in the world hereafter. This is not of course to deny that relationships habitually based upon deference and cooperation could not in certain circumstances breed hostility and conflict.

I

Population and resources in
pre-industrial France

Historians have too often allowed their interest in dramatic political events to obscure more fundamental historical realities – the continuities in those very economic and social structures which so profoundly shaped political systems. France remained an overwhelmingly agrarian society with, even in the eighteenth century, the rural population representing around 85 per cent of the total population. The pace of change was slow and subject to regression, with the farmers barely able to produce sufficient food to support themselves as well as the élites and town dwellers who depended upon them. Throughout the centuries considered in this chapter, although productive techniques in both agriculture and industry improved and the organisation of communications and trade became more efficient, there were no fundamental structural changes in the mode of production and distribution of commodities. The process of capital accumulation was inevitably limited by mass poverty. The repeated cycles in which population growth first stimulated increased production, but was then brought to an end by shortage of food and demographic crisis, are proof of this. Only towards the end of this long period, in the eighteenth century, can signs of fundamental change, and the emergence of a new, far more productive economic and social system be detected.

Societies employing relatively simple technologies tend to experience slow change. Lack of information renders judgements concerning the pace of this change hazardous, with such key indicators as the yields of arable crops clearly varying considerably between places and from year to year. Recent research suggests that between the ninth and thirteenth centuries, cereal yields might have doubled from around 2.5 to 4 per seed, reflecting the stimuli of population growth and increasing trade. Food supply was generally adequate, and its nutritional quality probably improving. However, instability and uncertainty were constant characteristics of traditional society. With such small seed to yield ratios, a reduction in the harvest of say a third below 'normal' meant that the available food supply had been halved, since half of the remaining corn had to be retained as seed. For the longer term, these centuries of relatively secure subsistence encouraged earlier marriage and population growth, so that pressure on food resources was again evident by the late thirteenth century and certainly in the fourteenth century. For wheat, yields varying between 2.5 per seed in the Alps, and an exceptional 8–9 on the fertile plains north of Paris were characteristics of the early fourteenth century. Productivity was stagnant, reflecting an inability to improve technology to the degree necessary to produce a lasting increase in per-capita output or to protect food supply. Traditional agricultural systems were certainly more flexible than is often assumed. They were able to respond to growing population and enlarged market opportunities by means of an accumulation of minor changes. In most areas nevertheless, poor communications meant that there was little stimulus to produce for markets outside the community and strong pressures to ensure its own supply of food. Agricultural systems thus developed by farmers making the best of local natural resources, in response to an essentially short-term perspective. The peasant concentrated upon the production of cereals, keeping only those livestock required for milk, meat, wool or as draught animals. His essential aim was to provide for the subsistence needs of the household. Innovations in terms of new plants or work practices were only accepted where they did not threaten the existing equilibrium. The constant problem was how to maintain the fertility of the soil. The small numbers of livestock limited the supply of precious fertilising manure, and forced farmers to leave one third, or, on poor soils, as much as half of the land fallow each year in order to rest it and to provide pasture. Caring for the soil was essential if disastrous long-term consequences were to be avoided. In the shorter term removing land from cultivation was an often intolerable burden for the poor, and had to be imposed by collective pressure. The shortage of draught

Plate 1. Peasant ploughing (end twelfth century). Note the wheels and metal ploughshare. Horses tended to remain a luxury for centuries longer and oxen or cows were used as draught animals

animals and prevalence of light ploughs meant that successful farming depended on back-breaking human activity, using hand-tools. Only in Flanders, due to the close presence of urban markets, the use of town-waste as fertiliser and relatively high crop yields, were farmers able, during the middle ages, to break out of this unproductive system, to suppress the fallow and cultivate root crops as feed for higher densities of livestock. The slow replacement of oxen and human labour by horses together with the use of iron plough tips especially in the larger farms and in northern France from the late twelfth century allowed more rapid, deeper and repeated ploughing, which resulted in increased yields, but the horse was costly, its health was fragile and it required far more feed than the ox. Not until the eighteenth and early nineteenth centuries were these processes to become generalised.

The great period of land clearance which had begun around the year 1000 reached its apogée in the thirteenth century. The landscape was transformed as forest contracted under the axe and flame – and in spite of its value as a source of building materials, fuel and sustenance for animals and human – as marshes were drained, and terraces cut into hillsides. This represented the continuing struggle to maintain a

balance between population and food supply. It was then that most of
the network of some 35,000 communities which exist today was
created. These developments were the result of population growth, but
also stimulated by favourable, that is relatively dry and mild, climatic
conditions and the slow growth of trade in the conditions of greater
security which followed the end of the Viking incursions in the north
and those of the Saracens in the south. The sense of greater security was
then reinforced by the growth of royal authority over warring barons.
A limited commercialisation of the economy occurred. The process
was gradual, varied in form over space and time and was far from
linear. In general local markets multiplied. Coinage, the essential
means of payment, circulated increasingly widely although, from our
perspective, slowly. It also remained in short supply because of the
limited production of bullion and the tendency of those who obtained
it to hoard such a scarce and useful commodity. From as early as the
tenth century, but especially in the middle of the eleventh century,
traders in luxuries such as spices, ivories and rugs from the East, or in
wine – an eminently commercial crop wherever waterborne transport
facilities existed (as in the Bordeaux region) – as well as in the more
bulky foodstuffs, created increasingly well-trodden earthen trackways
between the various little towns. These developed in privileged
geographical positions at crossroads or bridging points. They included
Marseilles, Rouen, Arras, Orléans and Paris – the sites of Roman cities
which had declined from the fourth century. More generally, it would
become increasingly impossible to live in complete autarky, not only
because there were products like salt and iron which needed to be
purchased, but also because of the demands of *seigneurs*, the Church
and especially of the state for the payment of dues and taxes. The
peasant was forced into the monetary economy.

   The crucial intermediary role of the towns as markets for locally
produced foodstuffs needs to be stressed, but so too does the miniscule
size of most of these towns by twentieth century standards. To
contemporaries, Paris in 1320 with some 200,000 inhabitants appeared
monstrous. It had doubled its size in two generations as the centre of
royal government, and because of its river network it was the major
regional commercial centre. The growth of towns was most evident in
the north between the basins of the rivers Maine and Escaut and that
of the Seine, and linked to the maritime trades in wine, salt and wool.

Lille, Douai and Arras and such other stages in maritime trade as Bruges, Rouen, La Rochelle, Bordeaux, Bayonne and Marseilles all had 15–40,000 inhabitants. Increased agricultural productivity favoured the growth of trade, and a widening in the range of activities, as well as the development of urban social hierarchies based upon wealth. This distinguished merchants from the small shopkeepers and artisanate and from the often turbulent journeyman and labourers. Relatively prosperous periods, like the twelfth century, saw the widespread construction – using local materials – of solid housing and improvements in diet. Total population grew to around 20 millions by the end of the thirteenth century and population densities probably quadrupled from around 10 to 40 inhabitants per square kilometre, levels which would not be surpassed until the technological revolution of the late eighteenth and nineteenth centuries.

These changes were associated with fundamental continuities signified above all by a demographic regime characterised by high rates of birth and of mortality, low celibacy, relatively late marriage, low illegitimacy and low pre-marital conception, and by the dominance of the nuclear family. Population remained susceptible to harvest failure, and undernourished people – particularly the very young and the old – were all too likely to fall victim to dysentery, diarrhoea, respiratory complaints and all manner of common illnesses. Epidemic crises were also frequent – smallpox, bubonic plague, influenza, typhoid, typhus and malaria. The depredations of war have to be added to those of famine and disease as soldiers not only murdered civilians but consumed their food stocks and spread infection. The frequency of these crises, the suffering they engendered, and the limits they imposed upon population growth, made them fundamental features of traditional civilisation. The recurrence of subsistence crises, due to a complicated mix of economic, social and political factors was repeated proof of an inability to ensure that food production kept pace with growing population. The diversification of crops in a subsistence polyculture remained for most farmers the essential means of safeguarding their families from the impact of a climatically induced famine, but as population densities grew, the risk of harvest failure increased as more and more arable land had to be devoted to the cultivation of basic cereals, further reducing the density of livestock and supply of manure, and, crucially, productivity per head. At the

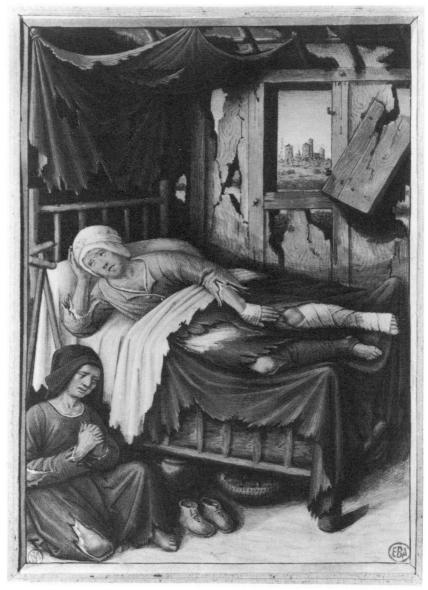

Plate 2. Misery: the wars, famines and epidemics of the period of
the Hundred Years War reduced the population by around 40 per
cent. Miniature attributed to Jean Bourdichon

same time a fragmentation of farms and a growth in the numbers of landless occurred, increasing the vulnerability of much of the population. Prosperity or misery, life or death remained fundamentally dependent on a good harvest. The impact of harvest failure varied considerably. It was likely to be especially severe in its effects when population densities were already high, and in the absence of alternative food resources, or where these had been depleted by two or three successive poor harvests. Wet summers were a particular threat to the cereals harvest, cold springs to the vine, drought to pasture. Mortality increased and birth rates fell as people adjusted to changing economic prospects and marriages were postponed.

Dependence on the harvest promoted a sense of submissiveness to nature and to the Divine Will. Most adults had experienced severe *mortalités* during which family and friends had been decimated by famine or disease. After two or three relatively benign centuries, by the late thirteenth century, there were already signs of extreme population pressure on resources in many regions as prices and land values rose and manufacture, attracted by cheap labour, spread into the countryside. It is possible that a general cooling of the earth's surface reduced levels of productivity, and certainly there were severe famines in 1309–11 and 1315–17. The impact of poor harvests was magnified by the effect of speculation and panic buying on prices in societies where reserves were limited by low yields and the lack of storage facilities, and where transport difficulties meant that it was slow and costly to move foodstuffs from one region to another. Impoverishment constantly threatened much of the population. Not only was starvation a prospect but undernourished people were exposed to the impact of disease and in cold winters to hypothermia. Debility, psychological misery and premature ageing were common. Repeated high mortalities were proof of the precariousness of human life. The solidarities of the family and community were often vital to survival but subsistence crises were also a major cause of disorder. Resentment was thus expressed against those – landowners, seigneurs and merchants – with surpluses to sell, or whoever – lords, priests and officials – failed in their duty to protect the poor. The arrival of the Black Death in 1347–48 massively increased mortality. Its repeated visitations were the main cause of a lengthy period of declining population which lasted in most areas until around 1450, and during which population levels fell in many communities by between a third and a half. There were 50,000 victims of its last French visitation – to Marseilles between 1720 and 1722 (around half of the population). The plague, and the hideous death it brought, in particular impressed itself on the human psychology. In these circumstances the contemporary preoccupation with death, and preparation for it in life, is hardly surprising.

The devastating combination of subsistence crises, plague and war in the fourteenth and fifteenth centuries substantially reversed previous trends towards population growth and had a profound impact on settlement and the rural landscape, on crop systems, property ownership and on social relationships. Only with the restoration of peace and a reduction in the virulence of the plague would gradual demographic recovery occur. The reduction in population pressure itself brought easier access to resources, better living standards and greater independence for the poor. Earlier marriage resulted in more births, but the impact was delayed by high infant mortality. Thus recovery was to be slow and only clearly evident from the 1450s, continuing in spite of the famine and epidemic of 1480–82. It was also patchy and especially evident on the rich cereal-growing plains of the north, those areas most integrated into commercial networks. Population within the present borders of France again reached about 20 millions by 1515 (16–17 millions within the then existing frontiers), and fluctuated around that level for the next two centuries. This phase of recuperation from the successive disasters of the fifteenth century lasted until the 1570s. Already by the early sixteenth century there were signs, including rising prices, of intensified population pressure on food resources and of the greater susceptibility of the poor to famine. Around that time a renewed cycle of subsistence crises began as overpopulation, underemployment and declining productivity intensi-fied the impact of poor harvests, whilst the situation was considerably aggravated by the brutality of the soldiery during the wars of religion and the Frondes. Subsequently most regions enjoyed some recovery from about 1600 to the 1640s, and many until the 1670s, with the most notable exception, the north-east, again devastated by war. The reign of Louis XIV would however end with two very difficult decades marked especially by the disastrous harvests and intensely cold years of 1694 and 1709–10, with stagnation prolonged in most areas into the 1730s. These proved to be the last major famines, although dearth, with an often severe impact on diet and resistance to disease, continued to affect the poor. Even these only moderately severe and demographically significant *crises de subsistance*, when cereal price rises of the order of 50–150% occurred rather than the tripling of earlier periods, were sufficient to cause considerable misery and unrest. The crises of 1788–9 and 1846–7 were particularly notable in terms of their economic, social and political impact.

From around 1730–50 France nevertheless entered into a period of sustained population growth and of demographic transition. Population grew rapidly from a maximum of 22 millions in 1715 to 28 millions in 1789. The chronology and rate of change varied considerably between regions but even if Malthusian crises continued to effect the rate of population growth until the mid-nineteenth century, their impact was much less marked than previously. Moreover wars were to be largely fought beyond the frontiers, and in the absence of religious motives, were far less barbaric than previously. Growth was especially rapid between 1745 and 1770. Crises were less frequent and not as lethal, and an excess of deaths over births far less common. The reasons were complex but included the slow, albeit cumulative, increase in agricultural productivity favoured by relatively good climatic conditions, improved communications and the more efficient distribution of foodstuffs, together with administrative assistance to the poor to provide them with subsidised bread or work and the ability to earn the means of payment, and the spread of rural manufacture as a means of supplementing incomes gained from the land. Epidemic mortality was not reduced by improved medical care but by marginal improvements in diet and in nursing, by government action through *cordons sanitaires* to prevent the transmission of disease and by changes in the virulence of the diseases themselves. Improved conditions and demographic expansion were especially evident in the north, east and south-east, whilst, in contrast, high mortality and a recrudescence of violent demographic crisis from the 1770s occurred in Brittany and parts of the centre (Orléanais, Berry and Touraine). In an intermediary region made up of Normandy, much of the Paris basin and parts of the centre and south-west, if mortality was lower than in Brittany, it combined with the beginnings of the voluntary restriction of births to reduce rates of population growth. Everywhere, frequent undernourishment meant continued susceptibility to murderous nutritional disorders, whilst the crises which occurred with growing frequency in the last three decades of the century, if not as spectacular as those of the previous century, were still evidence of widespread poverty and of physiological misery, of renewed population pressure on resources and a resultant degradation of living standards, and of the continued vulnerability of a low productivity agricultural system to climatic fluctuations. The fundamental factor in the economic cycle remained the state of the harvest.

Moreover in a predominantly rural society high population densities meant a plentiful supply of potential tenants and labourers; they implied growing subdivision of the land, and impoverishment. The development of rural manufacture and of seasonal migration was evidence of a desperate struggle to make ends meet. In such a situation those who controlled scarce resources, and especially access to land, were in a very strong position. Population pressure allowed them to demand high rents and to pay low wages. Demographic conditions thus had a vital impact on the division of income between social groups, and influenced the availability of resources – income and manpower – for the state.

From around 1730–50 a long period of economic growth began which, if it did not initially involve significant technological innovation, nevertheless served as a prelude to the structural change in the economy which was to take place in the nineteenth and twentieth centuries. The major stimuli to change were to be population growth, rising prices and growing internal trade facilitated by the improvement of communications and the increased supply and the more rapid circulation of money. Reductions in the cost of transport of a product had the effect of reducing its price to the consumer and enlarging its market. Increased external trade also played its part. As so often in the past, following the demographic crisis which marked the late seventeenth and early eighteenth century and the restoration of the balance between population and food supply, economic expansion (initially recovery) could begin once again. What distinguishes this period, in France as elsewhere in Western Europe, from its predecessors is that the increase in activity was to be relatively rapid and that it was to be sustained. There was to be no repetition of the crises, so effectively described by the English clergyman Thomas Malthus, in which the growth of population and of production in agriculture and industry was decisively reversed by harvest failure, epidemic and war. It is this which identified the eighteenth century as the beginning of a new epoch with the onset of a period (*c.* 1730–*c.* 1840) of slow, interrupted but gradually accelerating transition to industrial society, which would eventually result in a transformation of the human condition.

In agriculture, still by far the predominant source of employment and income, change took the form of land clearance, the slow spread of buckwheat in the poor soils of the Massif Central and Brittany, of maize in the south-west, of the potato and of agricultural fodder, and the reduction of fallow particularly in the north. The most optimistic estimates (those of J.-C. Toutain, *Le produit de l'agriculture française,* 1961) are of an increase of 60 per cent in agricultural production between 1701–10 and 1781–90. There must be some doubt given the shortcomings of the sources of information and the continued technical stagnation of most farms well into the next century. Moreover, communications difficulties continued to restrict commercial incentives largely to the river valleys and plains. Geographical conditions were the basis of major regional disparities. Besides a small minority of large landowners and wealthy peasants found particularly in the relatively urbanised north and the Paris region, there was a mass of small-scale peasant farmers whose essential objective remained family subsistence, and who frequently found themselves in debt as part of the daily struggle to achieve this and to pay taxes, rents, and seigneurial dues. In spite of a fashionable interest in agronomy, large landowners in general had little incentive to invest in agriculture. As population grew, peasants competed to rent farms and hire out their labour. Nevertheless, a process of piecemeal, unspectacular change was taking place. Growing population and enhanced commercial opportunities together with rising prices stimulated efforts to increase production.

The rural population was also becoming more than ever reliant upon supplementary activities, including temporary migration, carting and the manufacture at piece-rates for urban merchants of a variety of products including cloth, nails and cutlery. This growing diversification of employment provided additional resources and helped make possible the continuing rise in population. Economic historians have linked this process of 'proto-industrialisation' to industrialisation proper in some areas as urban merchants initially taking advantage of cheap sources of rural labour, were able to accumulate capital and begin very slowly from the 1780s to adopt British techniques and to mechanise production. The expansion of manufacture had taken place along similar lines in previous periods of population growth. That in this case it was to be sustained and transformed is what needs explanation. Although according to one estimate (J. Marczewski, 'Le produit physique de l'économie française de 1789 à 1913', *Cahiers de l'I.S.E.A.*, 1965) the production of manufactured goods increased by 4.5 times between 1701–10 (a period of depression) and 1781–90, it is clear that this occurred almost entirely on the basis of traditional techniques either in small urban workshops, closely dependent in the larger towns on self-regulating guilds, certainly anxious to protect their privileges and monopolies, but responding to an expanding market by intensified specialisation and division of labour, or else dispersed through the countryside, and everywhere employing predominantly human or animal power, supplemented exceptionally by wind or water. The key figure in this expansion was the merchant organising the distribution of raw materials and the finished product. Properly speaking this was a period of commercial rather than industrial capitalism, and its prosperity remained closely dependent upon that of agriculture. The towns were essentially commercial and administrative centres. Some of them nevertheless experienced considerable growth due to immigration, so that by 1789 just under 20 per cent of the total population, some 5,400,000 people might be classified as urban. The rather diffuse network of large towns together with a mass of smaller centres provided a framework not only for economic activity but for increasingly close administrative control. Paris, which by the sixteenth century had between 200–250,000 inhabitants (about 1.5 per cent of the French population), by the middle of the seventeenth century had a population of c. 550,000; by the end of the following century it had grown to 650,000 (2–2.5 per cent of total French population) reflecting, in the absence of major demographic crises in the eighteenth century, a process of accelerating urbanisation, accompanied by the embellishment of the nation's major cities.

French economic development during the eighteenth century was very respectable, making France the world's foremost economic power. In manufacturing the rate of growth – at around 1.9 per cent per annum – was probably higher than that for Britain (c. 1.2 per cent). If

British technology was already more advanced, it would be during the Revolutionary-Imperial period that a major gulf developed. The British lead in agricultural productivity was generally more pronounced, and this was reflected in superior living standards. More efficient communications, more developed markets, higher agricultural productivity and per-capita demand for manufactures, had already created production bottlenecks in textiles and in metallurgy which had stimulated technical innovation and the rapid diffusion of the new technology. Britain was first to begin the transition away from a civilisation based on water and wood as sources of energy and heat towards one based upon coal and the steam engine. France was to remain a follower for much of the following century but was to be impelled by a similar competitive technological imperative.

The distinction between economic and social structures and political institutions is of course to some degree an arbitrary one, with the latter embedded within, rather than distinct from, the former. However this is the background against which state building occurred, against which we must write our political history. These are the factors and conditions which largely determined the resources of men and money that were to be available at any particular time.

2

Society and politics in medieval France

The Kingdom of France emerged slowly out of the ruins of the Carolingian Empire. The Treaty of Verdun in 843 divided the empire between the sons of Louis le Débonnaire and established a western kingdom which would gradually reserve for itself the name of France. Chroniclers like the monk Aimoin at Fleury-sur-Loire around the year 1000 created a tradition identifying this *Francia* with Roman Gaul and described it as the rampart of Christianity. The subsequent creation of modern France, the work of centuries, would be inspired by the dream of a reconstitution of the Kingdom of Charlemagne. There were many obstacles to the survival, let alone the enlargement of any political unit. Initially poor communications and lack of information, low population densities, small revenues and the absence of salaried officials made it impossible to bind together large territorial units. Government was inevitably decentralised. A period of political and territorial fragmentation ensued which lasted into the twelfth century. To a very substantial extent the evolution of the various lordships and principalities was determined by the results of war, and their social structures shaped by organisation for war. People looked for security to local lords, and they themselves to regional princes, often as in the case of Flanders, Burgundy and Aquitaine, the heirs of territorial commanders established by the Carolingian Charles the Bold. This fragmentation, clearly evident in the ninth century, was taken a stage further from around 900 as former royal administrators, the local counts and subsequently the *castellans* who had served as their deputies took advantage of rivalries between their nominal superiors to carve out for

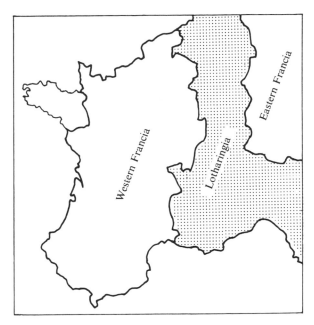

Fig 3 The creation of France. I The Treaty of Verdun 843

themselves increasingly autonomous power bases. At every level in society men sought protection from their more powerful neighbours, sometimes hoping to play one off against another and creating an intermixture of often conflicting obligations destructive of any sense of political hierarchy. Thus, to take an extreme example, around 1150 the Count of Champagne was the vassal of ten different seigneurs (including the King of France, Duke of Burgundy and Archbishop of Rheims). Great nobles would continue for centuries to affirm their autonomy, and seek allies to help them to maintain it. Forms of contractual relationship, of clientage, were created, especially in the north, in which the weaker became the vassals of the more powerful. They agreed to perform military service and offer counsel, and to provide financial aid in return for protection and justice. In this process kings, princes and counts sought to reinforce their own power by binding warriors, and particularly the mounted knights who formed the core of any army, to themselves. The award of a fief, with land and its revenues, occurred at a ceremony whose rituals and religious nature, with oaths often sworn over holy relics, was intended both to reinforce the sense

of obligation between the contracting parties – the *seigneur* and his
men – and to publicise its existence. However, the proliferating
numbers of castles – initially wooden towers on a mound for shelter
surrounded by a pallisade and ditch (motte and bailey) and from the
eleventh century stone keeps – was indicative of a continuing fragmentation of power, of widespread insecurity and of mounting
anarchy. The fief and its surrounding lands, soon came to be regarded
by those controlling it as an hereditary possession. Fortresses served
both to protect and to ensure control over local populations. They
were also key elements in the incessant struggles between *seigneurs* for
control over territory which often degenerated into brigandage or
vendetta. To curb this disorder the Church sought to encourage the
ideals of Christian knighthood, whilst at the same time a sense of
belonging to a distinctive social order developed amongst those
mounted warriors able to control land and resources and to equip
themselves properly for the wars which were their *raison d'être*. A
shared ethic or code of conduct evolved. Further signs of a growing
group cohesion can be seen in the development of marriage strategy as
a means of avoiding the sub-division of fiefs and of creating networks
of solidarity, and of a sense of pride in lineage. By the middle of the
twelfth to early thirteenth century a largely hereditary privileged order
of nobles existed. In spite of the ability – particularly in periods of
economic expansion – of non-nobles to purchase fiefs and develop a
noble lifestyle and of the king to create nobles, the nobility increasingly
became a relatively closed caste which survived until the night of
4 August 1789. It included both heirs of the Carolingian aristocracy and
those *châtelain* families which through vassalage and war had acquired
the hereditary right to a fief.

In contrast peasants settled on these lands owed a 'cens' in money or
produce, were obliged to make use of the lord's oven, mill or wine
press, and were required to serve as soldiers, to construct fortifications
as well as to work on land directly farmed by the lord. They gained
access to plots of land by providing their lords with the resources to
guarantee their safety. Thus lord and peasant accepted binding
obligations but on a very unequal basis. By the eleventh century most
peasants were reduced to the status of serfs by their need for security
and protection. Although in the less densely settled south, the power of
lords over the land was less complete, in the north it was presumed that

all land was held in fief. The accepted custom was that of 'No land without seigneur'. Serfs suffered from restrictions on their rights of movement outside the community, and depended on their lord's permission (obtained on payment of a tax) to marry or pass on their possessions to their children. These were measures designed to preserve the economic integrity of the *seigneurie*.

Exploitation by the lord was restrained primarily by his self-interest in the continuing capacity of his serfs to fulfil their various obligations in cash and kind together with the Christian commitment to provide charity. The conditions of the rural masses clearly improved during periods of prosperity or when, following demographic disaster, land was in plentiful supply, whilst the supply of labour to work it had diminished. In these situations lords were prepared to make concessions. A process of emancipation of serfs was clearly under way as early as the twelfth century, and was largely completed after the Black Death, although the obligation to pay seigneurial dues was to survive until 1789. In the meantime the economic, social and cultural subordination of the peasantry was punctuated by minor incidents of violent resistance in the dark of night, and about which the historical documents are largely silent. A repertoire of actions existed, reflecting the strength of community traditions and organisation, and an appreciation of the opportunities for verbal or violent protest. There were also occasional mass uprisings or *jacquerie*. The brutality displayed by both the insurgents and those who suppressed these risings revealed the force of pent up tension and perhaps also, in some periods, the emotional instability of populations subject to the terrors of famine, plague and war.

The relationships contracted during this period of 'feudalism', lasted from the ninth into the twelfth century and clearly corresponded to the weakness of the state and of its capacity to offer protection and justice. They represented both forms of economic exploitation and of political control, as the lord levied tolls, fees at markets and fairs, enjoyed the profits and power of justice and generally extended his authority over formerly free peasants. Many of the forms of social obligation created were to survive until 1789, although their significance was to alter with changing social and political structures. For a mass of humble folk the payment of dues to seigneurs and tithes to the clergy continued to be justified by the need to maintain the warriors

and priests who provided protection in this world and, in the case of
the clergy, hope everlasting.

Even in this period of fragmentation of state power however the
ideal of monarchy survived. In 987 on the death of Louis V, the last
Carolingian, assemblies of nobles and bishops held at Compiègne and
Senlis had offered the crown to Hugh Capet, a powerful magnate,
Count of Paris, Senlis, Dreux and Orléans. He, by persuading his peers
to accept his son, Robert, as his heir, quickly began to turn elective
kingship into hereditary monarchy. However, it had not been intended
that the Capetians should gain much more than symbolic authority.
The decline of royal influence continued. The lords of Brittany, the
Massif Central and southern France largely ignored the king's
existence, their sense of independence reinforced by the ethnic and
cultural distinctiveness of the populations they sought to control.
Centrifugal forces remained dominant with the king enjoying little
more status than any other territorial prince and engaging in constant
wars for land and power. The strength of the Capetians in northern
France was based essentially upon the lands held or dominated by the
king and his ability to secure vassalage both within the Ile-de-France
and its immediate surrounding area (for example from the counts of
Anjou, Blois and Soissons). It depended too on possession of the castles
which served as vital power bases. It was frequently menaced by the
ambitions of local *castellan* families like the Montlhéry and Mont-
morency, as well as by neighbouring territorial princes like the counts
of Anjou and Blois-Champagne or the dukes of Normandy and
Flanders. The last two were especially threatening, because through
strenuous efforts they enjoyed much greater success than the Capetians
in maintaining feudal hierarchy and central authority. They insisted
upon the performance of homage and military service and maintained
close control over high justice and the Church. As always, however,
much depended upon the strength and personality of individual counts
or dukes. In Normandy the death of William the Conqueror in 1087
was followed by a period of political confusion and breakdown of
central authority as Robert Curthose and William Rufus disputed the
inheritance. Nevertheless, strengthened by their position as kings of
England, the dukes refused to do homage to the French king until well
into the twelfth century and periods of serious hostilities occurred
between 1109 and 1113, and 1116 and 1120. The survival of Capetian

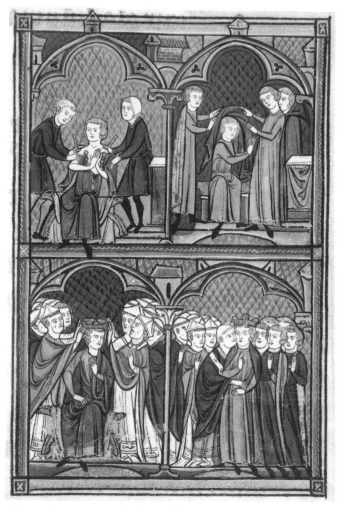

Plate 3 Coronation of a king of France. Anointment with Holy
Oil distinguished the Capetians from other territorial lords,
giving their claims added legitimacy. Miniature from mid-
eleventh century

authority came to depend upon carefully constructed systems of
alliance.

In this situation the one distinguishing feature of the Capetian king
was his sacred character. He alone was the Lord's anointed. It was,
nevertheless, to be centuries before the Capetian monarchs were to

achieve even a fragile political hegemony. This depended upon the establishment of a real military and political dominance over the princes and nobles who remained, at least nominally, royal vassals. It required the development of the administrative, financial, judicial and military systems necessary to initially assert, and subsequently maintain, royal power. The beginnings of this process are evident from the late eleventh century. It was inevitably slow given both the practical difficulties and the countervailing efforts of local magnates to use similar methods to affirm their own rival territorial power. In its essence this period, the second feudal age as the great French medievalist Marc Bloch labelled it, was characterised by the growing ability of the crown to use feudal institutions in its own interests. Anarchy was replaced by growing institutional order.

The growth of population and of economic activity was of crucial importance to the accumulation of royal power during such key periods as the late eleventh to early twelfth century and early fourteenth century, during the reign of Philip Augustus (1180–1223), Saint Louis (1226–70), and Philip the Fair (1285–1314). When the king's men were finally installed in Lyons in 1312 population densities were higher than they would again be before the eighteenth century. The Capetians moreover benefited from the location of their territories in a fertile region crossed by waterways and roads. The development of state institutions can be closely associated with the growth of an exchange economy. Both depended upon the improvement of communications, more rapid circulation of money and enhanced productive capacity. A long-term process of increased economic activity resulted in the growth of revenue from the royal domain, from feudal dues and the administration of justice, tolls and taxes. Relationships throughout society were being monetised. This permitted the development of a salaried and dependent bureaucracy and larger, more effective armies. Princes were able to pay officials, hire mercenaries and build increasingly complex and expensive stone fortresses. Practically, the main causes of administrative reform were the needs of war. The old principle that the king should live off the income of his own domain failed to provide the resources for political expansion or for the creation of a permanent armed force to supplement the feudal levy. Such measures as the confiscation of Jewish property in 1306 or that of the Knights of the Temple in 1307 were only a temporary palliative.

Philip Augustus and Saint Louis were able to levy extraordinary taxes to finance their crusades, and the principle once breached could never be fully restored. Other wars justified new impositions. The growth of bureaucracy moreover meant increasing peace-time expenses. From the reign of Philip the Fair both direct (especially the *taille*, which in some areas fell on property, in others on persons) and indirect (for example drink, livestock and salt) taxation were tolerated as a quasi-permanent means of financing the long wars against the English. On occasion, especially in the violent fourteenth century, the pill was sweetened by the summoning of Estates-General representing nobles, urban bourgeois and clergy who might be persuaded of the need to levy taxes. The principle of permanent taxation, however, remained unacceptable and royal attempts to introduce new taxes a potent cause of discord. There remained additionally the practical problems of estimating the scale of the resources which might be taxed, and for the taxpayer of obtaining cash – a scarce resource. The main features of state development were nevertheless control over a growing territory; the development of central administrative and judicial systems; and enhanced influence over and the ability to make use of the institutions of the Church resulting from the victory of gallicanism over the ideal of papal theocracy.

The area under Capetian control thus gradually expanded from its original territorial base in the Ile-de-France. Within these domains the king and his entourage had traditionally sought to maintain their authority by travelling between castles and manors, directly supervising their administration and holding court. From the middle of the eleventh century administrative units, *prévotés*, were created, each administered by *prévôts* as the agents of royal power. The period between the twelfth and the fifteenth centuries was one of transition during which a feudal–seigneurial governmental system began to transform itself through the development of its legislative functions and the accretion of bureaucratic forms of administration into a monarchical system, which survived in its essentials until the Revolution. The reign of Louis VI (1108–37) saw the further development of the royal court from the king's entourage into a more effective organ of government. The court remained the centre of political activity, attracting the able and powerful and, through its culture, influencing the lifestyle of the upper classes. Louis VI and his advisors, the Abbot

Suger of St Denis, and Raoul de Vermendois nevertheless made an effort to restrict the hereditary claims of noble families to particular offices and sought to define their bureaucratic functions. In spite of this affirmation of public power, and development of administrative organisation, it remained impossible and would have been unwise to exclude powerful territorial lords from the Council, the supreme organ of government. Personal relationships continued to be of fundamental significance. The obvious danger was that, especially during a royal minority, or where the king was weak, rival groups would develop within the Council and paralyse the administration.

Other twelfth century innovations included the creation of *baillis*, despatched into the provinces as roving inspectors and judges, and the growing use of written documents allowing the more effective recording and transmission of information and instructions. Nobles as well as clerks needed to acquire literacy. A gradual osmosis resulted between the culture of the schools and that of the court and with it the emergence of a civilisation based on classical values and those of chivalry. Rather than following the court in its perambulations, a permanent central organisation of professional administrators dependent upon the monarch, composed of clergy and minor nobles with some legal training, was gradually created. Paris, a city which owed to its geographical location its already considerable commercial and strategic significance, now increasingly well fortified, assumed the functions of a capital city.

From the middle of the thirteenth century under St Louis, a king inspired by the religious ideals of the 'royal lawmaker' (*roi justicier*), and especially in the early fourteenth century, specialised institutions born within the royal court began to achieve a more independent existence, as the volume and complexity of their activities increased. The *Parlement* established by St Louis next to the Sainte-Chapelle, constructed 1246–48 as a reliquary for the Thorns with which Jesus had been crowned at his crucifixion, assumed the role of the sovereign court of appeal presiding over a hierarchical system of royal courts. During the fourteenth century it would acquire responsibility for remonstrating against royal ordinances which its members felt did not 'confirm to reason'. This, together with the *Chambre des comptes* to supervise financial administration, were signs of the professionalisation of legal and administrative personnel. They were to be supplemented from the fifteenth century by additional parlements created largely in peripheral provinces acquired during and in the aftermath of the Hundred Years War. Their creation recognised both the particular susceptibilities of newcomers and served as a means of integrating them more effectively within France. In these various ways the activities and influence of the royal administration became increasingly pervasive. This was combined with insistence upon the better organisation and procedure and essential fairness and superiority of royal justice in comparison with that offered in the seigneurial and ecclesiastical courts. From the thirteenth century the king as suzerain took advantage of growing political strength to insist upon the right of appeal from the seigneurial to royal courts and from the fifteenth century upon the Crown's duty to abolish seigneurial courts guilty of abusing their powers. This was bitterly resented as a threat to the dignity and status of the seigneur, to his authority over subordinates and to his income. The ecclesiastical courts claimed jurisdiction in cases involving clerics, in crimes against religion, in marital affairs, and many disputes over property. The effort to reduce their competence was closely linked to the gallican struggle against the claims of the papacy to enjoy political supremacy over kings.

In spite of growing royal power, basic economic and social structures ensured that government remained decentralised. The primary function of the monarchy was the administration of justice as the essential means of preserving public order. With a small central bureaucracy, in an era of poor communications, it remained inescapably dependent upon the cooperation of local élites, and particularly municipal magistrates and rural seigneurs. As late as 1535 there were only around seven to eight thousand royal officials (including those in minor positions: one official for every two thousand inhabitants). Most poor people in any case avoided the judicial system, and continued to do so well into the nineteenth century. They preferred to regulate their affairs within the community and to avoid the costs, waste of time and risks of interference by an external authority ill-equipped by its culture and language, experience and sympathies to understand the concerns of ordinary people.

Strong and effective personalities like Louis VI or Philip Augustus were able to tighten the ties of vassalage and re-affirm its hierarchical character. They were willing to take judicial and if need be military action against insubordinate or disloyal officials or territorial lords. Many castellans lacked the military means to resist this royal centralisation, and reconciled themselves to acting as the king's agents in the administration of justice, the collection of taxes and the raising of soldiers and as the protectors of the Church. In contrast with kings and princes who were able to avoid the sub-division of their property by inheritance, lesser nobles were weakened by the passing of each generation. In a period of economic expansion many minor nobles were impoverished by their growing taste for luxury and as a result their dependence on their feudal superiors increased. The crusades, a continuous movement spread over three centuries, reduced internal violence by means of the removal and indeed premature death of many young warriors. In contrast to earlier trends, a process of concentration of power, in the hands of territorial princes as well as the king, was under way. The doctrine of monarchical superiority was clearly enunciated by Louis VI's adviser, Suger, the Abbot of St Denis, who insisted that vassals of the king's vassals owed primary allegiance to the monarch, placed at the summit of the feudal hierarchy, rather than to their direct seigneurs (as was the Anglo-Norman practice). This ran contrary to established custom according to which 'the vassal of my vassal is not my vassal', and took well into the thirteenth century to win acceptance. Philip Augustus, however, felt able in 1202 to use his rights as feudal seigneur to require homage from King John for his territories – Normandy and Aquitaine – in so doing weakening the authority of the English king over his vassals in those provinces. Any apparent increase in the power and prestige of the king made it more likely that vassals engaged in disputes would appeal to the monarch as the feudal arbiter, rather than taking matters into their own hands. Such appeals could be used to justify military expeditions into regions formerly outside royal control, such as the Mâconnais in 1160. War in these cases was the means of implementing judicial decisions, and it was by use of the law that the king was able to impose his authority on, and even confiscate the lands of major, princely vassals. In a changing social and political context kings were able to use the feudal system, which had originally emerged out of the weakness of the central power, in order to restore their authority. Their growing success could be seen in the response of vassals to the call for troops to defend the kingdom against the Holy Roman Emperor Henry V in 1124. Increased

Plate 4 Return of Philip Augustus to Paris after his victory at
Bouvines. Fifteenth-century miniature

attendance at the king's court was another sign. For much of the
eleventh century the great nobles and bishops had deserted the royal
court, leaving it to the turbulent minor nobles of the Ile-de-France.
This situation clearly began to change with the re-affirmation of royal
authority by Louis VI. There was a growing concern to give advice to
the king, an interest in acquiring office, and a desire to share power.
Increasingly status came to be determined by the Crown.

The reign of Philip Augustus represented a decisive stage in the
development of the French state in terms of its territorial expansion
and ability to subdue powerful rivals, most notably the Angevin
Empire created by Henry II of England. The crucial importance of
personality in the development of affairs can be seen from the way in
which Philip Augustus was able to take advantage of quarrels between
Henry II and his sons, which in themselves encouraged and also

represented complex feudal divisions within the Plantagenet domains. Subsequently, although defeated by Richard (died 1199) he enjoyed major successes against the indecisive and unpopular John and his various allies. This culminated in 1214 in victory over the English king at La Roche-au-Moine, followed by the defeat at Bouvines of Otto IV, Holy Roman Emperor, and his Flemish and English allies. These victories ensured a major shift in the European balance of power and a massive reduction in the power of the English king. In contrast, the conquered territory substantially enhanced the financial and manpower resources of the French monarchy. The revenue of the Crown increased by 160 per cent between 1180 and 1203, a development which itself required the enlargement of the central administration. Louis VIII (1223–26) was able to complete the conquest of Poitou and additionally to extend royal power into Languedoc, justifying the latter by the Church's condemnation of the Cathar heresy and the Crown's responsibilities as defender of the faith. Marriages and the dowries they brought were another means by which the crown acquired territory. Philip Augustus in 1180, for example, obtained the Boulenois and Artois on his marriage to the niece of the Count of Flanders. The failure of the marriage of a brother of St Louis and the heiress to the Count of Toulouse (in 1229) to produce issue led to Toulouse becoming part of the royal domain in 1271; it was by marriage, too, that Philip the Fair acquired Champagne and Brittany in 1291. The Dauphiné, in contrast, was acquired in 1349 by purchase. This continuous growth in the royal domain represented an accumulation of resources and of power.

Ideologically the enhancement of royal power was supported by a Church anxious to secure social order, and insisting upon the sacred rights and responsibilities of a monarch who through his coronation at Rheims became the Lord's anointed. From the late tenth century the Church had used the threat of excommunication in a largely vain effort to secure respect for 'the Peace of God' and had supported the king in his role as guardian of peace. In a period of monarchical weakness it had preserved the traditions of bureaucratic administration and provided an alternative institutional structure. It too shared in the benefits of the return to order and prosperity which made possible the reconstruction of the great cathedrals of Paris, Rheims, Chartres and Laon. Through its network of parishes and its involvement in the daily life of the population, the Church provided an explanation of the

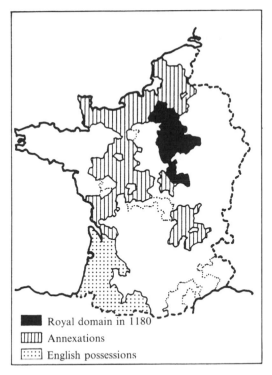

Fig 4 The creation of France. II The reign of Philip Augustus, 1180–1223

universe, norms of behaviour for rich and poor, and justified the social system in terms which continued to be used throughout the Ancien Régime, namely that God had divided mankind into three – those who prayed, those who fought, and those who worked. The interdependence of these groups was the basis of social and political order. Those who worked were required to serve and maintain the others in return for prayer and protection. Salvation was the reward for fulfilling their obligations. The role of the monarch as a military leader, and the sacred nature of his functions moreover ensured that the Church would insist upon the masculine character of monarchy. Women were regarded as physically and emotionally unsuitable to hold power.

The relationship between state and Church, although essentially based upon interdependence, with many churchmen (initially because of their virtual monopoly of writing) occupying positions in the royal

court, was also plagued by conflict of interest, by resentment on the
part of the Church of the use by kings of rights of appointment to
monasteries and bishoprics as a form of patronage, and suspicion on
the part of kings of the papacy's claim to exercise supreme authority on
earth, as the representative of God, *le Seigneur*. The reforms introduced
by Pope Gregory VII and his successors in the second half of the
eleventh century had sought to improve the quality and sense of
personal commitment of the clergy, but also to secure greater
independence from secular interference and to affirm the Pope's
spiritual and political supremacy through the right to excommunicate
and depose kings. Better communications had helped make closer
papal control over the provinces of the Church possible. The rise of
royal power, however, made this intolerable, leading in particular to a
bitter conflict between Philip the Fair and Pope Boniface VIII over the
taxation of the clergy, and the right of the king to discipline clerics.
This dispute in which a prominent role was played by the new
university-trained lawyers, well versed in Roman law, saw the
emergence of Gallicanism, the theory of the temporal independence of
the state, and the liberties of the Church of France, as a counter to
theocratic ideals. Philip the Fair insisted that he held his throne directly
from God, and was supported by a meeting of the three orders (Estates-
General) convoked at Notre-Dame de Paris in 1302. The weakness of
the papacy in the fourteenth century, including the period of
'Babylonian captivity' in Avignon (1309–77), and the existence of rival
popes between 1373 and 1418, allowed the further affirmation of these
Gallican liberties. This culminated in the Pragmatic Sanction of
Bourges in 1438, an agreement by an assembly of the clergy to
substantially restrict papal authority and fiscal exactions in France.

Thus, over a period of three centuries the kings of France had
succeeded in asserting themselves militarily and ideologically. There
remained, however, substantial threats to the survival of their power.
Even when the various principalities had been brought under closer
royal control they retained their own customs and laws, rights
confirmed at the time of their accession to the royal domain.
Geographical variations in legal custom would until the Revolution
reflect the political divisions of the eleventh and twelfth centuries and
earlier. The legal traditions of the south, where written law and Roman
usages were dominant, differed significantly from those of the north,

where custom remained uppermost. These differences were reinforced by linguistic variations with the *langue d'oc* of southern France far closer to Latin than the *langue d'oil* of the north. Moreover, and in spite of the development of the administrative power and resources of the monarchy, distance, slowness of communication and the small size of the royal bureaucracy restricted effective central control. The possibility remained of resistance to the royal authority from over-mighty vassals, and urban or rural communities. This, especially where combined with English interference, threatened anarchy in a militarised society in which the government was far from achieving a monopoly of armed force. Thus in 1314 leagues of nobles were organised in Brittany, Picardy, Burgundy and Champagne to demand respect for provincial customs and to protest against taxes. The political danger was increased when delegates from these areas met together, but fortunately for the Crown, they were unable to agree upon a common strategy. On an altogether different scale was the series of events known as the Hundred Years War.

For some 130 years, from 1335–40, a succession of famines, plagues and wars plunged four successive generations into misery and despair and threatened the very existence of both dynasty and state. Rising population densities meant that problems of food supply were anyway inevitable. The arrival of the bubonic plague in Western Europe in 1347 carried off perhaps a third of its inhabitants, and the first murderous epidemic was followed by several others at intervals of about fifteen years. Whilst the Hundred Years War did not result in an enormous number of battlefield deaths, the armies carried disease with them whilst the guerrilla warfare and the widespread brigandage which accompanied the collapse of ordered government destroyed homes, livestock and crops and brutalised populations. This combination of events caused severe economic and social disruption.

In these circumstances, just as in the eleventh century, the search for security encouraged renewed fortification and intensified localism. Forms of 'bastard' feudalism, of clientelism, developed with the towns to a far greater extent than previously playing a key role as military centres, places of refuge and sources of money. The weak attached themselves to patrons more powerful than themselves. The inevitable immediate result was a weakening of royal authority. In the longer term the wars were again a powerful force in stimulating improvement of the royal administration. Although medieval armies were small compared with those of later periods – with the 100,000 raised in the summer of 1340 representing the largest – they were substantial in relation to the resources available. Attempts to raise taxation were, however, always dangerous and likely to provoke discontent amongst those nobles who were not part of the growing bureaucracy and who continued to insist that the monarch should live off the revenues of his domain. In 1356–58, during the captivity of John II and due to the weakness of a government discredited by defeat at Crécy and Poitiers, the dauphin, the future Charles V, was faced not only with dissent from the nobles but also that of the merchants of Paris led by their *prévôt* Etienne Marcel, and by the complaints of the provincial estates meeting at Paris and Toulouse. In periods of monarchical weakness and crisis, such bodies were inevitably more assertive. Efforts to conciliate élites (noble, urban bourgeois and clergy) through provincial estates and Estates-General such as those of 1343 and 1355–56, ran the risk of giving a platform to critics determined to limit the arbitrariness of royal officers. They felt able to demand regular meetings, the right of consent to taxation or the summoning of the feudal levy, and a role in the selection of royal officers; demands the dauphin Charles finally proved unwilling to accept. These developments coincided with peasant uprisings (*jacqueries*) which threatened much of the Paris region, as the rural population protested against both royal taxation and the exactions of a nobility which had proved itself incapable of protecting its dependants against marauding bands of soldiers. The divergent interests of these groups, and the widespread desire for strong government and social order, helped to promote a temporary recovery. However, the minority of Charles VI in the 1380s and his subsequent insanity at a time of profound European-wide demographic and economic crisis provoked another round of war, revolt and massacre and, following a truce in 1388, renewed English intervention in 1412.

The wars themselves were caused by problems of suzerainty and conflicting claims to the throne of France. In 1293–97 Philip the Fair had sought to crush his most dangerous vassals, the king of England as Duc de Guienne, and the Count of Flanders whose power was based on the commercial and industrial prosperity of the Flemish cities. Edward I had managed to retain Guienne but had felt obliged to render homage

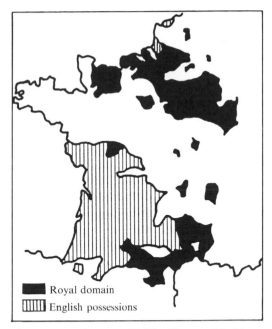

Fig 5 The creation of France. III The Treaty of Brétigny 1360

for it. Flanders had been severely punished militarily and financially.
Philip died in 1314. By 1328 his three sons were also dead, and the direct
line of Capetian succession extinguished. The alternative claimants in
this situation were Philip's daughter, Isabelle, whose son Edward III
had recently succeeded to the English crown, and her cousin Philip,
Count of Valois. His claim, as Philip VI, was recognised by an assembly
of leading nobles and clergy meeting at Vincennes, because he was an
adult male, and as a means of excluding the King of England. At this
stage Edward III's primary concerns were with restoring order in
England itself and retaining what was left of Guienne. In 1329 at
Amiens he paid homage. His laying claim to the throne of France in
1337 was probably conceived of as a potentially lucrative military
adventure and a means of securing the English wool trade with
Flanders, of protecting the Plantagenet heritage in the south-west, and
of diverting the energies of the warlike English barons onto the
Continent.

At Crécy (1346) and Poitiers (1356), poorly organised and ineptly
commanded French armies suffered major defeats which must have

Comme il se mettoit alabz̄y.
Pour regarder dessus la Ville.

Il luy vint dire ung de ses gens,
Monseigneur vous pouez a plain
Veoir vr̄e Ville dorleans.
Comme sil la tint en sa main.
Et tout acoup soudainement.
Ung canon si vint lors ferir.
Ledit conte si ruddement.
Que tost apres le fist mourir.
Quant la Ville sceut les nouuelles.
De la mort qui ainsi aduint.
Len sen esbayt a merueilles.
Car len ne sceut dont cela vint.
Qui le canon vers lui Jecta.
Len ne peut scauoir ne cognoistre.
Mais quoy quil en feist prouffitta.
Car cestoit le grant caen et maistre.
Qui pour la mort ne se trespas.
Dudit conte qui estoit le chief.
Les anglois nen bougerent pas.
Ains sentretindrent de rechief.

appeared as God's judgement. At Poitiers the French king, John the Good (II) was taken prisoner. In the ensuing negotiations for his release although Edward III did not demand the French crown, he forced John to abandon half of his kingdom, including Normandy. The dauphin, the future Charles V, however, refused to recognise this agreement and war-weariness on both sides led to a compromise treaty signed at Brétigny in 1360 which left the English king, in return for freeing John II, with much of the south-west and a mound of gold, but neither Anjou nor Normandy. The peace was short-lived. In 1368 Charles V was able to take advantage of resentment amongst the barons of Aquitaine at efforts by the English to impose a centralised administration and increase taxation, and of their appeal to him as suzerain to adjudicate. Ten bitter years of war followed during which the English territories in Aquitaine were gradually reduced to a small area in Gascony around the ports of Bordeaux and Bayonne, tied to England by the wine trade. Only in 1388 was a lengthy truce agreed, lasting until 1412 when an English expeditionary force ravaged parts of Normandy and Anjou. This was followed in 1415 by the much more serious efforts of Henry V. He took advantage of the intermittent madness of Charles VI and the rivalry this encouraged between the princes of the blood. Henry V's first campaign culminated in the slaughter of the French nobility at Agincourt and was followed by a further invasion in 1417. At Troyes in 1420 a treaty was signed by which Henry V married Catherine, daughter of Charles VI, and was recognised as heir to the French crown. In 1422 his youthful successor, Henry VI, became king of both England and France.

The bases for this duel monarchy were however weak. The settlement was not unnaturally rejected by the French dauphin, calling himself Charles VII, who controlled the west, centre and Midi. Moreover, given the limits to English military strength, it was fundamentally dependent upon the support of a French party associated with the Duke of Burgundy. In 1429, inspired by the initial successes of Joan of Arc, the French recovery gathered pace. Duke

---

Plate 5 The siege of Orléans. Joan of Arc was to play a major role in the liberation of the city, one of the wealthiest and most strongly fortified in France. Artillery was used by both sides. Late fifteenth-century miniature

Philip the Good, anxious about the impact of war on Burgundy, made a separate peace in 1435, and in the fifteen years that followed, the English cause met growing resistance and suffered defeat after defeat, losing Paris itself in 1436. Areas formerly under English rule were encouraged to accept the restoration of French sovereignty by relatively moderate treatment. Along with other areas recently incorporated into the kingdom, they received parlements with, on the model of that of Paris, important administrative and judicial functions.

The dramatic succession of famines, plagues and wars over a period of at least 130 years had reduced the population from 16–17 million to about 12 million. If the social structures of an overwhelmingly rural society remained substantially unaltered, the process of adjustment to such an intense and prolonged series of crises ensured that the economy was more commercialised and the state more bureaucratic. The economic and political importance of the towns had grown. The wars themselves had done much to enhance both dynastic loyalty and by means of the monarchy's calls for support against the English, a diffuse sense of French identity. From the 1450s there began a long period of economic, political and demographic reconstruction and growth which, although interrupted by the wars of religion, and those under Richelieu, by the Fronde at the beginning of Louis XIV's reign and the wars at its end, was to be sustained.

3

Society and politics in early modern France

The misery caused by the long wars against the English and widespread internal disorder led to the construction of an ideal of good government, a vision of a state strong enough to impose order. This combined the glorification of monarchy by historians, artists and architects, with renewed efforts to subdue the military nobility by offering it employment in the royal service. Although bitter disputes over taxation continued, royal impositions were gradually accepted in principle and for the 'common good'. The closing years of the reign of Charles VII (1435–61) together with that of Louis XI (1461–83) constituted a major phase of political reconstruction, when growing economic activity facilitated a major increase in the revenue of the state – with tax income increasing from some 1.7 million livres tournois in 1439, to 2.3 million in 1449, and 5.1 million in 1482. The establishment of a secure income and the necessities of war would from 1439 allow the creation of a permanent army of 12–15,000 men, equipped with artillery, which reduced dependence on the feudal levy (finally abolished only in 1697). This constituted a first step towards the emergence of a state monopoly of armed force. Growing centralisation required the more effective support of administrative and judicial officials by military personnel, and by 1515 the 16 million inhabitants of the kingdom were governed through an administrative structure which, including soldiers and dependants gave sustenance to some 600,000 people, about 4 per cent of the total population.

The recovery of royal power was marked also by the notion that the king was 'Emperor in his Kingdom', by the re-assertion of the

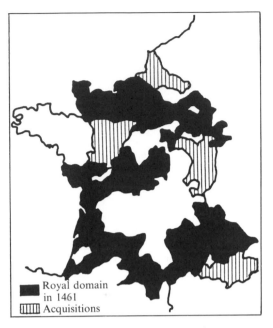

Fig 6 The creation of France. IV The reign of Louis XI, 1461–83

sovereign rights of royal courts, by an effort to make justice more
coherent, cheaper and more popular, and by the efforts of a king like
Louis XI to choose his own dependent officials, a policy bitterly
resented by those nobles who felt excluded; but whose opposition he
was strong enough to crush. Much of the old nobility had anyway
disappeared during the wars, providing opportunities for upward
mobility by successful soldiers, and wealthy *bourgeois*, prior to a
renewed closure of the noble order in the late sixteenth century. The
end of the fifteenth century also saw the disappearance of the
principality of Burgundy with the death without male heirs of Charles
the Bold in 1477, although the settlement which followed resulted in
the definitive loss of most of Flanders. In 1491 the marriage of Anne of
Brittany to Charles VIII finally extinguished the last autonomous
princely state, no longer able to preserve its independence by taking
advantage of the quarrels between England and France. It was all in
marked contrast to the political fragmentation of the year 1000, or the
threatened dissolution of the kingdom during the Hundred Years War.
The impact of geography, of provincial particularism and the defence

of noble privilege of course remained firm restraints on the affirmation of royal power. However, during the minority of Charles VIII the regent Anne de Beaujeu felt confident enough to convoke the first truly national and representative Estates to Tours in 1484, with one deputy from each order and each bailliage, establishing a form of election not dissimilar to that of 1789. The right of these delegates to present their *cahiers de doléances* (lists of grievances) and to discuss government policy was also established. Yet although deputies docilely voted taxes, the promise to recall them in the following year was not kept. Whilst accepting its responsibilities before God, the monarchy remained unwilling to justify its actions before men. The evident optimism of humanistic writers in the early sixteenth century, their pride in the rediscovery of antiquity, and rejection of the barbarism of the more immediate past, and the apparent prosperity and material well-being of much of the population should not moreover blind us to the fragility of an equilibrium threatened by population growth, war and religious dissent.

The long reign of Francis I (1515–47), like those of his successors Henri IV and particularly Louis XIV, was to be marked by the determination of a strong and over-confident personality to impose his will on France, and on Europe. Whilst rehabilitating Paris as his capital, Francis like Louis XI was attracted to the Loire valley. At Chambord he created a palace which provided a carefully constructed symbol of royal glory, a fit setting for courtly life and a vital centre for the distribution of patronage, and a potential means of subordinating the aristocracy. The ordinance of Villers-Cotterêts in 1539, through its insistence on the use of French in place of Latin in official documents, accelerated the process by which French became the daily language of local élites, the *lingua franca* of trade, and slowly, in a centuries long process of diffusion, completed only by compulsory education towards the end of the nineteenth century, the language of the masses. In creating the administrative state the kings of France were creating the nation. However the dream of European hegemony and the rivalry which developed between Francis and the Habsburg Charles V, was to embroil the country in a succession of external wars and closely related internal disorder, lasting until 1661. The situation was envenomed by religious dissent. In an era when almost every aspect of life was influenced by religious belief, and when the Roman Catholic Church was the repository of so much influence, the development of Protestantism was a matter of grave and often passionate concern. Inevitably religious disputes reflected pre-existing social and political divisions. Francis I was a sceptic in religious matters. His successor Henri II (1547–59) was a man of faith. For both, however, the Church was a major political instrument and source of revenue, and as such, had to be protected. There was also the obvious danger that religious disputes would encourage or serve as a pretext for political disaffection. Factional divisions at the centre were reflected in struggles between the clients of great men in the provinces which often degenerated, whatever the apparent political and religious justification, into little more than banditry.

Protestantism involved the demand for a religion based upon the Bible and deliverance from an oppressive clerical institution. For conservatives the defence of social order inevitably involved the protection of religious and moral orthodoxy, and was the primary responsibility of the king as the Lord's anointed. Failure would render him unworthy of his high office and served as the justification for the establishment of the Holy League by the Guise family in 1576, to oppose the accession to the throne of the Protestant Henri of Navarre. The geography of adherence to Protestantism is not easy to explain. In part it reflects the regional influence of major magnates such as the Montmorency-Châtillon and Bourbon families and the impact of religious disputes upon conflict for political power within the nobility. The royal council itself was divided by bitter factional rivalry. Most Protestant churches were initially to be found in the south and west including Normandy. The eventual north–south divide, with Protestants increasingly limited to the region around Montauban, Nîmes and La Rochelle, was to be the result of military defeat and subsequent persecution. Protestantism appealed to perhaps a fifth or quarter of the population at some time or other and in particular to relatively literate urban communities of professional men and artisans. These churches developed only rare linkages with surrounding rural societies – most notably in the Cévennes – where adherents were often partly motivated by the desire to eliminate the tithe.

A complex of factors combined to explain the defeat of Protestantism. They include the opposition of a monarchy which through its Concordat with the papacy in 1516 had already gained supremacy over the Church and was able to control the appointment of bishops and abbots and strictly limit papal financial exactions. In comparison with parts of Germany, the press and universities appear to have exercised a less dynamic role in the diffusion of ideas. Perhaps, too, clerical corruption was less scandalous whilst Calvinism failed to appeal to popular religious sensibilities as effectively as Catholicism. By the 1560s the Protestants were already too weak to achieve dominance but as yet too strong to be eliminated. The wars of religion which ensued would represent a massive crisis of monarchical authority.

Under these pressures royal government underwent a process of partial disintegration, particularly following the death of Henri II in 1559, which left a minority succession. This was a situation which encouraged the ambitions of great magnates. The sacred character of the monarchy could be rejected, on religious grounds, by both Catholic and Protestant critics. At its most extreme this was seen in the various justifications offered for tyrannicide. More seriously there occurred a collapse of central control over the decentralised and increasingly faction-riven administrative and judicial systems. Insecurity and the violence and bitterness generated by civil war were symbolised by the St Bartholomew's Night massacre of 5–6,000 Protestants in Paris and elsewhere on 27 August 1572. This only served to prolong the conflict in spite of the already clearly inferior military position of the Protestants. Murder, rape, torture and looting exemplified how completely the values of religion were forgotten in these wars of religion. In the regions worst effected, particularly in the east, the likelihood of food shortage and epidemic was greatly increased by foreign intervention and the movements of armies.

The sense of crisis was deepened in 1589 by the accession of the Protestant king, Henri IV. Catholic nobles were conscious both of the threat to their faith and to the privileges and rights they had previously derived from the monarchy. Henri, a master of compromise, sought however to conciliate his opponents. He was greatly assisted by a widespread desire for the restoration of order, best represented perhaps by Jean Bodin in the *Six livres de la République* (1576) in which he declared himself to be a partisan of an 'absolute power' capable of imposing its will and restrained only by respect for God's command- ments. A strong current of opinion favoured support for the legitimate king and resented Spanish intervention in support of the Catholic

Plate 6 The sacking of a farm: a classic image of the misfortunes
of war. The soldiers break down the door, murder the men, rape
the women, and carry off whatever takes their fancy

League. This sentiment was reinforced amongst both nobles and urban
élites by the apparent threat of anarchy represented by the radicalisation of the League in some northern cities and by peasant violence.
The political situation improved to a significant degree following the
decision of Henri IV (in 1593) to accept the Catholic faith, combined
with the Edict of Nantes which provided Protestants with politico-
military guarantees in the shape of towns which they were to control.
Another major innovation of the reign was the *paulette* by means of
which the sale of office, a revenue-raising device employed for over a
century, was regularised. Offices were to become inheritable on
payment of a fee. However humble, office conferred both status and
privilege upon its holder. Higher offices, frequently mere sinecures,
conferred nobility. In the short term this served to reduce magnate
influence on the bureaucracy, restricting the ability of great lords to
construct dependent clienteles. In the longer-term, private-property in
state-office and the creation of a largely self-perpetuating élite, was to
become a major obstacle to judicial and fiscal reform. This was partly
because of the multiplication of the number of venal offices, on a scale

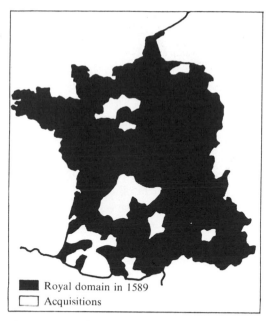

Fig 7 The creation of France. V Expansion of royal domain during the reign of Henri IV, 1589–1610

unsurpassed in Europe, to meet the costs of war in the seventeenth century. The system, which allowed the ennoblement of successful bourgeois families, diverted them from trade into the legal or administrative professions. Although their presence was bitterly resented by established nobles, it did however allow for continuous upward mobility, for a constant renewal of the élite, and the creation of a certain sense of common interest within the propertied classes.

The assassination of Henri IV in 1610 removed a strong and effective ruler. Under the regent Marie de Medici, and then Louis XIII (1610–43), faction rivalry initiated a return to anarchy, only gradually brought to an end between 1625 and 1642, when the cardinals Richelieu and then Mazarin sought to restore effective central leadership. Richelieu crushed Protestantism as an effective military force and brought the wars of religion to a final end. This period also saw the early development of the use of royal *commissaires*, the forerunners of the later *intendants*. These functionaries, provided with considerable supervisory and remedial powers as agents of the Royal Council, at this

stage merely detached on temporary missions, held non-venal com-
missions, and were dependent upon the crown in a way that the mass
of royal *officiers*, holders of venal (that is, purchased) office were not.
Their more extensive use was to be necessitated by the continuing
impact of external war against Spain (the Thirty Years War, 1618–48).
This resulted in massive tax increases (possibly as much as four-fold in
the 1630s) provoking a renewal of popular protest made all the more
dangerous in the case of the *Fronde* (1648–52) by the simultaneous
expression of grievances by elements of the great nobility and
magistrature irritated by the aggressive methods of the two cardinals
and the aggrandisement of their families.

This was another instance of grave economic distress and massive
popular discontent leading to violent opposition in both town and
country to the financial exactions of seigneurs and clerics and especially
the demands of government. The lack, or else excessive cost, of legal
redress, where royal *officiers* were interested parties, often seemed to
leave little alternative. The expression of discontent took various
forms. Animals might be maimed, hay-ricks set on fire, seigneurial or
royal agents beaten up, or contempt expressed for the offender in
various ways, such as ribald songs, the more structured use of 'rough
music' (*Charivari*) or through burning in effigy at carnival. The latter
was a customary means of expressing a grievance, part of a recognised
litany of protest, a useful means of letting off steam, and thus less likely
to meet with official repression. In the absence of an effective local
police and backed by a sense of communal solidarity, such actions
might at least ensure that landlords, seigneurs, the collectors of tithes
and taxes behaved with prudence.

Even so, following a poor harvest, the pressures on wide sections of
the community could become intolerable. The well-being even of
normally prosperous peasants and artisans might be menaced and the
very existence of the poor threatened. The anxiety and bitterness and
the emotional instability which resulted could overcome any lingering
fear of official retribution and provoke brutal protest, leading
occasionally to major revolts. These were likely to involve mostly
peasants with a leavening of urban artisans, tradesmen and impecunious minor nobles and professional men. They developed especially
where there were no local garrisons, or when, because of war, troops
had been transferred to the frontiers. The most notable risings occurred

in Guienne and other south-western provinces in 1548, in Dauphiné in the late 1570s, in Normandy and Brittany and again in the south-west in the 1590s, in the south-west once more in 1624 (Quercy) and in 1636–37, the most serious of all, the *Croquant* revolts affecting a wide area between the rivers Loire and Garonne, followed in 1639 by the revolt of the *Nu-Pieds* in Normandy. The rebels used community structures and economic networks as a basis for organisation, and employed custom and religion as justificatory beliefs. The general climate of opposition to authority certainly encouraged such action, particularly against tax collectors. New taxes, or rumours of such, were enough to cause church bells to be rung, emissaries from various communities to meet and crowds to march. The strength of popular feeling can be explained by the pressure imposed by a monetary tax on a predominantly subsistence rural economy. It forced peasants to search desperately for something to sell or for remunerative employment, often depriving them of foodstuffs they could well have eaten, or forcing them into debt. Revolt was most likely in wartime, when taxes, which had anyway been more or less arbitrarily imposed on a community by outsiders, for purposes they rarely understood, were increased. These revolts, although a serious threat to social order, rarely posed a threat to the social system. They represented a demand for the easing of burdens and for 'justice'. Most seigneurs shared the anti-fiscalism of the protestors, themselves viewing taxes as a threat to the payment of rents and feudal dues. Peasants were unable to escape from a profound sense of dependence on landowners and the clergy. In the end, the localism and limited objectives of these rebellions meant that they were easily suppressed once sufficient military force had been gathered and local élites had finally become frightened that turbulent crowds might turn on them, and were willing, once again, to cooperate with royal officials.

In spite of these disorders, the administrative machine survived and continued however inadequately to function. It could serve as the basis for an eventual restoration of the crown's authority. Indeed the wars which had increased the state's financial needs had intensified governmental impatience with such intermediary bodies as the provincial Estates and municipalities and encouraged authoritarianism on the part of its officers. The later seventeenth century was to see the virtual disappearance of large-scale armed revolts, the reinforcement

LVDOVICVS XIIII DEI GRATIA FRANCIÆ
ET NAVARRÆ REX CHRISTIANISSIMVS,

Plate 7 Louis XIV in 1660 aged twenty-two, already marked by a
sense of his personal dignity. Painting by Wallerand Vaillant

of the repressive apparatus of the state combined with less onerous
fiscal demands, and the development of a better-disciplined society due
to the spread of education and more effective religious socialisation
associated with the Catholic reformation. Subsequently the most
serious cause of popular protest was to be high food prices, leading to

demonstrations in market places, attacks on food transports, and on merchants suspected of speculation. The numbers of such incidents increased into the eighteenth century as commercialisation and the profit motive came into conflict with the subsistence needs of the poor and traditional conceptions of morality. They remained common until the improvement of communications, modernisation of marketing systems, and greater security of food supply established in the middle of the nineteenth century.

To a greater extent even than that of Henri IV the reign of Louis XIV (1643–1715) is obscured by myth. It can however safely be characterised as a further attempt to bring to an end the political fragmentation and social anarchy symbolised by the Frondes. The king's greatest success was to be this internal pacification achieved in the early years of his reign. On assuming personal control of government in 1661, Louis appeared to be immensely energetic but also dangerously avid for glory. In the continuing struggle against the Habsburgs the French enjoyed the advantage of a relatively homogeneous kingdom with interior lines of communication, and the more effective mobilisation of resources. However, initial success, followed by territorial expansion and the threat of French predominance, only alarmed the rest of Europe. Permanent mobilisation for war would eventually bring disaster, but this too had its positive side in that foreign armies were largely excluded from French soil, the French army itself was more regularly paid and better disciplined, and the nobility more fully employed – both in the army, and at court – than ever before, in the service of the state. The disarmament of noble châteaux and of the towns commenced by Richelieu and Mazarin also continued, achieving for the first time an effective royal monopoly of armed force.

In many respects Louis XIV was only operating a system of government created by his predecessors in which the role of the monarch, as the Lord's anointed, was to serve as the symbol and source of unity. To this end he was able to employ and, generally to control, the upper nobility (*haute noblesse*) at court and in the provincial governorships and higher military commands which were their due, and to channel the bellicose energies of the lower nobility into the king's service in an army which was now more effectively royal and less an instrument of the great nobility. The constant waging of war would satisfy the nobility's medieval perception of itself as the

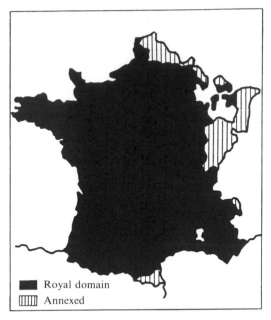

Fig 8 The creation of France. VI The reign of Louis XIV

warrior caste. The careful control of patronage systems and of the army allowed the king to purchase the loyalty of members of the élite or if necessary to use coercion. An image was constructed of an all-powerful monarch, of the Sun King ruling, in splendid isolation, from his massive and sumptuously decorated new palace at Versailles. Besides symbolising royal power and glory, Versailles provided a focal point for an aristocratic civilisation and for the diffusion throughout society of better manners and more restrained behaviour. Attendance on the king at court was the means of obtaining high office and pensions, of sharing in the royal bounty. The huge cost of construction was from the point of view of the monarchy money well spent. It increased the dependence of the upper nobility, and meant that they could be more closely supervised. It also ensured that kings were to be more than ever isolated from other forms of reality.

Another major act, of both direct political and symbolic significance, was the renewed assault on Protestantism culminating in the revocation of the Edict of Nantes in 1685. This was probably inevitable. The provisions of the Edict had already been substantially whittled away.

The existence of an armed state within the state was clearly intolerable. After 1622 only La Rochelle and Montauban remained under Protestant control. The Peace of Alès in 1629, whilst it confirmed the Edict of Nantes, suppressed the right to maintain even these towns as places of safety. By then too the Protestant party had been weakened by many desertions, most significantly by its noble leaders, many of them afraid of losing access to royal patronage. The Catholic counter-reformation, which only really began to make its impact on France from the first decade of the seventeenth century, was also beginning to have profound effects, imposing a new order on a Church, which had by now recovered most of the resources usurped or lost during the Wars of Religion. In 1685 Louis XIV, convinced of the validity of the principle 'One faith, one king, one law', was able to revoke the Edict with little risk of serious resistance, although the emigration of Protestants including many merchants and manufacturers (although partly compensated for by the influx of refugee Irish Catholics), had adverse economic consequences.

That Louis XIV could make effective use of this political system reflected both his own ability, his determination to exclude potentially troublesome magnates from his Council in favour of dependent members of a relatively new bureaucratic nobility, and the heart-felt desire of the better-off to avoid a renewal of internal anarchy. Both king and nobles were imbued with a more clearly defined sense of social hierarchy, in which the king stood indisputably at the summit and could appeal to the honour and loyalty of his nobles. A carefully constructed etiquette increased the social distance between them. Although disputes still occurred, their significance was limited both by the superior power of the monarchy and the involvement of most noble families, whether of the old 'sword' nobility or of the substantially new judicial-cum-bureaucratic 'robe' nobility, in the state service. The nobility developed a growing confidence that their needs were best served within rather than against the state. This compact would survive for as long as the élites remained sure that the monarchy was protecting their vital interests.

This development of Absolutism (a late eighteenth-century label), a crucially important stage in the process of state building, involved an increase in the interventionist capacity of the central power, by means of the further development of bureaucratic administration, although

Louis XIV and his successors would continue to face many of the same obstacles, including those of distance, poor communications, and inadequate resources, as had their predecessors. They had to work within the limits set by established institutions and extremely varied and heterogeneous laws and customs, and by the bounds of a pre-industrial society. The implementation of the policies of the central government in the provinces depended especially upon the *intendants*, recruited amongst aspiring young noble members of the Privy Council. Each was responsible for one of the thirty-three major administrative units (*généralités*) with subordinate officials (*subdélégués*), usually local nobles, under their orders, each administering an *élection*. They supervised all aspects of general and increasingly of municipal administration, including justice and the assessment and collection of taxes. These few agents of the central administration depended upon the willing cooperation of local notables, both nobles and commoners, men who owed their influence to their personal wealth, ownership of property and influence within their communities, as much as to their offices. At the base of the judicial hierarchy were the 70,000 seigneurial courts. In most circumstances the representatives of the central government were thus still local men and behaved as such. Family connections and local solidarities provided permanent obstacles to the development of bureaucratic government. Conflicts over jurisdiction and rivalries between governmental institutions abounded, exacerbated by the successive creation of new, and often venal, offices, which greatly increased the cost and slowed the processes of administration and justice. Covert disobedience and the failure to implement instructions, replaced open defiance. The situation of the *intendants* was made all the more difficult by the inadequate numbers of police. Lyons, with 150,000 inhabitants, for example, employed only 84, and the countryside was secured by a royal corps of mounted constabulary (the *maréchaussée*) with a national strength of only 4,000. Community self-regulation was the ideal. Where substantial disorder threatened, there was no alternative to calling in the army, but this could take time and was resisted by military commanders. For all these reasons the *intendants* were forced to adapt to local circumstances. By the 1780s they were experiencing a gradual decline in their authority as a consequence of weakness at the centre, due to the growing assertiveness of the nobility and the institutions within which noble interests were best represented.

The shortcomings of the system were especially obvious in the frequent partiality and cruelty displayed in the administration of justice. Moreover reform was extremely difficult. The purchase of office only reinforced the sense of independence of the mass of office holders (*officiers*). Governments did not dare suppress venal office, nor could they afford to buy out office-holders. At best a strong king, like Louis XIV, could use patronage to control such key institutions as the few remaining provincial Estates and the parlements, which were both the highest courts of law in their particular regions but also responsible for the registration of government edicts which was necessary before they acquired the force of law. However the failure of kings to summon an Estates-General between 1615 and 1789 and the absence of a representative and consultative institution at the national level seriously weakened relationships between the monarchy and its leading subjects.

In this situation internal administration remained 'a dialogue between the crown and a series of local elites, institutions and social groups, each one jealously guarding its traditions and undeniably legal privileges' (Mettam 1988). In the towns various groups (*officiers*, corporations, and so on) were accorded privileges in return for payment and service as part of the royal administration. In the countryside the key role remained that of the noble *seigneur*. The exercise of power at local and regional levels continued to depend to a large degree upon their social structures and upon relationships both within élites and between them and the social systems they sought to dominate. What was willed at the centre was not necessarily implemented in the locality. This was especially evident in the crucially important administration of finance. War and preparation for war were constant features of the *ancien régime* state. Its costs were the main charge on the budget – rarely below one-third, often over one-half, reaching 70 per cent during wars. The frequency of conflict, the introduction of a form of conscription (1688) and the growing size of armies (reaching 500,000 during the reign of Louis XIV) continually increased the strain. Due to the fiscal exemptions enjoyed by the nobles and clergy, the burden of taxation was borne primarily by the peasants, those least able to bear it. The situation was made even worse by the high cost of levying taxes, which depended upon the holders of venal office or, in the case of indirect taxes, on tax farmers – consortia of businessmen under contract to the crown – both operating through thousands of personal agents. These groups were at least as interested in personal profit as in serving the state. The efforts to encourage manufacture and colonial trade associated with Colbert were part of a drive to increase income as the means of achieving military supremacy. Their impact on state revenues was at best marginal and on economic structures it was negligible. Increasingly recourse was had to the Paris capital market, leading to an accumulation of debt which it would prove difficult to service and to a growing dependence of the crown upon its financiers. The cost absorbed 15–20 per cent of the budget for most of the eighteenth century, but an unsustainable 49 per cent by 1788. The mutual interest of (mainly recently ennobled) financiers and the leading noble families who provided most of their capital in preserving such a profitable system was to prove a constant obstacle to reform.

The reign of the Sun King came to an end with an intense social crisis caused by the burden of taxation at a time when, as in 1694, harsh weather and repeated harvest failure, or between 1708 and 1710 an accumulation of military and natural disasters, would in any case have had a devastating demographic impact. Almost twenty-five years of war was finally concluded by a state of mutual exhaustion and the treaties of Utrecht and Rastadt in 1713–14. In contrast with these calamitous decades the remainder of the eighteenth century, and in particular the years from about 1745 to about 1770, was to be characterised by economic and demographic recovery, and long periods of internal peace and order. Yet although in the closing decades of the century there were some signs of technical innovation in both farming and manufacture, and in spite of the fact that easier climatic conditions, improved communications and the better distribution of foodstuffs limited the intensity of subsistence crises, the basic economic and social structures of a pre-industrial society survived. France remained a predominantly agrarian society, with manufacturing dispersed in small workshops in both town and country, and the entire economy dominated by the harvest. The legal hierarchy of a society of orders remained intact, justified as it had been around the year 1000 by the distinction between those who prayed, those who fought, and those

Plate 8 Construction of a road. Painting by J. Vernet (1774). The movement of people and goods was made easier due to the *corvée* (1738), establishment of the *Corps des Ponts et Chaussées* (1750) and substantial government investment

who worked. In a strictly hierarchical – though not entirely immobile – society, the poor were kept in their place by dependence, fear and the sense of inferiority which underlay resignation and outward respect. Similarly the political institutions of the *ancien régime* changed only very slowly with precedent being used to considerable effect by the defenders of vested interest. Nevertheless, and in spite of the slow pace of social change, these formal structures were coming to be seen as increasingly anachronistic.

It has become more and more unfashionable in recent years to emphasise the social causes of the Revolution of 1789. In place of the familiar Marxist view of a struggle between a declining nobility and a rising bourgeoisie, historians have increasingly come to stress the interests nobles and bourgeois had in common, as well as the divisions of interest within each of these groups. They have quoted Turgot's observation that, 'The cause of privilege is no longer the cause of distinguished families against commoners, but the cause of the rich against the poor' (1776) and have described the emergence of an élite of *notables* of which nobles were only a part. In a society which defined itself in terms of orders, there were groups at the summit of each order which tended to distinguish themselves by their wealth, status and power, from the rest of their order. Nobles and wealthy non-nobles had shared interests in landownership, a common life-style and the enjoyment of privilege. The bourgeoisie remained an essentially pre-industrial class, being composed mainly of landowners, professional men, financiers and merchants and, far from being hostile to nobility, wealthy commoners were engaged in the process of acquiring noble status as the ultimate mark of their personal success. The problem, if this was the case, will be to explain why the lines of conflict as they were drawn in 1789 would largely separate noble and bourgeois. The rapid collapse of the regime, paralleled perhaps only by the events of 1989–90 in Eastern Europe, is surely inexplicable without consideration of the underlying social tensions.

The French nobility was certainly not a declining social group. Many nobles were at the forefront of innovation in both agriculture and industry. Successful business and professional men still sought nobility as the ultimate symbol of achievement. Although these *nouveaux riches* newcomers were often resented, particularly by impoverished families of ancient lineage, the nobility was a relatively open élite which continued to renew itself. Land remained by far the main source of income, and most families restricted themselves to traditional investments in land and in office and enjoyed the benefits of rising prices from about 1730. Some of the most illustrious families, like that of Orléans, were nevertheless increasingly prepared to invest in the most dynamic sectors of the industrial economy, in textiles, mining and metallurgy. Like any social group, the nobility was divided – between wealthy and impoverished nobles, court nobles and provincial gentry, old and new, and into political clienteles and family clans – into groups which had differing perceptions of their vital interests. The mass of provincial nobles resented the power and ostentation of the great court families (some 4,000 people) who monopolised pensions, favours, and senior positions in the army and bureaucracy. Families of old lineage poured scorn on the pretentions of the recently ennobled, many of whom would within the course of two or three generations nevertheless succeed in fully integrating themselves, an achievement frequently symbolised by the move from judicial office (robe nobility) to military service. Many other noble families could barely make ends meet. Some were unable to afford the education or the investment necessary to acquire office, or the equipment essential to a military career. Only their pride, the cult of honour, the sense of belonging to a race apart, given a semblance of historical credibility in such books as the Comte de Boulainvilliers, *Essai sur la noblesse de France* (1732), by the right to wear a sword, and the family pew in the village church, allowed them to maintain a 'social distance' between themselves and the peasantry. The poor nobles faced the eventual prospect of being forced to take on degrading manual or money-making activities which might well lead them into *dérogeance* or the loss of noble status and privilege including the tax exemptions made all the more important by their possessors' impecunious position. The great majority came somewhere in between these extremes. For them a decent income, education and culture, were the means of keeping up appearances. The division of inheritances to favour the eldest son and a carefully planned marriage strategy, including the dispatch of unmarriageable daughters to a nunnery, were crucial means of keeping family possessions intact.

The number of nobles by 1789 has been variously estimated at between 110,000 and 350,000 (1–1.5 per cent of the population). In

France, unlike Britain, titles and noble status descended from the father to all his children. Acceptance of the lower figure would suggest that one in four of noble families had acquired nobility during the eighteenth century, a relatively high rate of upward mobility, but if the higher estimate is accurate only around one in twelve families had been recently ennobled, which would support a more plausible view of the second order as a relatively self-contained, though far from closed, caste. Compared with other social groups the nobility's privileges and distinctive values gave it a greater sense of corporate unity and of moral superiority. Its traditional commitment was to service in the state bureaucracy and in the army. The latter was regarded as the most honourable of its functions, through which its members repeatedly sacrificed their lives and justified their fiscal and seigneurial privileges. As had been the case from time immemorial nobles occupied all the important offices of church and state – of sixty-five ministers in office between 1718 and 1789 only three were non-nobles, although others came from recently ennobled families. Nobles were thus both the agents of a centralising royal power and, in the provinces, its most determined opponents. It would take the Revolution to impose a greater sense of unity.

The bourgeoisie too was an extremely diverse group. In current usage the term, (when it was not used in the technical sense to designate an enfranchised citizen of a city), was applied to the property owner or *rentier*. To *vivre bourgeoisement* meant to live primarily from unearned income, and to share the aristocratic disdain for those who worked with their hands. Often such people belonged to the charmed circle of holders of ennobling office, admission to which required the wherewithal to purchase, but also useful contacts and family connections. Others either did not desire or more likely could not afford the cost. Although the structure of the bourgeoisie varied with the range of economic and administrative functions of a particular town, its wealthier members were inevitably few in number and formed a relatively coherent group, living in close proximity in newly constructed mansions, furnished in the latest style, meeting socially and intermarrying. Below them in status came the less successful *négociants* (men of commerce), *marchands* (traders, manufacturers, putting-out and retailers) and professionals and the lower middle class of shopkeepers and self-employed artisans. There could be little sense of solidarity amongst such diverse groups. The latter were men who took pride in their 'art', in skills acquired through a long apprenticeship. Both they and the journeymen they employed shared in a sense of moral community which limited the tensions between master and man and distinguished them both from the members of other trades and especially from the mass of unskilled labourers, desperately striving to make ends meet. In a town like Orléans in 1789 *négociants, marchands*, officials, professional men and shopkeepers made up 7 per cent of the active inhabitants and master-artisans 30.8 per cent. Although only 16 per cent of the population lived in towns, most of which were small and essentially medieval in appearance, the dynamic impact of these places as economic, administrative, political and cultural centres should not be underestimated.

If the nobility frequently represented a goal and a model to aspiring members of the middle classes, they might also often resent its arrogance. The most prestigious path to nobility was through the purchase of ennobling office. Necker calculated that there were some 4,000 of these. It was also necessary to withdraw from 'degrading' money-making activities or manual work and to adopt the life-style of a landed gentleman. Even then the process of assimilation could take two or three generations. Moreover economic prosperity, growing wealth and increased competition for ennobling office, at the same time as institutions like the parlements were becoming more exclusive, tended, as the eighteenth century progressed, to reduce the opportunities for promotion and to exacerbate hostility towards the established nobility, particularly at the local level at which noble hauteur was most likely to be experienced. This does not mean that the bourgeoisie, before 1789, was becoming class conscious. Certainly however some of the better educated and more self-aware landowners, merchants, *rentiers*, and professional men were attracted by meritocratic and egalitarian ideas, and were increasingly resentful of noble privilege.

In spite of the emergence of something akin to class structures based upon income and socio-professional origins, the old concepts of 'honour' and 'dignity' continued to influence social relationships. Aristocratic pretensions and insistence upon legal and social distinctions were a cause of tension. Nobles of ancient lineage saw themselves as belonging to a race apart, with its identity maintained by breeding and a cult of honour. These pretensions were inevitably resented both by the newly ennobled en route to assimilation and especially by those commoners aware of aristocratic disdain. The path to social promotion and final respectability was in practice obstructed by all manner of pitfalls. The number of ennobling offices was always relatively small. Economic depression might spoil the best laid plans. Lawyers, landowners, *officiers*, large merchants (*négociants*) and *rentiers* were however essentially conservative in their outlook and their resentment was only beginning to find political expression before the pre-revolutionary crisis. In part this was a response to the so-called 'noble reaction', an effort to preserve noble predominance in appointments to civil office and senior positions in the army. Nobles felt that they – and they alone – were the natural counsellors of the monarchy, and that they had a right and indeed a duty to serve. Their privileges were thus a just reward for service. In many respects the label 'reaction' is a misnomer. It did not take the form of a deliberate offensive on the part of the privileged. Nobles were behaving much as they always had. However, it does convey accurately a growing disquiet about their behaviour amongst other social groups. The *loi Ségur* of 1781 (largely a codification of earlier measures), restricted direct entry into certain commissioned ranks in the army to men belonging to families which had been noble for at least four generations, with the aim of creating an officer corps imbued with traditional martial values. The law had little practical consequence. Even before the decree about 95 per cent of officers were nobles. It served nevertheless as proof of growing noble exclusivism to non-nobles, and indeed to the recently ennobled, against whom it was primarily directed. Other features of this 'noble reaction' had an impact on rural life.

Towards the end of the century it is estimated that the nobility owned 20–25 per cent of the land, the clergy 6–10 per cent, the bourgeoisie around 30 per cent and peasants 40–45 per cent. In a period of rising prices land was an attractive investment, possession of which, moreover, secured social status. Much of the noble and clerical property was concentrated on the fertile northern plains, whilst the proportion owned by peasants tended to increase towards the south. To the north-east of a line from Caen to Lyons nobles owned about 30 per cent of the agricultural land, whilst to the south-west their share rarely exceeded 20 per cent. In some localities, particularly close to large towns, the proportions were much higher. For many landowners, there was little incentive to invest capital in agricultural improvement, especially when rising rentals might be supplemented with income from seigneurial dues or office-holding. By these various means the relatively small number of noble families were able to appropriate perhaps one-quarter of the revenue from agriculture. This economic power was reinforced by the social and political power conferred by seigneurial justice and the support they enjoyed in case of dispute from an administration itself constituted of nobles determined to defend the social order. The conditions of peasant life varied considerably from region to region according both to ecology and to the division of property. They made up about three-quarters of the population but, following payment of rents, seigneurial dues, tithes and taxes, were left with little more than one-third of the income from the land. Other key factors influencing their situation included tenurial arrangements, involvement in rural manufacture, different habitat structures, communal practices and cultural traditions, and legal status, with around one million serfs in the Franche-Comté and Nivernais whilst other peasants were free agents. Significantly however only a minority, perhaps one-third, had access to sufficient land to maintain their families. The remainder were forced to rent land or sell their labour in order to subsist. Population pressure and the continuous parcellation of smallholdings drove many peasants into destitution, allowing landlords to increase the size of their estates, whilst at the same time further subdividing holdings to increase the number of tenants on short leases. As in previous periods of demographic recovery, the intensification of commercial relationships and the move towards production for sale enhanced the value of the basic economic resources and intensified the competition to control them. Some landowners were encouraged to develop more rational and remunerative means of exploiting their economic resources, through improved farming methods, greater commercialisation of the product, investment in the exploitation of raw materials on and under the land (particularly water, wood and coal), and attempts to increase the returns from rentals and seigneurial dues (assisted by better surveying, mapping and accounting techniques). In a period of growing population pressure on resources, the rise in rents and prices led to a deterioration in the situation of the growing numbers of poor, struggling to obtain access to land, employment or at least charity. Such conditions inevitably increased the hostility of the mass of the population towards those, whether nobles, bourgeois, clerics or the better-off peasants, who appeared to be accumulating land and to be exploiting the scarce resources they controlled at the expense of the rural community. As always such pressures stimulated peasant resistance although this inevitably came from a position of weakness in the face of seigneurial justice and noble domination of the judicial and administrative system.

Resistance took various forms including law-suits over such matters as the enclosure of common land and the restriction of customary rights of usage in forests, and increasing criminality in what remained, in spite of growing literacy and the Church's efforts to encourage greater self-control, a harsh and brutal world. Both provide evidence of a more combative spirit and of resistance on the part of the rural poor to the development of a capitalistic agriculture. This was especially evident when, after a poor harvest, the rise in food prices caused by panic buying and speculation made the burden of rents, seigneurial dues, tithes and taxes, which even in a good year extracted anywhere between one-third and one-half of the peasants' gross revenue, all the more intolerable. There was certainly nothing new in this, nor in the tendency of the poor to explain their misery by personalising their problems and blaming in particular the parasitic activities of merchants, seigneurs and the clergy. The seigneurial presence with its courts of law, the right to levy dues and labour service, its irritating monopolies, hunting privileges and pomp, was particularly strong in the north, east and centre-east but much less so in the Massif Central and south. It must all have seemed increasingly redundant when the seigneur no longer offered protection against marauders and when most of his judicial functions had been rented out to local lawyers or taken over by the monarchy. Although these rights were frequently owned by commoners the system nevertheless remained closely identified with the nobility. It was in these areas in which the seigneurial system was most burdensome that the capitalistic pressures to acquire land and to maximise returns were also most intense. The tithe payable to the Church in contrast was particularly high, at around 10–12.5 per cent of the crop in the south-west, whilst averaging 7–8 per cent for France as a whole. Taxation was another burden borne primarily by the peasants, who were additionally required to perform labour service on the roads, billet and transport troops and serve in the militia. If there were no major anti-taxation revolts in the eighteenth century, there was certainly bitter resentment, especially of indirect taxes like the *gabelle* on salt. The burden of protest had however clearly shifted from resistance to the demands of the state to defence of communal interests against the increasingly capitalistic practices of landlords and *seigneurs*, of merchants and farmers.

It was nevertheless the financial problems of the state which were to cause the final crisis of the *ancien régime*. The demise of Louis XIV had been followed by the regency of Philippe d'Orléans (1715–22), with subsequently, from 1726 to 1743 a long period in which the Cardinal de Fleury served as Louis XV's (1715–74) leading minister. The essential characteristic of this period had been its relative freedom from external war. These were years of administrative reorganisation and fiscal stability and, in spite of the failure of Law's schemes for financial and budgetary reform and for the repurchase of venal office, of declining expenditure and taxes. They were an interlude between the wars of the Sun King and the series of wars – the War of the Austrian Succession (1741–48), the Seven Years War (1756–63), and the American War of Independence (1777–83) – which by bankrupting the state brought on the Revolution. Typically the peaceful years have been relatively neglected by historians.

Eventually Louis XV would prove to be too weak and the Cardinal de Fleury too old (at ninety) to resist the pressure from courtiers to enter the War of the Austrian Succession on the side of Prussia against the hereditary Habsburg enemy. Military failure then and subsequently was undoubtedly a blow to the monarchy's prestige. The Treaty of Paris which brought the Seven Years' War to an end was particularly humiliating. Successive defeats and a growing state debt reflected as much as anything the lack of effective political leadership. This was also the case internally where every effort to improve the state's financial position through increased taxation met with opposition from the privileged classes. This was voiced both by the *parlements*, of which there were thirteen, 'sovereign' courts of law which served as final courts of appeal, together with twenty-five other more specialised sovereign courts, generally dealing with fiscal matters. Once having purchased their offices, the members of these courts were irremovable,

Plate 9 The battle of Fontenoy during the War of Austrian Succession, 11 May 1745. The Marshal de Saxe presents captured flags to Louis XV. Painting by Horace Vernet

and had a long tradition of opposition to the monarchy, expressed in the form of *remonstrances* or criticisms of various legislative proposals, and by refusals to register laws, without which they were inoperable within a court's jurisdiction. Although the king could force registration (by means of a procedure known as a *lit de justice*) parlements could thus delay the implementation of legislation and publicise their grievances. Parlements also had extensive administrative responsibilities in their localities and this could bring them into conflict with the royal bureaucracy. Historically their members were usually divided amongst themselves, and unable to stand up to a determined government. From the 1750s, however, they appear to have voiced increasing criticism of government policy. In the 1780s they were to serve as a focal point for the development of the political crisis, serving above all to express noble dissatisfaction. Most members of the parlements inherited their offices and were already nobles (for the period 1775–90 this was true of 97 per cent in Toulouse, 90 per cent in Grenoble, 82 per cent in Paris, with much smaller proportions elsewhere), whilst membership conferred nobility upon the remainder.

As nobles they were determined to safeguard their liberties, privileges and property, but additionally they were imbued with vague ideals concerning their duty to protect the constitution and the people against royal 'despotism'. This mixture of liberal principles and the defence of privilege attracted considerable public support. The Parlement of Paris had claimed the right to verify taxation in 1763–64. Subsequently provincial parlements had protested against government policy and even gone on strike.

By the end of 1769 the budget deficit had reached 63 million livres, and the following two years' revenue had been spent in advance. In this desperate situation, and in order to circumvent opposition, Louis XV, for once, acted with determination. His chancellor Maupeou decided in February 1771 to exile the Parlement of Paris to the provinces and to set about replacing the parlements with salaried officials dependent upon the state. The Abbé Terray began the work of tax reform and by 1774 the budget was almost in balance, and the state's credit restored. This was the moment at which Louis XV died. His young successor, a weaker man dominated by his courtiers and anxious to avoid unpopularity, abandoned Maupeou's reforms just at the moment they began to take effect. The monarchy had thus lost the political initiative. Although, following the chastening experience of Maupeou's reforms, the parlements were for many years to be more circumspect in their opposition, they were simply biding their time. Frequent requests continued to be made for an Estates-General, or at least provincial Estates, to consent to taxation. This all helped to feed the growing current of criticism evident from mid-century, most notably in the seventeen volumes of the *Encyclopédie* published between 1751 and 1765. Its 150 contributors, inspired by the belief that progress was possible through the development of human reason, rejected appeals to the traditional authority of custom or religion, and insisted upon rational criticism of established institutions and behaviour. Typically the Abbé Coyer in his *La Noblesse commerçante* (1756) ridiculed justifications of seigneurial privilege based upon the age-old military role of the nobility. All this contributed to the development of a complex intellectual climate which served to justify all manner of discontents. These writers, the so-called *philosophes*, however, lacked a political programme. They favoured monarchy because of its supposed social utility, but many nobles and professional bourgeois desired a wider participation in government. This resulted in the development of a doctrine, based very much upon Montesquieu's *Esprit des Lois*, which demanded both the enlargement of their own constitutional role to include approval of legislation and of taxation and the protection of the 'fundamental laws' of the kingdom, and at the same time condemned 'despotism', a debased form of monarchical government. In effect a new political culture seems to have begun to emerge from the 1750s. Its proponents certainly did not see themselves as revolutionaries, but played the dangerous game of expressing contempt for established values, and presented new ideas on such matters as the duties of government and on the role of the propertied classes, with little thought for the possible practical implications of their views. Meritocratic rather than egalitarian, they nevertheless supported greater civil liberty and freedom from the constraints of administrative regulation and from the restrictive effects of corporative organisation on economic activity, with 'happiness' as the objective and 'reason' as the means. As a practical matter, reform of the legal system was widely supported. It was assumed that the abolition of conflicting jurisdictions and complex judicial procedures would make justice available to all. They were particularly bitter critics of the Church which seemed to exemplify the irrational and superstitious, and to serve as the enemy of reason.

The impact of the Enlightenment is not easy to assess. It undoubtedly proved to be fashionable in educated circles – noble and non-noble – particularly amongst the younger generations, gathering in provincial academies, upper class *salons*, and the socially more diverse masonic lodges, reading rooms and *cafés*. It faced little in the way of structured, intellectual opposition. The spread of literacy, and the existence of a relatively well-educated professional bourgeoisie had created a wider audience than ever before for new ideas. Even so it is difficult to determine how far down the social hierarchy new ideas percolated. In intention at least, the Enlightenment was not directed at the mass of the population. Its proponents were suspicious, and indeed frightened, of popular unrest. The use of the apparently universalistic language of rights and justice, however, encouraged the popularisation of new ideas amongst an increasingly literate middle class and artisan audience, in simplified, and often distorted form, through pamphlets and by word of mouth. Although an irritation, censorship proved largely ineffective. It is worth remembering, though, that most of the population was untouched by new ideas, and that even in the educated classes many, especially amongst the older generations, and away from intellectual circles, were left indifferent or hostile. Traditional and religious ideas continued to hold sway. Although declining in significance, religious works retained their predominant place amongst the output of the printing press, merely hinting at the weight of conservatism in this 'age of enlightenment' in which too most of the population remained totally or functionally illiterate. Similarly the image of the 'good king (*roi-père*)' retained its potency. If anything went wrong, and especially when food prices rose, the fault was not the king's, but that of his incompetent or evil-intentioned ministers. Thus the efforts of Turgot in the 1770s to reduce the regulatory powers of the corporations, to establish freedom of internal trade in cereals and more generally to create a framework which would encourage economic activity, and thereby increase government tax revenue, met with considerable opposition from bureaucrats and the parlements afraid that deregulation would lead to increased popular disorder and themselves subscribing to popular fears of a speculative 'famine plot'. In the very imperfect market conditions which prevailed, because of poor communications, it was perhaps inevitable that the poor harvest of 1775 and rising prices, together with suspicion of Turgot's intentions, should provoke widespread protest, the so-called 'flour war', which contributed to his subsequent dismissal and the restoration of market regulation.

Enlightenment ideals were not however without their influence in governing circles, as can be seen from the abolition of judicial torture and the extension of civil rights to Protestants. Many of the major reforms of the legal system implemented after 1789 were already under discussion. Criticism itself achieved respectability and many of the leading critics were integrated into the establishment. Contemporaries nevertheless were left with an overwhelming sense of governmental inflexibility in the face of the mounting wave of criticism which characterised the 1780s, a movement encouraged paradoxically by the self-interested criticism of monarchical 'despotism' voiced by such privileged noble institutions as the parlements. This itself was largely a response to the opportunities provided by the state's deteriorating financial situation and its increasingly desperate search for remedies.

Although the figures are all very approximate because of the absence of effective central budgetary control, it has been estimated that by 1788, in a year of peace, 26.3 per cent of government spending was military in character, and 23.2 per cent civil, whilst a massive 49.3 per cent was absorbed in funding government debt (against a more 'normal' 15–20 per cent). Public opinion frequently blamed the growing debt upon the extravagance of Queen Marie-Antoinette and the court, and this indeed made up over 5 per cent of total expenditure. The primary cause of the financial crisis was however the cost of war and of preparation for war. The future stability of the French kingdom had required the avoidance of military commitments. But Louis XVI had ardently desired French participation in the American War of Independence as a means of gaining revenge for the defeats of the Seven Years' War. The successes of French arms were financed by Necker mainly through loans, which were to weigh heavily upon the financial system. At the same time, proposals to increase taxation of the privileged classes were blocked by the parlements. The government's reluctance to proceed with these was increased, moreover, by the fact that most of the projected reforms would have resulted in a short-term loss of revenue. Even as awareness of the problem grew in ministerial circles, a tendency remained for the king and his Ministers of War and the Navy to spend without counting the cost. Nevertheless, by the summer of 1788 the government was effectively bankrupt and in August the financial Controller General Lambert was obliged to suspend interest payment on the debt. Consideration of the need to adapt an archaic system of financial management and tax collection to the needs of a modern state could clearly not be postponed for much longer. It had long been clear that tax revenue could only be increased significantly by reducing the exemptions on direct taxation enjoyed by the clergy, nobility, various urban corporations, and so on, and by bringing the collection of indirect taxes, hitherto farmed out to private companies, under direct state control. The *taille*, the major direct tax, was levied almost exclusively on the peasantry, and had effects counter to the policy of encouraging increased productivity as an alternative means of increasing tax income. The obstacles to reform were both technical and social. Although France was probably less heavily burdened by taxes than Holland or Britain, public opinion was convinced of the contrary, in part because of the complexity, diversity, and regional variations in the type and scale of taxation, all of which contributed to a sense of arbitrariness. Holland and Britain also had the advantage of more effective credit institutions and governments which, enjoying greater public confidence, were able to mobilise loans at a lower rate of interest. Socially, the major obstacle to reform was the nobility. Certainly many nobles were prepared to contemplate change in return for a greater share in political power, but in practice whatever course of action ministers took seemed to face opposition from some segment of a social élite whose intransigence might seem to mark a growing sense of insecurity regarding its own status. The last desperate effort to overcome this resistance was to lead directly to revolution.

PART 2

THE DUAL REVOLUTION: MODERN AND CONTEMPORARY FRANCE

The causes of the French Revolution have been endlessly debated. Assessment of its impact has resulted in this century in the adoption of two successive orthodoxies. First the Marxist, the most recent major advocate of which was the late Albert Soboul from his Chair of the History of the French Revolution at the Sorbonne. This portrayed the Revolution as bringing about the final, and much delayed ending of the feudal system. The way was open for the emergence of modern capitalist society. Subsequent efforts to set the Revolution within a broader chronological context have led to a questioning of its significance as an historical event. Although the revolutionaries clearly sought to remove some of the institutional obstacles to the development of a market economy, it appears that France in 1815 was not so very different from France in 1789. It remained an essentially pre-industrial society dominated by a landed élite. It was only subsequently, as the pace of socio-economic change accelerated, that a fundamental social transformation occurred. Even then the complex of developments associated with industrialisation evolved far more gradually in France than in either Britain or Germany. This insistence upon the significance of continuities across the revolutionary period has led historians, and most notably François Furet, to stress the importance of its ideological and political rather than socio-economic impact. A recognisably modern political culture was created and widely diffused during these tumultuous years. Sovereignty was transferred from the king to the nation. Amongst the problems this caused was that of defining the 'nation', and the means by which it would intervene in politics. In the search for a solution a variety of constitutional proposals were considered. In the process the words left and right, conservative and radical took on new meaning. A wide range of political allegiances was created, and a set of agendas with which to inspire political activists from that day to this, although these have of course been repeatedly reinterpreted to suit changing social and political conditions. The French Revolution might then best be conceived as an integral part of a dual and permanent revolution whose bases are both economic and political. It has inspired both hope and fear, at times with a dangerous, religious intensity. As a result it was not until the Fifth Republic that a genuine consensus on institutions was to be established. It is the impact of this dual revolution that we shall be concerned with in the next section of this book.

4

Revolution and Empire

The collapse of absolute monarchy was to be sudden and shocking to contemporaries. It heralded two decades of revolutionary turbulence and war, after a century or more free from serious internal disorder. Moreover the stability of the social and state systems of most European countries were to be threatened and a new political culture established which still shapes our thought and action. Inevitably explanations of these events have varied. The 150th anniversary of the Revolution in 1939 was marked by the appearance of Georges Lefebvre's *Quatre-Vingt-Neuf* (subsequently translated as *The Coming of the French Revolution*). For its Marxist author, the revolution represented the seizure of power by the *bourgeoisie*, a class created by the centuries' long development of capitalism in French society. That the representatives of this class were able to seize power, to destroy aristocratic privilege and establish civic equality, was due to the collapse of monarchical power. This had occurred because of the unwillingness of the landed aristocracy to contemplate fiscal and institutional reforms which would have reduced their privileges, and the ability of bourgeois political leaders to take advantage of mass discontent in the countryside and amongst the urban poor, particularly in Paris, in order to defeat aristocratic and monarchical reaction. Lefebvre in effect identified four revolutionary movements – that of the aristocracy which prevented monarchical reform, that of the bourgeoisie, the urban revolution symbolised by the storming of the Bastille, and the peasant revolution.

They were interlinked, but each had its own distinctive objectives. This remained the dominant view amongst historians for some twenty years, until challenged by Alfred Cobban in a lecture entitled *The Myth of the French Revolution* in 1955. Cobban denied that the Revolution involved 'the substitution of a capitalist bourgeois order for feudalism'. He believed that it represented an effort by the traditional landowning and professional middle-classes to gain access to office and political power. Rather than promoting the development of capitalism, the revolution represented a major setback. Although condemned out of hand by Lefebvre as the work of a political reactionary, Cobban's essentially negative assault on the established view stimulated an extensive and ongoing debate. The appealing certainties of a narrow class-based explanation have been lost for ever, as historians have identified both the vital interests which nobles and bourgeois had in common, and the divisions of interest *within* both social groups. It has come to be accepted that political events – the calling by the king of an Assembly of Notables, and the preparation for and meeting of the Estates-General in 1789 – revived and reinforced a complex of social tensions concerning the management of property and access to political power and focused the discontent of the middle classes, urban workers and peasants on the aristocracy. Whilst the actual outbreak of the Revolution has to be linked to a fortuitous combination of particular events, its fundamental causes were certainly deep-rooted in the structure of French society and its political system. The government's failure to cope successfully with mounting fiscal problems had substantially reduced its prestige at the same time as this apparent ineffectiveness increased interest in proposals for constitutional reform. Support for the government from many of its normal adherents declined, and with it, its capacity for either reform or repression, so the mobilisation of opposition proceeded apace, culminating in the revolutionary overthrow of the *ancien régime*.

In theory at least, the French governmental system was based upon absolute monarchy, with the king's rights limited only by divine law. He was the source of all laws and of administrative authority, and had the right to appoint all officials, to declare war or peace, and levy taxes. Louis XV declared in 1766: 'Sovereign power resides in my person alone. To me alone belongs all legislative power with neither any responsibility to others nor any division of that power. Public order in

Plate 10 Louis XVI in his coronation robes. Painting by Joseph-Siffred Duplessis

all its entirety emanates from me, and the rights and interests of the nation are necessarily bound up with my own and rest only in my hands.' As the clergy, present in every community, constantly reminded the population – this was God's will. One of Louis XVI's major achievements was to substantially weaken this age-old popular veneration for the person of the monarch.

In practice, as we have seen, severe limitations were imposed upon the powers of the central authority by the relationship of interdependence which existed between the king and social élites. These provided the senior personnel for the civil service and army, and for judicial institutions including those sovereign courts, and most notably the parlements, which claimed to act as guardians of the fundamental laws of the kingdom. Other limiting factors included the small size of the dependent bureaucracy, and the fact that many officials had purchased their entitlement to office and saw this as conferring considerable independence upon themselves. There was also the sheer physical difficulty of receiving information and maintaining control over a large territory with poor communications, although substantial road improvements had occurred during the eighteenth century. In other words there was a marked and dangerous contrast between the monarch's political responsibilities and the resources available to fulfil these, and nowhere was this more evident than in the areas of primary governmental responsibility: the maintenance of justice; the waging of war; and the levying of taxes to finance these functions.

Effective government involved a continuous process of compromise between the king, social élites and office holders. The reconciliation of complex conflicting interests was never easy. A solution of the grave problems facing the French monarchy in the late eighteenth century would have required leadership of an extremely high standard, which the mediocre Louis XVI had neither the ability nor training to provide. Neither did he have the strength of character necessary to choose and consistently support an effective chief minister. Such a delegation of authority would have appeared to Louis to be inconsistent with his divine right to rule. This fundamental weakness of absolute monarchy, its excessive dependence upon the abilities and will of whoever inherited the throne, was intensified by the absence of an effective system for coordinating the activities of ministers and of a routine for presenting matters for the monarch's consideration. His interventions in government were unsystematic, frequently ill-informed and subject to court intrigue. A king who hardly stirred out of Versailles, except to hunt, was physically, and more important psychologically out of touch with the problems of his kingdom. As a result his policy decisions reflected the influence of a small circle of aristocratic advisers who regarded him with contempt and who were willing to contemplate only those reforms which did not threaten their own social status and political power. Ministerial stability and consistent policies were always at the mercy of faction struggles within this inner circle.

On 20 August 1786 Calonne, the Controller General, warned Louis XVI that the state was on the verge of financial collapse. According to his – uncertain – calculations, revenue in 1786 would amount to around 475 million livres, and expenditure to 587 millions. A rise in debt on that scale could not be funded for long. There were a number of policy alternatives. These included economies: the scope for these was limited, however. Debts and debt interest had to be repaid or confidence in the financial system would collapse. Savings on the military account would threaten France's international position. Reductions in spending on the royal household and on public works were possible, but would nowhere nearly cover the deficit. Another possibility was increased taxation, but the widespread feeling that the burden was already excessive and the bitter opposition likely from the privileged classes made this a politically hazardous course of action. Calonne concluded that, 'it is impossible to tax further, ruinous to be always borrowing and not enough to confine ourselves to economical reforms and that, with matters as they are, ordinary ways being unable to lead us to our goal, the only effective remedy, the only course left to take, the only means of managing finally to put the finances truly in order, must consist in revivifying the entire State by recasting all that is vicious in its constitution'. In a *Summary of a Plan for the Improvement of the Finances* presented to the king, Calonne, borrowing from the earlier schemes of Turgot and Necker, proposed a massive re-organisation of the state, according to rational principles. His plan, as approved by Louis XVI in the autumn of 1786, proposed to introduce a land tax to be levied in kind at harvest-time, and from which no one should be exempt, although otherwise nobles would continue to enjoy substantial tax exemptions. In an effort to conciliate the élites, the plan proposed to create a network of local and provincial assemblies elected by landowners which would distribute taxation and supervise public works – but always under the strict control of the government's *intendants*. Measures were also to be taken to stimulate economic activity through the abolition of internal customs barriers and improved roads, as well as by relaxing controls over the grain trade. In the short-term, and to deal with the pressing problem of indebtedness, Calonne proposed raising more loans which could easily be repaid once his reforms began to take effect.

In order to secure support for these measures and overcome likely opposition to registration of the new laws in the parlements, Calonne proposed to convoke an Assembly of Notables, whose 144 members would be selected by the king from amongst 'people of weight, worthy of the public's confidence and such that their approbation would powerfully influence general opinion'. Such a hand-picked body he seems to have assumed could be expected to see reason, and would appreciate that the nobility as such, and its social and political pre-eminence were certainly not under attack. Indeed this would have been inconceivable to a government composed of the king and his nobles.

The assembly, made up of princes of the blood, bishops, leading nobles, magistrates and representatives of provincial estates and some cities, opened at Versailles on 22 February 1787. It was soon clear that Calonne had badly misread the situation. Its members distrusted him, partly because of his predecessor Necker's more optimistic assessment of the financial situation. They demanded detailed accounts. These representatives of the privileged classes were prepared to accept reductions in their fiscal privileges, but only in return for political reforms in the direction of representative government. Calonne sought to justify himself in a pamphlet which only further alienated the notables and angered the king, who, typically, failed to support his minister against court intrigue and adverse public criticism. Calonne was replaced by Loménie de Brienne, Archbishop of Toulouse, whose efforts to secure support for reform enjoyed no greater success. The notables were dismissed and Brienne appealed instead to the Parlement of Paris. But its members, from self-interest, and supported by a public hostile to likely tax increases, only joined in the attack on government. Whilst they would accept some of the proposed reforms – freeing the grain trade, commuting the *corvée* (labour service on the roads) to a tax payment, and the establishment of provincial assemblies – they opposed the major fiscal measures and claimed that only an Estates-General could sanction new taxes. They had in mind a body of the kind last summoned in 1614, voting by order, with its proceedings safely controlled by the nobility and clergy.

Efforts to command the Parlement's compliance by means of a procedure known as a *lit de justice*, followed by its exile to Troyes, provoked widespread protest. Brienne, apparently anxious to avoid confrontation, abandoned the land tax and thus, it seemed, the need to summon an Estates-General. More forceful measures were also introduced. On 8 May 1788 the Keeper of the Seals, Lamoignon, forced the registration of edicts which heralded the creation of a new Plenary Court to assume many of the parlements' functions and which would effectively emasculate them. The response was an extension of the so-called 'aristocratic revolt', in which nobles and members of the provincial parlements encouraged protests against ministerial 'despotism'. Public opinion was inflamed by a wave of pamphlets critical of the ministry and calling for constitutional reform. In Rennes and Grenoble, rioting was so serious that troops were called in. Determined repressive action would probably have mastered the situation, but the growing loss of public confidence in the regime revealed by the indiscipline of noble army officers (setting a bad example to their subordinates which would subsequently rebound on them), by the general unwillingness to subscribe to a new loan, and the imminent bankruptcy which threatened the government as a result, led Brienne to accept calls for an Estates-General and to fix a precise date for its meeting – on 1 May 1789. Recognising his failure, he submitted his resignation. A new ministry under Necker abandoned the reforms under way. The parlements were restored. It is at this point, in August 1788, that the existing monarchical system can be said to have been discredited completely. The king and his close advisers seem to have lost any will to reform or to impose order on the nation. A dangerous vacuum of power existed. The question now was who would dominate the Estates-General which it was assumed would introduce substantial constitutional reform.

The crisis was further intensified by a series of poor cereal harvests in the 1770s and 1780s, culminating in that of 1788, a year of drought followed by disastrous storms. The abundant wine harvest only led to glut and collapse of the price of what was for many peasants their only marketable crop. Cattle disease added to their problems. In 1788–89 the maximum cyclical increase in wheat prices was of the order of around two-thirds above the minimum of 1786 (it had been 100 per cent in 1770, and would be again in 1812 and 1817). As families were forced to spend growing proportions of their shrinking incomes on basic foodstuffs, so demand fell for building work, for textiles and the other products of numerous rural and urban workshops. The 1786 Anglo-French trade treaty increased the supply of manufactured goods at just the wrong moment. For much of the population, employment and earnings collapsed at the same time as the cost of living substantially increased. In normal times a wage earner might spend around 70 per cent of his income on sustenance. In Paris where a loaf of bread weighing four pounds cost 9 sous in August 1788, it cost $14\frac{1}{2}$ sous by February 1789, at a time when a workman lucky enough to remain in employment earned perhaps 20–35 sous a day. A miserably cold winter made the situation all the more difficult adding the problem of keeping warm to that of finding the wherewithal to purchase sufficient food. Insecurity and misery spread beyond the mass of habitually impoverished people into the ranks of normally quite comfortably off artisans and farmers.

In this situation there was frequent recourse to the traditional means of expressing a sense of grievance and of exerting pressure on the authorities to provide assistance. From January, and particularly from March 1789 and throughout the *soudure*, the period when the product of the previous year's harvest was almost exhausted and the coming year's not yet brought in, riots in market places, the looting of bakers' shops, attacks on grain shippers, the enforced sale of grain and bread at a 'fair' price, were common. These movements represented the widespread fear of hunger, the intense anxiety of the masses in a pre-industrial society, faced as they were with the permanent threat of destitution and informed by the persistent folklore of dearth with its tales of people dying of hunger or reduced to eating rotten food, grass and weeds. Beggars were everywhere, voicing the age-old threat to burn down the homes of those refusing them alms; crime multiplied. Although urban workers were capable of organising strikes, as the silk weavers of Lyons had shown in 1786, it still seemed that the most effective action they could take to improve living standards – given the scale of the increase in food prices – was pressure to reduce prices rather than to increase wages, that is they reacted primarily as consumers. From the government's point of view the most serious disorders were the Reveillon riots in Paris. These were caused by an imprudent remark by Reveillon, a wallpaper manufacturer, expressed at an electoral meeting, and subsequently distorted, in favour of wage reductions. Rumours spread and on 27–28 April 1789 serious riots occurred, finally quelled only by military action which killed or wounded some fifty people. Throughout the spring, in fact, the army was constantly deployed to prevent or repress disorder and suffered growing fatigue and, because of doubts about government support, a loss of morale in the process.

Social tension was particularly inflamed by the fact that some individuals – bakers, merchants, farmers and landowners – actually appeared to be profiting from the general misery, by hoarding grain and thus forcing prices to rise. Merchants who naturally sought to profit from price differentials between places, and were encouraged to do so by the authorities, were accused of depriving people in the areas in which the grain originated. The increased transport of grains which inevitably occurred in periods of dearth, seemed to many to prove evil intent. So too did the fact that price increases were proportionally far greater than the shortfall in the crop – the result of both speculation and of the panic buying up of stocks by consumers. All these factors reflect the underdeveloped character of the commercial system in an age of poor communications. The development of commercial capitalism had already intensified differences of interest between the more acquisitive and successful urban merchants and manufacturers and their workers, and in the countryside between landlords, the more substantial farmers and the remainder of the community. Now, at the moment in March 1789 when throughout the country members of the three estates were meeting to prepare their lists of grievances (*cahiers de doléances*) for the meeting of the Estates-General, a widespread sense of injustice, hatred and suspicion influenced debate.

The government's response to the subsistence crisis had been to protect and encourage the grain trade (which gave consumers the impression that it was protecting speculators); and additionally to allay fears by suspending exports, making bulk purchases abroad and offering import subsidies. Particular efforts were made to provision Paris. As a result of these policies rumours spread that ministers were involved in a so-called 'famine plot'. The belief that powerful people were plotting with the grain merchants to punish the poor and secure huge profits reappeared during every crisis. Although the identity of the plotters varied between places, reflecting local social tensions, in a period of political crisis it was inevitable that ministers, who were already the targets of so much criticism, should now be blamed for the ultimate social crime – a plot to starve the people. Inevitably, too, governments which normally claimed the credit for prosperity were now blamed for misery. Poverty, together with the famine plot mentality, also made the payment of seigneurial dues and tithes as well as taxes, all the more intolerable. This, together with declining economic activity, sharply reduced the government's revenues. Popular attitudes during the economic crisis thus reflected, in extremely distorted fashion, the existing political situation, whilst the economic crisis itself made a substantial contribution to the politicisation of the urban and rural masses.

It was against this background that the preparation for the meeting of the Estates-General proceeded. On 25 September 1788 the Parlement of Paris declared that the constitutionally correct form for its meeting would be that of its predecessor in 1614, and in consequence each estate would deliberate and vote separately, and each would be able to veto the proposals of the others. This inevitably disappointed those whose model had been the British parliament or American state institutions. Amongst these so-called 'patriots' there emerged a particularly influential 'Society of Thirty' drawn from amongst the habitués of the socially prestigious Parisian *salons*. Of its fifty-five known members, fifty were nobles, almost all from old-established families, many of whom had previously felt excluded from office by court intrigue. In contrast with the desire of most aristocrats simply to limit the power of absolute monarchy, through the strengthening of traditional institutions which they had habitually dominated, such as the parlements, the provincial estates and the Estates-General, these 'patriots' adopted the model of British constitutional monarchy as a more liberal, and more efficient means of securing the predominant position of a wealthy, and not exclusively noble, élite. Not surprisingly, they were particularly influential amongst an audience drawn from the well-off, educated middle-classes.

Through the circulation of pamphlets and model *cahiers de doléances* the 'patriots' attempted to gain support for alterations in the procedure of the forthcoming Estates-General. They demanded that the Third Estate should have as many representatives as the other orders, and by implication, that voting by head should replace voting by orders, thus destroying the noble veto. In response, an alarmist memoir signed by the princes of the blood, whilst offering to renounce fiscal privileges, attacked such proposals as 'likely to sacrifice and humiliate your brave, ancient and worthy nobility' and as an affront to the monarch himself. It warned the king against a possible revolution in the principles of government leading to an attack on property. This document, which would serve for both nobles and their opponents as a sort of aristocratic manifesto, revealed both the willingness of many nobles to make concessions and accept the loss of their privileged fiscal position, but also their determination to preserve as much as possible of their social status and political power. By the end of 1788, the parlements also were clearly anxious about a possible threat to their own privileges, and were becoming more supportive of the monarchy.

Although many nobles welcomed a campaign against royal 'despotism' and were prepared to accept the loss of some of their privileges, most were unwilling to renounce aristocratic predominance within the Estates-General. In other words they were unwilling to share the political power which appeared to be within their grasp. Thus the Parlement of Paris was prepared to concede increased numerical representation for the Third Estate but not voting by head, whilst contradictorily the second Assembly of Notables convened by Necker in November 1788 was willing to accept voting by head but rejected numerical equality in representation. Without this the representatives of the Third Estate would remain in a strictly subordinate position. This debate on representation had the crucially important effect of re-aligning the political conflict. In response to noble exclusivism the 'patriot' opposition was increasingly hostile to both parlements and the privileged in general. The growing number of resolutions, petitions and pamphlets written by men who were to achieve national prominence like Sieyès, Volney, Roederer or Rabaut de Saint-Etienne, as well as by a mass of more anonymous figures, was indicative of a rapid process of politicisation and the development amongst educated non-nobles, members of the Third Estate, of a sense of common purpose. Most influential of all was probably the Abbé Sieyès' pamphlet, 'What is the Third Estate?' His answer was 'everything' – in the sense that it was 'a complete nation' which could survive without the other two orders. 'Nothing can function without the Third Estate; everything would work infinitely better without the others.'

But, Sieyès continued. 'What has it been until now in the political order?' The answer – '*nothing*'. 'What does it ask? *To be something.*' In conclusion he went so far as to suggest that when the Estates-General came together, the Third Estate might meet apart from the other two estates and re-constitute itself as a National Assembly competent to discuss and decide upon the affairs of the entire nation. This tract would come to serve as the programme of the 'patriot party' – not an organised party in the modern sense but a variety of groups, some, especially in Paris, already meeting as *clubs*. These provided a forum for speakers who had already achieved political notoriety – publicists like Brissot, *philosophes* like Condorcet and liberal nobles like Lafayette, La Rochefoucauld, Talleyrand and Mirabeau. A similar effervescence was evident in such provincial centres as Aix, where Mirabeau's 'Appeal to the people of Provence' appeared, or Arras, which saw the publication of Robespierre's pamphlet, 'Appeal to the people of Artois'. The convocation of the provincial estates of the Dauphiné in June 1788 also contributed to an increasingly vigorous debate. Its deputies, meeting at Vizelle, had determined that in future representatives ought to be elected, rather than sitting as of right, that voting should be by head, and that the Third Estate should have as many deputies as the two other estates together. These proposals were accepted by the government and would serve as a precedent both for the campaign to establish estates in other provinces, and for the debate on the Estates-General. All this had the effect of provoking a growing alarm, and also an intransigence amongst nobles. The very nature of the political process was changing. As the expression of bourgeois resentment of privilege grew more commonplace and more extreme, so the alarm of members of the orders of clergy and nobles was intensified, and their determination to defend their distinctions and power reinforced. Social and political polarisation was developing rapidly.

Necker's announcement in the *Result of the King's Council of State of 27 December* that the representation of the Third Estate should equal that of the clergy and nobility was welcomed, but failed to satisfy 'patriot' opinion. Voting by head would only be implemented if all the orders agreed, which seemed unlikely. It was in response to this that Sieyès' pamphlet *What is the Third Estate?* had vehemently denounced the nobility and clergy for their unwillingness to recognise the rights of their fellow citizens. Ominously the journalist Mallet du Pan observed that, 'The public debate has changed. Now the king, despotism, the constitution are merely secondary: it is a war between the Third Estate and the two other orders.' Efforts by members of the Third Estate to secure equal representation in the provincial estates of Provence, Guienne, Franche-Comté, Artois and Brittany added to the controversy and led in January 1789 to fighting in the streets of Rennes between law students and supporters of the nobility. This clash was precipitated by the obvious and arrogant unwillingness of the Breton nobility to accept a compromise. A pamphlet entitled 'Discourse on the nobility of the Breton parlement' (December 1788) already referred to 'the dangerous insurrection of the Third Estate'. Significantly the deputies elected to the Estates-General by the Third Estate in Brittany would be marked by their intransigent hostility towards the nobility. Meeting regularly as the Club Breton, joined by like-minded 'patriots' and corresponding regularly with their electors, they would made a significant contribution to the radicalisation of opinion both in the National Assembly and in the urban centres of Brittany.

On 24 January 1789 the government decreed that deputies to the Estates-General would be elected by each order in the *bailliages* and *sénéchaussées*, that is within the basic administrative units. Although the regulations were extremely complex, with numerous variations, in most areas the members of the First and Second Estates would attend their electoral assemblies in person, whilst for the much larger Third Estate every male taxpayer over twenty-five years of age would be allowed to participate in a primary assembly to choose two delegates for every hundred households who would subsequently take part in a *bailliage* electoral assembly. Most of the electoral assemblies were held in March and April 1789 against a background of economic crisis, widespread social disorder and political agitation. The government made no attempt to influence the outcome, leaving it to be determined by local circumstances and the influence of political ideas spread by numerous pamphlets.

Information on the numbers voting is fragmentary. In rural parishes around Rouen only 23 per cent of those eligible voted. In the city itself it was 40 per cent. In Alsace 55–60 per cent turned out in Strasbourg and Colmar. Surprisingly, only around 30 per cent voted in Paris, suggesting perhaps that political awareness was much less developed than historians have sometimes led us to believe. Those who attended the secondary assemblies of the Third Estate were inevitably drawn overwhelmingly from amongst the more literate, educated and better-off members of particular communities and a dominant role in debate was taken by those who possessed the skills and confidence necessary to address public meetings – lawyers and officials in particular. Of the 1,318 deputies who actually took their seats in the Estates-General, 326 were members of the First Estate of clergy. In comparison with the previous assembly of 1614 a far higher proportion (220) were members of the lower clergy, that is parish priests rather than the bishops and abbots, canons and monks who had habitually ruled the Church. Amongst the 330 nobles, a high proportion, 166, were essentially army officers, indicative of a determination amongst the previously powerless minor provincial nobility to curb the court aristocrats and *parlementaires* who had always assumed the right to speak for them. Significantly only 22 members of parlements were elected in what were often extremely tense and quarrelsome assemblies. The result was no doubt affected by the exclusion or withdrawal of many recently ennobled office holders – a fact that they bitterly resented as they took their places amongst the Third Estate. Although the meeting at Versailles would reveal that around 90 of these noble delegates were politically liberal, a large majority of the Second Order's representatives, if not entirely intransigent, were nevertheless quite clearly conservatives determined to preserve noble pre-eminence, and to maintain their social distinctions. Amongst the delegates of the Third Estate, with its representation doubled to 661, 214 came from the liberal professions (including 180 lawyers). There were relatively few businessmen (76 merchants, 8 manufacturers and 1 banker). The remainder mostly described themselves as landowners – a characteristic shared by almost all the deputies of the Third whatever their professional labels. It would however be delegates with a legal education, many of them the holders of venal office – a relatively uniform group in terms of training, culture and interests – who would dominate the Third Estate at Versailles.

The elections, together with the preparation of *cahiers de doléances* which accompanied them, further stimulated political debate. They were especially effective in allowing the penetration of new political ideas into the countryside. More generally they created a dangerous sense of expectancy. Why was the king asking for a statement of grievances if it was not his intention to do something about them? This led to a widespread assumption that seigneurial dues, tithes and taxes were about to be abolished, which frequently led to an immediate refusal to pay. Although the *cahiers* expressed great confidence in the king's intentions, they also helped to disseminate the increasingly widespread belief that a more liberal political system, a more egalitarian society, and improved material living standards were soon to be created. This belief inevitably represented a threat to the stability of the political system.

The *cahiers* themselves constitute a mass of documentation (some 60,000 were prepared) which, used with care, can provide important insights into the attitudes of substantial parts of the population towards society and politics on the eve of a major transformation of French institutions. The assemblies of the First Order were, unlike the existing deliberative bodies of the Church, overwhelmingly representative of the parish clergy, who in many *bailliages* seized their opportunity to voice a range of accumulated grievances against the bishops and monastic priests. They condemned the impropriation of tithes and their own low incomes, criticised pluralism and non-residence, favoured diocesan government through elected synods, and more open access to the highest positions in the Church. Greater emphasis was placed nevertheless on the issues which united the clergy. For example they were determined that Catholicism should remain the established religion and that the Church should retain control of education. They were hostile to the growing toleration of Protestants. The influence of secularising 'philosophic' ideas was clearly the cause of some anxiety. There was also a widespread willingness to accept a reduction in the fiscal privileges of the Church.

The *cahiers* drawn up at the meetings of the Second Estate reveal a similar willingness to renounce fiscal privilege (89 per cent of noble *cahiers*) as well as a desire to replace absolute with some form of constitutional monarchy. The existing system of government was condemned as despotic and corrupt, with this blamed not on the king but upon those ministers and courtiers who misinformed the monarch, wasted resources and monopolised office. The solution seemed to lie in the regular meetings of an Estates-General, in ministerial responsibility to the elected body as well as to the king, and in reform of the legal system to ensure the protection of individual liberty. Nobles, however, generally assumed that *they* would play the predominant role within the new institutions and retain their monopoly of high office in the bureaucracy, army and Church. Most noble *cahiers* insisted that voting in the crucial Estates-General which would introduce these political reforms, should take place by order – as a means of defending 'the just prerogatives of the nobility and the clergy' (the noble deputy d'Eprémesnil) – although a significant proportion accepted the re-placement of voting by order with voting by head (38.76 per cent). Only 5 per cent of noble *cahiers* favoured equality of opportunity – probably most did not even consider the possibility – in comparison with 73 per cent of urban Third Estates *cahiers*. On the issue of seigneurial dues it appears that nobles were divided between those with sufficient wealth to accept the loss, and the mass of country gentlemen (*hobereaux*), less well off financially, who also made it a point of honour to defend the signs of their superior social status. Nevertheless the most striking feature of these noble *cahiers* is the large area of agreement with those of the Third Estate – on the creation of a liberal and constitutional state.

The electoral process itself had contributed substantially to the politicisation of the bourgeoisie which prepared the urban *cahiers* of the Third Estate. In the towns, their preparation was dominated by such organised groups as the guilds, corporations and municipal councils who focused in particular upon local grievances. In addition they clearly favoured the regular convocation of Estates-General and voting by head, together with the abolition of noble fiscal exemptions and privileged access to office, as well as measures such as the abolition of internal customs barriers to stimulate the economy. On such matters as the abolition of seigneurial dues, of venal office or trade guilds, on the abolition of tithes or the confiscation of Church property, these *cahiers* were far more circumspect. They were reluctant to attack property rights and, if anything, favoured limited reform rather than drastic change. It was the *cahiers* from the larger urban centres which were the most concerned with politics. They favoured constitutional government, the voting of taxes by an elected assembly and equal liability to taxation, and were more likely to support the abolition of the seigneurial system. Typically the representatives of the corporations – masters and journeymen – whilst condemning most other forms of privilege, insisted upon the retention of their own rights to control entry into their trades and levels of production in order to restrict competition.

The rural *cahiers* – the great majority – although often following urban models, were mainly concerned with specific local grievances, with the burden of seigneurial dues, of the tithe and especially what they saw as excessive taxation. Tension within the rural community – between rich and poor – was rarely represented in *cahiers* prepared by members of the rural bourgeoisie or the better-off peasants, although protests against the enclosure of common land and the denial of customary rights of access to the poor were not uncommon. More frequent was the expression of rural–urban hostility, based upon conceptions of the towns as the residence of tax officials, merchants, of the 'parasitic' higher clergy and the absentee landowners who exploited the peasantry. Nevertheless, the fundamental institutions of the *ancien régime* were not really questioned.

The clear conclusion to draw from an analysis of the *cahiers* is the surprising degree of agreement between the representatives of the three estates. Fiscal and judicial reform, more open access to office and a modicum of representative government would probably have satisfied most of the population. The obvious question then, is why, if this emerging consensus existed, France was drawn nevertheless into revolution? An essential part of the answer is the failure of the royal government to respond effectively to the appeals being made to it.

THE DEBATE ON A NEW CONSTITUTION

With absolute monarchy discredited and the creation of a power vacuum, a struggle developed between nobles, who in practice had shared political power with the monarchy through their quasi-monopoly of office holding, and non-nobles, who in questioning aristocratic privilege were demanding equal rights of access to political power. The political crisis, beginning in 1787, which had had the immediate effect of reinforcing noble opposition to the monarchy had, through the process of election of deputies to the Estates, the preparation of *cahiers* and the pamphlet war these produced, stimulated an increasing assertiveness on the part of educated non-nobles. The growing tension and mutual suspicion was immediately apparent amongst the deputies who gathered at Versailles on 4 May 1789 to attend the Estates-General. In these circumstances the government's failure to provide effective leadership was to prove disastrous. Speeches by the king and by Necker at the opening session of the Estates-General proposed no programme. Whilst accepting, in vague terms, that there might be a case for some reforms, they warned against hasty action, and did nothing to resolve the immediate issue of voting procedures. Such ineptitude left widespread feelings of disappointment and disaffection.

The procedural difficulties which immediately ensued reflected and exacerbated existing divisions. In the absence of a clear government lead on the question of voting, representatives of the Third Estate, led by those from the Dauphiné and Brittany who had for the past twelve months been engaged in conflict with the authorities and who were particularly hostile to noble pretensions, determined to establish their position by pressing for the verification of credentials in common. The First and Second Orders initially rejected this unseemly pressure, although talks on procedure continued until the nobility's decision (by 206 votes to 16) on 20 May that the vote by order and a mutual veto were fundamental rights and essential to the security of the monarchy and the safeguarding of liberty. Finally, on 10 June, Sieyès proposed to a meeting of the Third Estate that if agreement could not be reached, then it should proceed to scrutinise the election results alone. This was adopted by 493 votes to 41. The decision which followed on 17 June to adopt the title National Assembly (by a vote of 491 to 93) was indicative of the development of wider ambitions, made evident by its resolution authorising the continued collection of taxes. The majority of the deputies of the Third Estate, although essentially moderate men, were determined to make their influence felt and to implement constitutional reform. There could be no doubt now that the sovereignty of the king and the social status and power of the nobility were being challenged.

Faced with a direct challenge to his authority, Louis XVI determined to hold a special session of the Estates-General on 23 June, at which he intended to present a programme and regain the initiative. However, even this backfired because officials forgot to inform the Third Estate that their meeting place would be closed until this royal session. Arriving on 20 June for a meeting, deputies assumed that the closure of the hall must be the result of a royal plot and gathered instead on an indoor tennis court. There they took an oath not to disperse until constitutional reform had been achieved. It seems to have been the king's original intention, on Necker's advice, to propose voting in common on important issues, regular convocation of the Estates, their consent to all new taxes, tax reform, decentralisation of local government by means of a network of provincial estates, together with guarantees of individual liberty and of equal access to official positions. These conciliatory proposals might have been effective. But, under pressure from the queen and his brothers, the king instead quashed the Third Estate's decisions of 10 and 17 June. His fundamental assumptions about his own rights and duties, as well as those of the privileged orders, no doubt made him unsympathetic towards reform proposals. He furthermore insisted that the separation of the orders must be maintained, and that if on occasion they could engage in common meetings, the privileged orders were to retain their right to veto proposals which affected themselves. The deputies of the Third Estate, bitterly disappointed, were left more determined to resist than ever. Necker, who had pointedly absented himself from this royal session of 23 June, was dismissed on 11 July.

The nobility, most of whom had welcomed the king's speech, were alarmed by the government's failure to disperse a Third Estate whose members, in arrogating to themselves the title of National Assembly, so obviously challenged its authority. The determination of this assembly to resist royal pressure was encouraged when it was joined by most of the clerical deputies and, on 25 June by forty-seven liberal nobles. On 27 June, hoping to gain time while troops were moved into the Paris region, the king ordered the remaining clergy and nobles to join the National Assembly. The news was greeted with enthusiasm in Paris, but Louis would never willingly concede the loss of his sovereign powers, and had determined to resort to military action. This might well have succeeded, if it had not been for the intervention of the popular classes. Moreover, the growing collapse of discipline within the army and the strength of opposition to the monarchy clearly imposed limits on its capacity for coercive action.

The government's inability to control the widespread subsistence disorders in the spring and early summer of 1789 had already attracted mounting criticism from the propertied classes. The belief that the king would listen to the grievances expressed in the *cahiers* had only encouraged popular protest, and refusals to pay seigneurial dues, tithes and taxes. The demonstrators themselves blamed the government for its apparent unwillingness to assist them, whilst at the same time it offered protection to the merchants and speculators who appeared determined to starve the poor. The continuing rise in the price of bread was increasingly explained in terms of an aristocratic plot. The machinations of the privileged order were seen as intended to punish the poor and to obstruct the workings of the Estates-General from whose gathering many expected better times. Rumours were additionally generated by the government's decision to reinforce military garrisons in the Paris region with, wherever possible, mercenary regiments. In the meantime, however, due to the pressure of continuous activity and lack of firm leadership, discipline and morale in such key units as the French Guards in Paris were deteriorating, intensifying the crisis of confidence amongst the king and his advisers. Continued political agitation was fired by the dismissal of Necker, regarded by 'patriots' as the only man capable of solving the regime's financial problems, and the only minister committed to reform, by high food prices and talk of an impending military coup. These fears led to rioting in Paris on 12 July, involving the burning of the hated internal-customs posts and efforts by crowds, composed of shopkeepers, small traders, and workers to arm themselves in order to resist royal tyranny. The search for arms led on 14 July to an assault on the royal fortress of the Bastille, in which many deserters from the French Guard participated. This was to be of considerable symbolic significance. Of more immediate practical importance was the establishment by solid middle-class citizens of a 'Permanent Committee' to replace a royal municipality clearly overwhelmed by events, and to create a citizens' militia to preserve order and protect the city against attack. The dual objectives of this militia represented the ambivalence of the propertied classes – afraid of popular disorder, but dependent on their troublesome allies for support against the king and his soldiers.

The news from Paris, the sense of expectancy it created, and the breakdown of central power, together with those rumours which combined the age-old belief in a famine plot with fear of nobility, encouraged a new paroxysm of unrest in the countryside. Normandy and lower Maine, parts of Flanders, upper Alsace and Franche-Comté,

Plate 11 The taking of the Bastille, 14 July 1789. Anonymous
painting

the Mâconnais and Dauphiné, were the regions particularly affected.
The peasantry sought to defend the interests of the village community
against the exactions of a panoply of exploiters including landlords,
seigneurs, tithe and tax collectors, and capitalistic farmers and
merchants. Areas like Languedoc, where the burden of taxation,
seigneurialism and commercialisation were less intense, seem to have
been far less affected by this outbreak. Although there was little
personal violence, hundreds of noble châteaux were looted and
burned as peasants searched for hidden stocks of grain, and destroyed
the records of seigneurial obligations. Often a festive atmosphere
prevailed as peasants celebrated a victory for popular justice. The
economic crisis had created widespread misery and fear of starvation.
The preparation of the *cahiers* had encouraged hopes and aspirations
for a more secure existence. Now that this seemed to be threatened by
the determination of the king and his nobility to preserve their
exclusive rights, direct action seemed justified. Panic spread – turning
between 20 July and 6 August into the manifestation of popular
hysteria which historians have labelled the 'Great Fear' – with
rumours that the château burning was the work of marauding brigands

Plate 12 Châteaux burning as their owners flee, summer 1789. Anonymous engraving

intent on murder, pillage and rape and the destruction of the ripening crops. Throughout the provinces, as in Paris, municipal administrations and civic militias were created in an effort to restore order. They were armed with weapons seized from arsenals or freely handed over by troops. Local élites had clearly lost confidence in the ability of the monarchy to fulfil its fundamental responsibility for the maintenance of order and furthermore suspected the sincerity of both the king's and the aristocracy's commitment to constitutional reform. The composition of these new bodies varied from place to place, according to the character of local élites, the balance between political groups and the degree to which popular pressure was exerted. They represented not only a determination to preserve social order but also the

Assemblée Nationale,
Abandon de tous les Privilèges:
a Versailles Séance de la Nuit du 4 au 5 Aout 1789

Plate 13 The night of 4 August 1789: a social revolution. The
Constituent Assembly votes for the abolition of the seigneurial
system. Engraving by Helman after Charles Monnet

dissolution of royal government. They would look to the National
Assembly for inspiration, rather than to the monarch.

On 16 July the war minister, the Duc de Broglie, advised the king
that the army could no longer be relied upon. The regime had lost its
monopoly of armed force. In despair the king recalled Necker and in
front of an armed crowd, on the steps of the Hôtel de Ville in Paris,
donned the tricolour cockade which united the white of the Bourbon
family with the red and blue of the city. He furthermore accepted the
appointment of the 'patriots' Bailly as mayor, and Lafayette as
commander of a militia whose new title of National Guard signified its
political aspirations. On 4 August the National Constituent Assembly,
as it now called itself, with clergy and nobles such as the Duc

d'Aiguillon and Comte de Noailles to the fore, accepted the need to abolish the seigneurial system. In what Georges Lefebvre referred to as the 'death certificate of the old order', deputies decided to entirely destroy the feudal regime and thereby to abolish serfdom, labour services, seigneurial justice and exclusive hunting rights and banalities, together with, or so it initially appeared, all seigneurial dues and tithes. These were measures intended to pacify the countryside. In the cold light of day, however, deputies, many of whom had profited personally from the system, were to have second thoughts. A committee was established which confirmed the abolition of all forms of personal servitude but required peasants to repurchase dues which were based upon a more or less fictitious 'contractual relationship' and therefore represented property rights. The price was established at twenty-five times the annual value, a rate which satisfied no one. Moreover it was stipulated that arrears owed from the past thirty years would have to be paid, a decision which encouraged a further wave of attacks on châteaux. Peasants who had neither the resources nor the inclination to compensate seigneurs, generally tended to ignore the Assembly's second thoughts. Redemption payments were only rarely paid. Finally, on 15 July 1793, in the aftermath of another massive wave of rural protest caused by poor harvests and suspicion of noble intentions and because of the need to stimulate support for the war effort, dues were finally abolished without compensation by the Convention. These measures implied a major re-casting of social relationships. As well as causing substantial financial loss for seigneurs, they destroyed the legal basis for noble power in the countryside.

On 26 August a Declaration of the Rights of Man and the Citizen was promulgated. It provided an inspiring statement of principle as well as representing the fundamental determination of deputies to make their revolutionary intentions clear to the world. In affirming a commitment to the rule of law, to equality before the law, to representative government, to freedom of speech within limits set by the law, and to equal access to office, it represented an assault on the legal basis of privilege and of monarchy. It also guaranteed private ownership of property as one of the 'natural and imprescriptible rights of man', and as the basis of social and political order. This was after all an assembly made up of men of property. Thus although a decree of 19 June 1790 abolished hereditary nobility and a whole panoply of measures threatened noble privilege, they were to survive as a major status group with much of their wealth intact. The ideal of the Constituents was to create a situation in which individuals would henceforth be free to dispose of their talents and property, restricted only by the stipulation that their actions should do no harm to others. Measures were introduced to stimulate economic activity. These included the ending of restrictions on the grain trade (August 1789), the legalisation of loans at interest (12 October), and suppression of the craft and mercantile guilds and of official controls on manufacture (loi d'Allarde, 2 March 1791), reforms which had been discussed for decades. The abolition of venality (11 August 1789), with far from generous compensation, cleared the way for a thoroughgoing re-organisation of the administrative system. The complex chaos of conflicting jurisdictions which had made up the *ancien régime* administration had long been subject to criticism. The rational restructuring which ensued, provided for a hierarchy of communes, districts and departments. The other guiding principles, representing a reaction against absolutism and a determination to weaken the power of the executive, were decentralisation together with the election of officials. The basic ideals of popular sovereignty and elective rep-resentative government were recognised by a law of 14 December 1789. It stipulated that deputies and officials were to be elected by 'active' citizens, those paying the equivalent of three days labour in taxes. The poorest, propertyless members of society, who lacked the independence thought to be a prerequisite for voting, were to be excluded. Even so a mass electorate was constituted, made up of 4.3 million electors, including 77,590 in Paris. The essential restrictions on political participation were the higher (ten day) tax qualification required of those eligible for office and particularly the principle of indirect election. The limits to the deputies' radicalism were also evident in such measures as the Le Chapelier law (June 1791), which banned workers' associations and strikes as restraints upon individual freedom, and in the use of force against hostile demonstrations.

The revolution had nevertheless passed its point of no return. Fundamental commitments had been made to the principles of equality before the law, the sovereignty of the nation and representative institutions. An unprecedented series of changes had occurred in political and social institutions. A new political culture had been created. It was quite clear that the deputies intended to restrict substantially the powers of the monarchy, although the search for a compromise with the king would continue; indeed the alternative was unthinkable for some time to come. Yet, in spite of these massive innovations, a broad consensus in favour of the Revolution existed from which only a small minority of nobles and higher clergy were excluded. In this situation Louis XVI had little alternative but to make concessions whilst part of his court, headed by his brother, the Count of Artois, finding the situation intolerable, made up the first wave of émigrés. They would soon be joined by growing numbers of noble army officers – some 6,000 – unable to tolerate indiscipline or from 1791 to take an oath of loyalty from which the king's name had been omitted. Although many officers remained and would, like the young Napoleon Bonaparte, benefit from accelerated promotion opportunities, these émigrés constituted the cadres for counter-revolution.

RADICALISATION OF THE REVOLUTION

This immensely creative phase would be followed by what 'revisionist' historians like François Furet since the 1960s have tended to dismiss as an unnecessary aberration, a process of political and social radicalisation, culminating in the Terror. This 'popular' phase of the Revolution, upon which Marxists like Soboul tended to dwell, is now deemed to have prevented the liberal compromise between noble and non-noble élites which had seemed possible in 1789. The revolutionary militants of the Year II, with their egalitarian values and commitment to the defence of the Republic against its internal and external enemies have been marginalised, and dismissed as hooligans. Aspects of the Terror were certainly odious but some historians like Pierre Chaunu, supported by the conservative media, have gone much further in presenting the Terror as the first step towards the twentieth century revolutionary terrorism represented by Stalin's *gulags*. Frequently exaggerating the number of deaths they have described the repression of counter-revolutionary movements in the Vendée as heralding Nazi genocide. This essentially ahistorical, and indeed hysterical approach, can only be understood as a feature of the politics of the reactionary right of our own time. It ignores the threat posed to the achievements of 1789 by the reactionaries of that time and their foreign supporters.

Although the challenge to privilege and the sense of expectancy this had produced had undoubtedly created a powerful political dynamic and widespread social tension, it was above all the counter-revolutionary menace which provoked the radicalisation of the Revolution.

Efforts to set the Revolution within a longer-term context, as a means of assessing its significance, have also led to a denigration of the revolutionaries' achievement. However even if it has to be accepted that 'the cost of the Revolution' was high and that in spite of widespread suffering little was achieved in terms of the modernisation of socio-economic structures, that continuity massively outweighed change, and indeed that France remained an essentially pre-industrial society in 1815, it must also be granted that a new political culture was created and new institutions established which, centred on conceptions of the rights of man, were to fundamentally affect, and for the good, the ways in which we conceive of social relationships.

The continuing collapse of the authority of the royal government was another major reason for the radicalisation of the Revolution. It proved unable to offer an effective lead to contending groups within the Assembly, ensuring that whatever initiatives did come developed out of that body itself. This was to be a process fraught with difficulty. The inspirational phrases of the Declaration of Rights were one thing, the implementation of practical measures of reform and the solution of the financial problems which had occasioned the summoning of the Estates-General were another. It was soon clear that it was easier to overthrow one regime than to reach agreement on what should replace it. The debate on the new system of government and the inevitable competition for power which ensued would open up increasingly bitter divisions amongst the country's new rulers; assisted by the pressures of war, it would promote major political re-alignments and a process of politicisation which threatened to bring the masses into politics. There were certainly pressing problems. These included the need to re-define political authority and to re-establish effective government. To a substantial degree the policy decisions taken by the Assembly reflected its social composition. Most deputies were relatively well-off and anxious to safeguard a social order still conceived of in basically agrarian terms, as well as to preserve the monarchy as the essential guarantor of this social order. The solution incorporated into the

Constitution of 1791 was to accord considerable formal authority to the king as head of the executive whilst seeking to control its use by insisting that royal orders were valid only if counter-signed by ministers who were responsible to the elected assembly as well as to the monarch. The king's right to veto legislation could only delay its implementation (for two to six years) and did not apply to financial bills. These stipulations reflected a fundamental lack of trust, which made the harmonious working of the new system extremely unlikely.

The disorders which had preceded and accompanied the revolution and the widespread refusal to pay taxes had greatly intensified the government's financial problems. The Constituent Assembly summoned originally to solve these, felt obliged to take exceptional measures. On 2 November 1789 it had determined to adopt a proposal made by Talleyrand, Bishop of Autun, that church property be sequestrated. In March 1790, as the financial crisis deepened, it was decided to issue treasury bills (*assignats*) repayment of which would be guaranteed by the value of the confiscated land (*biens nationaux*). Subsequent over-issue of this paper currency would lead to its rapid devaluation. The impact of these measures was to be considerable. The Assembly had certainly not planned to threaten the existence of a Church still seen as the basis of moral order. It had been intended that the clergy, as well as the educational and charitable work they supported, should be provided for by the state. There was little sympathy nonetheless for either the 'useless' contemplative religious orders or even the teaching and charitable orders widely regarded as wasteful and inefficient, and their dissolution was to follow (decrees of 13 February 1790 and 18 August 1792). Unfortunately, although the various assemblies were full of good intentions in the spheres of education and welfare, their achievement was an essentially negative one. The pressing financial needs of war would soon frustrate any real achievement although the principle of state responsibility for the provision of public assistance and in particular of free and obligatory instruction as the means of promoting enlightenment, civic virtue and linguistic and national unity survived to inspire the left throughout the following century. More immediately, from October 1789 the Assembly began to take an active role in the reorganisation of the Church. This and the guarantee of freedom of worship enshrined in the Declaration of Rights threatened the autonomy and exclusive rights of

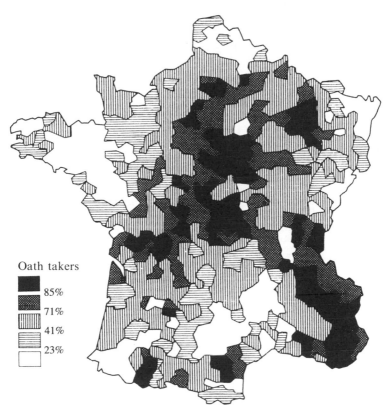

Oath takers
85%
71%
41%
23%

Fig 9 The Civil Constitution of the Clergy (percentage of oath takers)

the Catholic clergy. The Civil Constitution of the Clergy (July 1790) extended the principles of administrative reform to the Church by providing for the election of clergy by the departmental electoral assemblies. The Church was to be subordinated to the state and to civil society in ways the Pope could not accept. Pius VI temporised but the oath of loyalty required of priests in their new position as employees of the state (decree of 17 November 1790) was too much and he felt obliged to condemn the reforms in March–April 1791. Initially priests had often welcomed the democratisation of the church but the papal decision forced many of the 50–60 per cent who had already accepted the oath to retract. Their original decisions had to a considerable degree reflected the attitudes of their parishioners towards the revolutionary regime and significantly, a map representing these juror–non-juror decisions in 1791 would continue to correspond quite closely to those illustrating the left–right political divide throughout the nineteenth century. The increasingly anti-clerical and then anti-religious policies introduced, as the authorities sought to impose their will on the Church, would reinforce the determination of many communities to defend their right to a parish priest, the vital intermediary between man and God. More than anything else this created the potential for mass resistance to the Revolution.

Until at least the summer of 1790 however, and with the exception of the formerly privileged classes, there was widespread support for a regime which had eliminated or eased the burdens of seigneurial dues, tithes and taxation. The revolutionary land settlement was to be an important element in this creation of a pro-revolutionary party. The confiscation of Church property, and subsequently that of émigrés (only about half of whom were nobles) by a decree of 3 June 1793, would affect around 15 per cent of the national territory. Although it had initially been intended to facilitate access by the poor to property by dividing estates into small portions and allowing payment over twelve years (decree of 14 May 1790), the urgent need to increase state revenue led instead in May 1791 to the requirement of a deposit of 30 per cent and the balance over four and a half years with sale to the highest bidder. The more egalitarian decrees of 3 June 1793 and 4 Nivôse Year II had little impact and were soon reversed. Thus, not surprisingly it was those with money to spare who were best placed to take advantage of the favourable opportunity to purchase provided by such extensive sales. The impact on social structures varied con- siderably between regions according to the amount of land for sale. Church property had been particularly extensive on the rich northern plains, reaching 30–40 per cent of the land in Picardy, but falling to as little as 3 per cent in parts of the south. The majority of nobles, perhaps as many as four-fifths, sat out the revolution, intensely annoyed by their loss of titles (decree of 19 June 1790), power and status, and frequently insecure and frightened, but suffering little further material loss after the abolition of seigneurial dues. Subsequently many former émigrés were able, by one means or another, to partially reconstitute their estates, but there can be no doubt that the nobility as a group lost

Table 4.1. *Share in landownership (per cent). Department of Nord*

	1789	1802
Clergy	20	0
Nobles	22	12
Bourgeois	16	28
Peasants	30	42

heavily as a result of the Revolution. This was especially the case in a frontier department like the Nord. Georges Lefebvre estimated that shares in land ownership there evolved as shown in table 4.1.

The Nord was unusual in the share purchased by peasants but even there it was bourgeois purchasers, that is existing landowners, professional men, merchants and manufacturers, who acquired two-thirds of the land sold, increasing the economic dominance of many towns over their rural hinterlands. Landownership offered security and enhanced social status as well as providing a decent income. Although a considerable number of better off peasants were able to acquire land, the situation of most of the rural population remained little changed as a result of the Revolution. This fact engendered bitter disappointment and a determination to oppose the implementation of decrees like that of 10 June 1793, which sought to facilitate enclosure and the division of common land. It was widely seen as an attack on customary collective practices crucial to the survival of the poor. The revolutionary conception of property as an individual right free from restriction had little support in many rural communities. The rural masses were to remain divided in their attitudes to a revolution which had seemed to promise so much and given so little. Although they would remain bitterly hostile to any hint of a restoration of seigneurialism or of the tithe most peasants lacked a real sense of positive commitment and soon relapsed into an indifference towards those political affairs which did not directly affect them. Even so the national debate on the characteristics of the new regime, together with competition for power between individuals, families, clan and social groups in countless towns and villages ensured that the political crisis would be prolonged.

Initially, within the Constituent Assembly there had been an almost universal commitment to monarchy, although significantly Louis XVI was now deemed to reign not only 'by the grace of God' but also 'according to the constitutional law of the state'. The debate continued concerning the nature of the monarchy and the respective powers of the king and the elected assembly, that is about who should hold power. Loosely organised groups argued over the forms of the new political community. A majority of socially conservative politicians like Lafayette, Bailly, Sieyès, Talleyrand, and even Mirabeau who secretly took the king's money, were anxious to finish the Revolution by conciliating the king. The more radical deputies increasingly looked outside the Assembly and towards the popular classes of Paris for support. There the level of mobilisation of the masses, low at first, rapidly developed due to the activities of political clubs, meeting in such places as the former Cordelier and Jacobin convents, and the printing of innumerable newsheets. Competition, initially between nobles and non-nobles and subsequently between such bourgeois groupings as Feuillants, Girondins or Jacobins, and their various efforts to win popular support resulted in a democratisation of politics, but additionally in the escalation of conflict. Influenced by the professional men and journalists, who spoke in the clubs, popular societies were created which increasingly agitated for a wider franchise, for referenda and the right to recall deputies. The lower middle-class traders and artisans, and the skilled workers who largely made up these groups shared both a growing commitment to democracy, contempt for the moderation of the Constituent Assembly and suspicion of the king. This was evident as early as 5 October 1789 in the action of the crowds which forced the monarch to move from his palace at Versailles to the Tuileries in Paris. The Assembly followed. This would allow the exercise of continuous popular pressure on both. A process of political education, and indeed of the politicisation of everyday life was underway. The content and objectives of politics were being transformed.

It rapidly became evident that Louis XVI, while he might make concessions under pressure, remained an unwilling participant in the process of political reform. Suspicion of the monarch and his advisers grew, reaching a peak when, on 21 June 1791, the royal family tried to escape from France leaving behind them a justificatory memorandum complaining about the limits imposed on the royal right of appointment to office, on the king's ability to veto legislation, on his freedom to conduct diplomacy, and about the growing influence of the radical clubs. For many this so-called flight to Varennes (where the king was arrested) finally broke the spell of monarchy. At the same time the evident desire of a large number of deputies to continue to seek an accommodation with the discredited king intensified political tension. In the Assembly moderates like Barnave were anxious to preserve a strong monarchy from fear that a republic would herald a degeneration into anarchy. Radicals like Danton, Desmoulins and Robespierre, on the other hand, agitated for the trial of a king they claimed had proved himself to be a traitor and a perjuror. On the streets rising social tension was clearly evident. On 17 July a peaceful crowd which had gathered on the Champ de Mars to sign a petition against the rehabilitation of the king was brutally dispersed by middle-class National Guards commanded by Lafayette. They left behind some fifty dead. At this stage nevertheless many former liberals were themselves advocating the radical step of establishing a republic. By the time the Constituent Assembly had completed its work and given way to a Legislative Assembly with the promulgation of the constitution on 13th September 1791 the monarchy was widely discredited.

The period during which this sat (1 October 1791 – 20 September 1792) was short but of crucial importance. It saw the abolition of the monarchy, and a further radicalisation of the Revolution in a situation of war, threatened counter-revolution and the popular disorder consequent upon a poor harvest and inflation. The members of this assembly were all new to national politics, the Constituent Assembly having excluded its members from re-election. There were fewer clerics and (ex-)nobles, although most deputies came from the prosperous land-owning and professional middle classes with experience in local government. A large majority would doubtless have favoured moderate policies. Thus 250 of the 745 joined the Feuillant club and only 136 the Jacobins and included in this latter number were future Girondins, a group which came to owe its label to the fact that many of its leaders including Vergniaud, Guadet, Gensonné and Ducos represented the Gironde department. In spite of their differences, the deputies were overwhelmingly committed to the defence of the principles of 1789. For this reason even moderates, as *patriotes*, believed in the urgency and legitimacy of repressive measures against the émigré nobility and non-juror clergy – the *aristocrate* party, and sided with the Jacobins rather than the more cautious Feuillants. They also shared in the decision taken on 20 April 1792 to take military action against the émigrés gathering on the frontiers and the 'despots' who supported them. This decision which, in effect, forced war on the European powers was very much influenced by internal political strife. The king accepted the decision in the hope that the Revolution would be defeated and destroyed. Lafayette and his associates believed that the prestige derived from a successful war would allow them to crush the Jacobins. Brissot and the Girondins, convinced that there was an international conspiracy to restore the *ancien régime* by means of invasion and internal subversion, took faith in the capacity of a revolutionary army to overwhelm its opponents and liberate Europe. This was a dream which attracted most Jacobins, with Robespierre, warning of the dangers of war in the Jacobin club, almost a lone opposition voice. In the event the military situation rapidly deteriorated, making it necessary by July to declare the fatherland in danger (*la patrie en danger*). By this time the differences between those deputies who still sought a compromise with the king and those political militants determined to secure victory at all costs had become unbridgeable. In August, following the publication of a threatening counter-revolutionary manifesto by the Duke of Brunswick, commander of the invading Prussian and Austrian army, popular support grew for action against the king, other subversives and corrupt politicians. A conflict of authority developed between the Assembly and the Paris Commune and radical clubs as news was received of Prussian military successes on the eastern frontier and fear grew of counter-revolutionary plots. On 9–10 August some 25,000 members of the popular societies and of the now democratised National Guard attacked the Tuileries Palace, massacring 600 of the king's Swiss guards and securing the imprisonment of the monarch. Lafayette who attempted to march on Paris and restore constitutional monarchy was deserted by his troops. The growing threat of invasion and fear of treason led between 2 and 6 September to the massacre of some 1,400 political prisoners held in Parisian prisons. Most conservative members of the Legislative Assembly fled leaving it under the control of a Girondin majority, which under constant popular pressure voted the suspension of the king from his functions and the summoning of a Convention to prepare

Plate 14 The attack on the Tuileries, 10 August 1792. Painting by
Jacques Bertaux

a new constitution which, now that the age of kings was finally over,
would guarantee liberty and popular sovereignty. It was to be elected
by manhood suffrage (with the exception of domestic servants deemed
to be lacking in independence) but again with the safeguard of indirect
election. In the succeeding weeks the Girondins ordered the deportation
of refractory priests, the final abolition of seigneurial dues without
compensation and the sale of émigré property – measures which the
king had previously obstructed. Even amongst those committed to
victory, however, there emerged differences over political and military
tactics which would lead the members of competing groups to accuse
each other of treason. In spite of these seemingly radical measures
therefore Girondin leaders were to be increasingly subject to criticism
by Parisian radicals because of their opposition to the uprising of 10
August and to the final dethronement of the king, and reluctance to
introduce controls over the supply of food.

The Convention was to govern France from September 1792 until
November 1795. Only around 700,000 of a potential electorate of 7
million participated in its election reflecting both popular indifference
and the limits to politicisation. Like previous assemblies it was made
up predominantly of comfortably off bourgeois. On 10 August 1793,

the first anniversary of the attack on the Tuileries, it promulgated a new constitution. Although its introduction was suspended because of the military crisis, this represented a determined effort to win popular support and provided for a unicameral legislature elected by direct manhood suffrage, which would itself elect an executive. The preamble guaranteed, in addition to the liberty proclaimed in the Declaration of Rights in 1789, the rights to public assistance, education and even to insurrection to resist oppression. This, the most democratic constitutional document of the period, was soon however overshadowed by bitter factional divisions especially between Girondins and Montagnards (the mountain dwellers, that is the radical deputies sitting on the left and at the top of the steeply banked seats in the assembly), the latter based on the Jacobin club and led by eminent members of the Paris delegation and most notably Robespierre, Danton and Marat. Both groups sought to appeal for support to the majority of uncommitted deputies, the so-called Plain. If there was a general consensus on such fundamental matters as the need to secure the protection of private property and to defend the revolution, and in favour of an aggressive foreign policy in order to bring 'fraternity and assistance' to the oppressed peoples of Europe, there remained explosive political differences. The Montagnards were convinced that their opponents were insufficiently committed to the campaign against counter-revolution and half-hearted in their support for the trial and finally the execution of the king which took place on 21 January 1793. The Girondins on the other hand suspected the Montagnards of planning to use violent popular support in order to establish the dictatorship of Paris over the provinces. As the military crisis deepened in the spring and summer of 1793 and exceptional measures to combat the internal enemies of the republic came to seem ever more necessary, so competition for power within the Convention grew more intense. News of the treasonable contacts between General Dumouriez and the Austrians and the popular demonstrations this provoked in Paris helped to establish parliamentary support for a purge of leading Girondins and for a terror directed at the nation's enemies. The more extreme Jacobins called on the 'people' to save the Revolution from the treason of the 'rich'.

The military effort caused massive problems. Armies had to be raised, equipped and fed. The state's financial crisis deepened. Printing

Plate 15 The execution of Louis XVI, 21 January 1793. The final symbolic breach with the *ancien régime* and an act in defiance of the crowned heads of Europe

more paper money (*assignats*) heightened inflation. In spite of the reasonably good harvest of 1792, the disruptive impact of war and inflation caused serious food shortages. The effort to mobilise men and resources would lead to growing internal dissent. In part this was due to the very scale of the effort implied by the universal call to arms (*levée en masse*) and, when the stream of volunteers became inadequate, by the growing resort to conscription. By the summer of 1792 there were already 400,000 men under arms, mostly enlisted since 1789. In spite of the massive emigration of nobles, the officers were mainly professional soldiers, owing their often rapid promotions to their own abilities and to the Revolution itself. Their victory over the Duke of Brunswick at Valmy on 20 September 1792 saved the Revolution and led to the 'liberation' of the left bank of the Rhine. Subsequent victory at Jemappes permitted the occupation of the Austrian Netherlands (essentially modern Belgium) but the threat this posed to the strategic and commercial interests of Britain and Holland led almost inevitably to war with these powers, declared by the Convention in February 1793.

The establishment of the system of government known as the Terror was a response to these difficulties, to the defeats of spring 1793, to the renewed threat of invasion and of counter-revolution and to the demands for decisive action articulated by the Parisian clubs and popular societies. It was intended as a temporary expedient. As a decree published in October 1793 put it, the government of France would be 'revolutionary until there is peace'. The will of the Convention was now to be enforced through ministers reporting to its committees and especially to the Committee of Public Safety, a kind of war cabinet exercising a general supervisory role, and to the Committee of General Security responsible for policing the country. These bodies would largely supplant the legislative body for as long as the emergency lasted. In the provinces they acted through both the elected local authorities and the popular Jacobin clubs although delegates of the Convention, the *représentants en mission*, had over-riding authority. Where necessary they could call upon the support of the army, national guards, or the armed civilian *armées révolutionnaires* found in around one-third of departments. The latter were composed of enthusiastic urban Jacobins determined to impose republican virtue and the style of an essentially urban revolution upon an often recalcitrant countryside. These developments represented something of a return to centralised government, a reinforcement of the role of the state, following the brief experiment with decentralisation, although of course in practice conditions varied considerably and the actual implementation of the Terror was far from uniform. There remained an inescapable dependence on the good will of local officials, themselves often heavily engaged in faction fighting and either indifferent to outside events or hostile to the growing interference by representatives of the state in the affairs of their communities. Support for the radicalisation of the Revolution appears to have been particularly widespread in the neighbourhood of Paris and other major cities, in the threatened frontier regions and in parts of the centre and south-west. 35,000–40,000 presumed enemies of the Revolution were executed or died in prison during the Terror, for the most part in Paris (about 16 per cent of the total), and during the ferocious repression of counter-revolutionary insurrection in the Vendée (52 per cent) and the south-east (19 per cent). These statistics however substantially underestimate the impact of frequently indiscriminate military efforts to clear the countryside of insurgents and all those who might lend them succour.

A large majority of those killed were manual workers or peasants, although proportionate to their numbers the nobility no doubt suffered most. The impact of the Terror was further intensified by widespread arrest and imprisonment (affecting about 500,000 or 3 per cent of the adult population) all adding to the sense of shock and creating intense anxiety even in the most isolated village.

Military mobilisation, the need to feed the growing armies and the disruption of the food marketing system caused by this, by civil disorder and inflation and by poor harvests added a sometimes overwhelming concern with subsistence to these other tensions. The diminution of purchasing power and widespread unemployment this would anyway have caused was made all the more severe by the loss of external markets due to the war. Rising social tension and widespread popular protest involving numerous market place riots and efforts to disrupt the commerce in foodstuffs threatened to disorganise the provisioning of the cities. Hostility towards a government which could not assure the sustenance of the poor grew. In this situation the Convention, although favouring free trade, felt bound in May and September 1793 to impose maximum levels on the price of grain and to make speculative hoarding a capital offence. Robespierre insisted that 'existence is the first of all rights' but these measures were intended to be nothing more than a temporary expedient, a concession to the war effort and to pressure from the Parisian shopkeepers, artisans and workers, the so-called *sans-culottes*, that is those who wore trousers rather than knee-breeches, and who by implication worked with their hands. In practice the lack of effective means of enforcement in the face of the ill will of merchants and peasants attracted by black-market prices and the obstructionism of many rural municipalities made the enforcement of price controls extremely difficult. The very attempt, combined with requisitioning however caused considerable agitation, so that the revolutionary government itself became increasingly anxious to end the experiment and this economic terror was noticeably relaxed even before the fall of Robespierre and was finally abolished on 24 December 1794.

Another manifestation of the Terror was the campaign of dechristianisation waged in some areas during the autumn of 1793 and spring of 1794. This combined intellectual anti-religious feeling with popular anti-clericalism and was further stimulated by association of the refractory clergy with counter-revolutionary fanaticism. It manifested itself in pressure on priests to resign their functions, in the destruction of religious images and the closure of churches, in the hunt for dissident clerics, and ultimately in the effort to create a new revolutionary cult of Reason and the Supreme Being. The effort to desacralise daily life also involved the introduction of a revolutionary calender which abolished Sunday. The effects varied. A great deal depended on the enthusiasm of particular *représentants en mission*. Certainly the credibility of the official constitutional church was destroyed and the habit of religious observance weakened in many places, especially one suspects in parts of the Paris region, Normandy, the Rhône corridor and areas of central France where the influence of the Church was often already tenuous. In many other places support for the clergy was strengthened in reaction to the assault on traditional religious practices.

In deciding on these various measures the Convention was to an important degree making concessions to the Parisian popular classes, the workers and masters of the Paris trades who had participated in every major demonstration from the taking of the Bastille. Only with their aid had the Revolution prevailed. The outbreak of war and counter-revolution had both radicalised the revolutionary leadership and reinforced its dependence on mass support. Political factions within the Convention could appeal to those outside its walls. Between 31 May and 2 June 1793 representatives of the organs of Parisian local government, of the *sections* and municipality, petitioned for the arrest of leading Girondins and for the more energetic waging of the war. A majority of deputies felt bound to agree then and again on 4–5 September when further demonstrations demanded the establishment of 'revolutionary government'. To impose food procurement and political repression, in the absence of a substantial state bureaucracy or monolithic party, the government had little alternative but to use the local popular societies and the *armées révolutionnaires* with their largely *sans-culottes* membership and reverberating slogans – *Guerre aux tyrans* (War on the tyrants), *Guerre aux aristocrates*, and *Guerre aux accapareurs* (hoarders or speculators). The clubs had proliferated, and by the Year II spread into many rural areas. Estimates of their number vary between 5,000 and 8,000 with anywhere between 500,000 and 1 million members, that is 1 adult male in 12 or 6, although regular activists must have been far fewer. Their leaders remained predominantly bourgeois professionals or landowners but, as a result of the process of politicisation, some democratisation was evident.

The *sans-culottes*, and particularly the more militant amongst them, were a socially disparate group with diverse interests, made up mainly of master-artisans, journeymen and shopkeepers, that is the better off, more literate elements amongst the popular classes. The poorest remained indifferent or else felt excluded. Locksmiths, joiners and cabinet-makers, shoemakers and tailors appear to have been amongst the most active. They were given a sense of unity by craft and neighbourhood loyalties and in some provincial cities and in the various *quartiers* of the capital were able to organise political action through meetings and demonstrations, and in Paris by means of regular meetings of the *sections*. They condemned, in the most ferocious terms, all those suspected of being luke-warm towards the Revolution and above all the 'rich and corrupt', all those whether aristocrats, financiers, landowners, merchants and speculators in general who were believed to be exploiting the poor. Their hostility was in part a diffuse form of class antagonism but they subscribed to a set of egalitarian moral values rather than a systematic political ideology. It seemed so obviously unjust that some citizens had substantial property whilst others endured constant insecurity, that some consumers had food and drink in plenty when others frequently went without. Their ideal was a community in which all should work and in which every family would gain status and security through the possession of a small property, where the rich would be deprived of their superfluity in order to provide for the poor. Although committed to the private ownership of property they believed that absolute rights of ownership should be restricted by the 'needs of the people'. This was symbolised by the question of bread which ought to be available to all at an affordable price. They demanded additionally the right to influence government decisions, not only through elected deputies who ought to be subject to recall where they diverged from their instructions, but by means of mass petitioning, a form of popular sovereignty which constituted an obvious threat to the rights of elected assemblies. The masses thus began to adopt and adapt the slogans and ideals of the political groups engaged in the struggle for power and threatened to become an independent political force. Neither in Paris nor the provinces however did the leaders of this movement give much thought to developing an effective means of coordinating their action. Their activities remained essentially local.

The primary link between this popular movement and the Jacobins was a shared commitment to the defence of the Revolution. The threat of counter-revolution initially represented by the émigré nobles, who had in 1789 gathered in Nice, Turin, Lausanne, Mannheim, Coblenz and Brussels and sought support from the European powers and who had begun to organise conspiratorial networks in France, was substantially reinforced by the growth of mass resistance to the Revolution. It seemed transformed into a 'vast conspiracy against the liberty of France and the future liberty of the human race' (Hérault de Séchelles). The reasons for this development were varied. One characteristic of the movement and indeed its fundamental weakness was its localism. Certainly there was widespread resentment of growing interference in communal affairs by the new administrators who through the army, urban national guards and the *armées révolution-naires* possessed a coercive power much greater than those of the *ancien régime* in many areas. Moreover from as early as 1790 much of the population began to feel that the sacrifices they were being asked to make far outweighed the gains they had made from the Revolution, although rejection of Jacobinism certainly did not necessarily imply support for an émigré and aristocratic counter-revolution. The main centres of mass support for armed opposition were to be characterised by the significance of the religious issue. Conflict frequently reflected pre-revolutionary tensions. In the Midi and especially the Montauban and Nîmes areas, as early as spring 1790, there was a reaction against the growing Protestant role in local affairs and rumours that Catholics were about to be massacred encouraged renewed sectarianism. These movements together with subsequent attempts to raise the peasants of the Lozère and Ardèche in July 1792 and at the beginning of 1793 were crushed with relative ease. Elsewhere support for those clergy who refused to accept the Civil Constitution was a more dangerous threat. In areas of intense faith the refractory priest represented the religious idealism of his community, and had powerful and important functions to perform. Efforts by outsiders to deny this were bound to be resisted. Even then, as a cause of counter-revolutionary mobilisation, religious issues have to be considered alongside disappointment with the revolutionary property settlement, hostility towards taxation and conscription and the requisitioning of foodstuffs and horses in return for increasingly devalued paper money. Peasant land hunger was such that even in areas where they supported refractory priests they often did not hesitate to acquire former church property. Where the land settlement was favourable to influential groups within the village community they tended to favour or at least not actively to oppose the Revolution. Where in contrast they felt deprived of the opportunity to purchase land particularly by bourgeois speculators from nearby towns their frustration was intense, particularly when even the abolition of the tithe failed to benefit tenant farmers who found it reincorporated into their rents. In the west, widespread violence occurred in the spring and summer of 1791, developing in 1793 into full scale rebellion in the Vendée and southern Anjou and to a lesser degree in parts of Brittany and Normandy. This lasted into 1796 and intermittently until 1799 and beyond. Conscription and especially the decree of 24 February 1793 added fuel to the flames of resentment, stimulating widespread rioting and guerilla attacks on the bourgeois purchasers of confiscated property (*biens nationaux*), on officials and their local supporters. It was most dangerous where rural artisans and peasants accepted the leadership of nobles with military experience. The relationship was often a tense one. Even where artisans and peasants apparently fought for the same cause as nobles this certainly did not mean that they favoured the restoration of the *ancien régime* in its entirety.

The danger to the Revolution was exacerbated by 'federalism'. To many moderates it appeared as though a minority of deputies, supported by the Paris popular movement, were usurping the rights of the nation's elected representatives. The democratisation of local government and the emergence of a relatively 'extreme' popular Jacobinism and the threat this posed to established social relationships caused widespread alarm. A movement of resistance to the Terror thus developed in the spring of 1793. It attracted liberal royalists but mainly involved socially conservative republicans in cities like Bordeaux, Lyons, Marseilles, Nîmes, Montpellier, Toulon and Caen, with upper middle class leaders anxious to defend liberty, order and property against the threat of anarchy implicit in proposals for an agrarian law to involve land redistribution and to levy forced loans on the 'rich'. At a time when events in the Vendée as well as external war were imposing intense strains on military resources this new threat to the survival of the Republic was regarded by Jacobins as a particularly heinous form of treason. When, in desperation, the federalists of Lyons and Marseilles appointed royalists to command their armies and those at Toulon called in the British and handed over much of the French fleet in the process, they clearly exposed themselves to the prospect of brutal retaliation.

By August of 1793 around twenty departments were affected by royalist or federalist activity. Shortages of troops ensured that the central government lost control over large areas. Nevertheless the Republic was to survive. The uncoordinated military effort mounted by the federalists was easily overcome. The Vendéans, able to mobilise some 30,000 men, were militarily a greater problem, but by the end of the year their main effort had been crushed. Continued guerilla activity – the *chouannerie* in parts of the Vendée, of Brittany and Normandy – so difficult to entirely terminate where activists enjoyed the advantages of local knowledge, a protective topography and community support, only intensified an increasingly vicious cycle of massacre and reprisal and created enduring hatreds.

For as long as the Revolution seemed threatened, an overriding sense of unity survived amongst its defenders. Military success against both external and internal enemies in the autumn and winter of 1793 however allowed the fissures to break open. Faction fighting was intensified. From as early as the autumn of 1793 Danton and his supporters pressed for a relaxation of the Terror. In contrast Hébert appealed for its intensification. Both of these groups were isolated politically by Robespierre and his supporters and their leaders guillotined in March–April 1794. The Committee of Public Safety was also determined to restore governmental authority in the capital and to control the popular movement which placed it under constant radicalising pressure. This became easier as many militants were incorporated into the burgeoning bureaucracy and army. Others were either too frightened, disillusioned or fatigued to continue their political involvement. A considerable loss of spontaneity was probably inevitable. Between January and April 1794 the leadership and organisation of the Parisian popular movement was destroyed and with it some of the most committed supporters of revolutionary radicalism.

Plate 16 Emergence of the conservative republic, Thermidor
Year II (28 July 1794). Troops loyal to the Convention arrive at
the Hôtel de ville in Paris to arrest Robespierre. Engraving by
Helman, after C. Monnet

Subsequent efforts by surviving *sans-culottes* militants to resort to
force to defend their conception of popular democracy were rapidly
crushed. By their success the Jacobins had however isolated themselves
from the mass support which had brought them to power in the
summer of 1793. Furthermore the Terror had been acceptable to most
members of the Convention only as an expedient. The military
victories of June–July 1794 won by the superior generalship of officers
promoted on merit, by weight of number and because of divisions
amongst the allies, ended the immediate threat of invasion and made
revolutionary terrorism much less tolerable. A majority of deputies
found increasingly abhorrent Robespierre's apparent determination to
turn terror into a permanent form of government, a means of creating
a new moral order. They objected too to the judicial murder of some
of their own and particularly Danton. Who could feel safe? The
Committee of Public Safety was itself divided, along both personal as
well as political lines. When on 26 July 1794 Robespierre denounced
Cambon, Billaud and others in the Convention they vigorously
defended themselves and attracted vocal support. On the following day

the assembly voted the arrest of Robespierre and his associates, and secured their rapid execution. This reassertion of the sovereign powers of parliament was followed by the curtailment of the powers of its committees. The administration and National Guard were energetically purged of both suspected Jacobins and *sans-culottes* and the popular societies subjected to repression or closure. Political prisoners were released and the surviving Girondin deputies recalled. These events, in the month of Thermidor Year II in the revolutionary calendar marked the beginning of the transition to a more conservative regime.

THE CONSERVATIVE REPUBLIC

The context was one of widespread and extreme misery with the worst subsistence crisis since 1709 caused by the poor harvest of 1794 and the long and harsh winter of 1794–95. Popular risings in Paris on 1 April and 20–23 May 1795 caused, above all by the desperate desire to reduce bread prices but employing the slogan 'Bread and the Constitution of '93', were easily crushed by the army and the national guards of the better-off western *quartiers* of the capital. This marked the end of the *sans-culottes* as a significant political movement for some thirty-five years. On 23 August it was decreed that the surviving political clubs and popular societies should be closed. Cold, hunger and repression had taken their toll. Recourse was increasingly had to the arbitrary judgements of the military courts. The subsequent conspiracy to seize power led by Babeuf, a proponent of the abolition of private property, ended prematurely with his arrest in May 1796 and provided yet another excuse for the detention of suspects. The Convention was now able to complete its task of preparing yet another constitution. The democratic constitution adopted but never implemented during the summer of 1793 had come to appear dangerously egalitarian. The Constitution of the Year III in contrast provided for the election of a binary legislature made up of a Council of the Ancients and a Council of the Five Hundred with a system of indirect election in which around one million men, or about 20 per cent of the primary electorate were eligible for election to departmental assemblies, whose 30,000 members ultimately selected deputies. Manhood suffrage had come to be seen as a recipe for anarchy or despotism. Furthermore as a safeguard against a possible royalist election victory it was further stipulated that initially two-thirds of the deputies to be elected to the *Conseil des Cinq-Cents* and *Anciens* should be members of the Convention. The commitment to equality before the law survived, and property rights were firmly guaranteed, but this document was silent on the rights to work, to assistance and to an elementary education which the Jacobins had previously insisted upon. These were to be the responsibility of the individual and not the state. Indeed the final ending of the economic controls associated with the Terror seemed to confirm the regime's indifference to popular suffering. Executive authority was conferred on a Directory of five, although in order to prevent a repetition of the dictatorship they had just endured deputies were now determined to enforce a rigorous separation of powers.

This was to be a regime constantly aware of the threats from both the Jacobin left and the royalist right, and desperately in need of a social and political base it could call its own. The danger implicit in its balancing act was rapidly made clear. Resentment of the Convention's perpetuation of its own power led to a royalist rising in Paris on 5 October 1795 forcing the regime to look to the left for support but this only served to alienate those moderate notables who were its natural constituents.

The alliance with the left could anyway only be a short-lived tactical manoeuvre. Although the monarchist threat would on several occasions promote efforts to increase republican unity, anxiety within governing circles that this might encourage the rebirth of the alliance between the Jacobins and the popular classes always led to a renewal of repression. Similarly openings to the right, as in the case of the decree of 21 February 1795 establishing freedom of conscience in religious matters, were hedged around with too many restrictions to enjoy real success. The monarchist menace certainly seemed very real. It could be seen daily in the dress, affectations and arrogance of the so-called *jeunesse dorée* (gilded youth) in Paris. It manifested itself in continued insurrection in the west against which a reinforced military effort under Hoche was deployed, with as many as 100,000 men sweeping through the countryside in flying-columns in the spring of 1795. In communities in the Rhône valley and throughout the southeast the excesses of former Jacobin militants were avenged. They were subjected to ostracism and intimidation and not infrequently murdered. If 1795 was the bloodiest year of this White Terror it continued until at least 1802 and represented both revenge and the reassertion of social hierarchy. The purge of Jacobin sympathisers from the administration and the widespread collapse of local government in the face of desertion, draft dodging and brigandage left former militants cruelly exposed. Overt royalist political activity was also evident. In spite of the inept intransigence of Louis XVIII's demand in the Verona declaration of 24 June 1795 for a restoration of the 'ancient constitution', subsequent elections revealed considerable support within the wealthy electorate for monarchists. So much so that on 4 September 1797 – the so-called *coup d'état* of 18 Fructidor Year V – the Directory felt obliged to annul the election results in over half the departments and to reactivate legislation against émigrés and priests as well as to engage in a further purge of the administration. The Constitution had been violated.

The so-called Thermidorian and Directorial regimes have generally received a bad press. However the seriousness of the problems they faced ought to be borne in mind. Ending the Terror did not end the problems caused by civil and external war, and by poor harvests. Although the Directory made substantial progress towards ending the financial instability caused by the massive depreciation of the *assignat*, repeated purges of both the bureaucracy and of parliament considerably weakened the authority of the central government and left it increasingly isolated. It survived for as long as it did due both to the ability of men like Barras and Carnot and especially because of the divisions and weakness of its adversaries. There were however obvious dangers in a situation in which war and its own isolation forced the government to increasingly rely upon the support of the army. Military victories which kept most of the army outside France and engaged in a systematic policy of looting and living off the land certainly eased the regime's financial difficulties. Moreover its senior officers were opposed to both a royalist restoration which would threaten their own status and to a Jacobin revival which would seek to reimpose civilian control over their activities. Ominously however efforts to control the generals were often contemptuously rejected. The revolutionary army had been transformed into an increasingly professional force, divorced from civilian society.

THE CONSULATE AND EMPIRE

By the end of the 1790s the Republic in the persons of its squabbling politicians was discredited. There was a widespread desire even amongst deputies for strong government which would more effectively safeguard social order, whilst respecting personal liberty and equality before the law, that is the fundamental gains of 1789. There was little agreement as to how these objectives might be achieved. Various groups were however looking for the support of an influential general. Bernadotte, Joubert, Moreau, and then Bonaparte were all cast in this role. For Sieyès and his faction, frightened by a neo-Jacobin renewal of the Directory in June 1799, Bonaparte had obvious virtues. Besides his talent as a soldier, he possessed useful contacts within the intellectual and political élites, and was popular both in the army and amongst civilians. Using the pretext of a Jacobin plot, the legislature was persuaded to transfer itself to Saint-Cloud, just outside Paris, and once there, on 18–19 Brumaire 1799, surrounded by troops and pressured into establishing a ruling Consulate made up of Sieyès, Ducos and Bonaparte. The coup had been planned as a means of affirming the authority of Sieyès and his supporters but it was rapidly to become evident that real power lay in the hands of Bonaparte, the man with military support. The constitution of the Year VIII (1799) provided for his appointment as First Consul for ten years with substantial executive power. Although virtual manhood suffrage was also recognised, as before democracy was kept at bay by means of the indirect election of candidates for a legislative assembly (*Corps législatif*) selected by a senate that was itself formed by cooption. Moreover the press and political activity were subject to constant and effective repression. In order to avoid possible difficulties with the legislature, provision was made for a plebiscite, with its results carefully manufactured, as the means of legitimising these arrangements. Although Bonaparte owed his power to the army, his regime, whilst certainly authoritarian, was not to become a military dictatorship. The supremacy of the civilian administration was to be preserved even if much of its energy was to be absorbed in the incessant task of providing the means for waging war.

The immediate problem was to impose governmental authority upon a country plagued by widespread banditry and political dis-affection and in which local administrators had lost confidence. A combination of military action against royalist insurgents in the south and west, together with concessions to Catholics to allow Sunday worship, and a generous amnesty for both royalists and Jacobins, sought to impose order and create a consensus in support of the new regime. This was followed by measures which would permanently increase the effectiveness of the administration and represent another important stage in the creation of a centralised state – an *Etat bureaucratique*. A law of 7 February 1800 established the prefectoral system. This involved the creation of a depoliticised, hierarchical structure whose officials, as the representatives of the state in each department, would enjoy high salaries and status. The revolutionary principle of the election of local officials was replaced by their imposition from above. Significantly 40 per cent of the 281 prefects appointed between 1800 and 1814 would be *ancien régime* nobles. Financial confidence was to be restored by means of the more efficient collection of taxes (law of 24 November 1799) and the establishment of a central bank. These measures represented major steps towards the creation of a modern centralised bureaucracy. In spite of his own ignorance of administrative and financial matters Bonaparte proved willing to accept the reforming proposals of experienced administrators like Lebrun and Gaudin, the latter – at Finance – a former collaborator of Necker. There had also been considerable progress in the preparation of new legal codes before the establishment of the Consulate. These would both confirm the basic principles of personal liberty and legal equality established in 1789 and seek to protect and to regulate the transmission of private property which, following the destruction of the society of orders, had become the essential source of social status. They provided France for the first time with a uniform legal system. The prestige of the regime was further heightened by a string of military victories leading to the Peace of Lunéville (8 February 1801) which restored French dominance over Northern Italy and the left bank of the Rhine, and to the Treaty of Amiens (25 March 1802) with Britain. In the longer term neither Austria nor Britain would be able to tolerate the prospect of French hegemony. More immediately however peace released troops for internal repression in combination with which Bonaparte felt able to take further conciliatory initiatives. In April 1802 an amnesty was offered to all save one thousand émigrés providing that they took an oath of loyalty and accepted the revolutionary land settlement. Furthermore a concordat, finally published at Easter 1802, was negotiated with the papacy and from a position of strength. It represented Bonaparte's cynical appreciation of the value of religion as a means of social control. It also made it easier for Catholics to accept his government and substantially weakened the royalist cause. Whilst recognising the preeminence of Catholicism as the religion to which most of the population adhered, the Concordat provided for extensive state control over the clergy. It was nevertheless generally welcomed as bringing to an end a period of vicious conflict between Church and state which had threatened the very basis of established religion. Even Napoleon's subsequent occupation of the papal states and excommunication by the Pope failed to shake this new internal consensus.

On 6 May 1802 the senate, in gratitude for Bonaparte's achievements, proposed that his authority be extended for a further ten years; the *Conseil d'Etat* (state council) instead suggested a plebicite to ask the nation to establish him as consul for life with the right to nominate his successor. In this way legislative bodies, made up of wealthy property owners but repeatedly purged until they were composed overwhelmingly of proven adherents of the regime, gave power to Bonaparte as a means of avoiding the uncertainties of election and parliamentary government. The mass of the population, after years of repression remained indifferent. The establishment of the hereditary Empire on 18 May 1804 was another means by which those who served the regime sought to increase their security in response to a series of royalist assassination plots. Although it had little real effect on the institutions of government, it had immense symbolic value in bringing the era of revolution to a close. The new monarchy like the conservative republic which preceded it was to be an authoritarian, repressive regime, devoted to the preservation of the social status quo.

Napoleon's essential objectives remained the establishment of effective government, the reinforcement of social hierarchy, assuring French military and political predominance in Europe and the secure establishment of his dynasty in France. Alongside the wealthy a new status hierarchy based upon service to the state was to be constructed. Its future members, drawn from the middle and upper classes, were to be trained in the lycées (law of 1 May 1802) under close state supervision. Their achievements were to be recognised with mem-

Plate 17 Austerlitz, 2 December 1805, confirmed French military predominance following the occupation of Vienna, a fact recognised in the Treaty of Pressbourg. The Austro–Russian force was defeated with the loss of 37,000 dead and 30,000 prisoners; 8,000 French troops lost their lives. Engraving by J. Rugendas

bership of the Legion of Honour (May 1802) and of the imperial nobility (1808). The prospects offered by the extended Empire attracted men from a variety of social backgrounds. Former *ancien régime* nobles made up 22 per cent of the new nobility, 20 per cent would come from the popular classes, and 58 per cent from the bourgeoisie. Shared objectives served to reduce political disunity. Although most members of the old nobility chose to remain inactive, as time passed few families were unrepresented in the civil adminstration or officer corps. The regime's successes and growing air of permanence encouraged many nobles to overcome their initial disdain for the 'usurper'. The bourgeoisie continued as under the *ancien régime* to view office holding as a primary means of achieving upward social mobility.

As the administration became more effective, so the regime became more dictatorial. Representative institutions were largely ignored, although membership of the departmental electoral colleges, which from 1802 was restricted to the 600 most heavily taxed men in each

Plate 18 Napoleon distrubuting Europe between his brothers.
Engraving by Gauthier

department (mainly landowners, wholesale merchants and lawyers) was valued as a source of status. At the top, the emperor's growing intolerance of dissent led to the replacement of able ministers like Chaptal, Talleyrand and Fouché and left the regime increasingly dependent on the will and ability of the dictator. In the short term religious peace, social order, material prosperity and the seemingly endless list of military victories protected the regime from dissent. Those workers whose age, family responsibilities and luck in the draw enabled them to escape military service benefited from the reduction in the size of the labour force and rising wages. Urban consumers and most of the rural population benefited from the series of good harvests between 1802 and 1810, a period of prosperity for which the regime claimed and frequently received credit. Perpetual war was however to lead to the Empire's collapse. The determined effort to impose French political and, through the Continental System, economic hegemony on Europe was bound to be resisted. Napoleon's reorganisation of the army between 1800 and 1804, his careful preparation for war and tactical genius offered only temporary advantage. His opponents learnt

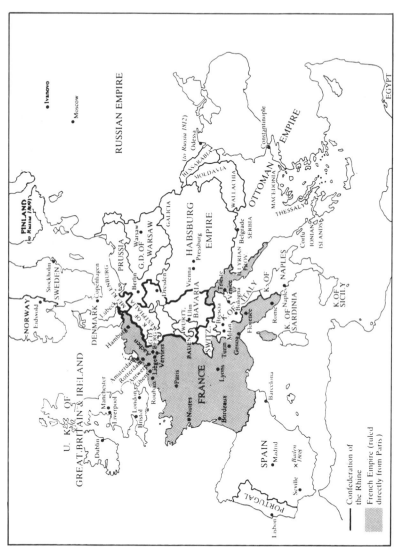

Fig 10 Apogée of Empire, 1812

RUSSIAN EMPIRE

• Ivanovo

• Moscow

FINLAND
(to Russia 1809)

NORWAY

• Edsvold

Stockholm •
SWEDEN

U. K. OF
GREAT BRITAIN & IRELAND

Dublin •

Manchester •
Liverpool •

Bristol •

London

Antwerp
Ghent

Amsterdam
Rotterdam

Roubaix

DENMARK
Copenhagen •

Lübeck
MECKLENBURG

Hamburg •

K. OF WESTPHALIA

Berlin •

PRUSSIA

G.D. OF
WARSAW

Warsaw •

Dresden •

GALICIA

Verviers

FRANCE

• Paris

• Nantes

Lyons •

Bordeaux •

K. OF
BAVARIA

WÜRTT.
Ulm

BADEN

SWITZ.

Munich •

Vienna •

HABSBURG

EMPIRE

Pressburg •

ILLYRIAN
PROV.
Trieste

K. OF
ITALY

Turin •

Genoa •

Milan •

Bologna

Venice •

Florence •

Rome •

K. OF
NAPLES

• Naples
K. OF

K. OF
SARDINIA

K. OF
SICILY

SPAIN

Madrid •

× Baden
1808

Barcelona •

PORTUGAL

Lisbon •

Seville •

MOLDAVIA

BESSARABIA
(to Russia 1812)

WALLACHIA

Odessa •

Belgrade •

SERBIA

OTTOMAN

EMPIRE

Constantinople •

MACEDONIA

THESSALY

Corfu
IONIAN
ISLANDS

EGYPT

Confederation of
the Rhine

French Empire (ruled
directly from Paris)

their lessons the hard way, but learn them they did. The numerical advantages offered by the size of the populations of military age in France and its annexed territories were lost as the armies retreated and with the declining ability to make the defeated pay, so the costs of war, in terms both of men and money, increased and with this came growing political opposition.

The strength of this opposition is difficult to gauge. Administrative reports generally told the emperor and his ministers what it was presumed they wanted to hear, repeatedly stressing the people's loyalty and great love for their ruler. There were three main elements of political opposition – republicans, royalists, and most dangerous of all the war-weary. Following earlier repression and especially a wave of arrests in 1801, republican and popular opposition had largely been relegated to the verbal, to little more than anonymous yells of 'Down with (*A bas*) Bonaparte' and private discussion by groups of old Jacobins. Police surveillance and occasional prosecutions combined to create an atmosphere of fear and to encourage restraint. Royalist groups, of which the Knights of the Faith (*Chevaliers de la Foi* (1809)) were the most notable, were more active, engaging in assassination plots and creating underground networks linked with émigrés and the British. Within high society contempt for the regime was frequently expressed in the privacy of the home. Many of those who had rallied to it and held office had done so on a conditional basis and only for as long as there was no alternative. Even within the army generals like Bernadotte, Moreau and Pichegru had long questioned the motives of a man who had been prepared to abandon his troops, first in Egypt in 1799 and then in 1812 in Russia, and who appeared to be making excessive demands upon the army for his own personal glory.

War-weariness increased rapidly with the failure of the Russian adventure and during the defensive campaigns of 1813–14. The British blockade intensified the commercial crisis which resulted from the poor harvests of 1811–12. An extremely harsh winter added to popular misery and discontent. The burden of taxation, increasing from 1809, became all the more difficult to support. Draft-dodging increased. It had been a far less serious problem for most of the imperial years than during the Republic or Directory. More effective policing and the greater prestige of the regime saw to that. Those who could afford to were able anyway to hire replacements. It is worth noting too that

Plate 19 The crossing of the Berezina, 25–29 November 1812, a crucial moment in the disastrous retreat from Moscow. Lithograph by Victor Adam

between 1800 and 1814 conscription took only some 7 per cent of the total population, a high enough figure but not when compared with the 20 per cent taken between 1914 and 1919. However by the end of 1813 the allies had crossed the Rhine, and Wellington was advancing through the Midi. Even the normally docile *Corps législatif* voted in favour of peace on the basis of France's 'natural frontiers' (essentially those of 1792) in December (by 229 to 31) and had its session adjourned for its pains. Through 1813–14, as casualties mounted and morale declined, the refusal of young men to report for duty once more became a major problem. Endemic guerilla warfare in the west revived as unwilling conscripts provided a continuous stream of recruits. In many parts of central France too the call to arms to defend the nation by the distant government in Paris seemed threateningly irrelevant to daily life. Together with widespread subsistence disorders and unemployment this contributed to a renewed breakdown in law and order, particularly in the still under-policed countryside. Defeat and internal disorder threatened the conditional loyalty of the propertied classes predicated upon the promise of social order and prosperity. On 31 March 1814, in spite of an often brilliant defensive campaign the allies entered Paris; on 2–3 April the senate and *Corps législatif* voted to deprive the emperor of his throne. On 6 April his own marshals forced him to abdicate at Fontainebleau. This collapse represented a massive withdrawal of support by the notables. The masses remained to a large degree indifferent to the proceedings. As Napoleon had himself predicted when asked how the people would react to his disappearance: *On dira Ouf*!

A new constitution was now prepared by the senate, a body made up of imperial dignatories, officials and landowners, many of them former members of the old revolutionary legislatures. The proposals which emerged, the bases for a new constitutional Charter, closely resembled the constitution of 1791 providing as it did for a constitutional monarchy, but with the king enjoying considerable power as head of the executive, and incorporating the other crucial gains of 1789 including equality before the law, freedom of religion and the press, and guaranteeing the revolutionary land settlement. The lower house of parliament was to be elected on a very restricted franchise, ensuring that only the wealthy – those with a 'real' stake in society – would share in political power. Under pressure from the allies and in order to secure the restoration of legitimate monarchy, Louis XVIII felt obliged to accept this compromise. The Charter was proclaimed on 4 June.

It took a considerable degree of incompetence on the part of the restored monarchy and its supporters to make Bonaparte popular again. The need to reduce substantially the size of the administration and army in a France restricted to its old frontiers and requiring only a peace-time military establishment, was used as a means of purging the potentially disloyal, of rewarding supporters and placing trusted personnel in key positions. This caused considerable resentment particularly as it seemed to herald a far more thoroughgoing counter-revolution. In the countryside there were widespread rumours about the repossession of their land by former émigrés and the reimposition of feudal dues and tithes. Napoleon was able to take advantage of this and of his continued popularity in the army. His return from exile on the island of Elba on 1 March 1815 seems to have revived radical anti-noble, anti-clerical, and nationalistic feeling – a neo-Jacobin revival which caused great anxiety amongst 'respectable' property owners. These notables were also appalled at the prospect of renewed war. Thus, in order to win the support of these essential cadres, Napoleon himself felt obliged to promise the establishment of a constitutional, parliamentary regime in an 'Additional Act' similar in many respects to Louis XVIII's Charter.

Support for the emperor's return remained however far from universal. It was most whole-hearted in the north and east which had suffered from the allied invasion. Elsewhere the response was often indifference or active opposition as in those coastal regions which anticipated a renewal of the British blockade and especially areas in the south and west in which popular opposition first to the religious policies of the Revolution and subsequently to conscription had been most intense. It was in these regions that often brutal reprisals would be taken against Bonapartist sympathisers when Waterloo brought this new adventure – Napoleon's Hundred Days – to a bloody climax. This overwhelming defeat forced the emperor to abdicate for a second and final time on 22 June 1815 and was followed by his imprisonment at a safe distance, out in the Atlantic on the island of Saint Helena.

This did not however mean the end of political upheaval in France. The Revolutionary – Napoleonic era had destroyed old landmarks and had fundamental effects on the ways in which people thought about politics. Precedents had been established, allegiances formed which were to be passed on to succeeding generations. The fears and aspirations which had been generated created agendas for the following century. The masses had entered the political arena. They had learnt about the relevance of political affairs to their daily lives and about political organisation. It would prove impossible for even the best organised of police forces to reverse this entirely. The sense of emergency which had led to the Terror exacerbated political polarisation, for or against the Revolution. The crucial importance of state power had never been as obvious. Moreover during the Terror, and in subsequent periods of conservative reaction, administrative reforms occurred which were to enhance significantly its capacity for social intervention. In recent years it has become fashionable, and not only amongst politically conservative 'revisionist' historians, to decry the significance of the Revolution (and by implication of revolutions), to seek to reduce it to the status of a passing epiphenomenon – the Revolution as continuity – with few lasting effects and these essentially negative. There are indeed good grounds for arguing along these lines.

The abolition of guilds, banning of workers associations and removal of internal customs barriers had seemed to lay the foundation for economic liberty. Many landowners and peasants had benefited from the abolition of tithes and seigneurial dues. Successive upheavals had however created an atmosphere of uncertainty less conducive to entrepreneurial activity other than of a speculative character. The needs of war led to the reimposition of controls. Soaring inflation threatened paralysis. The desire for security and an active land market encouraged the diversion of capital from commerce and manufacture, with industrial production probably reaching its lowest level in 1796. Subsequently greater internal security and the widening of the frontiers provided better opportunities, but the maritime war, in which British domination was more complete than ever before, had devastating effects on the ports and their hinterlands, previously the most dynamic sectors of the economy. The prosperity of the first part of the Empire was geographically restricted and always fragile. It was terminated by the poor harvest of 1810 and the deteriorating military situation. To a large degree it represented merely recovery from the losses of the revolutionary period. Although localised examples of innovation and growth can certainly be identified most notably in the Paris, Rouen, Lille and Mulhouse areas, protected by war from the full rigours of British competition, French technology increasingly fell behind that of its rival. The basic pre-industrial structures of the French economy remained unchanged, with the predominance of a low productivity agriculture, of slow and high cost transportation systems and frag-mented commercial networks and small-scale manufacturing. The gradual processes of change represented by growing commercialisation and increasing productivity, already evident in the previous century, were if anything slowed rather than stimulated.

In social terms too it seems quite correct to stress the continuities between the pre-revolutionary period and the early nineteenth century. It was the structure of the élite which was most dramatically affected by the Revolution and Empire. Even there the impact was limited. The decline of the society of orders was already well under way before the Revolution. The abolition of noble privilege confirmed as much as completed this process. Although the substantial land transfers which occurred reduced the economic and social power of the nobility and church their main consequence was to consolidate existing patterns of

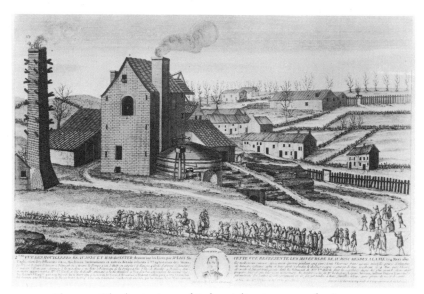

Plate 20 The beginnings of industrialisation: a coal mine near Liège. Note the use of a steam engine for drainage, and the anxious crowd gathering following news of an accident on 29 February 1812

landholding and the position of the rich, amongst whom the nobility remained conspicuous. In a still primarily agrarian society in which the wealth necessary to fund the appropriate life-style, and to provide the education which allowed access to the professions or political office, was derived primarily from the land, it followed that the social élite, this class of *notables*, even if enlarged by the inclusion of many non-nobles, retained many of its pre-revolutionary characteristics. Certainly the years after 1789 had provided opportunities for upward mobility, particularly through state service and speculation on the value of land and military supplies, but the aspirations of the new men had been defined according to models established by the old. The social élite of the early nineteenth century, like that of the eighteenth was the creation of complex processes of inter-penetration between families with established status and those with ambitions. The Revolution had however created an intense sense of insecurity. Political conflict, competition for power, had left bitter divisions within this élite and had awakened the more or less clearly formulated aspirations of other groups. Thus although it is important to reject the exaggerated notion of revolution as the essential 'motor of history' in the Marxist sense, this should not lead us to ignore its massive impact on the political and ideological scene. It would take generations to work through the agenda it had established and the effort to do so would profoundly mark the succeeding century as the proponents of *movement* to complete the revolution, clashed with the supporters of *résistance* to further change.

5

The nineteenth century: continuity and change

1815 saw the restoration of the Bourbon monarchy in the person of Louis XVIII, brother of the king executed in 1793. This was far from representing a return to the pre-revolutionary status quo. The gains of 1789, constitutional monarchy, representative government and equality before the law were recognised in the charter granted by the king to the nation. In many other respects too the agenda for political debate throughout the forthcoming century had been set during the long years of internal strife and external war between 1789 and 1815. Sustained political mobilisation had created a new political culture. Those who had directly experienced these events transmitted durable mental habits to their children. A wide range of political options had emerged including reactionary Catholic monarchism, commitment to the liberal principles of 1789, *sans-culottes* egalitarianism, Jacobin nationalism and Bonapartism. Each of these signified adherence to highly selective references and images of the Revolution (the Declaration of the Rights of Man, the execution of the king, Robespierre, Bonaparte and so on) which signified fundamentally different value systems, around which political 'parties' (not organised bodies until the 1900s) coalesced and wider support might be mobilised. In effect the ways in which people perceived and thus behaved continued to be substantially influenced by their conceptions of the revolutionary–imperial period. Over time and between social groups these ideas underwent frequent more or less conscious re-interpretation under the impact not only of political but of processes of socio-economic development already under way during the old century and accelerating in the new. The chronology of change in the economy and society was however very different from that in politics. The history of the nineteenth century thus has to be looked at against the background of two revolutions, the industrial as well as the political.

ECONOMY AND SOCIETY

Revolution and war had distorted earlier patterns of growth. Maritime blockade had largely destroyed the prosperous overseas trade, whilst industries contributing to the military effort or with their markets enlarged by frontier changes had prospered. Within the reduced boundaries of 1815 essentially pre-revolutionary patterns of growth were resumed. Growing population and urbanisation stimulated the commercialisation of agriculture. Productivity gradually increased as the more intensive cultivation associated with mixed farming was introduced. In manufacture artisanal, workshop production developed through increases in the numbers of workers employed in both town and country, as well as efforts to increase productivity by means of greater specialisation, but additionally through concentration and mechanisation and the beginnings of structural change and modern industralisation. This represented the onset of a lengthy period of transition from an economy dominated by agriculture and artisanal forms of manufacture towards an economic system in which, in spite of important continuities with the past, industrial production predominated.

In many respects however the economic and social structures of the ancien régime survived until the 1840s. The events of the Revolution had done little to change an essentially pre-industrial economy with low levels of productivity, a system which remained susceptible to frequent crises induced by poor harvests, the resultant sharp rise in food prices and decline in demand for manufactured goods. Structural change in the economy was stimulated both by rising levels of demand caused by population growth and a slow rise in per capita incomes, and by the impact of technological innovation on the supply of agricultural and manufactured goods. At first gradually, and then with increased rapidity from the 1840s to 1850s, a series of innovations occurred effecting most notably communications with the railway and electric

Table 5.1. *National income at constant prices (in 1905–13 francs)*

Years	Total national income (millions of francs)	Per capita national income (francs)
1825–34	10,606	325.6
1835–44	13,061	380.5
1845–54	15,866	443.0
1855–64	19,097	510.9
1865–74	22,327	602.0
1875–84	24,272	644.2
1885–94	26,713	696.6
1895–1904	30,965	794.7
1905–13	34,711	876.4

telegraph, in the organisation of commerce, and in the production of textiles, in metallurgy and engineering. The adoption of steam as a relatively cheap, flexible and plentiful source of power was a striking feature of these developments. In total they represented the transition from a civilisation based upon wood and water, to one built upon coal and the steam engine as the primary sources of heat and energy.

There is no simple explanation of these economic changes. The British example was of course an important stimulus due to the threat of competition, although this was restricted by protection, and the simple desire to emulate. Economic change in France has nevertheless to a large degree to be explained in terms of the specific French context, in relation to particular geographic conditions, market structures and the supply and cost of the factors of production. Nineteenth-century growth differed from that of previous centuries in that it was sustained and involved major structural changes in both the economy and society. One crucial characteristic was the substantial increase in per capita production revealed in table 5.1. The statistics should be treated with caution but they can be treated as indicators of general trends.

Sustained growth meant breaking out of the vicious circle which in a traditional society resulted in a low real income because of low per capita productivity, caused by low levels of investment in capital equipment, which in its turn was the result of low levels of demand due to low real income. The problem was intensified by a tendency for population growth to accelerate in the early stages of development, at a time when industrial growth, and the provision of employment opportunities outside the agricultural sector, remained slow. To a substantial extent per capita income and the whole cycle of economic growth depended upon rising agricultural productivity both to feed this population and to provide resources for industry. A long period of increased demand was necessary to encourage economic innovation, the shape of which was determined by the range of techniques available and the capacity of potential innovators to make use of them, itself determined by the availability of capital and of labour with the appropriate skills. Early innovation must be considered within the context of established local and regional economic systems. New techniques tended to be more readily accepted the more easily they fitted into existing productive systems, the lower their capital cost and the greater the possibility of financing them through self-investment. In effect modernisation involved not the substitution of 'modernity' for 'tradition' but the interpenetration of various attributes of both.

The structure of demand was decisively transformed by transport innovation, which increased the size of potential markets by reducing the cost of transporting commodities. There can be no doubt that the effectiveness of all forms of transport was substantially increased from the 1840s. The means were provided for the cheap and rapid movement of goods, of people, and, through the telegraph and press, of information. Progress had undoubtedly been made before the construction of a railway network, but the traditional forms of transport had constituted a major obstacle to the development of a more unified market and a major disincentive to increased production. Comparisons might be instructive. Britain, a much smaller country, possessed the advantages of a relatively dense waterway system which facilitated the establishment of an integrated market. France had more in common with a large land mass like Germany, in which the railway played a major role in stimulating changes in market structures. Improved communications additionally reinforced the importance of towns as economic centres, as poles of growth attracting enterprise, capital and labour, and as markets for both agricultural and industrial products, and amongst towns the existence of a more clearly defined functional hierarchy. It would be too much to describe the railway as a necessary pre-condition for the substantial extension of markets, but transport changes without doubt profoundly affected the spatial structures of economic activity. Large-scale production is dependent upon access to large markets. Prior to the development of the rail network, high transport costs made it difficult to break out of an economic system based upon small-scale production for localised demand. The exceptions were regions close to the sea or waterways, with relatively easy access to markets. The new forms of transport also tended to favour these already more developed areas of plain and valley with their higher productivity, incomes and investment potential. A 'dual' economy thus emerged as investment tended to be concentrated in the more dynamic regions. The more 'modern' and the more 'traditional' sectors were not isolated from each other, but were distinctive in terms of the scale and capital intensity of production. These differences were most marked in agriculture, between the more market-centred capitalistic farms and peasant farms orientated towards the satisfaction of family needs.

The basic factors influencing demand for agricultural products were the growth of population and per capita consumption. Prior to the communications revolution, in a predominantly rural society with low average incomes, diet and patterns of demand were slow to change. Subsequently change accelerated. The process of urbanisation, in particular, meant that an increasingly small part of the population was able to produce its own food. Consumer demand in the growing towns, together with improved access to urban markets provided a major stimulus to innovation in agriculture. Change was inevitably slow in traditional agricultural economies, based as they were on delicate internal balances. Groups of plants needed to be integrated in such a way as to facilitate the division of labour throughout the farming year. Of even greater importance was the production of a range of commodities in a polycultural system. Plants with different vegetative cycles provided some guarantee against the failure of any one crop due to bad weather. Innovation, although never absent, normally depended upon almost certain confidence that the replacement of one element in the cultural system would not upset the equilibrium of the whole. The peasant cultivators who dominated much of French agriculture, concerned above all with family subsistence, required empirical proof of the value of innovation before engaging in it themselves. The reduction of risks was the primary concern rather than profitability. Innovation occurred, normally by means of a slow accumulation of experience, usually gained in the first instance by the larger farmers who possessed sufficient land and capital to take risks. However, and in spite of often poor access to markets, not even the most traditional of peasant families could isolate themselves entirely from commercial considerations. It was necessary for every family to cultivate a cash crop or else hire out labour, work in rural industry or have recourse to temporary migration, to obtain the cash resources vital for the payment of taxes or purchase of necessities which were not produced locally. Even the most isolated regions were engaged in trade. The diversity of French agriculture is partially revealed by map 11. In the earlier part of the century farmers efforts continued to be concentrated upon the production of basic foodstuffs. Only from mid-century did their interest markedly shift towards the production of meat and dairy products and wine, trends indicative of a growing responsiveness to changes in the structure of demand as living standards generally improved.

The initial improvement of access to markets through construction of the primary rail network took place between the 1840s and the 1870s. This and the provision of secondary rail and road links encouraged substantial increases in productivity and in commercialisation. The combination of growing production with high and rising prices brought prosperity. In the last third of the century, however, falling prices combined with rising costs of production to cause a severe crisis and a decline in the rate of increase of productivity. The establishment of more integrated national and international markets, and the stimulus to increased production had resulted in overproduction, especially of wheat and wine. Recovery commenced in the mid-1890s but was hesitant and limited. Tariff protection was reintroduced to limit competition from imports and substantially reduced the pressure to innovate. In many respects French agriculture on the eve of the First World War thus remained archaic. This was particularly evident in the survival of large numbers of small peasant farms and in those regions which remained relatively isolated and where natural conditions were not favourable to innovation and the creation of a modern agriculture. Yet in spite of the limits to change, the period from the 1840s was one of crucial significance for the long-term evolution of French farming, a period which saw the final disappearance of the age-old subsistence crises, and in which the operating context for farmers

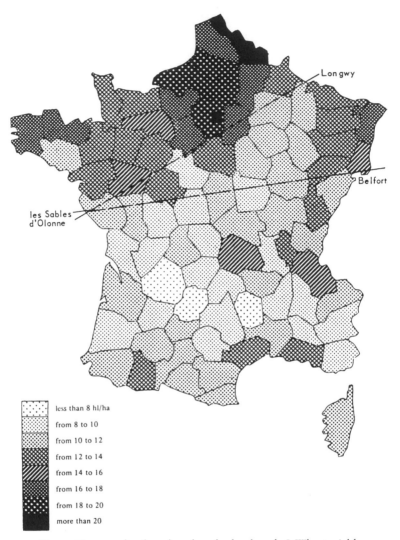

Fig 11 France: developed and underdeveloped. I Wheat yields in 1840

was transformed and more substantial innovation occurred within the space of three or four decades than had previously occurred in as many centuries. This marked a decisive break with the past.

The development of French industry like that of agriculture has been frequently compared with that of British and found wanting. This approach does however have its limits. It fails to take account of differences in social and economic structures leading to different but equally rational forms of industrial growth. Estimates of nineteenth-century growth rates vary considerably (between 1.8 per cent and 2.9 per cent per annum). Production nevertheless seem to have increased six times over by 1913. The period 1815–46 appears to have been one of slow, regular growth, interrupted by minor fluctuations; 1846–51 was a period of major political and economic crisis, followed from 1852 to 1857 by a period of rapid growth. The years 1858 and 1859 were a time of depression, succeeded from 1860 to 1882 by slow growth interrupted by the war of 1870 and the resultant political crisis. Another period of depression from 1882 to 1896 ended in 1897 with the onset of a lengthy period of prosperity terminated only by the Great War. The main factor affecting growth rates appears to have been technical innovation and the investment of capital, which brought about fundamental changes both in the structure of the economy and in productivity in particular industrial sectors. Industrialisation represented a response to changing market conditions, to new opportunities and competitive pressures which stimulated innovation. Technological change was influenced by a complex of factors, including the scale of demand for the product, the comparative cost of labour and of machinery, and the availability of capital. Until the very end of the century, with the development of electro-metallurgy and chemicals on a large scale, technology was only marginally influenced by science. In practice it developed by means of the piecemeal application of new developments, and their adaptation to the particular circumstances of time and place. Once introduced, new equipment (such as the steam engine) was employed for fifty years or more, although with occasional modifications. The major exceptions to these generalisations occurred with the construction of large-scale integrated metallurgical establishments, and the development of the railway network, in which advanced technology in the form of the steam engine was integrated into what was otherwise a labour intensive form of transport. Technological changes in these two sectors had fundamental effects on the whole economy through the provision of large quantities of iron and steel and the availability of a low cost means of bulk transport.

Nevertheless there was no abrupt change in the structure of French industry. The most obvious method of responding to increased demand

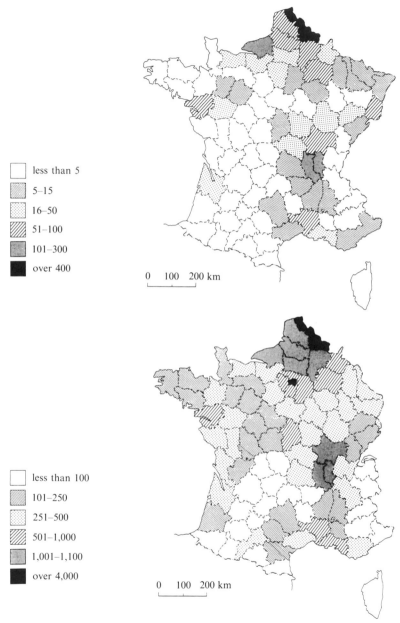

Fig 12 France: developed and underdeveloped. II The steam engine as an indicator of industrialisation. Number per department in 1841 and in 1878

is simply to produce more in the same old way. This is not necessarily perverse or lazy, but can represent an intelligent use of existing resources. In the French case this extension was encouraged by the availability of cheap labour, and the continued fragmentation of the market until at least the 1850s. The structure of demand was complicated. It depended not only upon the size of the population and its per capita income but on a mass of decisions about expenditure and upon personal taste. Poor communications had meant the survival of a decentralised market and thus the dispersal of production. In general, artisans and merchants produced and redistributed goods to geographically limited hinterlands. Inefficient, high cost producers were protected from competition by high transport costs. The nineteenth century saw a rapid expansion of trade as part of a process of improved communications, market integration, and transition from relatively closed to more open local communities. The demand for such goods as iron tools and cotton garments rose with farm incomes and especially technical innovation which reduced their cost. This had vital effects in terms of the creation of substantial homogeneous markets, high levels of demand for standardised products, and the promise of high profits. However the rate of increase in demand for industrial products continued to be influenced by the relatively slow growth of population, by the survival of a low productivity peasant agriculture, and by the immobility of population and slow growth in towns. The situation was worsened by depressed agricultural prices between 1817 and 1851. Additionally throughout the century the distribution of a large part of total income in the form of rents, interest and dividends and, conversely, the restraints imposed on the growth of earned incomes helped to preserve a highly individualised bourgeois demand for luxury products which hindered the development of mass production. To some extent export markets compensated for the limitations of internal demand. However, continuity with the rapid growth of exports in the eighteenth century had been broken through the loss of markets during the revolutionary–imperial wars. After the disasters of this period exports increased primarily where they were not in competition with British factory production, that is particularly in the markets for high quality goods like silks and *articles de Paris*. Even so France remained second in the world for the export of manufactured goods until 1870.

From the 1840s the pace of change accelerated. This was characterised by the growing predominance of factory over artisanal forms of production and of the industrial economy over agriculture. For many small producers the spread of capital intensive methods of production heralded a period of crisis and decline. The rate of growth in large-scale mechanised industry between 1835–44 and 1855–64, for example, has been estimated to have been twice as great as that for industry as a whole. In twenty years its share of the total industrial product rose from one-quarter to more than one-third. Small-scale enterprises were disadvantaged in an increasingly competitive market by their inability to enjoy economies of scale, their poor links to commercial networks, low profit margins and limited access to external credit which made innovation difficult and left them vulnerable to short-term economic fluctuations. The enlargement of markets and the growing complexity and cost of technology both favoured large enterprises, yet the small managed to survive largely by means of greater specialisation. The growth of the service sector was another important feature of economic modernisation, involving the concurrent development of communications, financial and commercial networks. Structures and habits were transformed as the volume of goods produced and marketed multiplied. The traditional fairs declined. As the scale of production increased and investment levels rose, manufacturers adopted less passive attitudes towards their markets. They started to prospect for new customers – the commercial traveller appears in the 1820s – and to advertise their wares. The growth of a mass circulation press was vital in this respect. The retail trade too was transformed by the establishment of growing numbers of shops, including the first department stores.

In all these ways the pre-industrial economy which had survived until the middle of the nineteenth century was transformed and in the process a major social revolution occurred. The transformation of economic structures made possible considerable improvements in living conditions and changes in attitudes to life, the effects of which were clear in the decline in birth as well as mortality rates. In addition the town replaced the village as the main place of residence. France was however to be distinguished amongst the industrialising nations of the nineteenth century by its relatively low rate of population growth. This meant that in comparison with contemporary third-world countries population pressure on resources was far less intense.

Table 5.2. *Population increase (1750–1911)*

Year	Population (millions)	Year	Population (millions)
1750	21	1861	37.4[a]
1801	27.3	1872	36.1[a]
1821	30.5	1881	37.7
1831	32.6	1891	38.3
1841	34.2	1901	38.9
1851	35.8	1911	39.6

[a] Affected by territorial changes.

Within the period 1815–1914 three major phases of evolution can be identified. The first, from about 1815 to about 1848 was characterised by slow economic change. Although agricultural productivity rose, in many regions population increase maintained dietary standards at low levels. This was essentially a period of continuity compared with the second half of the eighteenth century, with both high (although declining) death and birth rates. It culminated in the intense mid-century economic, social and political crisis between 1846 and 1851. A second period roughly corresponds to the Second Empire and was characterised by accelerated industrialisation, the transport revolution, rapid urban growth and increased migration from the countryside. Living standards certainly appear to have improved although an earlier tendency for birth rate to decline seems to have levelled off. The third period, from about 1871 to 1914, saw a renewed decline in birth rate, with the impact on overall levels of population partly compensated for by reductions in mortality as economic development brought further improvements in living conditions. During these years migration from the countryside grew far more intense. This description of general trends must not however be allowed to conceal regional variations in demographic behaviour. The date and extent of transition from a pre-industrial to more modern patterns varied significantly and was influenced by a complex of factors in addition to economic change.

Urbanisation was accompanied by the transformation of towns, which had remained almost medieval in character, to recognisably modern urban centres. This was a complex development with the character and scale of growth depending upon pre-existing socio-economic structures, which were far from homogeneous, and the nature of regional economic change. Whilst stressing the importance of urbanisation, it is also important to remember its relative slowness in comparison with other parts of western Europe. The period of revolution and empire had been one of stagnation, and the growth rate of towns in the first half of the century was probably lower than it had been for much of the eighteenth. Nevertheless 25.5 per cent of the population was classified as urban in 1851, and the proportion had reached 44.2 per cent by 1911.

The most notable development was the growth of Paris. In 1851 3 per cent of the French population lived in the capital and its suburbs; by 1911, this had risen to 10 per cent. The economic structure of the city had become increasingly complex. In the early decades of the century artisanal forms of production had been dominant. Subsequently heavy industry had developed, particularly engineering and chemicals, on the northern and eastern outskirts, while inner-city areas, although continuing to shelter the various artisanal trades, proved increasingly attractive to the development of administrative, financial and commercial enterprise. All these activities encouraged in-migration although the cost of housing tended increasingly to force most low-wage earners to reside in the more peripheral *quartiers*. The development of mass transport facilities from the 1870s, with suburban railways, tramways and finally bus and underground services, made it increasingly feasible to live some distance from one's place of work. Migration to the towns had always occurred. Its primary cause had been rural poverty. Industrial and commercial development in the nineteenth century substantially increased urban labour needs, at the same time as the transport revolution and technical change had promoted industrial concentration at the expense of the employment in rural industry on which so much of the population in the countryside had come to depend. The towns became more attractive because of employment opportunities which offered higher wages, greater security, less hard work (especially for women), and increased leisure. Their attractiveness grew especially from the 1850s as urban living conditions improved, and as better communications made the rural population more aware of the contrasts between urban and rural life.

This process of socio-economic transformation was inevitably accompanied by major changes in popular culture and behaviour, of which secularisation and rising mass literacy are only the most obvious indicators. The Church had less immediate relevance in an increasingly urban environment and when dependence upon nature was becoming less absolute; education was of increasingly obvious practical value in an industrialising, more commercial and highly administered society. For the élites who took the crucial decisions concerning investment in schools, instruction promised to be the most effective means of 'civilising' the masses and of safeguarding their own power.

SOCIETY AND POLITICS

The abolition of legal privilege in 1789 had left wealth as the primary social distinction. The continued importance of traditional forms of wealth creation meant that France remained in 1815 dominated by a pre-industrial social élite predominantly made up of landowners, nobles and non-nobles, many of whom served or had been employed in the government service, together with a rising proportion of professionals and business-men. This was an élite recognisable as such by the possession of certain generally desired attributes including wealth, social influence and political power, and which served as a reference point for other social groups. In national politics the predominance of these *notables* lasted until the 1870s. It corresponded to the survival of traditional social structures and patterns of behaviour which were only slowly transformed by economic change. It was enshrined, throughout the period of consitutional monarchy (1815–48), in an electoral system based on a property qualification. This was the means of avoiding popular sovereignty and the threat posed by the poor and ignorant to what was perceived to be genuine liberty, and to Christian civilisation itself. Property symbolised capacity. Lack of property represented proof of intellectual and moral inadequacy. The system furthermore facilitated the maximum exercise of personal influence. The *notable* was typically an individual whose status depended on position within the local community, and upon the presumption by members of this community that he had the ear of important persons in government. His social status, life-style and education were such as to allow him a foot in both the local and the enveloping national society. In general these *notables* were opposed to the extension of political rights to the poorer classes and with even greater determination resisted any threat to their rights as property owners. They constituted a powerful conservative commitment to *résistance*. Their wealth and education allowed them to exercise substantial influence as politicians, officials, landowners, employers and dispensers of charity (in a pre-welfare state). This access to multi-faceted means of exercising pressure and influence gave them tremendous advantages in the political game. For them, and probably most of the population, the experience of revolution had been profoundly disillusioning. It had come to represent the confiscation of property, punitive taxation, conscription, an assault on the Church, the Terror and the threat of further social anarchy. Yet the nineteenth century was to be beset by the threat of revolution. This was largely because of widespread disappointment with what was felt to be the incompleteness of political and social change. Some of the discontented, those in favour of *mouvement*, were to gain satisfaction through the limited extension of the franchise in 1830, others by means of the introduction of manhood suffrage in 1848, more when the Republic was definitively established in the late 1870s. Moreover the structure of the élite itself gradually changed as the process of concentration in finance and industry created new conditions for amassing wealth. The scale of accumulation also changed. Although the absolute wealth of landowners did not decline before the 1870s to 1880s, relative decline began much sooner. The agricultural depression of the last third of the century accelerated the process. Landowners were slow to transfer their capital to more lucrative forms of investment. But if the structure of the élite of wealth changed and indeed, as we shall see, substantial political power was diffused down the social hierarchy, French society would remain fundamentally inegalitarian. Thus whilst it is tempting to focus upon dramatic political events, this should not lead us to neglect important continuities. Access to political power and especially to the key positions in government, parliament and the administration continued to depend on possession of the income and education which fitted men for public life. The cultural and political hegemony of the propertied classes was only ineffectively challenged. Privilege in these spheres was defended, if necessary, as in June 1848 or against the Paris Commune in 1871, by the brutal deployment of military force. The political history of nineteenth-century France can thus, to an important degree, be seen as a continuous search for stability. Eventually this was to be secured, but

only from the 1870s, through the establishment of a strong centralised
state, the Third Republic, better able than its predecessors to influence
and control the social groups and regional societies which divided the
nation, and this due to the modernisation of the techniques of
government, more effective political socialisation, the institutionalisation of protest, and growing legitimisation of the regime. The
functions of the nineteenth-century state thus remained essentially
those of its predecessors, of the *Etat-gendarme*, and above all the
safeguarding of law and order and the promotion of national unity.
However in order to achieve these objectives it was obliged to extend
its role in the sphere of public works so as to take advantage of new
communications technologies (rail and electric telegraph) which
immeasurably increased the effectiveness of political and administrative centralisation, and to develop a system of mass instruction
(most notably through the laws of 1833, 1850 and 1882) to ensure
greater cultural homogenisation and closer social control. The Third
Republic would emerge victorious from the great test of war in 1914
and survive until the even greater test in 1940. Before we can discuss
these events however something needs to be said about the complex
evolution of nineteenth-century politics.

THE RESTORATION

The return of the Bourbons in 1814–15 was due essentially to military
defeat. Not the most auspicious of beginnings. Although there was
little enthusiasm for their return it did at least bring peace. Moreover
Louis XVIII accepted the need to re-assure the social and political élites
by promulgating a constitutional Charter. This accorded to the king
powers far greater than those granted in the constitution of 1791. It
stipulated that 'the person of the King is sacred and inviolable' and
insisted that 'Executive power belongs to the King alone', including
the sole right to initiate legislation and to dissolve parliament at will.
It did however retain such key liberal provisions as the requirement
that the responsible minister countersign royal acts, and the need for
parliamentary consent to taxation, a powerful means of exercising
pressure. It furthermore promised to safeguard personal liberty, to
recognise equality before the law, to make provision for a legislature to
be elected by those whose capacity for rational decision making was

Plate 21 The royal family in May 1814. From left to right, the king's brother the Count of Artois (the future Charles X), Louis XVIII, his niece the Duchess of Angoulême (daughter of Louis XVI), and the Duke of Angoulême and Duke of Berri, both sons of the Count of Artois

guaranteed by the possession of property, education and leisure, and to recognise the basic freedoms essential for political debate. Equally important was the promise that established status and property rights would be respected, including those to land confiscated from the Church and former émigrés during the Revolution. Amongst the élites there was a general willingness to accept a compromise which protected them against both a return to the *ancien régime* and the dangers of popular sovereignty. Thus with the support of most senior military commanders and of royalist sympathisers in the administration, the change of regime was relatively easy. The masses welcomed the end of conscription and, as many believed, of taxation; businessmen, particularly in the ports, looked forward to renewed prosperity; but it was above all the nobility who fêted what they hoped would be a return to a mythical golden age in which their dominance had been unchallenged. The main effect of Napoleon's return during the Hundred Days and the re-awakening of popular revolutionary patriotism and of incipient Jacobinism was to reinforce concern about social order.

Opposition was slow to voice itself. This was partly because of the repression which had followed Waterloo, when the Bourbons in spite of previous criticism of the centralised imperial state had gratefully taken over the existing apparatus of surveillance and control. In addition the politically aware were initially uncertain about the character of the new regime. Besides the general desire for peace and order, most *notables* would probably have wished for a moderate constitutional monarchy, avoiding all excesses in domestic and foreign policy of the kind which had become only too familiar since 1789. Many non-nobles, whether landowners, professional or businessmen, or prosperous peasants, even if not enthusiastic adherents of the Bourbons were prepared to accept the regime provided it respected these basic aspirations. In contrast real enthusiasm was to be found amongst nobles and the clergy and members of other social groups subject to their influence. Encouraged by the king's brother, the Duke of Artois (the future Charles X) and his entourage, they were confident that at last they would receive compensation for the sufferings they had endured during the Revolution and be assured of predominance within the state and army. Many believed that it was God's will that France should be cleansed of the remains of Jacobinism and atheism. They were inspired by an idealised conception of a Christian society, with the château at its centre in every village.

The election of the first parliament of the regime, to be known as the *Chambre introuvable*, took place in an atmosphere of political terror in August 1815. Some 50,900 electors selected 402 deputies. Of these 78 per cent were clearly very conservative and amongst them 52 per cent were *ancien régime* nobles. Of the others most were not opposed to the regime but only to the exaggerated demands of its more extreme adherents, the ultras with their semi-secret organisation the *Chevaliers de la Foi*. Louis XVIII, influenced by Napoleon's former minister Fouché, was unwilling to risk the politically divisive measures demanded by the ultras. He dissolved the Chamber in September 1816 and partly through the use of government influence was able to secure the election of a far more moderate majority. Amongst its achievements were to be the electoral law of 1817 which by means of a property qualification created an electorate of 100,000, predominantly land-owners. The government proceeded with a purge of ultras from the administration and allowed the return of political exiles. Reconcili-ation could however go only so far. Liberal election successes frightened the ministry led by Decazes into introducing a more restrictive electoral law. Then the assassination, in 1820, of the heir to the throne, the Duke of Berri, the last in the direct line of Bourbons until the posthumous birth of his son, precipitated a crisis. Exceptional measures of repression were introduced, including detention without trial for three months, tighter censorship, and yet more restrictive electoral legislation. This accelerated the processes of political polarisation occurring between ultra-royalists and liberals, between nobles and non-nobles within the élite, and on a regional basis between the west and south and other areas. Above all, these developments signified the effective end of efforts to broaden the base of support for the regime and to rule by consensus.

Political tension was further increased by the accession of Charles X in September 1824. The new king had a conception of his rights and responsibilities hardly compatible with constitutional monarchy. He was supported by a ministry led by Villèle and an ultra dominated Chamber, three-fifths of whose members were nobles and one-half former émigrés, elected in 1824 in the aftermath of the assassination crisis. The majority was however to be riven with bitter divisions between the proponents of an aristocratic and clerical monarchy like La Bourdonnaye and constitutional monarchists inspired by Châteaubriand and these broad divisions themselves splintered by personal feuds and competition for influence and office. Measures such as a law against sacrilege and compensation for former émigrés whose land had been confiscated during the Revolution, and which liberals described as a fine on the nation imposed by a self-seeking noble majority, intensified suspicion. In the provinces official encouragement of ostentatious religious missions which called for a collective penance for the sins of the Revolution caused growing tension and noticeably altered the tone of political life. Manipulation of the electoral system to reduce the number of voters from 100,000 to 89,000 between 1817 and 1827, and the preferential treatment of nobles within an army and administration already considerably shrunken with the return to peace, further contributed to the fear that a return to the *ancien régime* was under way.

The cadres for opposition certainly existed amongst the displaced members of the former imperial service élite and officers retired prematurely on half-pay. In every little town, together with landowners

Plate 22 The restoration of moral order or Catholic reconquest, 1826. One of the many missions attempting to re-establish collective piety. Engraving by Massard, 'The solemn blessing of a cross'

and professional men, they met regularly in cafés and clubs to read newspapers and discuss their contents. Few republicans dared to openly express their ideas. These were essentially liberals committed to constitutional monarchy, who initially at least had seen the Bourbons as more likely to guarantee liberty and order than either Bonaparte or a republic. The death of the former emperor in May 1825 had left Bonapartists without an obvious leader. In most regions there appears to have been little sustained interest in politics outside this narrow circle of men with money and leisure. Police reports claimed that most liberals were lawyers or merchants, although because the electoral system required that candidates were wealthy and due to press publicity for parliamentary speeches their leaders tended to be members of the land-owning élite, mainly but not exclusively non-nobles.

The appointment in August 1829 of Polignac, a religious mystic, to head a ministry which, in the persons of La Bourdonnaye and Marshal Bourmont, symbolised defeat, national humiliation and the White Terror of 1815, and which ignored liberal electoral successes in 1827, completed the process of political polarisation. Its formation seemed to confirm the widespread suspicion that the king was plotting a coup d'état. In reaction the liberal association *Aide-toi le ciel t'aidera* (Heaven helps those who help themselves), originally formed to ensure the registration of voters, called for a nationwide refusal to pay taxes. Its moderate, legalistic leaders, men like Guizot, increasingly found themselves at the head of an alarming coalition which included young republican activists. Poor harvests, high food prices, unemployment and misery added to the sense of crisis. Two successive elections in 1830 returned majorities hostile to the government. Liberal deputies certainly did not want revolution and would probably have been satisfied if the king had been prepared to accept their verdict on Polignac and to recognise that his ministers should enjoy the confidence of parliament. Both sides were however determined to abide by their mutually exclusive interpretations of the Charter. The king believed that concessions would take him down the slippery road to revolution. He responded by invoking the emergency decree powers he possessed under the terms of article 14 of the Charter and introducing in July ordinances which tightened censorship, dissolved the newly elected chamber before it even met, revised election procedure to increase administrative influence, and reduced the electorate to its wealthiest quarter, to 23,000 made up of mainly noble landowners. This brought the crisis to a head. It forced members of the social and political élite to choose, unwillingly, between 'liberty' and the Bourbon monarchy. Although the liberal leadership included nobles like the Duke of Broglie and Count Molé, a large majority of nobles were undoubtedly sympathetic towards the king. Amongst the opposition wealthy landowners, former imperial officials and members of the liberal professions played leading roles. Once again constitutional conflict would be settled on the streets of Paris.

The liberals gave the signal for resistance with a poster, written by Thiers and Rémusat, calling in rather ambiguous terms for protest action. No doubt only peaceful protest had been envisaged but this was to degenerate into violence. The call to defend 'liberty' mobilised a disparate coalition drawn from the middle and working classes of the city. The first clash with *gendarmerie* attempting to disperse demonstrators occurred on the Place du palais royal around midday on 27 July. In the afternoon troops, exasperated by taunts and the stones thrown at them, seem to have fired without orders, and this was followed by bitter street fighting in the poor *quartiers* of the capital. Although the garrison amounted to some 11,000 men, contingency plans for dealing with a major insurrection had not been prepared and ammunition and food stocks were low. Marshal Marmont, the military commander, was both unpopular and unsure of himself. The army was not trained for street fighting. On 28 July three columns were ordered to converge on the *Hôtel de ville*, clearing barricades as they went. They achieved their objective, but the barricades were only reconstructed after they had passed. Isolated, tired and hungry troops began to fraternise with insurgents amongst whom there were many former veterans of the imperial armies. There remained the possibility of awaiting reinforcements from the provinces, but Charles X was increasingly disheartened by reports that they could not be depended upon either. Almost everywhere the royal administration simply collapsed, its members quickly replaced by representatives of the liberal opposition. On 31 July the king accepted the appointment of the Duke of Orléans as *lieutenant-général* of the kingdom in the hope of saving something from the débâcle, and on 2 August abdicated in favour of his infant grandson, the Duke of Bordeaux, withdrew the ordinances and agreed to new elections. It was too late.

Plate 23 Fighting in the boulevard des Italiens, 28 July 1830.
Lithograph by V. Adam

The Revolution had occurred because many essentially moderate
members of the élite had withdrawn their normal support from a
regime which had threatened the fundamental principles of representative government enshrined in the constitution. It had moreover
shown excessive favour towards one element of this élite, the nobility,
and in so doing threatened the status which other *notables* had enjoyed
since 1789. The loss of legitimacy which it had suffered as a
consequence appears to have influenced even its most determined
supporters and in part explains the lack of resolution of some officers
of the Paris garrison. Events had developed so rapidly and in such an
unexpected direction that opposition leaders were inevitably un-
prepared. A small group of liberal politicians, frightened by such
slogans as *Vive* (Long live) *Napoléon II* and *Vive la République* which
were interspersed with shouts of *A bas les Bourbons* and particularly by
the prospect of a renewed popular intervention in politics and the civil
and indeed foreign war which might ensue, vested Lafayette, the aging
hero of 1789, with command of a National Guard and established a
municipal commission to restore order. On 30 July to end the power
vacuum they had offered the throne to the Duke of Orléans on

Plate 24 Lafayette receiving Louis-Philippe at the Hôtel de ville, Paris, 31 July 1830. Painting by Eloi-Firmin Féron

condition that he agreed to respect the principles of constitutional monarchy. A proclamation written by Thiers presented the new king as 'a prince devoted to the cause of the revolution', as a 'citizen-king'. On 31 July Louis-Philippe appointed a government and convened a meeting of the Chamber of Deputies. On 8 August the Chamber voted in favour of a revision of the constitution which significantly altered the balance of power between king and parliament in the latter's favour. On this occasion the contractual character of the relationship between king and nation was clearly affirmed, with Louis-Philippe obliged to swear on oath to respect this revised and more liberal Charter.

THE JULY MONARCHY

In spite of the surprisingly rapid re-establishment of the authority of the central government, the political situation remained tense. Conflicts of interest were inevitable between the diverse groups which had overthrown the Bourbons. Having achieved their aims most liberals became political conservatives, interested in the protection of their personal liberty and property. However the *Liberté* for which many had fought had diverse meanings. In the aftermath of the revolution people felt free to discuss them in meetings and newspapers. Dissatisfaction was expressed with a new electoral law which reduced the tax qualification for voting from 300 francs to 200. This significantly reduced the weight of nobles within the electorate whilst enfranchising mainly landowners (who together with farmers made up about 56 per cent of voters in 1846), officials (about 8 per cent), professionals (about 10 per cent) and businessmen and a small majority of the more prosperous artisans (about 26 per cent). It continued to exclude the vast majority of lower middle-class, peasant and worker citizens. Thus whereas in Britain the 1832 electoral law had enfranchised one in twenty-five of the population, in France the corresponding figure was only one in one hundred and seventy, although growing prosperity gradually enlarged the electorate from 166,000 to 241,000 whilst the 1831 municipal election law gave the vote to some 3 million. This enlarged, but still small, electorate would consistently provide the regime with solid parliamentary support. However to some at least of those who were excluded this was all very arbitrary. Republican militants, still a small minority, complained about the way a rump of the Chamber of Deputies rather than a newly elected Constituent Assembly had taken the crucial constitutional decisions. Even within the government there were fundamental disagreements over the degree to which political liberalisation ought to be pursued. The Minister of Justice, Dupont de l'Eure, resigned and subsequently denounced the regime for 'repudiating its authors and natural supporters, and returning with an uncontestable prediliction to the traditions and the men of the Restoration'. In Paris a revival of the Republican press occurred. In the provinces the network of committees established to oppose the absolutist dreams of Charles X was partially reactivated. Moreover, and this to a large degree explains the increasingly conservative and indeed repressive character of the government, the revolution re-established the masses on the political stage. Official praise for their courage encouraged Parisian workers to take to the streets to demand the trial and punishment of Charles X's ministers but also through petitions and strikes to make such practical demands as higher wages, a shorter working day, and the banning of employment-threatening machinery. They were demanding that a regime which they believed they had put in place recognise the basic human right to a living wage. They were to be disappointed by the government's negative response, whilst living standards were to sharply deteriorate in the economic crisis which followed the revolution.

Popular demands were met with incomprehension by a government committed to 'the principle of the freedom of industry'. The seizure by workers of the city of Lyons in November 1831 and their slogan 'Live working or die fighting!' caused a great stir. The journalist Saint-Marc Girardin wrote that this insurrection had 'revealed a great secret', which was that 'the Barbarians who threaten society are not...on the steppes of Tartary...they are in the suburbs of our manufacturing cities'. The government determined both to end political agitation and especially to repress the growing numbers of associations created by workers to protect their 'rights', and to safeguard the longer-term by the introduction in 1833 of a major law on primary education designed to 'moralise' the lower orders. In response small groups of middle-class republicans began to look outside the narrow electorate for support and to politicise discontented workers through clandestine organisations like the *Société des Droits de l'Homme* (Society for the Rights of Man). This gradual coming-together of young republican militants and workers was to be vital to the intellectual development of both. It led to an inter-penetration of republican political ideas and those derived from a traditional artisanal corporate culture. This post-revolutionary period lasted until the law banning associations introduced in April 1834 and the wave of insurrectionary protest and increasingly brutal repression which followed, immortalised by Daumier's drawing of the massacre by troops and bourgeois National Guards in the Cloître Saint-Merri in Paris. It was to prove central to the development of a class-consciousness and an interest in republican politics amongst the lower middle class and artisans, and to a widening of support for the republican movement. In the immediate future however these developments were to be restricted and fragmented by governmental repression. Particularly from the 1840s, as the capitalistic transformation of the economy grew more intense and threatening to artisanal traditions and work practices, the socialist conception of a more egalitarian society based upon self-regulating producers' cooperatives, also attracted growing interest.

The political peace of the years which followed 1834 was due in part to firm, repressive government, but additionally to support from a narrow electorate for a regime which allowed them, through parliament, to represent their own particular interests. Successive governments sought to guarantee order not only through police activity but by means of economic protection, an essential 'conservative principle' (Guizot, the prime minister), and efforts to ensure prosperity on the basis of a major public works programme involving most notably railway construction. The king as head of the executive made full use of his powers, ensuring that ministers sympathised with his objectives. Governments, responsible additionally to parliament, sought to maintain majority support in part through the extensive use of patronage. The Orléanist monarchy lacked however the mystical appeal of its Divine Right predecessor. Support for it was to a much greater degree conditional. Nevertheless throughout its existence opposition both within and outside parliament was weak and divided. It ranged from the supporters of another Bourbon restoration, the legitimists on the right, to the republicans on the left. Its most numerous and vocal critics were drawn from the ranks of the 'dynastic' opposition and in newspapers like the *Siècle* they returned to the language of 1789 to attack the dominant *aristocratie bourgeoise*. Politicians excluded from power condemned the corruption of the representative process through the abuse of government influence in elections and, particularly following their dismal failure in the 1846 elections, sought to change the rules of the game by means of franchise reform, not to enfranchise the masses but to secure the wider representation of the property-owning middle classes.

The position of the regime was not as secure as it appeared. Even in the 1846 election there was substantial support for the opposition from lower middle-class voters in the major cities. Moreover its credit suffered from scandals in high places, from continuous opposition criticism of electoral corruption and the use of patronage to control deputies, and especially from the severe economic crisis beginning in 1845–46 and the widespread popular protest it caused. The image of prosperity cultivated by the regime was shattered and replaced by widespread pessimism and anxiety. Political agitation multiplied, as a result in particular of the 'banquet' campaign, its form a means of circumventing the laws against political meetings. This was initiated by members of the dynastic opposition like Odilon Barrot who favoured a limited extension of the franchise by means of a reduction in the tax qualification to 100 francs. These moderates however rapidly lost the initiative to republicans like Ledru-Rollin who at Lille in November 1847 demanded manhood suffrage. A true romantic he idealised the 'people' as the '*Ecce Homo* of modern times', whose 'descent from the cross' and 'resurrection' was close. To avoid bloody revolution he assumed that political changes would need to be accompanied by unspecified social reforms, which would end the people's suffering. The government's intransigence, revealed in an aggressive speech from the throne on 28 December, only encouraged more virulent opposition. In its turn this heightened conservative fear of 'anarchy' and 'communism'.

The banquet campaign, attracting widespread support in the centres of opposition strength in the north and east, was planned to culminate in a mass banquet in Paris. The government, afraid of disorder, banned the gathering, a move which was accepted with a certain sense of relief by liberal and moderate republican politicians. More anonymous and radical figures however called for a protest demonstration. On 22 February 1848 crowds of students and workers gathered at the Madeleine and on the Place de la Concorde and sporadic violence occurred as the police attempted to disperse them. On the following day elements of the solidly middle-class National Guard made clear their support for reform and alienation from a regime which seemed to represent the interests solely of the upper classes, the so-called *grande bourgeoisie*. This seems to have persuaded the king and his advisers of the wisdom of reform, and news of the replacement of the intransigent Guizot with the more liberal Molé as chief minister was well received in the ranks of the citizen militia. In contrast, the construction of barricades was underway in the working-class *quartiers*. The situation might nevertheless have been stabilised if it had not been for a fusillade fired at around 10pm, without orders, by nervous troops guarding the Foreign Ministry in the Boulevard des Capucines. An enraged population began to construct hundreds of barricades in the narrow, tortuous streets of the old city, easily blocked by an overturned cart, barrels and paving stones. In an attempt to save the rapidly deteriorating situation an increasingly indecisive monarch was encouraged to abdicate, and members of the dynastic opposition including Barrot and Thiers attempted vainly to establish a regency for his grandson. At the same time republican leaders at the offices of the newspapers *National* and *Réforme* were beginning to realise that a more radical outcome was now possible. On the morning of 23 February probably only a small minority of the Parisian population had been committed republicans. By early morning on 24 February there were 1500 barricades and a mass insurrection was under way against a king who 'murdered his people'. With the loss of confidence amongst the political leadership and in the absence of clear instructions, the efforts of Marshal Bugeaud to clear the streets soon lost momentum. He was forced to withdraw his increasingly disorganised forces towards the Tuileries. In the late afternoon, amongst scenes of great disorder and public euphoria a Provisional Government made up of well-known republican politicians and journalists was proclaimed by the crowds at the *Hôtel de ville*. The Second Republic, like the first was to have a major impact on political culture. The themes of the earlier revolution, slowly reinterpreted during decades of gradual economic and social change, were now to undergo accelerated revision. New perceptions of society and politics were to be created which were to determine the options available in the succeeding decades.

THE SECOND REPUBLIC

A revolution had occurred because in a situation of economic and social crisis the regime had lost the support of many even of its habitual adherents. As the desire for political reform had become more widespread the regime had failed to sanction concessions soon enough. A fortuitous incident had then finally destroyed its legitimacy for many at least of the citizens of its capital. To their great surprise a small group of active republicans had been able to take advantage of governmental collapse and to take over the reins of power. It was then that their problems really began. The members of this Provisional Government were divided socially, personally and politically. They lacked experience of government. A majority of moderates, with at their head the aristocratic poet and historian Lamartine, saw their role as essentially one of preserving order and administrative continuity, whilst otherwise keeping their acts to a minimum, until the election of a constituent assembly. The sense of expectancy amongst the crowds in Paris however ensured that even these cautious men felt bound to recognise manhood suffrage, the democratisation of the National Guard which meant arming the masses, and freedoms of the press and assembly. A minority, made up of Ledru-Rollin, the socialist Louis Blanc and the worker and secret society veteran Albert favoured more radical action. It was rapidly becoming evident that it was easier to agree on opposition to the deposed regime than on something to replace it with.

Alexis de Tocqueville later remembered Paris 'in the sole hands of those who owned nothing...Consequently the terror felt by all the other classes was extreme...the only comparison was with the feelings of the civilised cities of the Roman world when they suddenly found themselves in the power of the Vandals or Goths'. Outside Paris too news of the revolution came as a great shock and caused considerable alarm amongst those who still tended to associate the republic with the Terror. In the absence of any alternative the change was grudgingly accepted by conservatives, reassured in part by the presence of the likes of Lamartine in government. In contrast many, particularly amongst the lower middle and working classes, reacted with enthusiasm to what promised to be the dawning of a new era. This sense of expectancy created a difficult situation for a government concerned to establish its authority and anyway faced with massive problems. Amongst these were the organisation of elections and providing assistance to those thrown out of work by the loss of business confidence in the aftermath of the revolution. The political education of the masses proceeded apace in the host of newspapers, political clubs and workers' associations created to take advantage of the new freedom. Probably only a minority of workers and peasants conceived of politics in terms of institutions or a formulated ideology, but particularly in the major cities slogans in favour of the 'organisation of work' and the *République démocratique et sociale* were popular, representing as they did the demand for state assistance in the creation of a network of producers' cooperatives to replace capitalist exploitation. The discourse in Parisian clubs like Blanqui's *Société républicaine centrale* or Barbès' *Club de la révolution* was frequently extreme. The latter's manifesto announced that 'we have the republic in name only, we need the real thing. Political reform is only the instrument of social reform'.

These radicals were determined to prevent a repetition of what they regarded as the betrayal of 1830 and organised mass demonstrations in order to maintain continuous pressure on the government.

Already on 25 February the Provisional Government had recognised the right to work, appearing to promise far-reaching reform when all that was intended was the traditional expedient of charity workshops for the unemployed, providing low-paid manual work. So-called National Workshops were established in Paris and most other urban centres. The establishment of the Luxembourg Commission composed of representatives of government, employers and workers to enquire into working conditions and propose reforms reinforced the belief that major changes were imminent. In practice the main concern of the government was to promote economic recovery through the re-establishment of business confidence which required the preservation of public order and avoidance of 'socialistic' measures. The first of these objectives, together with the threat of foreign intervention to enforce the provisions of the 1815 peace settlement threw the regime into early dependence on the army. Widespread peasant protest against the capitalistic threat to customary agricultural practices had the same effect. Any lingering peasant hopes for sympathetic government action were soon destroyed by the introduction of a 45 per cent supplement to the land tax designed to help balance the budget and pay for the National Workshops. The government was increasingly isolating itself from potential mass support and reinforcing its dependence on social élites, which regardless of former political persuasion were now united by the desire to prevent social reform.

The introduction of manhood suffrage which at a stroke increased the size of the electorate from 250,000 to close on 10 million was the realisation of a dream for radicals. For the first time in history the entire male population, in a major state, was qualified to vote and, indicative of a growing political maturity, 84 per cent did so in April 1848. For conservatives it was a nightmare. In practice however the democrats were to be disappointed. In the absence of organised parties the choice of candidates in most areas, and especially in rural constituencies, remained dependent on the activities of small groups of politically experienced notables. Conservative organisation and propaganda was more effective. Many voters, faced with a plethora of candidates, turned to those whose wealth, education or functions gave them status in the local community, including the clergy. Indeed one result of the introduction of manhood suffrage was to establish a clear correlation between religious commitment and political conservatism, in opposition to what was represented as a challenge to the eternal values of religion as well as to social order. Where influence was insufficient then intimidation could be employed. The poor needed to be prudent. Republicans had little time to counter this before balloting on 23 April. A large majority of the successful candidates were to be conservatives, and former monarchists, even if, reflecting a continuing crisis of confidence, they adopted the republican label. Indeed when they met as a Constituent Assembly they elected an Executive Commission made up essentially of the more moderate members of the previous Provisional Government.

The election results inevitably caused great dissatisfaction amongst radicals. A major demonstration in Paris on May 15, which culminated in the chaotic invasion of the Assembly's meeting place by the crowd and the call for a committee of public safety to levy a wealth tax to finance the immediate creation of producers' cooperatives, strengthened the conservative determination to restore order. The National Workshops which to radicals symbolised the hope of a better world increasingly represented the revolutionary menace for conservatives – '80,000 workers paid by the state to learn about revolt in the idleness of the *cabaret*' – was one newspaper's description of the Parisian scheme. On 22 June their closure was announced. No effort was made to reassure the tens of thousands of unemployed that relief would still be provided. Indeed the government's threat to resort to force only reinforced the widespread disillusionment with legal political processes and the belief that with such an uncaring regime there was little alternative but to *recommencer la révolution*. On 23 June, inspired by the slogan 'Liberty or Death!', barricades were constructed throughout the poor eastern *quartiers* of the city. The insurgents had no overall plan, no collective leadership emerged, and the rising rapidly degenerated into a desperately fought defence of isolated neighbourhoods.

Estimates of the numbers involved vary, but a substantial number of men and women (perhaps 40–50,000) felt sufficiently disappointed with the outcome of the revolution to risk their lives in an attempt to establish a regime more responsive to their needs. They believed they were fighting for justice. Against them were ranged the forces of 'order' including National Guards from the wealthier western *quartiers*, about one-fifth of them workers; the Mobile Guard recruited from amongst young, unemployed workers who, not yet integrated into craft and neighbourhood solidarities, remained loyal to comrades and to the government which paid them; together with the regular army which was to become in the eyes of the propertied classes the 'saviour of civilisation'. Overall command was in the hands of the Defence Minister General Cavaignac who additionally, at the request of the Constituent Assembly, became head of government. Anxious to avoid a repetition of February when dispersed groups of soldiers had been overwhelmed, he concentrated his forces, a tactic which initially allowed the revolt to spread, and then when concentration had been achieved smashed the insurrection in three days of vicious street fighting. The artist Meissonier 'saw defenders shot down, hurled out of windows, the ground strewn with corpses, the earth red with blood...'. The Parisian left was to be decapitated for a generation. Whatever the precise sociological character of the conflict, contemporaries saw it as one between *bourgeois* and *peuple*, as a form of class struggle. According to de Tocqueville the insurrection was a 'brutal, blind but powerful attempt by the workers to escape from the necessities of their condition, which had been described to them as an illegitimate oppression...It was this mixture of cupidity and false theory which rendered the insurrection so formidable...These poor people had been assured that the well-being of the rich was in some way based upon theft from themselves'. The conservative press depicted the events as an outbreak of mindless savagery, as a rising fought for 'pillage and rape'. Their initial cry of triumph at the 'victory gained by the cause of order, of the family, of humanity, of civilisation' was mixed with fear and was soon followed by demands for more thorough repression. Political activity was severely restricted. The new constitution promulgated on 4 November 1848 provided for the election of a president with strong executive authority. The successful candidate on 10 December was however to be Louis-Napoléon Bonaparte, with 74 per cent of the vote compared with Cavaignac's 19 per cent. The emperor's nephew was able to take advantage of the cult of the great soldier and political leader created by an outpouring of books, pamphlets, lithographs and objects of devotion over the previous thirty years.

Bonaparte's appointment of a ministry made up mainly of figures

Plate 25 June 1848: barricade in the rue Saint-Antoine. Lithograph by Beaumont and Ciceri

associated with the Orléanist monarchy seemed to confirm his commitment to the so-called 'party of order'. The Constituent Assembly, its members aware of their growing political isolation and subject to pressure from the new government voted its own dissolution on 29 January. The elections which followed on 13 May were, especially in the provinces, far more politicised than those of April 1848. A clear right–left division emerged between a reactionary conservatism and a radical republicanism with the centre, the moderate republicans squeezed in between. The *démocrate-socialiste* or *Montagnard* movement, which might be seen as the first attempt to create a modern national party, incorporated both democrats and socialists determined to defend the republic and work for genuine social reform. In May some 200 Montagnards were elected and although this compared badly with the 500 conservatives the latter were nevertheless alarmed by such an unexpected radical success. Not only had the working-class areas of Paris or Lyons supported the 'reds' but so too had voters in some parts of the supposedly 'incorruptible' and conservative countryside. Where might this lead? An apocalyptic perspective of an eventual socialist electoral victory and of the threat to private property, religious faith and the family began to develop. Moreover in spite of constant repression, in some areas *démocrate-socialiste* organisation and propaganda in the form of newspapers, pamphlets, almanacs, engravings and songs, managed to survive. It presented a social programme, based on a few simple slogans which linked people's every-day problems to the political objectives of the left. Politics was made to appear relevant to the masses. State taxation, exploitation by the rich, the tyranny of capitalism in general and of usury in particular, were denounced. In a period of continuing economic depression the establishment of a *République démocratique et sociale* which would provide cheap credit to satisfy peasant land hunger and to protect those who felt threatened with expropriation for debt had considerable appeal. So too did the promise of free education, a guaranteed right to work and state support for the establishment of producer and consumer cooperatives. This was to be the road to liberation for the *prolétariat*. These measures were to paid for by means of higher taxation of the rich and the nationalisation of such key sectors of the economy as the railways, canals, mines and insurance companies. The ideal of a society of small, independent producers, that of the *sans-culottes* of 1793, was thus to be reconciled with the development of a modern capitalistic economy.

In response, conservative parliamentarians once more sought to change the rules of the political game. It was intolerable, as one judicial official put it, that 'the communists [be offered] the possibility of becoming kings one day through the ballot. Society must not commit suicide'. A new electoral law removed around one-third of the poorest voters from the rolls, and ever more intense action was directed at surviving left-wing newspapers and organisations, driving many of those which survived underground. Even this did little to relieve conservative hysteria. As the 1852 legislative and presidential elections came closer rumours of socialist plots abounded. The search for an alternative placed Louis-Napoléon as the incumbent president in an increasingly strong position. Although the constitution debarred him from a second term of office the conservative factions were unable to agree on an alternative. Moreover Bonaparte himself was determined not to hand over power with what he believed to be his historical mission, the regeneration of France, unachieved.

As head of the executive he was well placed to mount a coup d'état on 2 December 1851. Although directed against both the monarchist groups represented in the National Assembly and the radical republicans, the fact that only the latter offered resistance gave it an essentially anti-republican character. The coup could be seen as the culmination of a long period of repression directed at the left. In Paris only very limited resistance occurred, in part due to preventative arrests, in part to obvious military preparedness. Few workers were prepared to risk a repetition of the June insurrection to defend the rights of a monarchist assembly against a president who promised to restore manhood suffrage. Similarly only short-lived demonstrations occurred in other cities. However around 100,000 men, in some 900 rural communes and small towns, mainly in the south-east, did resist. They came from regions of predominantly small-scale peasant farming in which the difficulties caused by growing population pressure on the land had been intensified by the persistent problems of market-orientated activities like vine and silk cultivation, forestry and rural industry in general. More significant was the survival of clandestine democratic socialist organisations through which they were mobilised to defend the *République démocratique et sociale* and the new era of security and happiness which had been promised for 1852. The naïvety of their beliefs should not be allowed to detract from their very real faith in progress and the triumph of democracy. Their movements were easily crushed by the columns of troops which moved into the countryside once the security of their urban garrisons was assured. This was followed by a settling of accounts with the left, with over 26,000 arrests throughout France, and not too much attention paid to the rule of law. Conservatives had been badly frightened by grossly exaggerated accounts of 'red' atrocities. Now they gave thanks to God for their deliverance. Salvation seemed to be offered by the police-state. On 20 December a plebiscite was held to sanction the extension of the prince-president's authority. Louis-Napoléon was determined to secure a large majority. It was made clear to all officials that their continued employment depended upon enthusiastic campaigning. The basic theme was the choice between 'civilisation and barbarism, society and chaos'. In place of the era of disorder opened in 1848, a new period of order, peace and prosperity was promised. The result was predictable: 7,500,000 voted 'yes', 640,000 'no' and 1,500,000 abstained with opposition concentrated in the major cities. In symbolic promise of things to come the image of the Republic on coins and stamps was replaced by that of *Son Altesse Impériale Monseigneur le Prince-Président*. On 1 January 1852 at a solemn service in Notre Dame the Archbishop of Paris chanted the *Domine salvum fac ludivicum Napoleonem* as though the Empire already existed, and on 10 May new flags bearing the imperial eagle were distributed to the army. Relieved of their terror, the upper classes celebrated carnival in 1852 with great enthusiasm.

What was the long-term significance of the mid-century crisis lasting from 1846 to 1852? It had certainly aroused fear of social revolution and demonstrated the willingness of social élites to resort to violent repression to protect their privileges. However it also constituted an important stage in mass politicisation. The introduction of manhood suffrage had encouraged political mobilisation in support of both left and right. In spite of subsequent repression, it was during these years that the idea of the republic gained precision and mass support. Although substantial differences remained between moderates and radicals, they still, to an important degree shared the universalistic ideals of 1789–1794. The resistance to the 1851 coup d'état if it had much in common with 'primitive' traditions of popular protest, was nevertheless inspired by political ideology. *La Bonne, la République démocratique et sociale* had been, and with some success, presented as the means of creating a more egalitarian and just society. The coup had smashed these hopes. For the second time a Bonaparte, supported by the army, had destroyed a republic. Within a year, following another carefully orchestrated campaign, a second plebiscite (on 21–22 November 1852) approved the re-establishment of the hereditary empire which was proclaimed on 2 December, the anniversary of Austerlitz. Its constitution was based very much on that of the first empire, arrogating immense authority to the prince-president then the emperor.

THE SECOND EMPIRE

The intentions of the new Emperor Napoléon III have been the subject of frequent debate. The reputation of this strange man, inspired by a belief in his own destiny, suffered irreparably from the military disaster of 1870. He cannot however be simply dismissed as he was by Victor Hugo as *Napoléon le petit*. His objectives were clear – to de-politicise government through the establishment of a strong and stable executive power capable of promoting economic and social modernisation and by this means to 'close the era of revolution by satisfying the legitimate needs of the people' (2 December 1853). It was in the first decade, at least until 1857, that the personal power of the emperor was greatest. Ministers were convoked once a week to discuss an agenda he had prepared. They provided information. He took decisions. The tradition of ministerial responsibility to parliament gradually built up since 1814 was effectively annulled, and the *Corps législatif* rendered largely quiescent. These were years in which continued political repression and close cooperation with reactionary and clerical forces characterised the regime and in which elections were carefully managed through the support given to 'official' candidates. Even in this period, however, implementation of government policy was to be obstructed by a complex of, often conflicting, vested interest groups, as well as the practical difficulties of administrative control, finance and by vacillation on the part of the head of state himself. The new regime was in practice inescapably dependent on the artistocratic and *grands bourgeois* servants of previous governments. The majority of ministers were conservative ex-Orléanists (Magne, Fould, Rouher, Baroche). There were remarkably few genuine Bonapartists. As the former Orléanist prime minister Guizot pointed out, 'an insurrection can be repressed with soldiers; an election won with peasants. But the support of soldiers and peasants is not sufficient to rule. The co-operation of the upper classes who are naturally rulers is essential'. Napoléon appears to have assumed that the notables would rally to his government. He was, to an important degree to be disappointed. Indeed his frustrations are said to have led him to complain – 'What a government is mine! The empress is Legitimist; Napoléon-Jérôme republican; Morny Orléanist; I am myself a socialist. The only Bonapartist is Persigny and he is mad'.

Nevertheless, in the early years, strong government and political stability, accompanied by economic prosperity certainly enhanced the regime's status. The emperor's claim to be the 'saviour of society' was widely recognised throughout the property-owning classes. Much of the rural population upon whose electoral support he depended saw him as their emperor and, although republican historiography tended to minimise its significance, many workers were also attracted to the regime by the Bonaparte legend and the emperor's show of sympathy for the poor. His departure for the war in Italy in 1859 was greeted with a display of bellicose nationalism even in such centres of opposition as Paris and Lyons. The Second Empire thus enjoyed a broader consensus of support than had its predecessors. Election results suggest that this reached its peak in 1857 when official candidates received 89 per cent of the votes cast, although this represented only 60 per cent of registered voters due to large-scale abstention. Even then however prefects were anxious about public opinion, especially in the cities where supervision of the electorate was so much more difficult. Much of the support for the regime, particularly from the social élites had always been conditional and far from whole-hearted. It declined as the threat of a revolutionary upheaval receded. With order apparently restored notables would increasingly press for the re-establishment of a parliamentary system as the means by which they could participate more fully in political decision-making and protect their own vital interests. The growing number of critics therefore ranged from those who had initially welcomed the coup but no longer saw any need for

Plate 26 Napoléon III, the Empress, and Prince Imperial surrounded by their people. One of the numerous popular engravings. The image of Napoleon I, founder of the dynasty, can be seen in the background. Engraving by Léopold Flaming

authoritarian rule, including most notably socially conservative liberals, to republicans, the victims of the coup who rejected the Empire and all its works.

Republican opposition remained weak throughout the 1850s and for most of the following decade. The process of politicisation during the Second Republic had not, in most regions, lasted long enough to establish a permanent mass commitment to the Republic. Repression had been effective. Many former activists knowing themselves to be marked men had adopted a submissive pose. Administrative reports from the provinces in the 1850s were marked by a sense of security in sharp contrast with their alarmist tone prior to the coup d'état. In the 1852 elections republicans generally either voted for conservative opponents of the government or abstained. The moderate republicans Cavaignac and Carnot, elected in Paris, and Hénon, in Lyons, refused to take the oath of loyalty to the monarch and were unseated. Nevertheless, in most parts of France, republicans continued, cautiously, to meet, gathering at work, in bars and private homes and using the multiplicity of voluntary associations as a disguise for political activity. The cadres necessary for the eventual re-emergence of the republican party thus remained in existence or were re-constituted.

From 1860 the context for political activity was to be changed. The regime of Napoléon III, unlike that of his illustrious uncle, was not to take an increasingly authoritarian form. Significant steps were to be taken towards the creation of a parliamentary regime. Encouraged by his half-brother Morny, by Walewski the illegitimate son of Napoléon I and by his cousin Prince Napoléon, and anxious to create a constitutional regime less dependent on his own survival, the emperor conceded to the *Corps législatif* – by a decree of 24 November 1860 – the right to discuss the address from the throne at the beginning of each parliamentary session; and further agreed to nominate ministers without portfolio to explain and defend government policy before the elected assembly. Moreover its debates were now to be reproduced in full in the press according a much needed publicity to its activities. This was in spite of the misgivings of his more authoritarian ministers and especially Baroche, Fould and Rouher. In December 1861 Napoléon further responded to anxiety within financial circles about the growth of the national debt and Haussmann's unorthodox arrangements for financing the reconstruction of central Paris, by allowing increased parliamentary control over the budget. This provided a vital means of enhancing the influence of the representative assembly. Throughout the decade too, although repressive legislation remained intact, much greater tolerance was displayed towards the press. A new political climate was being created.

It seems likely that the emperor had always intended, once order had been restored, to introduce reforms designed to reconcile liberals and republicans to his regime. Authoritarian government was seen to be an obstacle to economic and social modernisation. Initially at least the policy of liberalisation represented confidence in the stability of the regime. However, the series of measures which included amnesty for republicans; alliance with Piedmont against Austria and in support of a 'Europe of the nationalities'; a loosening of the alliance between Church and state established during the Second Republic to further the development of mass primary education as a means of social control; the 1860 commercial treaty with Britain designed to intensify competitive pressures and to force the pace of modernisation; the enhanced role of parliament; and the legalisation of strikes, had complex and often contradictory effects. The realisation that the regime was unlikely to resort to brute force against its critics encouraged growing criticism from all those who felt that the new policies and the emperor's willingness to use his personal power threatened their vital interests. Amongst the most vocal were clerics anxious about the threat posed by Italian nationalism to the papacy's temporal power and political liberals concerned about the economic dislocation which might result from free trade and especially its impact on agricultural prices and on the metallurgical and textile industries. They demanded further liberalisation of political institutions to facilitate greater parliamentary control over government policy and restore the influence of established social élites.

The vitality of this opposition made it clear that the regime had failed to engineer a national reconciliation. In this situation Napoléon III, unlike his predecessors was prepared to adapt. Liberalisation became the means of re-assuring the élites upon whose willingness to cooperate the regime ultimately depended. The prolonged and at times apparently grudging nature of the process was to ensure that these predominantly conservative liberals were to prove less grateful than they might otherwise have been. Efforts by the regime to create an opening to the left only increased their suspicions. This involved

conciliatory overtures to workers through a discussion group established in 1861 by the emperor's nephew, the 'republican' prince
Napoléon-Jérôme, and the dispatch of a workers' delegation to the
London International Exposition in 1862 which led on to the
legalisation of strikes in 1864 and to growing toleration of illegal union
activity. It was however no substitute for conservative support. As this
weakened, the regime had little alternative but to make further
concessions to the notables' determination to re-establish the sort of
institutional arrangements which had made the July Monarchy so
responsive to their interests. Further liberalisation thus represented
concessions by the regime to pressure.

The increase in this pressure was clearly evident in the gradual
collapse of the system of official candidature, beginning during the
1863 parliamentary election campaign. The system was challenged in
the first place by an increase in the number of opposition candidates
and consequently of political agitation; and by the willingness of
clericals and protectionists, former government supporters with secure
local political bases, to criticise the regime. In the absence of the whole-
hearted support of local élites, electoral management became increasingly difficult. The electorate was encouraged to reject official
interference with the 'dignity' and 'independence' of voters. There
was a growing possibility that official 'advice' on voting might simply
be rejected, thus throwing the whole system into question.

The May 1863 elections saw the reconstitution of an extremely
heterogeneous, but increasingly effective parliamentary opposition,
which included the growing number of Legitimists determined to
defend the interests of the Church and willing to ignore the Bourbon
pretender the Count of Chambord's instructions to abstain from
political activity, irreconcilable Orléanist notables, independent liberals and republicans. Although only thirty-two outright opponents of
the regime were successful they combined with some of its more liberal
adherents to constitute a Third Party. Together with the scale of support
for opposition in the major cities this caused considerable disquiet
amongst the regime's supporters. Further concessions were made and most
notably the liberties accorded in 1868 to public meetings and the press.
The political context was again decisively changed. The more blatant
forms of administrative intervention in elections were now recognised
as counter-productive. Acts of political opposition had become far less

Table 5.3. *Legislative election results*

	Registered voters	Votes for government	Votes for opposition	Abstentions
1852	9,836,000	5,248,000	810,000	3,613,000
1857	9,490,000	5,471,000	665,000	3,372,000
1863	9,938,000	5,308,000	1,954,000	2,714,000
1869	10,417,000	4,438,000	3,355,000	2,291,000

risky than previously. There was an immediate and spectacular revival of newspapers and political meetings, most of them hostile to the government. The circulation of Parisian newspapers which had been around 50,000 in 1830 rose to over 700,000 in 1869 reflecting rising literacy and falling production costs as well as the political situation. Interest in politics was being renewed, bringing to an end the widespread indifference of the previous two decades. The outcome of the 1869 elections was a severe blow to the regime, and if compared with previous elections made the rise of opposition clear.

It was the results in Paris which particularly impressed contemporaries with only 77,000 votes for government candidates compared with 234,000 for opponents and 76,500 abstentions. Moreover the campaign was marked by the emergence of Gambetta, famous for his speeches for the defence in political trials, as the leading figure on the left. His espousal of a programme which included vague promises of social reform was accompanied by large, anti-regime demonstrations with crowds singing the *Marseillaise* and struggling with police and troops. This and a teleological view of history has led many historians to exaggerate the strength of republican opposition. The 1869 elections if they reveal the development of support for avowed republicans also suggest that there were definite limits to this. Thus of the seventy-eight declared opponents of the regime who were elected, only twenty-nine were republicans and the remaining forty-nine liberals. Furthermore, although it was the more extreme, indeed revolutionary, meetings and newspapers which made the greatest impression on the public, most leading republicans were moderates determined to avoid violence. These bourgeois republicans were as committed as government supporters to private property and a liberal economic system. Gambetta perfectly expressed their outlook in writing 'for us the victory of democracy with its free institutions means security and prosperity for material interests, everybody's rights guaranteed, respect for property, protection of the legitimate and basic rights of labour, the raising up morally and materially of the lower classes, but without compromising the position of those favoured by wealth and talent... Our single goal is to bring forth justice and social peace'.

His was a commitment to 'progress without revolution'. Socialist agitation in contrast was seen as likely to re-create the 'red menace' and as in 1848 to frighten the mass of small property owners and to provoke a repressive government reaction. Moderates like Favre, Simon and Picard, appear to have been willing to accept the liberal empire, to rely entirely upon legal forms of political action and to postpone the establishment of the republic to the indefinite future. Support for the republicans cannot be easily characterised. It existed in all social groups, but was predominantly urban and often the product of the continuing competition for local status between established and up-and-coming bourgeois groups. Even if every manifestation of discontent by workers should not be taken to represent opposition, industrial conflict and particularly the strike-waves of 1869–70 when troops were deployed against strikers, certainly increased tension. Although real living standards had improved since the late 1850s most workers continued to live in cramped and often squalid conditions and suffered from chronic insecurity. In contrast the rural population, with some regional exceptions, was much more likely to support the regime. Indeed opposition leaders largely explained its survival in terms of administrative manipulation of the ignorant peasantry. This led the liberal Prévost-Paradol to describe the regime as *la campagnocratie impériale* based upon 'rural imbecility and provincial brutishness', an expression of Parisian intellectual arrogance repeated in the republican Allain-Targé's claim that the future republic would need to re-educate the 'Thirty-five million brutes who compose the Nation to the rank of active citizens'.

The 1869 elections nevertheless revealed a growing threat of isolation to the regime. Amongst the newly elected deputies at least ninety-eight erstwhile government supporters were liberals whose views differed little from those of opposition deputies. Many of these supported an immediate demand for a government responsible to the *Corps législatif.*

Plate 27 The Schneider works at Le Creusot: a major metallurgical centre during the Second Empire with 15 furnaces, 160 coke ovens and 85 steam engines. Watercolour by Bonhommé

It was clear that concessions would have to be made to maintain the allegiance of social élites. These took the form of closer parliamentary control over both ministers and the budget. In practice ministers would in future need to ensure support in the assembly although constitutionally they remained responsible to the emperor alone. As one republican newspaper recorded with glee, 'the Empire of 2 December no longer exists'. These concessions were followed by a lengthy effort to form a government likely to enjoy both the confidence of the emperor and majority support in the Chamber, which culminated in the appointment on 2 January 1870 of a ministry headed by a former moderate republican, Emile Ollivier. Although opposition liberals like Thiers remained dissatisfied because of the emperor's retention of considerable personal power, most deputies saw this as necessary for the preservation of social order in a situation of growing social tension and political unrest. In effect the conservative 'Party of Order' of the Second Republic was reforming.

The early measures of the new government confirmed this con-

servative support. They included the final abandonment of the system
of official candidature; the dismissal of Haussmann, the controversial
Prefect of the Seine, to satisfy orthodox financial interests; of the
education minister Duruy to pacify clericals; the announcement of an
enquiry into customs legislation, which was seen as the prelude to a
return to economic protectionism; and determined efforts, involving
the use of troops, to restore a social order threatened by strikers in the
major industrial centre of Le Creusot and by republican demonstrations in Paris. Indeed for many liberals liberalisation had gone far
enough. They had been anxious to restore parliamentary controls over
the government as well as greater freedom for the press, but had
increasingly come to fear that liberty might be abused. The call for
revolution made in some sections of the republican press and at the
public meetings which had mushroomed in Paris, together with the
grossly exaggerated descriptions found in the conservative press
contributed to the creation of a 'red scare' just like that of 1848. A
similar process of political polarisation was also underway as the
clerical and liberal critics of the empire increasingly came to participate
in a broad conservative alliance. There seemed to be no alternative to
supporting the regime as the most effective guarantor of social order
and Christian civilisation, a point repeatedly made in official propaganda.

On 8 May 1870 a plebiscite was held. The electorate was asked to
decide whether it 'approves the liberal reforms introduced since 1860'.
The advocates of a 'yes' vote seem to have stressed the danger of
revolution rather than the achievements of the regime. Typically a
clerical newspaper in Alsace affirmed that 'Our *Yes* is to strengthen the
emperor against the reds'. The results were an overwhelming success
for the regime: 7,350,000 voters registered their approval, 1,538,000
voted 'no', and a further 1,900,000 abstained. To one senior official it
represented 'a new baptism of the napoleonic dynasty'. It had escaped
from the threat of political isolation. The liberal empire offered greater
political liberty but also order and renewed prosperity. It had
considerable appeal. The centres of opposition remained the cities,
with 59 per cent of the votes in Paris negative and this rising to over 70
per cent in the predominantly worker *arrondissements* of the north-
east. In comparison with the 1869 elections however, opposition
appeared to be waning. Republicans were bitterly disappointed. Even

Gambetta felt bound to admit that 'the empire is stronger than ever'. The only viable prospect seemed to be a long campaign to persuade the middle classes and peasants that the republic did not mean revolution.

In this situation the empire's final collapse was due to its incompetent management of foreign affairs. The Prussian triumph over Austria in 1866 had altered the European balance of power, and ever since, French public opinion had believed in the likelihood of a war by means of which France could re-assert its authority. When war came in 1870 it was however due to a series of errors by a government operating under pressure from conservative opinion. The hysterical response of the right-wing press to the news of a Hohenzollern candidature for the Spanish throne was a major factor in creating an atmosphere favourable to war. Although both the emperor and Ollivier might have been willing to accept a simple withdrawal of this candidature, conservative deputies demanded guarantees which Bismarck, in the infamous Ems telegram, refused in insulting terms. To have accepted this would have meant another humiliating foreign policy reversal and risked parliamentary disapproval which could have thrown into doubt the bases of the recently revised constitution and particularly the emperor's personal power. In this situation Napoléon, although aware that the military preparations were seriously defective, succumbed to pressure from the empress, from the foreign minister the Duc de Gramont, and from the more authoritarian Bonapartists and hoped that victory would further consolidate the regime.

The initial public response was indeed overwhelmingly positive. With the exception of a very small minority of revolutionary militants even republicans felt bound to rally to the national cause. Huge crowds singing patriotic songs gathered in the streets to see the troops off. The first defeats brought panic. The emperor's response to the developing military crisis was to replace the Ollivier government with one made up of authoritarian Bonapartists under General Cousin-Montauban. This could not alter the fact that the army was better prepared in terms of organisation, training and material for dealing with internal security problems than waging a major European war. Its mobilisation had been chaotic. It lacked adequate trained reserves. Its manoeuvres in the field suffered from poor staff work and a lack of effective coordination, which the emperor's well-meaning interference only made worse. *Elan*, the spirit of improvisation and the ability to muddle through, on which

Plate 28 Paris, 4 September 1870, following news of the defeat
and capture of the emperor at Sedan crowds gather in front of
the *Corps législatif*. Republican deputies declared 'the fatherland
in danger' and proclaimed the overthrow of the Bonaparte
dynasty. Painting by Jacques Guiaud

its leaders prided themselves, cost it dearly. The high command's
inability to achieve the concentration of forces, which alone might have
compensated for numerical inferiority, made disaster probably inevitable.

News of the defeat at Sedan and the capitulation of the emperor and
one major army was received in Paris on the evening of 2 September
and became public knowledge the following day. This failure utterly
discredited the regime. The small group of twenty-seven republican
deputies were supported by large crowds in demanding its replacement.
On 4 September these invaded the Palais Bourbon and drove out the
imperial *Corps législatif*. In such an uncertain political situation the
troops and police responsible for the assembly's security were unwilling
to use force against the crowds. Inspired as much by the desire to
prevent a take-over by revolutionaries as by the need to replace the
imperial administration a group of moderate Parisian deputies
proclaimed the republic and established a Provisional Government of
National Defence presided over by the military governor of Paris,
General Trochu, to continue the war. In the provinces the news of

defeat and revolution usually came as a great surprise but there appeared to be no immediate alternative to acceptance of the Parisian initiative. The Empire in its various manifestations had attracted widespread support. Liberalisation, together with its clear commitment to law and order had seemed likely to reinforce this. Military defeat however represented governmental failure on a scale sufficient to destroy its legitimacy.

THE THIRD REPUBLIC, 1870–1914

Once the republic had been proclaimed, its survival seemed to depend on a successful outcome to the war. There were however major obstacles to this, and in particular the shortages of trained troops together with their equipment resulting from the defeat and cata-strophic capitulations of the imperial armies at Sedan and Metz. Public morale never really recovered. Conservatives, in particular, questioned the wisdom of fighting a lost war partly because they feared that just as in 1791 this would lead to political radicalisation. This made the task of inexperienced republican administrators all the more difficult. Their appeals to the Jacobin tradition in order to justify new levies of men and increased taxes only intensified tension. In this desperate situation, with Paris under siege, the government was obliged to request an armistice and in February 1871 held elections essentially on the issue of whether or not to continue the war. The widespread desire for peace and social order, and the discrediting of both the Bonapartist and republican alternatives, resulted in a massive majority, especially in rural areas, for the mainly monarchist notables who had stood as peace candidates. This defeat for the republicans was to result in further serious difficulties.

In a Paris under siege (from 19 September 1870 to 28 January 1871), those adult males who had remained in the city, overwhelmingly from the poorer classes, had been armed and incorporated into a National Guard. The political radicalisation already evident in the closing years of the Empire was accelerated by the sense of betrayal resulting from the government's acceptance of a 'humiliating' peace, including a German victory parade through the city they and regular troops had so successfully defended, and the loss of Alsace-Lorraine. They were also

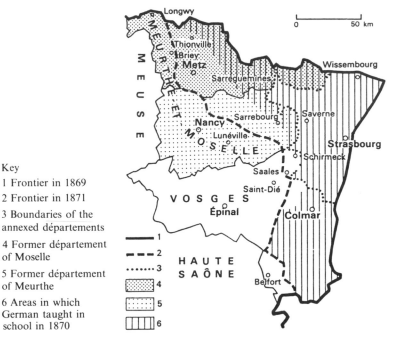

Key

1 Frontier in 1869

2 Frontier in 1871

3 Boundaries of the
annexed départements

4 Former département
of Moselle

5 Former département
of Meurthe

6 Areas in which
German taught in
school in 1870

Fig 13 The loss of Alsace-Lorraine

concerned about the future of the republic. The newly elected National
Assembly, meeting at Bordeaux on 12 February, had nominated a
government made up of the most moderate of republicans and led by
the arch-conservative Adolphe Thiers. The prospects for a *République
démocratique et sociale* seemed to be fading once again. The crisis
deepened because of the insensitivity of a government which decided to
end the National Guard pay that represented the only incomes of many
families until economic activity was restored, and threatened the
existence of many small businesses by requiring the immediate payment
of rents and commercial debts. Nevertheless the revolt which began on
18 March was largely unpremeditated. Initially it took the form of
popular resistance to a tactless and incompetently managed effort to
seize National Guard cannon parked on the heights of Montmartre.
Signs of disaffection amongst the troops involved caused a panic with
Thiers ordering a withdrawal to Versailles to await military reinforcements. The resulting power vacuum undoubtedly stimulated the
wider insurrection he had feared. Two rival political authorities came

Plate 29 The burning of Paris in an effort to obstruct the advance of government troops into Paris, May 1871. Amongst the buildings destroyed were the Tuileries Palace and the Hôtel de ville

into existence with the central committee of the federation of National Guard battalions in the city and the national government at Versailles, with each controlling its own armed force. On 26 March, following the failure of confused negotiations, insurrection turned into revolution with the election in Paris of the Commune. Fighting between the two bodies began on 2 April. In retrospect it seems clear that the Parisian movement, enjoying little provincial support and isolated by a military *cordon sanitaire*, was doomed. It was suppressed with extreme brutality by the troops of the imperial army, largely freed from German prison camps for the purpose. Ill-disciplined and poorly led National Guards were incapable of defending the city. The struggle turned into an increasingly desperate defence of isolated *quartiers* throughout an appropriately named 'bloody week'. In fierce street fighting the army lost 400 dead and 1,100 seriously wounded. No one really knows the number of insurgent casualties. Estimates vary between ten and thirty thousand, with most of them summarily executed after surrendering. In the following days and weeks more than 38,000 others were arrested.

Clearly for generals, as well as for monarchist deputies and moderate republican ministers, this represented an opportunity for a settling of accounts with political radicals whose calls for reform and revolutionary rhetoric had posed a threat to the established social order as well as with the criminal, rootless horde, the 'dangerous class', which they seem to have believed was plotting to destroy civilised society. As Jules Simon, the education minister so revealingly put it: 'June 1848, March 1871 – the same struggle'. On the other side of the political divide the Commune created a socialist myth of revolutionary heroism. More significantly however, this was to be the last of the great nineteenth-century revolutions. Emerging out of the particular circumstances of war and defeat, in the long term it represented little more than an interlude in the process whereby political protest was being institutionalised.

It remained to settle the precise character of the new regime. The struggle between the party of order, committed to a hierarchical society and to monarchical forms of government and determined on *résistance* to change, and those favouring *mouvement* in the shape of representative government and 'greater social justice' was to continue. Once the threat from the extreme left had, at least for the moment, disappeared, moderate republicans were once again able to distance themselves from their temporary monarchist allies. The essential reference points, the bases of two opposing political cultures, were once again the great myths of 1789. The elections held in February 1871 had returned an assembly, a majority of whose members (about 400 of 645) favoured the establishment of some kind of constitutional monarchy. They made some progress. Thus in May 1873 Thiers, whose government had crushed the Commune, had secured the withdrawal of German occupying forces through the payment of an indemnity of 5 milliard francs, and had begun the urgent task of reorganising the army, was replaced by more committed royalists, the Marshal MacMahon as president and the Duke of Broglie as prime minister. Thiers' fault had been to appear increasingly sympathetic to the notion of a conservative republic as 'the regime which divides us the least'. Yet once again, as in 1850, the royalists were to waste their opportunity and fail to achieve a restoration.

The obvious candidate for the throne, Charles X's grandson the Count of Chambord, in exile in Austria and out of touch with conditions in France, continued to insist on the replacement of the tricolour, 'the emblem of revolution' by the white flag and *fleur de lys* of the old monarchy. This refusal to compromise was supported in the National Assembly by some hundred Legitimist deputies, but not by the two hundred Orléanists undoubtedly committed to conservative politics but uncomfortable with the more extreme forms of Legitimist devotion to throne and altar. Faced with this intransigence, the monarchist leaders were forced to postpone a constitutional settlement and decided to wait until the death of the childless Chambord. The succession would then legitimately pass to the House of Orléans, securing it was hoped the natural fusion of the warring monarchist groups. In the meantime they were determined, with the assistance of the Church, to establish a regime devoted to re-establishing moral order. France needed to expiate the sins which had caused God to inflict military defeat on her armies. Religious revival seemed to promise both external, and through persuading everyone to accept the place in society which God had chosen for them, internal security. It was increasingly the defence of religion rather than monarchism which supplied cohesion and a sense of purpose to conservatives during these early years of the Third Republic.

In contrast anti-clericalism, added to their fundamental determination to defend the republic, provided a basic unity for the 150 republicans elected in 1871. Significantly there was no return to clandestine activity even in the repressive circumstances of the early 1870s. The institutionalisation of political protest, interrupted by the Commune, continued. Republican spokesmen insisted upon their own commitment to legal activity and asserted that the conservatives were reactionaries planning not only the restoration of the monarchy but that of noble privilege and the tithe. They would moreover lead France into another war in defence of the temporal power of the Pope. It followed that it was the republicans who were the true defenders of social order. Implicit in this was an effort to dissociate the republic from revolution. Even the radicals played down the question of social reform. The more prosperous circumstances of the 1870s encouraged them to replace their previous appeal to the *Petits* (the little people) against the *Gros* (the bigwigs) with concern for the interests of those whom Gambetta now labelled the *couches nouvelles*: the property-owning lower middle classes and peasants. These policies were to enjoy growing electoral success. By-elections meant that the composition of the Assembly changed quite rapidly. As early as July 1871, when elections were held in 114 constituencies, a further 100 republicans had been elected, indicating both how peculiar the circumstances of the February elections had been and also the real appeal of Thiers' conservative republic, which had after all smashed the Paris Commune. By January 1875 a conservative Catholic, Henri Wallon, was able to obtain sufficient support for a constitutional amendment in favour of the definitive establishment of the Republic. The constitution of that year sought to avoid the mistake of 1848 by ensuring that the president was elected by parliament and denied the authority accorded by a popular vote. In the aftermath of the Commune he was certainly granted substantial executive power but in practice assemblies, increasingly dominated by republicans, would insist upon their own predominance and the key role in government of a *président du conseil* (prime minister) dependent upon parliament. The 1876 general elections brought 340 republicans, elected especially in the east and south-east, into the chamber of Deputies, alongside 155 monarchists from rural areas of the west and north-west, around half of whom were by this time Bonapartists elected mainly in the south-west and representing a revival which had begun in 1873 and which would only end with the Prince Imperial's death in 1879 in the Zulu War. These circumstances meant that a final showdown between the republicans in parliament and the monarchist president of the republic could not long be postponed. In May 1877, following a vote of no-confidence, MacMahon dissolved the Chamber. The following October, and in spite of a return to a Bonapartist system of administrative pressure, the electorate returned 321 republican and only 208 monarchist deputies. MacMahon was obliged to invite the moderate republican Dufaure to form a government. Cohabitation was however to fail and when in January 1879 the delegates of the communes elected a republican majority in the senate, MacMahon finally accepted that his position was untenable.

This republican victory cannot be explained in simple sociological terms. Ideological divisions cut across those of class. It certainly represented a defeat for a traditional social élite made up primarily of noble and non-noble landowners, but which had also come to include many wealthy business and professional men or those with mixed interests like the Duke Decazes in finance and mining or the Duke of Broglie, chairman of the Saint-Gobain glass and chemicals company. Nevertheless a substantial portion of the economic élite, including financiers like Henri Germain or ironmasters like Dorian and Magnin had come to favour a conservative republic, as had the much larger numbers of business and professional men with local standing and influence, able to reach a mass electorate which had attained a significant level of political consciousness and which believed that its material and social aspirations would best be served by a republic.

The resignation of MacMahon was followed by a long period of conservative republican rule, lasting until 1898. The shifting alliances and repeated ministerial crises should not be allowed to obscure this basic reality. At the outset a programme designed to firmly establish a liberal–democratic political system was introduced representing, whatever its shortcomings, a major affirmation of individual liberty. In the absence of a modern party organisation, unity and a sense of purpose were conferred on moderate republicans by informal networks, electoral committees and newspapers presenting a simple ideology which associated the republic with indefinite progress towards liberty and material well-being. Restrictions on the press and public meetings and on the right to create associations, including trades unions, were eased (laws of 29 January, 30 June 1881 and 28 March 1884 respectively) and less repressive policies adopted towards strikes. Just like their predecessors once in power the republicans abandoned plans for administrative decentralisation and indeed the administration was purged of politically suspect figures who might otherwise obstruct the application of republican laws. A series of anti-clerical measures were introduced including repeal of the 1814 ban on Sunday work and the re-establishment of divorce, although the status of the Roman Catholic church as the established state church was not threatened. The *concordat* had its advantages. More important for the republicans was the establishment of a secular education system as the means of combating clerical obscurantism, of securing the emancipation of the individual and safeguarding the principles of 1789. For Jules Ferry his law of 28 March 1882 establishing free and obligatory primary instruction and removing religious instruction from the curriculum was 'the greatest social reform and...the most durable political reform'. He appreciated that education was an important source of

Plate 30 Peasants travelling by rail

power. To establish lay education was to provide the means for securing the *bourgeois* republic against both its clerical and monarchist enemies on the right, and against the threat of social revolution from the left, by inculcating fundamental notions of civic responsibility, patriotism and respect for law, property and order. In 1886 further legislation provided for the gradual replacement of clerics by lay personnel in all public schools.

The new regime was also very active in the economic sphere. It attempted to conciliate diverse interest groups by recognising their very real difficulties after the onset of economic depression in the late 1870s. Thus in 1878 Freycinet introduced a counter-cyclical public works programme concerned in particular to improve communications through the construction of branch railway lines and local roads. Criticised for its cost, it proved very attractive to the host of rural and small town voters. The re-introduction of protective customs tariffs by Méline between 1881 and 1892 similarly consolidated support for a republic which promised *progrès* and *bonheur* (good fortune). His policy represented a philosophical commitment to preserve the 'eternal', rural France against the corrupting impact of capitalism and urbanisation. Although combined with a populist attack on the monopoly powers of the banks and railway companies, in practice government policy provided for the fullest possible protection of the rights and vested interests of property owners combined with a *laissez-faire* attitude towards social reform. Moderate republicans were committed to a form of consensus politics which protected the status quo whilst enlarging individual opportunities for advancement. Together with the enhanced role of government as a provider of services, this encouraged a growing interest in politics. Deputies were clearly more than ever expected to do their utmost to cultivate ministers and obtain favours for their constituents. In spite of the creation of a stable political system, criticism nevertheless grew. In part this reflected a major political realignment as many solid middle-class and conservative republicans, having ousted the traditional élites, found that they had achieved their essential political objectives and now sought to defend their own privileged positions against more radical groups. As early as 1887 Rouvier, closely associated with big business, sought to establish a right of centre parliamentary majority. Although this failed because of differences over religious matters, it made evident the renewed interest of many moderate republicans in a broad conservative alliance in defence of social order. The electoral success of these *opportunistes* in 1893 allowed them to risk a breach with republicans to their left and resume the search for more congenial allies on the right. Younger men like Poincaré, Barthou and Delcassé with fewer emotional attachments to the past were more concerned about the rise of socialism than continuing the struggle against the clericals. The rash of anarchist outrages in the 1890s, which included the assassination of President Carnot, only encouraged this outlook. In the event the hoped-for realignment was not to occur.

For one thing the loss of electoral support in 1898 suggested that many voters would reject a move to the right. Mutual suspicion between conservative republicans and those further to the right over religious issues also survived and was intensified by the Dreyfus affair, as well as by the threat to the republic posed by the increasingly rabid nationalism of the extreme right and evinced by Déroulède's farcical attempt in February 1899 to persuade soldiers to participate in a coup and by the hostile crowd which in June insulted the President of the Republic, Loubet, at the Auteuil races. This, together with the evident moderation of many so-called Radicals, promoted instead a realignment towards the centre-left and in defence of the republic, which

Plate 31 The threshing machine: by far the most common machine introduced onto French farms in the nineteenth century. Painting by Albert Rigolet

resulted in the formation of the *bloc des gauches* for the 1902 elections to include most conservative republicans, including Poincaré and Waldeck-Rousseau, together with Radicals and reformist socialists.

The evolution of the Radicals bears examination. They had initially posed as the protagonists of the *peuple* (the ordinary folk) against the *grands* (the upper classes), proclaiming their fidelity to Gambetta's 1869 Belleville programme and demanding constitutional reform to abolish such remnants of monarchy as the presidency and senate; administrative decentralisation; the election of judges; the separation of Church and state; as well as social reform to include a shorter working day and pensions for the aged and sick to be financed by an income tax. They had condemned the *opportunistes* for their cautious religious policies and for their close links with big business. In practice however the absence of disciplined parties meant that the deputy's first loyalty was assumed to be towards his constituents. His primary responsibility was to obtain a fair share of new roads, schools and jobs. The boundaries between 'parties' were always fluid and ministerial instability the inevitable result. In such circumstances, and most notably perhaps in the aftermath of the 1885 election, when the Radicals actually held the political balance, their own internal divisions and indiscipline prevented them from making effective use of their opportunity. During periods of crisis for the regime such as that precipitated by the neo-Bonapartism of General Boulanger in 1889, or when, following the first ballot in the 1895 elections, a victory for clerical conservatives seemed possible, Radicals were prepared to cooperate with more conservative republicans and to respect *discipline républicaine*. In similar circumstances they participated in the Waldeck-Rousseau government of *défense républicaine* in June 1899. Their role was thus essentially a secondary, supportive one, except when Léon Bourgeois was able to form a government in October 1895 only to lose parliamentary support in the following April as a result of his rather modest income tax proposals, which deputies feared would create a dangerous precedent. These limited successes did however suggest that an effort to improve Radical organisation in time for the 1902 elections might pay a handsome political dividend.

The Radical Party had remained a *parti des cadres* based on informal groupings of local notables who dispensed patronage to their communities, rather than a mass party. Its parliamentary deputies would remain rather undisciplined, but something akin to a modern party electoral organisation was created in the rue de Valois in Paris. This was one factor contributing to the victory in 1902. The election of 233 Radical deputies inaugurated the great period of Radical administration in alliance with the *républicains de gauche* – in fact moderates who refused to accept the logic of Méline's *progressist* position that the defence of social order required an alliance with the right – and with the 43 socialists. This survived until 1909 with governments led by Combes, Sarrien and Clemenceau. It saw the first timid efforts to introduce old-age pensions but was above all characterised by a further assault on the Church, in large part in response to the Dreyfus Affair and the renewed threat to the republic from the extreme right.

The Affair had been caused by the prosecution by the army of a Jewish staff officer for spying. The evidence was always dubious but for conservatives upholding it it came to be synonomous with defending the honour of the army, the single institution which for them represented authority and order at home and patriotic endeavour abroad. Regarding themselves as the only true patriots they were hostile

Plate 32 A family dinner. Cartoon by Caran D'Ache illustrating
the furious disputes engendered by the Dreyfus affair

towards all those 'bad' French who questioned their chauvinism, and in particular socialists, trades unionists, Jews, and Radicals like Caillaux with their proposals for an income tax to finance social reform. They rejected the egalitarian values of the republic in favour of a mystical catholicism and a glorification of violence and war. The cult of Joan of Arc came to symbolise the spiritual union of *Religion* and *Patrie*. Former symbols of the revolutionary republic like the *Marseillaise*, the tricolour, and of course the army were appropriated by the right and its intellectual leaders Déroulède, Barrès and especially Maurras. Largely incorporating the personnel and ideals of traditional conservatism, this new right created a more potent political force than the right had known since the 1870s, one which was fundamentally anti-democratic and anti-parliamentarian in its demands for a strong executive power to overcome political and social 'factionalism'. The mixture certainly enjoyed some spectacular successes, including victory in forty-five of the eighty seats contested in the Paris municipal elections in May 1900, and gained considerable support amongst those groups which felt threatened by the evolution of modern society, including clericals, members of traditional élites and small businessmen.

The response on the left was to denounce clericalism as the enemy, and to attack its roots, the Catholic schools whose particularistic teaching was seen as a threat to national unity and republican institutions. Thus a series of measures was introduced, culminating in July 1904 in the suppression of the Catholic teaching orders and the closure of their schools, and in December 1905 in the disestablishment of the Church, terminating the Napoleonic Concordat which had recognised its special place in French life and compensated it for its losses during the revolution by paying the stipends of its clergy. This stimulated an intense but short-lived resistance to official inventories of Church property. Otherwise the right enjoyed only limited mass electoral support. The violent xenophobic and anti-semitic tone of their leading representatives alienated much even of their potential conservative and clerical constituency. Their significance should not however be underestimated for they were a contributory factor in placing nationalism and the growing German threat at the centre of the political agenda. A major political realignment was already well under way as support grew not only for 'patriotic' policies but in opposition to what was seen to be the growing 'social peril'.

Plate 33 Strike in the Nord coalfield: the use of troops as strike-breakers. Engraving from *L'Illustration*

Once the Radicals had achieved their 'final' victory over the *ancien régime*, their main preoccupation became the growth of industrial unrest. Clemenceau, who as minister of the interior had already inaugurated a repressive policy, became *président du conseil* in 1906. He was soon being denounced by the government's former socialist allies as the *premier flic* (cop) *de France*. His policy represented a fundamental commitment to the ethos and institutions of a *bourgeois* property-owning society and to social order. If the Radical conception of the role of the state was influenced by the egalitarian ideals of the revolution, so equally was it inspired by a belief in the rights of the individual in a property-owning democracy. Radical calls for social justice had long had an empty ring about them. Access to power and the improved material situation of many of their supporters had transformed the Radicals into an anti-revolutionary force.

How real was this socialist threat that so exercised both Radicals and more obvious conservatives? The socialists had taken some time to recover from the repression which had followed the Paris Commune. Nevertheless the election of a deputy in Marseilles in 1881 had been followed by steady growth and in 1914 socialist candidates would obtain 1,413,000 votes. In 1886 a parliamentary group distinct from the Radicals was formed which immediately prior to the war had 102 members. Conservative fears were none the less exaggerated. The socialist movement was constantly weakened by bitter sectarian squabbling. Even the creation of a unified socialist party – the *Parti socialiste unifie* known as the SFIO after its idealistic subtitle *Section française de l'Internationale ouvrière* (French section of the Workers' International), in April 1905, in a deliberate effort to establish a clear socialist alternative, could not resolve the many ideological and tactical differences within the movement.

Even more decisive in the realignment of internal politics than the supposed rise of socialism was the impact of deteriorating relationships with Imperial Germany, evident especially from the Agadir incident in July 1911. International affairs took pride of place amongst politicians' concerns, and resulted in the nomination of the conservative republican Poincaré as head of government in January 1912 and to the presidency in May. His efforts to form a 'national' government foundered on Radical hostility to the proposed presence of conservatives like Méline or of Catholics in government. With support from the right Poincaré nevertheless continued to prepare for a war he believed to be inevitable. Abroad this involved efforts to reinforce links with Russia, and at home to increase both the status and strength of the army and to develop a greater sense of national unity. The conservative press and mass circulation dailies like *Le Petit Parisien* contributed to the creation of an increasingly chauvinistic mood. Inevitably the debate on military organisation was shaped as much by internal political considerations as real military needs. The Socialists and many Radicals continued to resist the nationalistic xenophobia which threatened to restore the right to power, and made up the minority of 204 deputies who in August 1913 opposed the extension of military service from two to three years. The majority, made up of 358 deputies, was however determined that France should make an effort to match German military strength. Growing international tension was indeed promoting a more favourable attitude towards the army even on the left.

The April–May 1914 elections were fought on this conscription issue as well as the question of how to finance the growing military budget. The new Radical leader Caillaux, suspect to conservatives because of his desire to improve relations with Germany, increased their already venomous hostility by proposing recourse to income tax. The wealthy whilst insisting on the need for sacrifices were clearly unwilling to dip into their pockets to provide for national security. The electoral victory of the left with 342 successful candidates, including 102 socialists who had stressed the need to mobilise international working-class opposition to an imperialist war, was evidence of the strength of hostility to extended military service. In the last resort though the new government headed by the independent socialist Viviani, but dominated by Radicals, would prove unwilling to risk weakening the army by repealing the three-year law.

Significantly, during the international crisis in July 1914, following the Austrian Archduke Franz Ferdinand's assassination at Sarajevo, President Poincaré, on an official visit to Russia did little to encourage caution. His essential concern was to ensure united action against Germany. General mobilisation was ordered on 1 August and Germany declared war on 3 August. The population seems to have reacted more from a sense of resigned acceptance rather than with any great enthusiasm. Events had developed so quickly. Individuals felt helpless, unable to influence the situation. There was a widespread belief that the war would be short and a resolve to get the job done. The opponents of the republican regime both to the right and left rallied to the cause, the nationalists with the feeling that their warnings had been confirmed, the clericals confident that in this moment of crisis men would once again turn to the Church for hope and consolation, and the socialists in the belief that they were engaging in a just war of national defence in support of the relatively progressive French republic against an autocratic and aggressive German empire. Minor demonstrations against mobilisation occurred in thirty-six departments, mainly involving socialist and trades union militants, but the vast majority of activists were unwilling to contemplate action which might assist an enemy. They joined in a genuine *union sacrée*, a political truce from which however the various political and social groups would shortly seek to gain the maximum possible advantage.

Resolution rather than resignation, a patriotic *élan*, became the dominant emotion during the following two weeks as mobilised reservists left their home communities. Everywhere patriotic sentiments predominated over the anxiety caused by the departure of menfolk and breadwinners for the front. The strength of this initial consensus was evident from the very small proportion of men (about 1.75 per cent) who failed to report for duty. The government had expected that, given the strength of anti-militarism on the left, as many as 13 per cent might try to evade service. Indeed, since 1905 the police had been required to maintain a list of those, mostly syndicalist members of the *Confédération Générale du Travail* (CGT) trades union federation, thought likely to attempt to disrupt mobilisation and who were to be subject to preventative arrest in case of war. Especial concern had been shown concerning key groups like railwaymen, coal miners, workers in the docks and shipping, in the electricity industry and in the postal and telegraphic services, who might disorganise troop movements or cause economic chaos. In retrospect this concern seems exaggerated given the weakness of the trades union movement, the lack of rank-and-file support for revolutionary action and the complete absence of concrete plans to interfere with mobilisation. In the event too the Interior Minister decided that arrests were more likely to provoke than to prevent disorder. The process of mobilisation itself removed many potential troublemakers, the imposition of a state of siege and threat of repression restrained others, as did the sense of isolation in a nation committed to defending itself.

The ease with which mobilisation had occurred was evidence of the degree to which, in spite of social divisions, a sense of national community had been created. This was based on an overwhelming consensus in favour of such values as manhood suffrage and parliamentary democracy, the innate superiority of French civilisation, and an elemental love of France which involved a moral responsibility to defend the homeland. These sentiments had to a large degree been deliberately constructed through a combination of education, military service and the mass media. As the influential historian and educationalist Ernest Lavisse insisted 'if the schoolboy does not become a citizen fully aware of his duties, and a soldier who loves his gun, the teacher will have wasted his time'. Over centuries, but with increasingly more effect during the nineteenth century, a shared linguistic and mental universe had been created, and the minority of dissidents subjected to increasingly effective repression. In this process those who possessed political power had inevitably played a disproportionate part. It was above all their values and their social system, in which status and opportunity derived essentially from the possession of private property, which were now to be protected by war.

Power is exercised not only, or even primarily, through economic relationships but by means of the use of authority on a much broader front through a variety of forms of influence, by means of cultural hegemony and political control. The ability to mould opinion was a key aspect of social power – exercised through the development of a system of mass primary education from 1833, and through control over the media growing in importance as the source of information. This facilitated the establishment of a broad consensus on basic social values, which were presented as eternal truths. A key feature of this normative code was the institution of property, something which the wealthy élite had in common with much broader sections of the middle and lower-middle classes and the rural population.

Normally, even though apparent consensus might conceal pragmatic conformity rather than positive acceptance of the social system, repressive action was not needed to maintain the social and political subordination of the mass of the population. Order was maintained by the adverse reaction of most people to those who appeared to be breaking the rules. This is not to deny the significance of conflict most notably within élites and on the part of middle-class groups anxious to gain a greater share of power. The latter used the language of 1789, the language of democracy, in an effort to appeal to increasingly wide sections of the community, and to isolate the ruling group. Thus in 1838 the *Journal de Rouen* denounced 'the reign of the new landowning and financial aristocracy'. Similar themes were used throughout the Second Republic and Empire and with renewed vigour during the Third Republic. Yet the aims of middle-class republican politicians were inherently limited. They had a more democratic vision of society than those they sought to replace, but the ideal was still based on property, on respect for those values they shared with the old élite. They played the dangerous game of encouraging mass protest. The events of 1848, the Paris Commune and the rise of the socialist party in the closing years of the century provided a terrible warning of the dangers of political agitation and of the need to preserve social order. This served to restrain middle-class critics of the existing social system. The coming together of all those who possessed property represented an immense strengthening of the conservative consensus. Thus even though the élite of wealth might have lost its monopoly of political power, this wealth and its social position would continue to be guaranteed by the power of the state.

6

A time of crisis, 1914–1945

A long period of crisis and upheaval began with the outbreak of the First World War. The essential decisions on foreign and military policy were taken by a small group of politicians, career diplomats and soldiers, influenced by their perceptions of the intentions and military strength of their opponents and of their own internal political support. The most forceful single influence on foreign policy in the immediate pre-war years had been Poincaré. First as prime minister and then, during the crucial days of July 1914, in the supposedly decorative post of president, he was able, partly because of the incompetence and inexperience of prime minister Viviani and the foreign ministers Pichon and Doumergue, to insist upon the need to support Russia and respect the alliance upon which French security appeared to depend. Abandonment of Russia would have decisively shifted the balance of power in Europe in favour of the Triple Alliance.

The war came as a great surprise to the vast majority of French people. The order for mobilisation was greeted with less than enthusiasm. Reservists nevertheless obeyed the instruction to report to their regimental depots and were sent off by cheering crowds, convinced that France had been the victim of unprovoked aggression and that the war would be brief. The press was virtually unanimous both in publicising in the most condemnatory terms the crimes committed by the 'Teutonic barbarians' and in insisting upon the superiority of French arms and the power of the Russian 'steamroller'.

The socialist press which had so recently adopted a pacificist, anti-militaristic stance now informed its readers that 'the Fatherland, home of all great revolutions, land of liberty and freedom, is in danger'. Social and political differences seem to have been set aside and replaced by a common patriotism, the *union sacrée* for which Poincaré had appealed. Overwhelmed by the speed with which events succeeded each other, and persuaded by propaganda, most of the population were inspired to defend French civilisation against German militarism. A genuine consensus appeared to have been created which was given recognition at governmental level by the inclusion in its ranks of two socialists, the veteran Marxist Guesde and Sembat, and two representatives of the right – Delcassé and Millerand. The small minority of opponents of the war, leaderless and threatened with arrest, felt unable to resist the immense patriotic fervour. The Catholic concept of the 'just war' and invocation of the spirit of Joan of Arc was widely accepted, far more so than the clerical conception of this time of trial as an opportunity for the expiation of sins. The apparent religious revival which accompanied the outbreak of war was short-lived but the role of the Church in helping to maintain patriotic commitment should not be under-estimated. Neither should that of the schools and the pre-war processes of socialisation they had promoted and which were now being put to the test. This unique *union* was indeed to be severely strained in the following years. Intended, by the various political groups, to be a truce for the duration of what was expected to be a short war, its strength was greatly exaggerated in the press. In practice the various political and confessional groups retained their pre-war objectives and hoped to take advantage of the war to achieve them. Not unnaturally they disagreed about the nature and objectives of the war itself. Was it a defensive battle against a predatory and militaristic German Empire which should lead after its defeat to the establishment of a democratic republic, as much of the left supposed, or a struggle for survival between peoples in which France sought to defend itself against 'the instinctive savagery of German flesh and blood' (Maurras), as the right tended to claim? Although mutual suspicion rapidly re-emerged, the need to drive the enemy from French soil continued to provide a basis for cooperation.

Sustaining the military effort against the background of repeated military failure and the continuous attrition of trench warfare with its

Plate 34 The offensive tactics of 1914–15: massive casualties for minimal gains

damaging effects on morale was to impose a considerable stress on the social and political systems. Preparations for war had long been under way, and military mobilisation took place without much difficulty. However the superior tactics and training of the German army took their toll. The French armies were forced to retreat until Joffre managed to mount a counter-attack against the exposed flank of the enemy forces on the Marne in September, forcing them to adopt defensive positions and leading, through a process of 'leap-frogging', to the establishment of an unbroken line of trenches from Switzerland to the sea. By means of this 'miracle of the Marne' Joffre succeeded in establishing a strong position for himself in public opinion and in securing military primacy over the politicians in strategic decision making. Millerand, the War Minister was self-effacing before the military 'experts'. Joffre, giving full rein to the contempt for politicians so characteristic of military leaders, hardly bothered to keep the government informed of his plans. This early confidence in the high

Plate 35 Trench warfare: the aftermath of hand-to-hand fighting in the Meuse region

command was however to be sapped by its inability to live up to its promises. The wasting effect of a succession of ill-conceived offensives had a negative impact on military morale. The massive losses suffered at Verdun would eventually lead to the replacement of Joffre at the end of 1916, as a first step in the re-imposition of ministerial authority. Even then such problems as the nature of parliamentary control over ministers and the activities of an increasingly interventionist state, as well as the means of safeguarding civil liberties in time of war, were never to be satisfactorily resolved. Joffre's successor, Nivelle, was selected in part because he, as a Protestant and unlike most senior generals, was not suspected of hostility towards the republic, in part because he managed to convince politicians that he was the man of providence who would finally breach the German trench system. The bloody failure over which he presided on the Chemin des Dames almost broke the army.

It led to the mutinies of the spring and summer 1917 when elements of forty-nine divisions refused to take part in further attacks, although they remained willing to defend their positions. Under the strain of bombardment, fear of death, and a miserable existence a strong sense of grievance had developed concerning incompetent and arrogant officers, poor quality rations and inadequate leave. Political motives seem to have been largely absent, although paranoid and self-excusatory generals tended to blame everything on subversives. The harsh re-imposition of discipline was combined with improvements in conditions, whilst the soldiers' confidence in their commanders was at least partially restored by means of a number of carefully prepared offensives with limited objectives and consequently relatively few casualties. It was by such means that Nivelle's successor Pétain, the hero of Verdun, made his reputation as a caring general. As a result the French army was able to hang on during the desperate crisis caused by Russian withdrawal from the war and the reinforcement of the German armies on the western front.

The deterioration in the military situation was to have significant political consequences. The weariness evident at the front, together with the demands the war made on civilians, inevitably influenced morale. From as early as 1915 a minority amongst the Socialists, led by Marx's son-in-law Jean Longuet, had begun to question, not the commitment to national defence, but the unwillingness of the government even to consider the possibility of a negotiated peace and its evident determination to fight to the bitter end (*jusqu'au bout*). In response Socialist delegates were forbidden by the authorities to attend a conference of the Workers' International to be held on neutral territory in Stockholm in August 1917. This, together with rising working-class discontent with living and working conditions, gradually pushed the Socialists into opposition and led to the withdrawal of their ministers from government in September. November, however, saw the installation in power of Clemenceau, the incarnation of the Jacobin republic, motivated by an intransigent patriotism, and additionally determined to restore the authority of the civilian leadership over the military. He was supported by a parliamentary majority equally determined to secure the more effective prosecution of the war. The arrest for defeatism of the former Interior Minister Malvy and of the Radical leader Caillaux in January 1918, represented the culmination of a gradual shift of government towards the right, together with a loss of identity on the part of Radicals as they came increasingly to accept the nationalism of the right. Indeed for most of the population there appeared to be little alternative to fighting, to the finish, a war in which so many sacrifices had already been made. A negociated peace with an

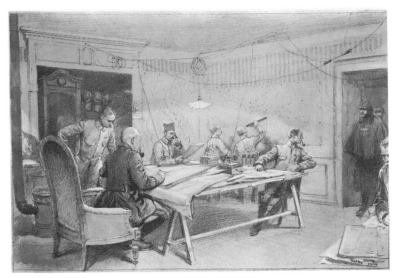

Plate 36 Senior officers planning – in isolation from front line realities. Drawing by Georges Scott

Plate 37 Mobilisation for 'total war': female munitions workers

undefeated Germany would have required territorial concessions to add to those of 1871. This was unacceptable.

In the meantime the unprecedented needs of the armies had to be met and the war had to be paid for. It was financed from the receipts of indirect taxation, through the floating of enormous loans and the printing of money. Of an estimated 157 billion gold (1913) francs of government expenditure between August 1914 and October 1919 it has been calculated that 45 billion came from tax revenue, 60 billion from defence bonds and the remaining 52 billion from various other forms of borrowing. The introduction of an income tax was successfully resisted by parliamentarians until 1916 and would only make a substantial contribution to government revenues after the war. The middle classes appear to have been more willing to contribute their sons than their wealth to the war effort. The impact was inevitably inflationary. The massive civilian effort was made all the more difficult by the loss to the enemy of major industrial regions in the north and north-east which had previously supplied 48 per cent of coal production and 58 per cent of steel. The economic achievement becomes all the more impressive if it is remembered that the 'short war illusion' meant that mobilisation plans had taken virtually no account of munitions production. There had been immediate manpower and raw material shortages. Some 63 per cent of male industrial workers had been called up for military service, including many with skills essential to war production. Priorities had needed to be urgently established resulting, for example, in the release from military service of around 500,000 key workers by the end of 1915. This had all called for the progressive extension of state intervention in the economy on an unprecedented scale, to fix prices, distribute raw materials, organise production and transport. A haphazard structure of old and new administrative organisations had been created, frequently in close cooperation with the employers' organisations. Indeed in an effort to maximise production, businessmen were offered large capital advances and the inducement of substantial profits. Even though these networks of control were to be rapidly demolished after the armistice, the experience promoted a certain amount of rethinking about the economic role of the state and the means of promoting greater efficiency. The war did not simply result in a waste of resources. In some sectors, and most notably steel, engineering, electricity and chemicals, the war effort and the high profits it offered promoted expansion and technical innovation. Nevertheless the losses caused by military action and the destructiveness of the occupation in Northern France, as well as the distorting impact of the diversion of resources to satisfying military needs, must be emphasised.

The occupation of the north, shortages of fertiliser and machinery, and above all the requisitioning of draught animals and the conscription of man-power, resulted in a sharp decline in agricultural production. The 1917 grain harvest, the worst of the war-time period, was about 40 per cent below pre-war levels. Although imports covered much of the short-fall, food prices inevitably rose, finally forcing state intervention and the introduction of rationing. In the meantime the incentive of high prices encouraged superhuman efforts on the part of the women, children and old men left in the rural areas. The producers of meat, vegetables and fruit in particular benefited, and many peasants were able to pay off debts, acquire land and perhaps enjoy a somewhat more comfortable existence. The separation allowances paid to servicemen's dependants, seem to have represented an unhoped for supplement to the incomes of many poor rural families. More than any other social group however it was the rural population which paid for the war with its blood, accounting for almost half the total casualties. This did not protect farmers from criticism. The urban consumers who faced the full impact of rising prices condemned their 'greed'. High food prices were clearly a major cause of discontent especially amongst industrial workers. The constant efforts of employers to increase productivity and lengthen the working day, justifiable in terms of the war effort, had of course the additional effect of substantially increasing profits and were bitterly resented by workers who claimed that wages were rising far too slowly in comparison with prices and that as a result their diets were increasingly inadequate for hard physical labour. Established male workers were also concerned by the employment of a growing proportion of unskilled labour. This threatened both their existing status and remuneration and future prospects. Many of these newcomers were women attracted to the ordnance factories by the prospect of higher wages, but often forced to supplement separation allowances insufficient for the needs of urban life.

In spite of these problems and inevitable social tension, the expression of anything other than unqualified support for the war effort remained for some time exceptional. By the end of 1916, if little enthusiasm remained, people on the home front seem at least to have adapted to the war. It had become routine. Once the original fervour had declined people got on with living, accepting even bereavement with a surprising degree of stoicism. They continued to find re-assurance in the optimism of the press, although as the war was prolonged soldiers developed an utter contempt for this *bourrage de crâne* (brainwashing). Certainly there were frequent complaints about the rising cost of living, although deprivation was never on such a scale as to threaten widespread protest. The failure of the spring 1917 offensive seems to have finally destroyed any lingering hopes that the war might soon end. The daunting prospect of endless war appeared. The middle classes, perhaps the most stridently patriotic, together with the peasants, perhaps the most resigned, appear to have accepted the situation. The former, in spite of the particularly high casualties amongst young officers and the material difficulties of families living on fixed incomes, had endured too much to draw back. Disaffection was most clearly evident amongst the working classes. The widespread sense of grievance concerning both working and living conditions was intensified by the impotence of the trades unions, bound as they were, initially by the *union sacrée* and then from January 1917 by compulsory arbitration procedures. This discontent only slowly took on political form. Many Socialist and trades union militants had been called up for military service, and those who remained were at first reconciled to inactivity for the duration of what, after all, was expected to be a short war. The first serious strike waves occurred in the Paris region in January and May–June 1917, mainly before the public became aware of Nivelle's disastrous offensive, and were essentially spontaneous, involving around 100,000 mainly women workers in the fashion trades and munitions. They were frequently condemned by union officials, many of whom as reservists risked being re-called to the front if they incurred the authorities' displeasure, and were easily brought to an end by the imposition of compulsory arbitration together with wage increases. Strikes in the Toulouse munitions factories and in the Loire basin were similarly short-lived. In spite of the stir caused by an unofficial May Day parade by five to ten thousand people along the Grands Boulevards in Paris during which shouts of 'Down with the war' were proffered, the vast majority of workers were not opposed to the war effort, although they were determined to protect their vital interests.

Nevertheless, following the Nivelle offensive pessimism certainly spread. The letters read by the postal censors revealed a definite sense of strain and of war-weariness, and with this, the not uncommon desire for a compromise peace. There were still however very few advocates of a peace at any price. With the Germans remaining on French soil and after so much sacrifice there seemed to be little alternative to fighting on until final victory. Prefects' reports blamed unrest mainly on 'social problems' and seemed confident that minor concessions to workers' demands would calm the situation. Anxiety about the impact of the Russian revolution on working class opinion was soon eased as it became evident that initial enthusiasm had turned to hostility as workers had become aware of its potential impact on the military situation.

A second strike wave hit munition factories in the Paris region in May 1918, involving well over 100,000 workers, although for the war effort the better organised strikes of miners and engineering workers in the Saint-Etienne area were potentially more serious. Again though there were few signs of support for revolutionary action. The obvious determination of the Clemenceau government to prosecute the war to a victorious conclusion had a positive impact on morale whilst the great German offensive in March encouraged a renewed rallying to the national cause. This last great German assault was halted by a desperate allied effort which finally broke the enemy army. The success of the counter-attack, which for the first time involved large numbers of fresh American troops and was effectively coordinated by Foch, the supreme commander finally accepted by the allies in the moment of ultimate crisis, together with the accelerating collapse of the Central Powers came as a great surprise to the allies who had planned on a final offensive in 1919. Victory at last seemed possible. The desire to drive the enemy out of France and to impose a salutary lesson on the invader by utterly smashing his armies and invading his territory was however soon tempered by a desire to save lives and bring the war to an end as soon as possible. The armistice which came into force on 11 November 1918 was celebrated with unrestrained joy.

THE INTER-WAR YEARS

The war was over. Its victorious outcome seemed to represent a triumph for republican institutions. It left France, in appearance at least, as the major continental European power. The humiliation of 1870 was finally effaced and the lost territories of Alsace-Lorraine recovered. Disillusionment would soon set in as the long-term implications of participation in such a brutal and bloody conflict became evident. This was indeed a Pyrrhic victory. The human cost was enormous. Almost eight million men had been mobilised and 1,322,100 (16.6 per cent) of them killed. Many others (some three million) had been maimed or debilitated by the experience. They and their families would never forget. Over one million were to receive invalidity pensions. The demographic impact was particularly severe in France which had mobilised 168 out of every 1000 inhabitants and lost 34 of these, whilst Britain had mobilised 125 and lost 16 and Germany mobilised 154 and lost 30. The effect, on a country already experiencing demographic stagnation, of the loss of so many young men (27 per cent of those in the 18–27 age group) and of the resultant decline in the numbers of marriages and births would be felt in the 1930s as the size of the active labour force and of the cohort of men of military age fell. The war also had a significant long-term impact upon the economy. In spite of the progress made in the early part of the century, France had gone to war in a state of relative backwardness in comparison with both Britain and Germany. Whilst the economic balance was not entirely negative in that much useful investment had occurred, it too remained decisively in the red. In 1919 levels of agricultural and industrial production were around 45 per cent below those of 1913. Resources had been destroyed or diverted to military use. Large areas of the most productive farmland had been devastated by battle, livestock driven off, towns and villages smashed. In the German zone of occupation over-exploitation and systematic destruction had massively reduced the productive capacity of mines and factories and the carrying capacity of the railway network. Disruption on this scale, and the harsh treatment of the population of occupied areas deprived of adequate supplies of food and fuel and subject to forced labour, would be a major cause of the mass exodus of refugees from the north in 1940. They were clearly not anxious to repeat the experience of German rule.

Plate 38 The cost of reconstruction: the ruins of Montdidier (Somme), June 1919

Reconstruction and redeployment would take time and money. Even so the process was achieved with surprising rapidity. Industrial production was restored to pre-war levels by 1924, and by 1929 was 40 per cent above the 1913 level. This was due to a combination of factors including the stimulus of reconstruction, the release of pent-up consumer demand and the rising exports made possible by the depreciation of the franc in world currency markets. It began to appear as if the war would only represent a brief interlude in a long-term process of economic growth. Indeed the statistics suggest that the war years and 1920s were in many ways a continuation of the dynamic period which had commenced in the late 1890s. The process of growth and concentration of production would however remain insufficient to eliminate the major structural weaknesses of the French economy. These resulted from a combination of demographic and demand stagnation, the survival of a large and inefficient agricultural sector, and of numerous small and medium-sized and, more to the point, poorly equipped industrial and commercial businesses. The existence of modern, large-scale enterprises within such sectors of industry as chemicals, electrical engineering or the motor industry, growing through the re-investment of their massive wartime profits, contrasted markedly with the cautious reluctance to invest of most entrepreneurs. As a result the average industrial machine in the 1930s was to be twenty years old, compared with seven in Germany. The cost of production remained relatively high and the employers (*patronat*) obsessed with the need to ensure continued protection against foreign competitors. Potential investors tended to prefer the relative security of government loans. Nevertheless patchy efforts to increase productivity were stimulated both by the relative prosperity of the 1920s and by the depression of the following decade when rationalisation came to the fore. Some idea of the scale of structural change is suggested by table 6.1.

The continuing movement of labour away from agriculture, the decline of artisanal production and indeed the shift away from industry towards the services so characteristic of a modernising economy can be observed in the figures in table 6.2. These reflect both the growth of a 'modern' bureaucracy, of the financial and banking sector and chain stores and also the burgeoning numbers of small shops and bars. Another characteristic of the period was the concentration of so much

Table 6.1. *Distribution of active industrial population (per cent)*

	1913	1938	Variation
Energy	4.0	6.2	+2.2
Building and construction materials	18.6	16.9	−1.7
Metallurgical industry and engineering	14.7	22.6	+7.9
Chemicals	1.6	3.9	+2.3
Textiles, clothing and leather	42.4	29.7	−12.7
Agricultural and food processing industries	7.8	9.6	+1.8

Source: J.-C. Asselain, *Histoire économique de la France*, II (1984), p. 74.

Table 6.2. *Structure of the active population (per cent)*

	1913	1938
Agriculture	37.4	31.4
Industry	33.8	32.3
Services	28.8	36.3

of this activity in and around Paris, a city increasingly 'swollen' with people, and the corresponding underdevelopment of the west, centre and south-west.

Technological stagnation was even more evident in farming than in industry. Mechanisation made slow progress. There were only 35,000 tractors in use in 1938. They were expensive and peasants, often still committed to the ideal of self-sufficiency, were reluctant to borrow. Most small farms anyway generated an income inadequate to support debt repayment. Farmers were insufficiently aware of their markets or of the potentially beneficial effects of investment. Cost-accounting was a complete mystery. Costs were high and productivity gains primarily the result of the removal of surplus labour through migration. Typically conservative landowners, afraid that this might both increase the cost and reduce the submissiveness of labour, condemned its morally corrosive effects. Cereal yields had by 1929–31 risen to 14.2 quintals per hectare, only slightly above the pre-war figure of 13.3 and well below the British and German averages (21.9 and 20.5 respectively). Although productivity was much higher on the large capitalistic farms of the

Paris basin and the north, it remained the case that the one-third of the labour force employed in farming contributed only one-quarter of the country's national income. The 1920s nevertheless were a decade of rising food prices, creating a sense of well-being within the rural population. The mind-broadening effect of the wartime experience was reinforced by easier access to local towns by train or motor transport and the beginning of rural electrification (from 1928). These stimulated improvements in diet, changes in dress and the decline of local customs although most peasants continued to put up with miserable housing conditions.

The war still had to be paid for. International debts incurred during its course, especially to the Americans and British, would need to be honoured. This was rendered all the more difficult by the wartime outflow of gold and foreign currency, by the sales of overseas assets and the substantial losses on investments resulting from the Russian revolution. Prices more than tripled during the war, and this had heralded a massive depreciation of the franc once wartime exchange controls were removed and public confidence in a post-war return to 'normal' was disabused. Faced with problems of such severity it is hardly surprising that French politicians looked to the peace treaty to provide not only long-term military security but to force Germany to make proper and adequate financial reparations for a war for which it was universally agreed it was to blame. The slogan 'Germany will pay' won near unanimous support. Disagreement with the allies about how much Germany should pay was to cause considerable resentment amongst people who felt that they had borne the highest cost in human sacrifice, as did evident German 'bad will' when presented with the bill. In the end France would receive the substantial sum of 10 milliard francs (1913 value) before payments were suspended in 1931, enough to burden Germany without satisfying the French.

Thus France emerged from the war victorious but seriously damaged. The capacity of social and political systems which had triumphantly endured the military threat was soon moreover to be tested by another crisis which would reveal in all sectors of society an overwhelming sense of caution, an inability to adapt, which together with increasingly bitter social and political relations, owed much to the experience of war. Whatever else had changed, French society remained profoundly inegalitarian. Information on inheritance suggests that half the wealth passed on from one generation to the next belonged to only 1 per cent of the deceased. It remained the case that in a society made up of roughly 14 million peasants, 13 million workers and 14 million members of the even more disparate middle classes, only the *grande bourgeoisie*, a fraction of the bourgeoisie as a whole, enjoyed real power. Birth, culture and ultimately wealth determined access to education; the great divider. The need for professional and cultural qualifications, together with correctness in dress and manners, comfortable accommodation and the ability to entertain and mix socially continued severely to restrict entry to important decision-making positions in government, administration and private enterprise. These attributes combined to protect position and to distance the less fortunate. The small number of upwardly mobile people succeeded because of ability, luck and a willingness to conform. The real threat to established order came, on the one hand from structural change in the economy, and on the other from the activities of political 'renegades', the largely middle and lower middle-class politicians on the left, who from a genuine commitment to a more egalitarian society or else as a means of enjoying electoral success were prepared to propose reforms which might destabilise the social system. Established élites could however at least count on the conservative instincts of most of those, whether peasants, shopkeepers, clerks or business and professional men, who prided themselves on the possession of property, however small, or of professional qualifications; of those who were determined to 'improve themselves' either directly or vicariously through their children, and who in various ways emulated their 'betters' and sought to distinguish themselves from the propertyless and uneducated. Thus, many of the skilled and better rewarded workers dreamt less of revolution than social promotion. They were encouraged by a mass circulation press and radio network which claimed to be non-partisan whilst diffusing an essentially conservative ideology.

The war had encouraged a rallying to nationalistic values and the 1919 elections brought overwhelming conservative success. Their advantage was reinforced by a new electoral system which benefited those parties capable of organising alliances. This had disastrous consequences for the left. The Socialist Party, isolated by its break with the *union sacrée* in 1917, and divided internally over its response to the Bolshevik revolution, rejected any sort of compromise with the 'bourgeois' parties. This forced the Radicals to negotiate agreements with conservatives and to form part of a *Bloc national*, whose most notable figures, Clemenceau and Millerand, stressed the need to continue the wartime *union*. In effect part of the political centre, which in 1914 had allied with the left, had now moved to the right. The creation of the *Bloc* signified both a greater willingness on the part of conservatives to accept the republican regime and the belief of many Radicals that the real threat to the established order came now from the left. Their rapprochment was symbolised by the emergence of an acceptable *modus vivendi* between Church and state. Although the Socialists' share of the vote rose from 17 to 21 per cent, under the new electoral system the number of seats they gained fell from 102 to 68. Furthermore many of those Radicals who had rejected an electoral alliance with the right were defeated. As a result the parties of the centre-right gained 450 of the 616 seats in parliament.

The outcome was the formation of a government led by Millerand, and from 1922 by Poincaré. Clemenceau had become impossible because of the accumulated hostility aroused by his anticlericalism, insistence on the need for continued austerity and increased taxes, and desire to establish a strong interventionist presidency. The government's aggressive foreign policy was marked by efforts to secure reparations and encourage separatist movements in the Rhineland. It culminated, in 1923, in the occupation of the Ruhr, a decision which alarmed public opinion to such a degree as to stimulate a move to the left which resulted in the electoral victory of the centre-left alliance, the *Cartel des gauches*. The campaign again revealed wide divisions amongst the Radicals, that is the fundamental instability of the key group in the political centre upon whose support governments depended for survival. But if they continued to differ on questions of social reform they could at least generally agree in 1924 on the need to work for a perpetual peace through collective security and the League of Nations, an approach which would come to be associated with Briand and which led in 1925 to the Locarno Pact by which Germany recognised, and the British and Italians guaranteed, the eastern frontiers of France. This was reinforced by the negotiation of defensive treaties between France and her Czech and Polish allies. Government by the centre-left was however only an interlude in a long period of conservative domination which lasted until 1932, and which was to be

Plate 39 The widespread fear caused by major strikes, in the aftermath of the Bolshevik Revolution, allowed conservatives to develop the theme of the man with a knife between his teeth during the November 1919 electoral campaign

dominated until 1929 by Poincaré and by his determination to ensure military security whilst at the same time eliminating inflation, balancing the budget and limiting the burden of taxation. These policies were combined with a visceral anti-socialism and a determination to associate it with the terrible menace of Bolshevism.

The formation of the *Union nationale* government in 1926, presided over first by Poincaré and then, after illness forced his resignation, by Tardieu and Laval brought, in 1928, the final acceptance of a law requiring compulsory protection against sickness. This had first been introduced in 1921, when, following the war it had represented a widespread sense of social obligation. Subsequent insistence on financing the measure through assurance revealed continuing middle-class opposition to any hint of social reform financed through taxation. Egoism was concealed by an appeal to the defence of 'moral order' and warnings about welfare dependency. The success of this approach was made all the more likely by the left's self-inflicted wounds. In the aftermath of the war membership of both the Socialist Party and the trades unions had initially increased, reflecting both a hatred of the regime which had involved the nation in a bloodbath and the belief in an imminent revolution. Since 1917 the socialists had been faced with the need to work out their attitudes towards Bolshevism. In the event the party split. At its Tours congress in December 1920, 67.3 per cent of delegates voted to adhere to the Communist International, ignoring Léon Blum's warnings about leftist extremism (*blanquisme à la sauce tartare*), and reducing the SFIO to 30,000 members. Their action was inspired by anti-war sentiment, by enthusiasm at the apparent success of the Soviets in establishing a new form of popular government and disillusionment with the repeated failure of the parliamentary approach to securing far-reaching social reform as well as with the evident 'careerism' of so many socialist deputies. The spread of disquiet at the brutality and demands for subservience made by the Soviet regime of foreign communists would encourage many of these errant comrades to return to the fold. This re-established the Socialist Party as the major proponent of social reform.

However the party would remain profoundly divided internally on tactics, between those favouring a rapprochement with the Communists, and a right wing closer to the Radicals. The impact of these divisions was increased when, following the failure of the general strike called in May 1920, the trades union federation, the *Confédération Générale du Travail*, also split, with a Communist minority forming a *CGT unitaire* in January 1922. Overall union membership collapsed from around two million in 1919 to 600,000 in 1921. As the left tore itself apart so electoral support declined, with Socialist candidates obtaining about one-fifth of votes cast in elections in the 1920s and the Communists one-tenth. The latter succeeded in establishing a well-organised movement with its bastions in the grim industrial suburbs of Paris and parts of the Cher and central France amongst workers who, if they largely enjoyed rising real incomes in the 1920s, continued to endure often appalling housing conditions and the rigorous and insensitive imposition of discipline in their work places. Nevertheless membership of the party declined from 110,000 in 1921 to only 30,000 ten years later. Its own internal unity was achieved at the cost of isolation from the rest of the political nation. It pursued a policy of class-based opposition not only towards the 'bourgeois' parties but particularly its main competitor for working-class votes, the Socialists, repeatedly described as 'social traitors'. The Socialists themselves, whilst not repudiating revolutionary ideals and language, and refusing to participate in government, meanwhile pursued an essentially reformist policy which involved electoral pacts with a Radical Party unwilling to contemplate substantial measures of economic and social reform. This tactical flexibility at least allowed it to benefit from the decline of support for the Communists in the towns and for the Radicals in the countryside.

For contemporaries the most threatening problems seemed to be posed by inflation and the inability of successive ministries to balance their budgets. The former was due primarily to the massive increase in government borrowing and in the volume of money in circulation (from 6000 million francs in 1914 to 37,900 million by December 1920) as a result of war and reconstruction. For almost eight years after the war internal prices had risen sharply whilst governments had repeatedly failed to come to an understanding of, much less to solve, the problem. This had furthermore resulted in a collapse in the value of the franc. The currency lost half its real value during the war and the decline sharply accelerated following the withdrawal of British and American support in March 1919. The growing lack of confidence only encouraged speculation and the flight of capital abroad. The failure of the French occupation of the Ruhr in 1923 to secure the payment of reparations added to the gloom. Between 1922 and 1926 prices again doubled. The international devaluation was even more marked with the pound sterling worth 25 francs in 1914 rising to 243 by July 1926. In this situation the real losers were the large numbers of rentiers, in a country still lacking a general system of old age pensions. The fixed income bonds they had traditionally favoured had, by 1926, lost five-sixths of their pre-war value. Otherwise the immediate effect of inflation and the consequent easing of the debt burden, together with

Plate 40 More conservative electoral propaganda. Blaming the Cartel des Gauches government for budget deficits and inflation. Poster by Jack

the stimulus afforded by devaluation to external trade, was to promote prosperity. Most social groups seem to have enjoyed rising real incomes, in the case of workers for example by somewhere between 9 and 26 per cent, but this did little to diminish the general air of pessimism caused by the constant rise in prices. The German hyperinflation of 1923 seemed to lend credibility to the most nightmarish visions.

Only with the formation of the Poincaré government in July 1926 did financial stabilisation occur. Its conservative composition and the support it enjoyed from the self-proclaimed *Union nationale* made up of Radicals and right wing deputies alone helped to reassure orthodox financial opinion which had had little confidence in the previous *Cartel des gauches* administrations led by Herriot. A combination of cosmetic and real measures followed, including tax increases, higher interest rates and reductions in government expenditure, together with, in June 1928, a partial return to the gold standard but with the franc at onefifth of its pre-war value, realistic enough to avoid the loss of competitiveness in international markets which had resulted from the overvaluation of the British currency in 1925. Success would however be short-lived. October 1929 and the Wall Street crash saw the onset of the most serious crisis ever to hit the capitalist world. The 1930s would bring a severe depression which would shatter many illusions about both the nation's internal stability and great power status.

The crisis was to effect France later than the other industrialised nations. The year 1930 was thus a prosperous one. Poincaré's stabilisation, that is devaluation, made French goods competitive on international markets, at least until the British devaluation in September 1931. The relative backwardness of the economy and the limits to its integration into world markets delayed the impact of the crisis. Furthermore, when it came, in terms of bankruptcies, falling production and unemployment, the crisis did not appear to be as severe in France as elsewhere. It was however to be more prolonged. The decade was to be one of perpetual crisis. Even in 1938 levels of industrial production were little higher than they had been in 1913. For this reason it might be said that France was the most seriously affected amongst the leading economic powers. Gross prices fell 46 per cent between 1929 and the cyclical low in spring 1935, whilst share values declined by 60 per cent. Industrial production was reduced by around a quarter, with such key sectors of heavy industry as steel-making experiencing a 40 per cent decline whilst consumer goods industries, with the notable exception of textiles, suffered far less. Falling prices were an obvious disincentive to investment. The unwillingness of manufacturers to replace old machinery reduced productivity and caused a 37 per cent decline in production of industrial equipment. Certainly in terms of unemployment, France suffered far less than Britain, Germany and the USA. Even if it is accepted that the official figure of registered unemployed needed to be doubled and that real unemployment was around one million concentrated especially in the Paris region, this constituted only about 2.6 per cent of the population compared with maxima of 7.6, 9.4 and 12.75 per cent respectively in the three leading industrial nations. These statistics all of course conceal withdrawals from the labour force especially by older workers and women, the repatriation of immigrants, and substantial underemployment due to reductions in working hours. Nevertheless many French commentators prided themselves on the more balanced character of the national economy, which retained so much of the population on the land. Yet agriculture too was experiencing its crisis, marked by falling prices, due essentially to the over-supply of both domestic and international markets. The price of vegetable products fell by 34 per cent between 1930 and 1935, and that of meat by 40 per cent. Landowners' rental income, farmers' profits and labourers' wages all experienced substantial decline.

Poincaré's stabilisation was thus to be a brief interlude in a lengthy period of disequilibrium. Once again budgetary deficits, now caused by falling tax receipts, led to depreciation of the currency on international markets but most political leaders, with such notable exceptions as the Socialist Blum and the conservative Reynaud, were to bitterly oppose planned currency devaluations of the kind used by Britain in 1931 and America in 1933 in order to stimulate trade. The passionate strength of opposition to devaluation as a 'swindle' which threatened the value of savings meant that it was an option politicians proposed at their peril. There was much more political mileage in denouncing it in the most apocalyptical terms possible. When, in 1934, Reynaud spoke in favour of devaluation, *Action Française*, the organ of the extreme right, with its habitual delicate turn of phrase, denounced him as 'vermin' with the 'mind and morals of a termite' and called for his imprisonment. As a result of this determination to preserve the international value, status and purchasing power of the currency and to avoid a return to the inflation of the 1920s, French products became increasingly uncompetitive in world markets. The country's share in an anyway sharply reduced volume of international trade in manufactured goods fell from 11.2 per cent in 1929 to 5.8 per cent by 1937. Efforts to stimulate trade within the protected markets of the Empire enjoyed some success, accounting for 25–30 per cent of exports by 1936–38, but could not adequately compensate for the loss of markets in the major industrial countries or prevent a growing reliance on imports of both foodstuffs and oil.

Enterprises dependant on export markets were the first to be affected by the crisis as economic activity declined in other countries. Their recovery was to be postponed by this unwillingness of successive governments to engage in processes of competitive international devaluation. Between 1929 and 1935 exports fell by 44 per cent in volume and a staggering 82 per cent in value. Internal demand was affected by falling agricultural prices, aggravated by excellent domestic harvests in 1932 and 1935. Declining sales and falling profits were an evident disincentive to industrial investment. A viscious downward cycle had thus been created with falling revenues and wages further reducing demand. Politicians, and economists, and not just in France, felt helpless, simply reacting to problems as they occurred. Although renewed budgetary deficits were a consequence rather than a cause of the depression, governments continued to be obsessed with the need to achieve balance and engaged in deflationary policies which further reduced demand.

Levels of personal consumption remained surprisingly high. This was largely because the nominal fall in national income of around one-third between 1929 and the depths of the crisis in 1935 was partly compensated for by a 20 per cent decline in retail prices. It could not however prevent the development of an intense sense of insecurity. Moreover the impact of the crisis obviously varied between social groups. Most adversely affected were the mass of small-scale peasant farmers, as real incomes from agriculture fell by 32 per cent. Many industrial workers enjoyed an increase in real incomes, although they were more aware of declining wage rates and the threat of un-employment. Business profits fell by around 18 per cent affecting most notably the mass of small manufacturers and shopkeepers, whilst the real incomes of landlords and rentiers with fixed incomes tended to rise. In general the wealthy retained their privileged position but in a society characterised by growing social and political tension.

A constant feature of the decade was governmental weakness. The multiplicity of parties and weak party discipline ensured that govern-ments were at the mercy of shifting parliamentary coalitions and that ministers spent most of their time trying to manipulate deputies. There were to be forty-two governments in the inter-war period, averaging only six months in power each and clearly unable to take a long-term perspective. The electoral system gave disproportionate power to the rural and small town electorate generally opposed to social reform which they perceived as most likely to benefit the urban worker, and to the taxation necessary to fund such measures. They tended to favour such parties as the Radicals, which although posing as a party of the left was unalterably conservative on economic and social questions, and whose deputies if they did not always lead, played a crucial role in the formation of every government. Parliamentary deputies in general, drawn overwhelmingly from the liberal professions, made considerable efforts to secure their constituencies by concentrating on local issues and seeking favours from ministers for their constituents. Governmental instability was certainly partly offset by bureaucratic stability, but the effect of this was to ensure a dominant role in policy formulation for senior officials drawn from the upper classes and inhibited by caution and respect for routine. This was a system of government peculiarly unsuited to coping with major crises and unable to contemplate, much less accept, the proposals for planning and a mixed economy coming from apolitical or even conservative technocrats like Detoeil, president of the electrical engineering company Thomson, or economists like Sauvy, inspired by a mixture of moral and scientific ideas, as well as from reformist trades unionists like Jouhaux, secretary-general of the CGT. Such ideas were rejected by a right committed to the free market and a left which conceived of the state as simply the agent of oppression. As a result the 1930s would see a growing loss of confidence in the regime.

The incoherence of government policy can be seen in the case of agriculture, where the problem was essentially over-production. Initially tariff protection was increased. The response to the good harvests of 1932 and 1933 was simply to falsify the statistics to avoid alarming the market. Prices nevertheless continued to fall and by June 1933 wheat, at 85 francs a quintal was half its 1929 price. The next step, in July 1933, was to impose a minimum price of 115 francs, but with insufficient funds and facilities available to allow the stocking of surpluses this short-lived policy only encouraged the development of an unofficial market on which wheat could be purchased at 60–70 francs. An effort was also made to reduce the supply of wine by means of restrictions on planting and an obligatory reduction in acreage but with little effect on prices. In other sectors of the economy, too, policies which ran counter to the supposedly overriding deflationary objectives of government policy were introduced, including measures to protect small shopkeepers against competition from chain stores. In the case of the trade deficit, rather than take measures to stimulate exports, that is act against the causes, governments sought to limit the effects by reinforcing protectionism from the summer of 1931. The sense of insecurity was so great that even habitual free-traders, including the representatives of the woollen and silk industries, were attracted by the prospect of autarky.

In May 1932 the electorate turned towards the left for a solution and the result was its greatest success since before the war with the return of 334 deputies including 157 Radicals and 129 Socialists, compared with 230 on the right. In spite of their rhetoric however the Radicals remained bitterly opposed to changes in taxation which might adversely effect their small business and peasant constituency. Radical ministers led by Herriot, committed to financial orthodoxy and to restoring business confidence, were as concerned as more obvious conservatives with the need to reduce government expenditure in order to balance the budget. This, their Socialist parliamentary allies could not support. Successive ministerial combinations failed to secure agreement. As the economic crisis deepened, ministers appeared helpless. The weak-willed resignation of a government led by Daladier following serious rioting in Paris on 6 February 1934 allowed the accession to power of a government of *Union nationale* which included Radicals but was conservative dominated and led successively by Doumergue, Flandrin and then Laval. This was even more obsessed than its predecessors with the need to prevent inflation through tough deflationary measures. It was vested by parliament with 'exceptional powers to ensure the defence of the franc and the struggle against speculation'. Its basic policy was to restore the competitiveness of French producers by reducing their prices. In seeking to achieve this it brutally cut civil service salaries by 10 per cent, reduced the interest payable on government debt, and with much greater originality decreed reductions in rents, and the prices of bread, coal and electricity. Between 1932 and 1935 there were to be eleven governments and fourteen plans for economic recovery, all based upon a combination of deflationary and protectionist measures intended to secure the economic and social status quo. The value of the franc was to be defended at all costs. Unfortunately the measures taken had the effect of reinforcing economic stagnation. Senior civil servants, and the representatives of the Bank of France, still privately owned in spite of its central bank functions, and leading industrialists like the Peugeots, de Wendels or Schneiders, all members of a narrow social élite, combined to exert their influence in favour of continuity.

Change was made all the more difficult by political instability which reflected the fragmentary character of the political system, and particularly of the Radicals who occupied the crucial centre position, and the ease with which undisciplined deputies could abandon governments which had in some way incurred their displeasure. In this situation politicians were reluctant to propose the substantial economic and social reforms, which in retrospect at least, the crisis would seem to have demanded. Nor were they willing to contemplate reforming the political system through a move towards presidentialism as a means of strengthening the executive vis-à-vis parliament. At most they might accept the need, as during the 1935 financial crisis, to grant temporary decree powers, in this case to a government led by Laval. To add to their difficulties governments were also faced with an alarming deterioration in the international situation. At Lausanne in July 1932 the great powers had recognised both Germany's inability to continue to pay reparations and her right to re-arm. In January 1933 Hitler became German chancellor and in October withdrew from the Geneva disarmament conference. By June 1934, as French military expenditure reached an all-time low, the government began to feel the need to increase arms procurement.

Amongst the middle classes, and especially the more wealthy and influential, this continuing air of crisis, fear of the loss of income and status, together with the sense of growing weakness in the international sphere, resulted in an alarming loss of confidence and the conviction that democracy had failed. Strong authoritarian government appeared to many to be the answer to the nation's problems. Once again the call for 'moral order' came from the right, uniting nationalism, clericalism, economic liberalism and anti-Bolshevism. Anti-parliamentary feeling was re-kindled by every electoral success the left enjoyed. The élite, those with economic power and substantial influence over governments, the civil service and the media, found it hard to accept that political power might be held by people whose objectives conflicted with their own. This sort of outlook had led in 1924 to the formation of the *Jeunesses patriotes* by Pierre Taittinger, organised on a military basis, uniformed and committed to street action. The analogy with fascism can easily be overdrawn but should not be ignored particularly in terms of organisation, objectives and forms of action. Such leagues were to attract growing support during the following decade. The most notable was to be the *Croix de Feu* initially an old soldiers' organisation

Plate 41 Members of the *Croix de Feu* parade in front of their leader, Lieutenant-Colonel de La Rocque. Founded in 1927 as an ex-soldiers organisation, from 1933 it recruited more widely and developed para-military structures

but which developed a much broader appeal to the middle classes and at its peak had 150,000 members. It was characterised by a fervent anti-communism and anti-socialism, with leanings to traditional Catholic conservatism and support for the established social hierarchy rather than the ideals of fascism. These leagues were the heirs of the extreme nationalistic organisations of the 1880s and like them were committed to the establishment of authoritarian government to replace the decadent, corrupt and ineffective republic. They were supported by influential personalities, including the surviving Marshals of France, and amply provided with funds by the employers' organisations and leading businessmen like the perfume manufacturer Coty and the industrialists Mercier and de Wendel, one of whose objectives in the early 1930s seems to have been to create a *Pétain mystique*. Of course not all ex-soldiers were attracted by the right. Many subscribed to the pacifism more typical of the left. There was nevertheless a widespread and visceral hatred of politicians and a desire for some kind of a re-

Plate 42 Members of extreme right-wing organisations clash
with police protecting the approaches to the Chamber of Deputies
in the Place de la Concorde, 6 February 1934. Around 15 were
killed and over 2000 injured.

birth of the *union sacrée*. However the sense of disenchantment with
the regime was never to be as intense in France as in Germany. The
economic depression was less severe, and the country had not suffered
a demoralising military defeat.

There were certainly moments of intense crisis. Early in 1934
the Stavisky affair, in which the fraudulent financial activity of a
naturalised Ukrainian Jew appeared to involve leading political figures,
provided an excuse for a campaign by the extreme right which
combined all its habitual themes, xenophobia, anti-semitism and anti-
parliamentarianism and hatred of the Republic. On 7 January *Action
française* inaugurated a series of demonstrations which was to
culminate on 6 February in a gathering of the various right-wing
leagues (*ligues*) in Paris. On that occasion when groups in the crowd
attempted to break through the police cordon protecting the approaches to the Chamber of Deputies a struggle developed in which 15
were killed and over 2,000 injured. The Radical prime minister,

Daladier, deserted by the leaders of his own party, subsequently resigned, creating a dangerous precedent in giving way to pressure from the streets. His replacement, Doumergue, was brought out of retirement to restore order and additionally to reform the political system. Instead however of pressing for the strengthening of executive authority in the immediate aftermath of 6 February, when such proposals would have gained widespread support, Doumergue allowed himself to be deflected by squabbles between the Radical and conservative members of his administration. The latter included most notably Tardieu, who as a member of previous governments actually appears to have channelled funds to the *ligues*. The senate too with its habitual irresponsibility made known its opposition to proposals which would have had the effect of reducing its ability to bring down governments. In the slightly longer term the most important consequence of 6 February was to be the formation of the *Front populaire*, as those parties most committed to the democratic republic, or frightened by what they saw as an attempted fascist coup, rallied to its defence.

There were of course major obstacles to the formation of a broad alliance of the left. The Communists, committed to class conflict and convinced that the depression was the last great crisis of the capitalist system, were particularly hostile to the Socialist 'traitors' who sought, through reformism, to divert the working class from its true goal. The Socialists in their turn would be extremely suspicious of proposals to cooperate in a *front unique*. In the past efforts to collaborate had always ended in a rancorous atmosphere of mutual recrimination. Moreover the Radicals and Communists were poles apart. In the immediate aftermath of 6 February, and with Radicals in the Doumergue government, these groups continued to hurl abuse at each other. Only at the end of June did the Communist leader Thorez, on instructions from a Moscow increasingly alarmed by the growing fascist threat, open the way for the formation of the Popular Front by calling for united action by all democrats. This was the means by which his party could escape from the isolation and ineffectiveness which had resulted from its class-war tactics. Together with a super-patriotic Jacobin dedication to national defence, which lasted until the signature of the Nazi–Soviet Pact in August 1939, it helped attract mass support. In the meantime, in July, an agreement was negotiated with the Socialists for mutual support in the struggle against fascism, war, and the deflationary policies of the Doumergue government. This was followed, much to the surprise of the Socialists and to the discomfort of the Radicals, by a call for an alliance between the working and middle classes. With unity against the international menace of fascism as the essential objective, the Communists were determined not to frighten the Radicals and were prepared to tone down their distinctive revolutionary programme.

The decision by the Radicals to enter a popular front depended on the outcome of an internal struggle between the supporters of Herriot, an opponent of cooperation, and the so-called 'Young Turks' of the party including Zay, Kayser, Cot and Mendès-France, supported by Daladier and strengthened by growing disenchantment with the existing alliance with the parties of the right. Agreement to cooperate was finally reached in June 1935 and on 14 July the three parties of the left symbolically joined together in a mass demonstration in Paris and furthermore established a committee to organise collaboration for the April–May 1936 electoral campaign. The main obstacles to agreement appear to have been the formulation of an economic policy dealing with the means of financing social reforms, the scale of nationalisation and the question of devaluation. The moderation of the compromise which emerged made it obvious that the essential objective of the Popular Front was to be the defence of republican institutions. It was profoundly disappointing for all those who had seen the unity of the left as opening the way for fundamental economic and social change, but little more could really have been expected when the parties to the agreement were so suspicious of each other.

The electoral campaign opened in April 1936 and was notable for the use made by party spokesmen of the radio to increase public awareness of the issues. It was to be full of contradictions. For the first ballot each of the parties belonging to the Popular Front retained its own candidates and programme, much of which was in flagrant dis-agreement with aspects of the joint programme the parties had agreed to present for the second ballot. Thus the Socialists offered substantial nationalisation and abolition of the senate, both of which were anathema to most Radicals. Internally the party was divided over both tactics, where as always there was a glaring contradiction between the party's revolutionary rhetoric and reformist proposals, and on such fundamental questions as whether it should drop its policy of non-participation in coalition governments if the alliance succeeded at the polls. The Communists whilst recognising the strength of the rank-and-file working-class desire for unity when in March they agreed to a merger between the two rival trades unions federations, otherwise gave absolute priority to the unity of the anti-fascist movement, for which it was essential to attract middle-class support. They had the advantage of offering the only reasonably coherent explanation of the economic crisis and could point to the Soviet experiment in planned growth as an apparent solution to the world's ills. The mutually agreed programme of the left included proposals to protect republican institutions such as the suppression of the *ligues* and the defence of lay education and of trades union rights. It attacked the deflationary policies previously pursued and presented measures designed to reduce unemployment and to improve the quality of working-class life including a public works programme, higher unemployment relief payments, and a reduction in the length of the working day. Together with tax reforms these policies would help restore purchasing power and stimulate economic recovery. It was also proposed to assist the rural population by means of official intervention in agricultural markets to secure higher price levels. The foreign policy of a Popular Front government would seek to promote disarmament and collective security through the League of Nations.

In sum this was a programme inspired by the American New Deal rather than by socialism. The only nationalisations proposed, those of the armaments industry and the Bank of France, were inspired by the desire to curb the power and influence of key conservative pressure groups. It was a moderate programme which offered genuine social reform whilst seeking to re-assure the small property-owning supporters of the Radical Party. Even so any hint of measures designed to reduce the power of conservative élites was found to create a storm of protest, and to stimulate a political mobilisation inspired by arrogance and anxiety. The employment by conservatives of 'the politics of fear' (Jackson) combined the themes found in the manifesto of a Parisian candidate of the *Fédération républicaine*:

> If the Popular Front is victorious;
> There will be a flight of capital;
> There will be a devaluation leading to total bankruptcy;

Plate 43 Léon Blum with members of his new Popular Front government outside the Elysée Palace in 1936

There will be anarchy;
There will be war;
For behind the Popular Front lurks the shadow of Moscow.

The election results were initially disappointing for the left. On the first ballot the Popular Front parties attracted 5,420,000 votes, only 300,000 more than they had obtained in 1932. The decisive factor was to be the disciplined way in which these voters rallied to the single candidate most likely to succeed in the second ballot on 3 May. This had the effect of giving the Front a clear majority of 376 seats to 222 for the parties of the right. In addition to solid working-class support the left had also gained voters amongst the lower middle classes, and especially in the south, the rural population. Although a clear swing of the electorate to the left had substantially increased the representation of both the Communists and Socialists in the Chamber, from 10 to 72 and 97 to 146 respectively, this had occurred partly at the expense of their Radical partners (reduced from 159 to 116). The survival of Popular Front governments would nevertheless depend on this nervous Radical rump.

On 4 May Léon Blum, as leader of the largest single party laid claim to leadership of a Popular Front government to be composed essentially of Socialists and Radicals, with the Communists deciding to remain outside the government on the pretext that their participation might cause panic. They committed themselves instead to loyal support and as the most radical element in the alliance enjoyed a ten-fold expansion in membership to 300,000 in 1937. In contrast Blum's basic assumption was that in the absence of a Socialist parliamentary majority he lacked a mandate to introduce fundamental social reforms. This, together with the realities of an alliance with the Radicals, allowed for only limited reformist measures. The Popular Front's electoral success and the formation of a government by Blum on 4 June 1936 had however created a widespread sense of expectancy, evident especially in an unprecedented wave of strikes and factory occupations involving around two million workers. The movement was essentially spon-taneous and localised. These were euphoric outbursts by workers for whom suddenly everything seemed possible. They were assertions of the dignity of labour, protests against harsh labour discipline and a demand for better working and living conditions and enhanced security.

Compared with the hopes and fears the government had inspired, the measures actually introduced in the summer of 1936 were moderate indeed. Initially they were dictated by circumstances and especially by the need to bring the strikes to an end. On the night of 7–8 June representatives of the employers and of the CGT met and signed the Matignon agreement. Both sides were frightened by their inability to control the workers' movements. They agreed on wage increases of 7 to 15 per cent, partly as a means of increasing purchasing power and stimulating economic recovery, and on recognition of trades unions' negotiating rights. These measures were to be supplemented by legislation providing, for the first time, for the right to two weeks paid holiday a year and for a forty-hour week, intended both to improve the quality of working-class life and to contribute to the reduction of unemployment. To extend the benefits of the new regime to the rural population an official marketing agency (the *Office interprofessionel du blé*) was to be created as a mechanism to stabilise and raise cereal prices. Less effective measures were taken to ensure that the Bank of France placed the national interest before those of its shareholders, whilst nationalisation of the armaments factories only added to the state of disorganisation in which they existed under private control. Blum had succeeded in provoking feelings of intense anxiety within the ranks of industrialists and financiers without increasing the government's ability to effectively control their activities.

The, probably inevitable, result was to disappoint many of the Communist and Socialist supporters of the Popular Front who condemned what they saw as Blum's excessive legalism. At the same time Radicals were disturbed by what had already been achieved. To operate within a basically liberal economic framework, and yet to introduce measures which threatened business confidence was to court disaster. In the absence of exchange controls, unacceptable to the Radicals, there was a massive outflow of capital abroad. Employers' efforts to minimise the impact of the Matignon agreements led to heightened social tension whilst the measures themselves significantly increased costs, reducing international competitiveness and provoking internal inflation. By September the devaluation of the franc (by 30 per cent) which the government had promised to avoid had become unavoidable. In the event it did little to increase the competitiveness of French firms suffering as they were from sustained under-investment. In an effort to restore business confidence and to reduce the strains with his Radical allies Blum, in January 1937, announced a 'pause' in the government's programme of social reform. This would do little to head off the growing conservative back-lash. Further tensions within the alliance were to be caused by the decision to commit substantial resources to re-armament in response to German re-militarisation of the Rhineland and over the question of whether to support the embattled Spanish Republic. When Blum asked for emergency powers to deal with the continued deterioration in the financial situation these were voted by the Chamber of Deputies but rejected by the senate. Blum resigned on 20 June 1937.

From then until the autumn of 1938 the Popular Front underwent a process of gradual disintegration as relationships between its constituent parts deteriorated. Initially as its parliamentary majority had survived the departure of Blum, the President of the Republic felt obliged to call upon the Radical Chautemps to form a government which until their final withdrawal in January 1938 would include Blum and other Socialists. Unable either to reverse or proceed with reforms,

Chautemps did little more than preside helplessly over new strike waves, a worsening in the balance of payments, and the growth of budget deficits due to the combined effect of increased military expenditure and falling tax receipts. Nationalisation of the railway companies to create the SNCF was simply a means of rescuing them from bankruptcy and on terms extremely favourable to their share-holders. In March, Hitler annexed Austria, as French politicians grappled with the internal political crisis caused by the Socialists' unwillingness to support Chautemps' request for decree powers to deal with the country's financial problems, and his subsequent resignation.

The rules of the parliamentary game required the Socialists to attempt to form an administration. Blum called for a government of national unity to prepare for a war which was beginning to seem inevitable. This was immediately rejected by conservatives determined to finally finish with the Popular Front. The second Popular Front government formed by Blum was doomed from birth and its leaders' proposals to introduce exchange controls and a capital tax only hastened its demise. President Lebrun called on the Radical leader Daladier to form a government in which the Socialists were unrepre-sented, although in the hope of keeping the anti-fascist front alive the parties of the left combined to pass a vote of confidence in the new ministry. Dissension over the Munich agreement, bitterly condemned by the Communists, would finally bring a formal end to an already insubstantial Popular Front.

Daladier's term of office was to be dominated by the deteriorating international situation, and by efforts to restore internal order. He relied upon liberal economic mechanisms to promote economic recovery. Determined action was however taken against strikers both by the police and employers anxious to root out 'trouble-makers'. It soon became clear that this was a government which depended on parliamentary support from the right, and that its strongest card was its much-trumpeted anti-communism. The newspaper *L'Ere nouvelle* could emphasise with delight on 1 November 1938 that 'the revolution of June '36 is well and truly over'. The language used is indicative of the degree to which the Popular Front had both reflected and above all stimulated a process of political polarisation. The hopes aroused on the left and amongst workers had created an apocalyptical vision of revolutionary anarchy on the right and amongst the property-owning classes, feeding on a resentment of a government whose policies seemed to favour the workers at the expense of the middle class. Parallels were drawn between Blum and Kerensky, their actions preparing the way for Bolshevism. The Popular Front was denounced as both a Jewish and a Communist plot. A group of extremist army officers organised as the *Comité secret d'action révolutionnaire* but better known as the *Cagoule* even planned a coup d'état. Although this was uncovered by the police in November 1937 it is significant that such military eminences as the retired marshals Pétain and Franchet d'Esperey, aware of what was happening, did not see it as their duty to report matters to the authorities. Another feature of this movement of resistance to communism was the creation of new parties of the extreme right. The *Croix de feu*, banned along with the other *ligues* in June 1936, transformed itself into the *Parti social français* and attracted 6–800,000 members with its demands for strong, authoritarian government. More clearly fascist in character was the *Parti populaire français*, with briefly some 200,000 members, created by the former communist Jacques Doriot. The political atmosphere was poisoned by a wave of verbal and occasionally physical violence, with even mainstream politicians like Tardieu or Laval echoing the sentiments of the extreme right.

It was against this background of bitter internal disunity that the Daladier government sought to cope with the crises caused by continuing economic depression, and by a deteriorating international situation. Industrial production continued to fall in the early months of 1938. In the aftermath of Munich however, and in the interests of national defence, numerous exceptions to the forty-hour law were allowed and compulsory overtime introduced. Moreover the senate was prepared to grant to Daladier the emergency powers it had refused to Blum. In supporting employers against strikers the government participated in their counter-attack against workers who had briefly challenged their exclusive right to manage their enterprises. This, together with the stimulus afforded by re-armament, undoubtedly contributed to the restoration of business confidence and to the beginnings of economic recovery evident from the autumn of 1938.

In September the British and French prime ministers, Chamberlain and Daladier, had abandoned Czechoslovakia to its fate, as the price, they hoped, of securing peace. On their return from humiliation at

Munich they had been greeted as heroes by the vast majority of their fellow citizens. Léon Blum himself undoubtedly expressed a widespread sense of confusion when he wrote: 'War has probably been averted. But in conditions such that I, who have never ceased to fight for peace ... can feel no joy ... and am torn between cowardly relief and shame'. There was a desperate desire not to repeat the slaughter of 1914. Conservatives, in France, traumatised by 1936, were also afraid that another war might provoke another revolution and many of them furthermore saw Nazi Germany as a welcome barrier to the bolshevisation of Europe. The German occupation of the rump of Czechoslovakia in March 1939 resulted in a major shift in public opinion. The long line of concessions to Hitler, beginning with acceptance of German re-armament in 1935, had only encouraged further demands. A new strategy seemed essential. It was agreed to guarantee the territorial integrity of Poland as a means of discouraging further German expansion which might well lead to war. British suspicion of the Russians however prevented the creation of an alliance which alone might have made the guarantee militarily effective. Tired of Western procrastination, and suspicious of their motives, Stalin signed an agreement with the Germans on 23 August 1939 which sealed the fate of Poland.

THE SECOND WORLD WAR

When war came on 3 September, following the German invasion of Poland, there were few signs of enthusiasm. Memories of the carnage of 1914 were only too fresh. Conservatives in particular resigned themselves to a conflict which threatened, by weakening Britain, France and Germany, to serve the interests of the Soviet Union. Their concern was intensified when the French Communist Party, belatedly receiving new instructions from Moscow, turned on 20 September from being the most active supporter of the anti-fascist cause into an outright opponent of a war which it was now claimed was the outcome of imperialist rivalry and of no concern to the working classes. The Party was proscribed for its pains and its parliamentary representatives imprisoned. The declaration of war was followed by a lengthy period of relative inaction, the 'phony war', on the western front. Solidly entrenched behind the fortifications of the Maginot Line, the French, with their British allies, remained on the defensive while the Poles, in whose interests they had supposedly gone to war, were crushed. They appear to have avoided offensive action which might, irrevocably, have committed them to war.

The apparent absence of danger only encouraged internal political dissent, in marked contrast to the *union sacrée* of 1914. On 19 March 1940, Daladier was forced to resign by a parliamentary vote of no confidence. He was blamed for the lack of military action, and by the right for the failure to rush to the defence of Finland against the Red Army. This possibility had been actively considered by the allies and would of course have involved them in a war of almost inconceivable danger with both Nazi Germany and Soviet Russia. Reynaud, an apparently more dynamic figure, took Daladier's place. The former prime minister nevertheless continued to serve as Defence Minister in a cabinet enlarged to include the representatives of as many political opinions as possible. The French war effort was to be beset by personal rivalries between ministers and military leaders, and by the absence of clear objectives. Whilst the allies plotted peripheral operations against Soviet oil installations and Scandinavian iron ore supplies to Germany in order to deprive it of the means of waging war, they were taken by surprise by the German invasions of Denmark and Norway and then by the opening of the Wehrmacht's offensive in the west on 10 May 1940.

The French High Command was singularly ill-prepared to meet a German assault spear-headed by concentrations of aircraft and tanks. It was those senior officers, like Pétain, who had exercised considerable influence on military planning throughout the inter-war years who bore the heaviest responsibility for the defeat of 1940. The experience of the previous war had convinced them that modern weapons offered the advantage to the defence. They were subsequently to lay the blame for defeat on the politicians, who had in fact from 1934 onwards sanctioned large increases in expenditure on defence. The Maginot Line, to which substantial portions of the defence budget had been committed between 1930 and 1936 was designed to maximise the advantages of defending armies. It was not extended to cover the frontier with Belgium even after the Belgian decision to opt for neutrality in 1936, and little else was done to prepare defensive positions along either the route taken by the invading German armies in 1914 or in front of the hills and forests of the Belgian Ardennes assumed to be impenetrable to large masses of troops. In the event of a second German failure to respect Belgian neutrality it was assumed that the relatively light manning of the Maginot Line would allow the concentration of manpower for the defence of Belgium and Northern France. In practice the allied forces which advanced into Belgium to meet the invasion were outflanked by German divisions which passed through the Ardennes and broke the weakly held French line at Dinant and Sedan. The crisis which ensued showed up the deficiencies of the High Command. The successive commanders-in-chief, Gamelin and Weygand, and General Georges commanding the crucial north-eastern front, were old and tired, and out of touch with the realities of modern warfare. Nothing appeared to have been learned from the *blitzkrieg* which had so rapidly smashed the Polish army the previous September. The French air force was both ill-equipped, partly due to the inefficiency of the aircraft industry, and poorly led. British aircraft were present only in small numbers. There was little appreciation of the offensive potential of concentrations of tanks and the substantial numbers available were largely dispersed in support of the infantry. Attempts to halt the German advance by means of the piecemeal commitment of inadequate reserves were doomed to failure. In spite of serious deficiencies in the air it was indecision at the top, incoherent command structures, inappropriate tactics, and poor training rather than inferior numbers or material which led to rapid and total collapse and which lost the Battle of France.

In five weeks the Germans took 1,850,000 prisoners. Some 92,000 servicemen were killed, a figure which testifies to the intensity of fighting in some sectors, but which was low in comparison with the murderous battles of the previous war. The roads towards the south were blocked by hordes of miserable refugees, as perhaps 6–7 million people left their homes and tried to escape from the expanding war zone, inspired in part by bitter memories of a previous German occupation. Essential services collapsed as officials left their posts and joined in the exodus. The Government, in need of a haven offering greater security than Paris, moved first to Tours and then to Bordeaux. Reynaud in desperation sacked generals and reshuffled his cabinet. The inclusion of a virtually unknown protégé of his, one General de Gaulle, an expert on armoured warfare, as a junior defence minister, was of little immediate significance. Far more important was the inclusion of

Marshal Pétain as deputy prime minister. By 12 June the Marshal, supported by Weygand the new commander-in-chief, was demanding an armistice. Weygand appears to have been obsessed by the need to safeguard the honour of the army, and, as in 1871, to preserve it intact as the means of securing social order and preventing a communist take-over. With the peculiar arrogance of the soldier posing as the guardian of the nation's soul, he vigorously opposed Reynaud's proposal that the defeated army should capitulate to avoid further useless sacrifice. This would have left the government with 'freedom of action' and the option of continuing the war from the Empire. Even as the struggle continued, blame for its outcome was being apportioned. Pétain condemned the Popular Front as the symbol and cause of national decadence. There can be little real doubt however that the main reason for defeat was the generals' own incompetence.

On 16 June an exhausted and rather brow-beaten Reynaud resigned in favour of Pétain. On 17 June the Marshal announced his intention to seek an armistice. His decision undoubtedly reflected a widespread belief that there was no alternative. A fight to the last which would have devastated France could hardly be contemplated. In this ca-lamitous hour the old hero of Verdun, around whom a potent myth had been created, appeared to his compatriots as a potential saviour. His offer, made to France during the broadcast announcing the armistice request, of 'the gift of my person, to attenuate her suffering' was received with deep emotion and gratitude. Although the cease-fire was not to take effect until 25 June organised resistance effectively came to an end. The war appeared lost beyond all hope. It was generally assumed that if the mighty French army could not resist the Germans, then the British would also, and in the very near future, be forced to sue for peace. In this situation it was hardly surprising that the departure of an obscure general, de Gaulle the under-secretary at the War Office, from Bordeaux to London on 17 June and his establishment of a French National Committee pledged to act as 'the provisional guardian of the national patrimony' went almost unnoticed within France.

The armistice terms were harsh. They were alleviated only by the German concern to prevent continued French participation in the war. For this reason it was clearly in their interest that the French government should remain in France rather than seek refuge in Britain

Plate 44 Paul Reynaud leaving a cabinet meeting, 21 May 1940. Within weeks his companions Marshal Pétain, the deputy prime minister, and General Weygand the commander-in-chief, would be pressing for an armistice

Fig 14 The division of France in 1940

or the Empire. Furthermore the continued existence of a French administration and police would substantially reduce the demands made upon German manpower. The French army was to be reduced to 100,000 men, equipped only to safeguard internal order. That portion of the fleet in home ports was to be de-mobilised. A substantial part of France, the most densely populated and productive, was to be occupied and an enormous levy imposed to meet the costs of the occupiers. French prisoners of war were to remain in German hands, in effect as hostages, until the final conclusion of a peace treaty. The subordinate position of the French government was immediately made clear, when in August 1940, and in apparent contradiction of the armistice agreement, Alsace and Lorraine were once more annexed to the Reich

Plate 45 The (re)-Germanisation of Alsace: a Nazi parade in Strasbourg in October 1941. Young men became liable for conscription into the German armed forces

and subjected to conscription and an intense programme of Germanisation. In the years that followed, German demands were to become ever more exorbitant and to involve the systematic exploitation of the French economy. The return to 'normal' which so many had so desperately desired was not to occur. The obvious reason for this was that the war did not end. The British, unexpectedly, kept on fighting. The Germans, unable to win air superiority, failed to launch a cross-channel invasion and were eventually to turn east in search of *lebensraum*. In the short term the essential concern of the occupying power was to make use of French resources and maintain a secure base for military action. In the long term, and once final victory was secured, France was to become the market garden and playground of Europe. It seemed better to keep the French in ignorance of these intentions and to encourage them to bargain in an effort to improve their position within a German-dominated Europe.

By many French people, particularly, but not exclusively, those on the political right, the defeat was blamed on national decadence. It did however provide an historic opportunity for change. The man to whom the nation now looked for leadership, Marshal Pétain, was, like so many military men, attracted by the notion of strong, authoritarian government. He had nothing but contempt for politicians and parliamentary politics. His government established itself, from 1 July, in the cramped and unsuitable hotel rooms of the spa town of Vichy. It expected soon to return to Paris. Pétain had been charged by a demoralised National Assembly, by 569 votes to 80, to draft a new constitution and been granted in the meantime 'full executive and legislative powers … without restriction'. He and his advisors began to plan a 'national revolution'. The 'constitutional acts' promulgated in July concentrated in the person of the Marshal the powers of both president and prime minister, with the right to designate his own successor and, in the absence of an elected assembly, the ability to exercise legislative powers through a Council of Ministers made up of his own nominees. Pétain, immensely flattered by the popular adulation he was receiving, was determined to rule in spite of his advanced years – he was 84 in 1940. He would remain politically alert. This was to cause considerable frustration amongst his younger associates. As his deputy he selected Pierre Laval, the archetypal Third Republic political manipulator and four times prime minister. Laval had little time for high flown notions of national regeneration. He was a pragmatist determined to establish better relations with Germany whilst at the same time preserving as much as possible of French sovereignty. His ambition led to his dismissal in December 1940, but after April 1942 he was, with German support, to become the dominant figure in the Vichy regime, although there is no doubt that major policy decisions still required support from the Marshal.

Pétain's own outlook can be summed up by the formula 'Work, Family, Homeland' (*Travail, Famille, Patrie*) which replaced the familiar republican device *Liberté, Fraternité, Egalité*. His dream was to restore the virtues of hardwork, honesty, and respect for one's social superiors, which he imagined had existed in rural society. Rather than fascism, the dominant note in government statements was the traditionalism associated with right wing movements like *Action française*. In many respects it echoed the Moral Order regime of the 1870s, it too established after a humiliating defeat. Even such anti-German nationalists as General Weygand could support what he believed to be measures essential to national regeneration, whilst

Plate 46 Marshal Pétain and Pierre Laval at Vichy in November
1942 accompanied by Cardinals Suhard and Gerlier. As in the
1870s following a previous catastrophic defeat Church and state
sought to collaborate in the re-establishment of 'moral order'

condemning the sort of indiscipline typified by de Gaulle's defiance of
the legitimate French government. Out of a mass of confused and often
contradictory designs, the intentions of the more dedicated adherents
of the regime can be discerned. Above all there was a continuing
conservative desire for strong government as an answer to the threat of
social revolution of which the Popular Front had been only the most
recent manifestation. They wanted élite rule, the protection of private
property, social harmony and order. They were above all united in
their hostility to those they blamed for the national humiliation,
including teachers, Jews, freemasons and 'Bolsheviks'. In these
circumstances the proper instruction of the young was regarded as
being of particular importance. It provided a means of protecting social
order and hierarchy. The position of existing élites would be secured by
restricting the already limited entry to secondary education and by the
re-affirmation of its exclusive classical basis. Other social groups
would receive an instruction which did not excite unrealisable
ambitions. Teachers who wished to retain their positions were obliged
to preach the virtues of the regime. Parental responsibilities were also

emphasised and efforts made to reduce the number of women working outside the home and to glorify the roles of housewife and mother.

Initially at least the Vichy regime enjoyed widespread support from a public dazed by the speed and scale of defeat. There was no real alternative. Pétain's government was furthermore the legitimate successor to the discredited Third Republic. But more than this the Marshal assumed mystical qualities as the father and saviour of his people. He alone promised protection from the invader. For much of the Vichy regime the combination of what appeared to be complete and utter defeat with the desire to preserve some semblance of normality persuaded most of the population to take refuge in the privacy of home and work, and to seek to make the best of things. Catholics in particular welcomed the regime's adoption of the Church's teaching on morality, the family and the importance of spiritual values, and its benevolent attitude towards religious education. Cardinal Gerlier, Archbishop of Lyons affirmed that 'if we had remained victorious, we would possibly have remained the prisoners of our errors. Through being secularized, France was in danger of death'. Although individual priests would censure Vichy and German policies, and especially the treatment of the Jews, the hierarchy would in general remain loyal to the regime, and as late as February 1944 would denounce resistance as 'terrorism'. For all these reasons the vast majority of officials and those army officers not demobilised or in prisoner-of-war camps remained loyally at their posts in France itself and throughout the Empire. Those servicemen who found themselves on British territory when France surrendered almost all decided on repatriation rather than continuing the struggle. Furthermore the British attack on the French fleet at Mers-el-Kebir on 3–4 July 1940, designed to ensure that it would never come under German control, aroused intense hostility towards the former ally.

There was however to be a continuous tension between the regime's traditionalist ideology and the practical problems involved in meeting the organisational and material needs of a modern urban society and satisfying the insatiable demands of the occupier. The economy was to be increasingly subordinated to German interests. By 1943 15 per cent of agricultural and 40 per cent of industrial output was exported to Germany and paid for largely by the French themselves in the form of occupation costs, made all the more burdensome by the overvaluation of the mark for exchange purposes. In that year French payments to Germany are estimated to have accounted for 36.6 per cent of the country's national income and to have amounted to the equivalent of one-quarter of Germany's pre-war gross national product, a figure which does not include the contribution made by the large numbers of French workers employed in Germany or the goods and services consumed by German troops in France. Indeed taking account of demand from the occupying forces, perhaps one-third of the French labour force was employed in meeting German needs. France in effect was making a massive contribution to the German war effort. In order to achieve this, the government whilst promoting the virtues of rural society and the 'return to the soil' as the essential bulwark against the advance of materialism, was at the same time obliged to encourage *remembrement*, that is the consolidation of small farms, in order to increase productivity. The peasant *corporation* created in December 1940 as a means of producer self-regulation rapidly turned into a bureaucratic machine for official intervention in the market. In industry, too, growing German demands called for a degree of planning which heralded the development of post-war technocracy. The paternalistic rhetoric, and the corporatist structures which were supposed to unite master and man, became effectively a cover for policies overwhelmingly favourable to businessmen. Trades union federations were banned in August 1940 and the few strikes which occurred, such as that involving miners in the Nord in May 1941, were brutally repressed. Many employers welcomed what they saw as revenge for the Popular Front and the restoration of their freedom to manage. For those with scarce commodities to sell, whether foodstuffs to the French or motor vehicles to the Germans, this was a time of rare opportunity. In an otherwise depressed economy the inducements to produce goods for the occupier were frequently irresistible. The return of Laval to government in April 1942 symbolised the victory of the pragmatists over the traditionalists and the practical abandonment of the dream. Although the regime continued until the end to benefit enormously from the personal prestige of Marshal Pétain, the motive force behind its activities increasingly changed from that of the restoration of France to participation in an increasingly desperate German-led crusade against the Bolshevik menace to Europe.

At the outset only a small number of avowedly fascist intellectuals,

Plate 47 French miners working under German supervision

men like Robert Brasillach, Pierre Drieu La Rochelle and Louis-Ferdinand Céline had openly welcomed German victory. They were as contemptuous of the former liberal democratic regime as of the traditional conservative values which the new government espoused.

As a result, they were to be kept at arm's length by Vichy until towards the end. They did constitute however the hard core of committed 'collaborationists'. For the Germans they were a useful threat, the basis of a possible alternative government, which could be used to put pressure on Vichy. Initially Paris with its German subsidised news-papers was the main focus of their activity. Former outsiders, they seem to have relished suddenly being invited to share the charms of Parisian high society. In Paris, too, Jacques Doriot's *Parti Populaire Français* helped organise the Anti-Bolshevik Legion of some 12,500 French volunteers who were to fight, in German uniform, against the Russians. Of these French fascists only Marcel Déat and Joseph Darnand were ultimately to achieve ministerial office in December 1943 as, re-spectively, Minister of Labour and Secretary-General for the Main-tenance of Order. They came into their own only as the traditionalist conservatives began to appreciate that the war was likely to end in defeat for Germany and to desert.

Collaboration was of course not simply a matter of politicians. The entire population had to adapt to German rule. Life is full of ambiguities. Collaboration could be a calculated form of behaviour or an accidental relationship. Frequently the nature of an individual's work, as a government official or in an engineering works, on the railways, in a café, made contacts with the occupier unavoidable. Most officials, at all levels, simply continued doing the jobs they had held before the war. Initially this was to safeguard their salaries and pension rights but it also represented respect for the apparent continuity of the French state. Subsequently sheer inertia, the lack of alternative employment, but additionally professional loyalty and a determination to preserve an ordered society, kept them at their posts. An effort was made to create a popular organisation committed to Vichy by appealing, in the Marshal's name, to First World War veterans formed into a *Légion française des combattants*. In practice it would be the inflated civil service which would serve as the dominant link between the government and the masses. At local level mayors were appointed rather than elected and councils purged. The increasingly difficult economic situation and growing shortages necessitated greater ad-ministrative intervention, supported by the apparatus of the police state. This was an assertion of the primacy of public administration over politics which delighted many officials even as it disturbed the

traditionalist proponents of regionalism and decentralised administration. Thus under Vichy an unelected social and administrative élite
was able to hold sway, imposing its control through the civil service,
the institutions of local government and the corporations. In the
absence of an electorate to win over it was especially well placed to
forward its own sectional interests.

Active collaboration involved only a small minority. At the
governmental level it was primarily, but not entirely, a response to
German pressure, as Vichy ministers, on trial for their lives, would
later emphasise. In the early post-armistice period in particular,
considerable scope for initiative was left to the Vichy authorities,
although even then, and in spite of the armistice agreement, effective
recognition of Vichy's sovereignty in the occupied zone would always
depend on the whims of the occupier. Thus the German authorities
prevented the extension of the youth organisation to which Vichy
attached so much importance as an agent of moral regeneration.
Collaboration nevertheless increasingly appeared to be the necessary
means of purchasing membership, and on relatively favourable terms,
of the new Europe which the Germans seemed to be constructing. On
24 October 1940 Pétain met Hitler at Montoire and in a speech on the
31 October proclaimed that 'It is with honour, and in order to maintain
French unity...that in the framework of an activity which will create
the European new order I today enter the road of collaboration'.
Moreover anger at the British attack on Mers-el-Kebir and the Free
French take-over in Equatorial Africa and a determination to preserve
the Empire increased interest in an accommodation with the Germans.
The determination to resist these incursions by force, revealed in the
successful defence of Dakar in September 1940 and the bitter struggle
in Syria in June–July 1941, did not however develop into a burning
desire to go to war with Britain as an ally of Germany, although
probably the most significant reason for this was Hitler's own
preference for the neutralisation of France and the avoidance of the
extension of the war to new fronts which would have followed French
intervention.

In return for collaboration, Vichy expected concessions on the
armistice terms and eventually a favourable peace treaty. The Germans
were not however prepared to respond to Laval's insistence on the need
to show the French people that collaboration brought benefits. His

failure in this respect, and Pétain's suspicion that he was accumulating too much power, led to his temporary removal from office in December 1940. This only served to confirm Hitler's suspicion of the sincerity of French intentions. The desperate search for a general settlement of Franco–German relations nevertheless continued. Darlan, who by February 1941 had emerged as the dominant Vichy minister, was an admiral inspired by the possibility that France might assume the maritime and colonial role of a weakened Britain. The return to power of Laval, Hitler's least unfavourite French politician, and as such increasingly independent of Pétain, represented a renewed commitment to the collaborationist strategy, but at a time (April 1942) when German awareness of the implications of a long war, was about to sharply increase the pressures placed upon France. Laval tried to use this situation to secure German concessions in return for 'intensive economic aid' and even broached the possibility of a military alliance 'to save our civilisation from sinking into communism' (13 December 1942). Negotiating from a position of extreme weakness Laval had little success, and following German entry into the unoccupied zone in November 1942 Vichy was, more than ever, reduced to the situation of a dependent satellite.

It was later to be claimed that Vichy had served as a 'shield' protecting France from even worse excesses, perhaps on the scale of those inflicted on Poland. The 'National Revolution' and the anti-masonic and anti-semitic legislation of 1940 were nevertheless in-digenous policies with the latter pre-dating by two years German pressure to contribute to the 'final solution' of the Jewish Question. Vichy anti-semitism tended to be nationalistic and Catholic rather than racialist and reflected the prejudices held by much of the population. The armistice certainly obliged the French government to repatriate Jewish refugees of German origin who had sought sanctuary in France, but the Statute of Jews of 3 October 1940 was an essentially French initiative. It debarred French Jews from elective office, from the civil service, teaching and journalism and imposed quotas on entry to most professions, although war veterans and some families long-established in France were judged to be sufficiently assimilated to be exempt. In addition though, and as a perverse means of preserving its tattered sovereignty, the Vichy regime increasingly implemented, as its own, the policies of the occupier. Jewish property in the occupied zone was seized with Vichy cooperation. From the summer of 1941 foreign Jews were rounded up and deported. These policies were then extended to the unoccupied territory as part of a policy of uniformising legislation over the entire country and in the hope that this spirit of cooperation would facilitate the extension of the civil authority of the Vichy state in the German zone. More mundanely, the regime was also anxious to share in the profits expected from the confiscation and sale of Jewish assets. Apologists for Vichy have pointed out that 'only' 26 per cent of the 300,000 foreign Jews resident in France, and only some 6,000 of the 150,000 French Jews, were deported, and certainly efforts were made to protect French citizens. Many were hidden, at considerable personal risk, by French families. It must be borne in mind though that the action taken against Jews occurred with the official cooperation of the French authorities and the active assistance of the police. The economic depression followed by defeat had reinforced xenophobia. Foreigners and Jews proved to be useful scapegoats.

The introduction of a scheme to encourage French workers to volunteer to work in Germany in May 1942 was certainly successful in securing a postponement of the German scheme for compulsory labour service, but only until August. In all some 40,000 mainly unemployed volunteers and 650,000 conscripts of the *Service du travail obligatoire* were to be sent to Germany, whilst in France itself close to 4 million people must at some time have worked for the occupier. However the efforts of many young men to escape from the STO had the effect of strengthening the growing hostility and even active resistance to both the French government and the German occupation regime. This growing problem of maintaining public order would force Vichy into increasingly severe forms of repression, into a war against its internal enemies which would do much to destroy its legitimacy. In this the French administration and its police, supported by the 45,000 volunteers of the *milice* formed in January 1943 to help maintain 'order', both engaged in a civil war and served as the agents of the occupiers. They were assisted by an immense wave of anonymous denunciations from people anxious to settle old scores, a development indicative of a deep sense of demoralisation.

The Vichy regime cooperated closely with the Germans as a means of preserving some autonomy, but also from a positive desire to participate in the struggle against communism and other forms of

Plate 48 Execution of young members of the resistance by German troops

'terrorism' and increasingly in the interests of simple self-preservation. Liberation by the allies threatened to turn France once again into a battlefield and bring with it the prospect of civil war. The growing success of the Red Army only reinforced this anxiety. It is likely that as many French men and women, in the police and groups such as the *milice*, participated in defending 'law and order' against 'brigands' in 1943–44 as did in active resistance. In all some 40,000 resistants or hostages were murdered, and 60,000 deported to concentration camps for 'Gaullism, Marxism or hostility to the regime', and a further 100,000 on racial grounds. With the appointment of Darnand as chief of security in December 1943 police action became increasingly brutal involving torture and the execution of hostages, although by this stage action against the resistance was even more decisively in German hands. The imminence of the allied landings only intensified the viciousness of repression, which achieved new paroxysms following D-Day, as in the panic of retreat, German forces only too frequently slaughtered innocent civilians as well as resistants.

Not even the clear breach of the armistice terms occasioned by the allied landings in North Africa and the subsequent German move into the unoccupied zone on 11 November 1942 deflected Vichy from the path of collaboration. The Germans were able to dissolve the armistice army virtually without resistance. In North Africa itself, however, Pétain's order to resist the allies had been countermanded by Darlan who just happened to be in the area. The army thus saved from destruction, although still commanded by mainly Pétainist officers, was to re-enter the war on the allied side. In France itself it became increasingly clear that the regime was not only becoming more and more a prisoner of the occupying power, but had also chosen the losing side in the war. Its only hope, and it became ever more unlikely, was some sort of a compromise peace. In the meantime it sought to defend itself against mounting internal opposition.

Resistance had been slow to develop. Most of the population had supported the Vichy government's efforts to make the best of a bad situation and had at first been pleasantly surprised by the unusually disciplined behaviour of the occupying forces. As it developed, resistance activity was to be characterised by its diverse origins and forms. Early landmarks included the clandestine publication in November and December 1940 of Henry Frenay's newspaper *Combat* and Robert Lacoste and Christian Pineau's *Libération* which did something to counter the otherwise paralysing feeling of isolation amongst potential resisters. Resistance had to be established from scratch and the learning process was to prove costly. This was the lesson of such rare public confrontations as the demonstration by students in Paris on armistice day 11 November 1940 and the miners strike in the north-east in May 1941, occasioned mainly by food shortages, but blamed by both the Vichy prefect and the Germans on Communist agitation. However it was not until June–August 1941, following Hitler's invasion of Russia and whole-hearted Communist commitment to resistance, that the occupiers began to show real concern. This marked the commencement of a vicious upward cycle in which acts of resistance were followed by savage repression which rapidly increased hostility towards the occupier. The deterioration in living standards, the unopposed entry of German forces into the unoccupied zone, and the conscription of labour for work in Germany, were to mark further stages in the development of resistance to both the occupier and increasingly, too, to a discredited Vichy regime. Growing Allied military success helped to establish a new climate of hope.

Resistance developed first in the cities amongst intellectuals and workers, groups which were from the beginning obvious losers to both German repression and exploitation and Vichy authoritarianism. There were also solid practical reasons given the relative impenetrability to the police of city *quartiers* like the *faubourg* Montmartre, les Halles or Belleville in Paris. It developed particularly in the occupied zone where the enemy was obvious, whereas in the south the existence of Vichy clouded the issue. The forms of resistance were diverse and inspired by a variety of motives. They were initially practised as a series of disconnected initiatives in particular localities by small groups of like-minded people related by kinship, friendship, profession, religious or political attitudes. In many, especially rural areas, it was possible to live in peace with very little contact with the occupier, although official food requisitioning would increasingly alienate the peasants. Loyalty to the Marshal and anti-Bolshevism limited the involvement of the politically conservative. However if members of the traditional élites were rarely involved, the role of the middle classes should not be underestimated. Support within all social groups would grow as part of a patriotic reaction against the increasingly obvious satellisation of Vichy and a humanitarian and often Christian-inspired response to German racism and brutality. Previous political convictions and the considerable local variations in the experience of occupation affected decisions. Initially the Socialists, reacting to the repression of the trades unions and the loss of civil and political rights, were probably the most active political grouping. The official Communist approach, inspired by the Nazi–Soviet Pact, was to avoid conflict with the occupying power whilst condemning the 'traitors' at Vichy. Even before the invasion of the Soviet Union, however, the clandestinely published *L'Humanité* was adopting an increasingly hostile tone, industrial sabotage was increasing and arms were being stock-piled in readiness. The final entry of the Communists into active resistance would have a substantial impact on both its numerical strength and combativeness. It would also establish the Party as a major political force. Although resisters, like the *milice*, were recruited from all social groups, it remained the case that resistance activity could often be seen as a means of continuing the class struggle. A mood of protest and hostility towards the better off was created amongst the poorer social groups by shortage and deprivation. Reinforcement of the authority of employers, the persecution of trades unionists and the extension of the working day were bitterly resented. Reduced levels of production, the lack of access to overseas markets, German purchasing and the reluctance of farmers to sell their produce on the open market when there was so little to purchase with their earnings, contributed to the creation of shortages on a scale not experienced since the late eighteenth century. Bread rationing was introduced in September 1940 and most necessities were rationed by the end of 1941. By 1943 the official ration amounted to only 1200 calories a day, well below the 1700 usually considered as the minimum necessary for good health. In the following year the crude death rate reached 19.1 per thousand compared with 15.3 before the war. The burden on women anxious to provide for their families and spending long hours standing in queues, was especially desperate. There was a growing obsession with meeting physical needs and inevitably those who could afford to resorted to the black market. Power cuts and shortages of heating fuel added to the widespread misery, whilst the intensification of police round-ups, deportation for labour service, and the toll taken by allied air raids, which eventually accounted for around 60,000 deaths, all added to the general feeling of intense insecurity.

The various resistance groups and networks created by local effort would increasingly respond to the external influence of the Free French and British and perform a range of functions including the collection of intelligence on troop movements, at which railwaymen were particularly adept; the distribution of tracts and newspapers; the establishment of hiding places and escape routes for political suspects, Jewish refugees and allied servicemen; sabotage and assassination. From 1943, in sparsely populated areas of the centre and south, guerilla activity would develop, involving large armed groups made up of young men avoiding labour service in Germany, stiffened by those rare army officers sympathetic towards the resistance and by experienced Spanish republican refugees. By the beginning of 1944 perhaps 30,000 were involved. All of these activities were extremely dangerous. The various groups were frequently penetrated by informers, and their members subject to torture and a miserable death if captured. They shared the added moral burden of knowing that the German authorities were also likely to visit retribution on their families and innocent hostages.

Cooperation between the various local groups was slow to develop due both to the added risk of exposure this would inevitably involve and mutual political suspicion. The London based Free French initially had little impact. The British and especially the Americans continued to keep open the possibility of negotiations with Vichy. Although Churchill had first supported de Gaulle only because alternative and more illustrious leaders failed to materialise, the General's consistent denial of the legitimacy of the Vichy regime, his total intransigence in defence of what he believed to be the vital interests of France, and the gradual strengthening of his military power, as parts of the Empire were liberated, slowly improved his position vis-à-vis the allies. It did little however to reduce what he regarded as an humiliating dependence. The situation of de Gaulle was nevertheless to be transformed when in May 1943 a *Conseil National de la Résistance* (CNR) was created, made up of representatives of political groups and resistance organisations. One of its leading figures, the former prefect Jean Moulin, a member of the Lyons-based and largely Catholic inspired group *Combat*, persuaded its members to declare their support for de Gaulle. They preferred to appeal to the Free French for the external support, and especially weaponry, they so desperately needed, rather than go cap-in-hand to the allies. Moreover de Gaulle was prepared to make the compromises necessary to increase his authority within France and particularly to commit himself to the re-establishment of democracy in the post-war period. The combination of growing support within the internal resistance, de Gaulle's determination to prevent a communist take-over in post-war France and the manifest incompetence of potential rivals forced the allies to accept the General's pre-eminent position and to recognise the status of the *Comité Français de Libération Nationale*. This was formed in June 1943 from a mixture of resistance leaders and former Third Republic politicians like Auriol and Mendès-France. It increasingly took on the character of a provisional government able to count on the allegiance of a regular army of 500,000 men formed in North Africa and equipped by the allies. Powerful internal political tensions would nevertheless survive as well as differences over both tactics and objectives. Most notably many Communists thought in terms of a future mass struggle not only against the German enemy but also the treasonable ruling classes as a prelude to social revolution. This was in marked contrast with the more conservative and cautious approach of the other groups concerned essentially to prepare for action to support the allied armies on some still distant day of liberation. As a result the communist *Front national* and *Francs-Tireurs et Partisans Français* tended to be starved of weapons and money in comparison with the resources sent by both the Free French and the British Special Operations Executive to the non-communist *Mouvements Unis de la Résistance* and its *Armée Secrète*. The struggle for power in the post-war world was already underway before the allied landings.

Assisted by overwhelming air superiority, allied forces were able to land on the coast of Normandy on 6 June 1944, to achieve a rapid military build-up and break out from their bridgeheads. Paris was liberated on 25 August and in the meantime Franco–American troops had landed in the south on 15 August and advanced up the Rhône valley. By the end of the year most of the country was free of German troops. The contribution of regular French forces to the initial landings had been limited, much to de Gaulle's disgust. Nor had there been a call for a mass rising by the resistance. Their essential role in the allied grand strategy was the extremely important one of delaying the arrival on the Normandy front of German reinforcements. Although the activities of both communist and non-communist groups had been quite successfully coordinated within the overall command structure of the *Forces Françaises de l'Intérieur* they had remained handicapped by a lack of military equipment. Paris, like many other towns was able to liberate itself as the Germans withdrew east. Eisenhower, the supreme allied commander, had planned to by-pass the city rather than risk involvement in a costly house-to-house conflict but this was to ignore the determination of resistance leaders, particularly the Communists, to play a more active role. The rising began on 19 August and was supported by the police, the supreme resistants of the last minute. In response Eisenhower felt obliged to rush Leclerc's Second French Armoured Division towards the city, and on 25 August the German commander, ignoring Hitler's orders to fight on in the ruins, surrendered. It had cost the lives of some 3,000 members of the resistance and civilians. In spite of playing an essentially subordinate and secondary role, this contribution of French forces to the liberation would do a great deal to restore national self-confidence.

In the face of the onslaught, the Vichy regime finally disintegrated. The government itself was forced by the German authorities to move first to eastern France and finally, as virtual captives, into Germany itself. At local level the administration simply tended to collapse with only small numbers of the more ideologically motivated officials and *milice* assisting in a last, often ferocious, round of persecution. Pétain's call on Frenchmen to remain neutral in the struggle was meaningless. His primary concern appears to have been to ensure an orderly transfer of authority, and to avoid internal strife. There remained a very real danger after so many years of misery and oppression that, as Pétain feared, the liberation would degenerate into a massive settling of accounts and into civil war. Indeed amongst both members of the resistance and the mass of more passive citizens who had associated themselves at the last minute with the anti-Nazi crusade, the prospect of liberation had created an immense sense of expectancy. In this situation the political left, strengthened by its association with resistance, appeared representative of the national interest. In part this had been fostered by the CNR's programme which promised to dismantle and to nationalise the 'feudal' economic empires, to involve workers themselves in planning for a greater and more fairly shared prosperity and to create a social security system. This implied a rejection of the self-centred individualism of the property-owning classes, and acceptance that poverty was as much the responsibility of society as of the individual.

Although members of every social group had participated in resistance, the traditional élites and major employers could not entirely escape from identification with Vichy. The right to a large degree collapsed with Vichy, and former supporters of the authoritarian Vichy regime faced what appeared to them to be the nightmare prospect of a communist-inspired social revolution. In practice the dangerous period following the collapse of one regime and the imposition of control by its successor, and in which a power vacuum existed, was to be short-lived. During it nevertheless perhaps 10,000 supposed collaborators were summarily executed, a high enough figure but far lower than subsequent conservative estimates which seem to have represented an attempt to tarnish the reputation of the resistance.

269

Plate 49 Execution of members of the *milice* in Grenoble in August 1944

Another 7,037 death sentences were pronounced by legally constituted courts although only 767 were carried out. 126,000 people were imprisoned, and 30,000 of these released before coming to trial. Many others, notably women who had associated with German boyfriends, were humiliated and paraded through the streets with shaven heads. Following an initial violent reaction those punished tended to be the makers of policy under Vichy rather than the executors, unless the latter had been overly zealous in their duties. Pétain and Laval were to endure extremely partisan trials. Even so their lawyers were able to offer a defence in terms of the two men's success in providing at least partial protection from the occupier. Another conservative myth was in the making. Both were nonetheless sentenced to death. Laval was shot but Pétain was to be reprieved on the grounds of his age and advancing senility. High profile groups like intellectuals and journalists suffered much more than the officials and businessmen who had been so essential to the workings of collaboration and who had often managed to turn it into a very profitable proposition. Although 11,000 civil servants were dismissed, most of them were to be reinstated by 1950; the machinery of government survived virtually intact. Continuity was essential to the smooth operation of the new regime. Moreover too many people felt guilty about collaboration in all its forms, large and small, for there to be sustained support for a massive enquiry and purge. The dead-weight of the state bureaucracy was soon re-imposed. Subsequently prosecution of the war to final victory and then reconstruction would take priority over retribution or indeed social reform.

As an allied victory had come to look increasingly likely people had begun to think of the post-war world. Within the resistance, a widespread determination had emerged to avoid a simple restoration of the pre-war social and political systems and to establish a more egalitarian society. Amongst those close to de Gaulle, as well as the former Vichyite officers of the North African army, there was considerable anxiety about the intentions of the many Communist dominated groups making up the largest and most dynamic segment of the resistance. Securing the authority of a new government was clearly going to be fraught with danger. The intention of the allies had been to secure the rear areas of the advancing armies by means of the establishment of their own military government. In the event a new institutional framework had been prepared by the *Comité Français de la Libération*

Nationale, which on 2 June had already declared itself to be the Provisional Government, drawing its members from a variety of political horizons, and including the Communists, both in recognition of the balance of power within the resistance movement and from a desire to establish a working political consensus. *Commissaires* had been carefully selected to replace Vichy prefects. At another level de Gaulle's triumphant reception in a succession of liberated towns, but above all in Paris on 26 August had legitimised his role as the embodiment of a resurrected French state. The provisional government's authority over the internal resistance was re-affirmed by the incorporation of its fighters into the regular army and from October by the disarmament of civilians. For their part the Communists were too committed to furthering the war effort to risk civil war. Moderation on their part also offered the prospect of mass support after the final victory.

The scale of de Gaulle's achievement was signified by the allied decision to treat France not as a collaborationist state but as a co-belligerent. The regime which most French people had welcomed in 1940 has in contrast to be accounted a disastrous failure. Its only slight and rather unexpected success lay in the development of economic planning. In spite of the 'return to the soil' rhetoric, the practical economic problems caused largely by German demands had forced a more interventionist role upon the state. The planning which some economists had previously declared might be a remedy for the pre-war crisis had become a necessity, and was to be substantially reinforced after the liberation to meet the equally pressing needs of reconstruction. It might have been otherwise if Britain had sued for peace as had been confidently expected. Even then however the best that France could have expected would have been the status of a favoured client state in a Europe subordinated to German needs. The Vichy regime as it emerged had shown itself to be committed to a reactionary politics which favoured existing élites and the Catholic church, largely at the expense of the poorer classes who in the Vichy scheme were to be subject to the paternalist and authoritarian controls, the corporatism favoured by the right. In practice they were to experience little more than shortages of necessities, harsh labour discipline, the loss of democratic rights and police repression. Vichy in effect constituted another round in the long civil war inaugurated in 1789. This particular round could be said to have begun in the 1930s with the economic crisis

Plate 50 Liberation: General de Gaulle walking down the Champs-Elysées on 26 August 1944

and to have climaxed with Vichy. It was the last in the series of crises between 1914 and 1945 which gave the period its fundamental unity. With it a long period of economic and social stagnation came to an end. In marked contrast the following three decades – the *trente glorieuses* – would bring sustained economic growth and social transformation.

7

Reconstruction and renewal: the *trente glorieuses* and beyond

The most obvious indicator of the scale and pace of economic and social change in the years since the end of the second world war is the transformation of the everyday environment. In 1945 the rural landscape was little different from that of the late middle ages, and the urban scene similar to that of the Second Empire, complete with overcrowded, run-down housing and nineteenth-century industrial landscapes. Between 1946 and 1985 population grew from 40.3 million to 55 million, 69 per cent of whom were concentrated in the towns compared with 51 per cent before the war. Large-scale construction of offices and housing changed the appearance of most towns. Many of the old factories had been demolished. People lived in much greater comfort, and most worked in less oppressive conditions. The automobile, symbol of this new age of mass production and greater personal mobility, was everywhere. Of course not everything had changed. Old and new co-existed, but the scale and pace of transformation was far more substantial than anything previously experienced. A decisive shift had occurred in the balance between continuity and change, beginning with post-war reconstruction, and from the 1960s involving more decisive steps towards modernity through rapid economic growth and structural transformation, new patterns of consumption and changing mentalities and the acceptance of substantially enlarged responsibilities on the part of the state. This all added up to a massive social revolution.

In spite of this the Liberation, which for so many members of the Resistance had held the promise of a new era of social justice, was instead, in a remarkably short time, to be followed by a restoration of the social and political relationships of the pre-war period. Many former *résistants* were to endure the sour taste of betrayal. More realistically it is hardly surprising that the heterogeneous coalition which came together in the struggle against the occupiers fell to squabbling once it was a question of determining the shape of reconstruction and the locus of political power.

There was nevertheless an important degree of consensus amongst the various political groups and within the reconstituted trades unions concerning reconstruction. Although it could not be indefinitely sustained, popular enthusiasm was boosted by speeches, newsreels and press articles praising miners, steelworkers and railwaymen. The shortage of labour was made good by longer working hours and rising productivity. To a large degree this was imposed by material conditions. The task seemed enormous, far greater than after the First World War. According to an estimate by the Ministry of Reconstruction the return to 'normality' would cost 4900 milliard francs or the equivalent of three years' pre-war national income. Other sources suggest that over one-quarter of the nation's wealth had been destroyed, compared with one-tenth during the earlier war. The depredations of war and German requisitioning and the long neglect of maintenance and of the replacement of capital goods resulted in shortages of such basic necessities as food and fuel. Industrial production in 1944 stood at 38 per cent of its 1938 level. First priority had to be given to the reconstruction of the transportation infrastructure which had been a prime target of allied bombing and resistance activity. At the end of the war only 18,000 kilometres (in disconnected sections) of the 40,000 of railway lines were serviceable and only one in five lorries had survived. The other major campaign to be fought was the 'battle for coal'. This remained the basic source of industrial and domestic fuel and in 1945 only 40 million tonnes were available (including imports) compared with 67 million in 1937. Although the shift to alternative energy sources was already under way, in 1950 solid fuels still provided for 74 per cent of energy consumption (90 per cent in 1913) with hydro-electricity supplying 7.5 per cent and oil 18 per cent. The restoration and modernisation of the

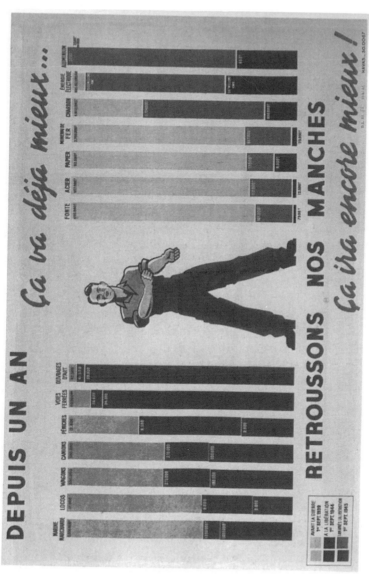

Plate 51 Reconstruction: the Communist Party calls for a further effort

steel and engineering industries were other pressing objectives. In this situation a high degree of state intervention in the economy was to be expected. The intensity of anti-capitalist feeling at the time of the Liberation made this inevitable. The *patronat* was blamed by much of the population for the defeat of 1940 and for collaboration and thus 'disqualified' (de Gaulle) from its previous pre-eminence. It had become necessary for the state to assume control of the 'levers of command' and direct investment not simply into reconstruction, but additionally into a programme of economic and social modernisation impelled by a now widely shared perception of France as a backward archaic society. A 'Malthusian' capitalist class which had already given ample proof of its shortcomings could not be trusted to ensure that France kept pace with other western societies. Nationalisation occupied a central place in the programme adopted by the *Conseil national de la Résistance* in March 1944 and this reflected a broad consensus created not only by the war, but in reaction to the pre-war economic crisis. Between December 1945 and May 1946 the major banking and insurance companies, gas and electricity utilities and the coalmines were added to firms like Renault, taken into state ownership because of its directors' collaboration. Compensation was paid to shareholders but generally at the prevailing, and very depressed stock market valuation. In spite of their great hopes the employees of these enterprises, whilst benefiting from a greater security of employment, otherwise saw little change in their relationship with their employers. Although state intervention in long-term planning was frequent, on a day-to-day basis the nationalised companies operated in much the same way as other enterprises.

Another feature of the period of reconstruction was the emergence of the Plan, contemplated, as we have seen, during the inter-war years, but which now, in such difficult circumstances seemed essential. The first was prepared by a team led by Jean Monnet and published in January 1947. It sought to define priorities, circulate information (collected by a massively extended statistical service), provide economic forecasts and develop contacts between businessmen, trade unionists and civil servants in order to create a dynamic climate for investment. This was not the planning Soviet-style which the French Communist Party favoured, but a form of technocracy by means of which officials who had received their professional training in the most élitist sector of higher education, the *grandes écoles*, attempted to ensure the more effective working of the capitalist system. In retrospect the establishment of direct links between government and particular sectors of the economy was far more important. The orthodox financial views of the Finance Ministry and governmental concern to restore business confidence as a means of promoting recovery rapidly re-assumed predominance. This was however within the new intellectual climate imposed by the widespread acceptance of Keynsian economic ideas, and which insisted upon the necessity of state intervention to promote growth and full employment. The age of the regulatory-state was to last until the early 1980s. The quasi-monopoly of statistical information possessed by the state made critical analysis of its activities difficult. Initially, too, there was no alternative, in the aftermath of war, to running up large trade deficits in order to secure the import of essential foodstuffs, raw materials and capital equipment. Only the introduction in 1948 of the Marshall Plan and the provision of aid on a massive scale by a United States anxious to promote European recovery would ease the strains. This act of altruism combined with self-interest helped confirm the growing fascination, sometimes combined with revulsion, for all things American, including the cultural manifestations of Hollywood and advanced industrial technology.

By 1947–49 the key economic sectors had been restored at least to pre-war levels of activity. To a large degree reconstruction was achieved at the expense of consumption. Thus in the effort to restore industrial supplies it was domestic consumers of coal, gas and electricity who suffered shortages. Bread rationing continued until 1949 although it was already becoming clear that domestic recovery combined with imports threatened the return of pre-war problems of agricultural over-production. The first Plan with its 'productivist' concerns sought to encourage an agricultural revolution by means of the tractor (137,000 of them in 1950, 558,000 by 1958 and 1 million by 1965) and chemical inputs, inaugurating a cycle of technical innovation largely financed by borrowing which would create an immense debt burden for farmers. Reliance on banks and on contracts to supply cooperative and food processing companies increasingly placed farmers in a dependent position. Certainly though considerable gains in productivity were achieved, at an annual rate of 6.4 per cent between 1949 and 1962, in part as a result of the shift from cereals cultivation into higher-value products like fruit, vegetables, meat and dairy products. At the same time the exodus of population from the countryside revived due both to mechanisation, and the growing attractiveness of urban life. The agricultural labour force fell from 36 per cent of the total in 1946, to 21 per cent in 1962, 12 per cent in 1972 and 7 per cent in 1982.

The phase of reconstruction can be said to have been completed by 1949–50 by which time the maximum pre-war levels of production, those of 1929, had been exceeded. The success of reconstruction was such that it provided a firm base for an unique period of sustained and accumulative economic growth marked by substantial gains in productivity, real incomes and mass purchasing power and by major changes in economic and social structures. In Western Europe only Federal Germany would surpass the French achievement. Subsequently the role of the state continued to be of considerable importance both in terms of direct investment and through the creation, partly by means of the Plan, of an encouraging climate for business activity. Prior to the establishment of the Common Market governments remained res-olutely protectionist using an arsenal of monetary controls to facilitate industrial expansion based upon a protected internal market, and employing deficit financing to maintain high levels of infrastructure investment as well as to stabilise the capitalist system.

Inflation was to be a constant problem. Deficit financing, expansion of the money supply both during and after the war, shortages and the early abandonment of many wartime controls, generated substantial price rises, fuelled by major wage increases as employees sought to protect their already diminished living standards. At the time in 1948–49 when, due to increasing production and effective controls, stabilisation appeared possible, the effects of the Korean war on world raw material prices set off a new inflationary round. Inflation certainly contributed to the revival of economic activity by widening profit margins and reducing the burden of indebtedness, but it also revealed something of the fragility of the economic recovery and the ineffective-ness of the political system, as well as contributing to rising social tension. Only with the action inaugurated by Pinay in 1952–53, which combined persuasion with controls and a successful loan to soak up excess capital, was inflation temporarily curbed. Greater financial stability stimulated a second cycle of growth, which was brought to an end from 1956 by renewed inflation caused by the rising costs of the war in Algeria, the impact of the Suez affair on the cost of oil and other raw materials, and the spending of a left-wing government committed to social reform. These factors combined to reduce French competitiveness in international markets and to severely dent business confidence.

In spite of these setbacks the conditions for largely self-sustained economic growth were being established as rising productivity pushed up both company and personal incomes and stimulated growing investment and consumer spending. The greater mobility of labour and its transfer from the less dynamic sectors of the economy like agriculture and textiles to the more productive, in per capita productivity terms, areas of chemicals, electrical goods, engineering and construction, was an essential part of this process, helping to ease the severe labour shortages evident until the entry into employment of the large post-war generations. Increasingly too France came to be integrated into the West European and Atlantic economies, initially through the General Agreement on Tariffs and Trade (1947) and the Organisation for European Economic Cooperation created to co-ordinate the disbursement of Marshall Aid, and later by means of the European Coal and Steel Community and finally through the EEC. The signature of the Treaty of Rome in 1957, against the advice of many businessmen, might appear something of a paradox, given the protectionist policies of post-war governments. It did however represent a further stage in the commitment to modernisation by providing access to new markets and through the intensification of competitive pressures.

In a situation of rapidly rising prices and with a growing deficit in external trade it was widely assumed that France would be unable to fulfil its engagements under the Treaty of Rome. Not only were tariffs within the Community to be eliminated within twelve to fifteen years (in practice by 1968) but the common tariffs levied on imports from outside the Community were to be reduced to the average prevailing in 1958, which tended to be below French levels. In compensation the Common Agricultural Policy, finally agreed in 1962, provided for price guarantees and income supports and due to tough negotiating by the French government was extremely favourable to its farming constituency. These measures, combined with the enlargement of the

potential market, were especially beneficial for large-scale farmers, the
10 per cent who already by 1968 produced 60 per cent of total output.
They also however provided a margin for survival for many small
farmers, slowing the process of structural change necessary to enhance
the international competitiveness of French agriculture. In 1973 60 per
cent of farms still had fewer than 20 hectares. Many families especially
in the uplands, the south-west and Breton interior remained impoverished and the situation was only gradually eased by migration and
measures like the Pisani law of 1960 which encouraged farmers to
retire. Peasant farmers (and small shopkeepers) were to be consistently
protected from the full impact of the free market although their
incomes remained subject to the vagaries of the climate, fluctuating
interest rates and changes in the CAP.

France proved able to meet its EEC obligations due to the
combination of a series of deflationary financial measures, including an
end to the indexation of prices and wages, together with a relaxation
of administrative controls and a partial restoration of market
mechanisms. The establishment, with the return of de Gaulle, of
strong political leadership with clearer objectives and prepared to
encourage, even enforce, industrial restructuring and modernisation
by means of investment in improved communications, cheap loans,
export credits and tax concessions was another vital factor. The overall
effect of the establishment of the Community was to promote a rapid
increase in trade between its six member states. Although farmers and
businessmen undoubtedly experienced considerable problems of adaptation in increasingly homogeneous and competitive markets the
benefits of integration were soon evident and the process increasingly
came to be seen as irreversible. Government policy sought to encourage
industrial concentration as well as agricultural restructuring and to
improve the infrastructure as the means of securing the country's
leading position in the new Europe. The results surpassed expectations,
with sustained economic growth at an annual rate of 5.5 per cent
during the first fifteen years of EEC membership, higher even than that
of West Germany (5 per cent), and levels of profitability which
encouraged high rates of investment. The French economy underwent
a major process of structural change, with industrial growth promoting
the modernisation of such services as banking and advertising.
Comparative advantage also had an effect. Thus the stimulus to change

was particularly effective in agricultural and food processing, in the automobile and aircraft industries, whilst the economy benefited from imports of German machine tools and consumers from Italian refrigerators and washing machines. The process of growth was further assisted by the relatively low price of raw materials and energy on world markets, and high levels of foreign, especially American, investment. At the same time this orientation towards a dynamic market for advanced high quality goods meant a shift away from the far less demanding third-world markets represented by the former Empire, with the franc area taking over one-quarter of exports in the late-1950s and only 5 per cent twenty years later. As the economic (and indeed the political) context changed it became inevitable that the role of the state exercised through the Plan, direct investment, price controls, subsidies and manipulation of the tax system, would be criticised from a liberal standpoint as inefficient and wasteful. In response, the emphasis shifted towards the creation of a climate favourable to private sector investment. The share of the state and public enterprise in total investment which had been 38.4 per cent in 1949–53 had fallen to 28.5 per cent by 1969–73. This policy was however partly contradicted by investment in a series of prestigious projects regarded as being of strategic national importance. In aerospace these included both military aircraft and the Caravelle airliner in the 1950s and subsequently the supersonic Concorde and the Airbus. The Ariane rocket designed to take satellites into space maintained a major French presence in one area of advanced technology as did massive investment in the nuclear power programme, in information technology, transport and armaments. This represented a determination, shared by all governments to stimulate continuous technological modernisation. The cost-effectiveness of these pro-grammes is difficult to estimate, not only due to the complexity of their impact but because so many inefficiencies are concealed by government support and the lack of genuine cost-accounting. In the case of the nuclear industry, secrecy has further inhibited discussion of such crucial matters as safety and the disposal of wastes.

Inflation would continue to be a problem throughout the 1960s, fuelled as it was by the massive extension of bank credits necessary to finance major investment programmes. Nevertheless from around 20 per cent in the 1950s the investment rate rose to 23.5 per cent of GDP per annum between 1965 and 1973, peaking at 24.7 per cent in 1974, a level unsurpassed in Europe. The result was the rapid introduction of more efficient methods of production which allowed the mass production of such consumer durables as the motor car, a former luxury which now became the most potent symbol of the new consumer society. In 1960 30 per cent of households already possessed a car. By 1973 this had risen to 62 per cent. Scientific advances, especially in chemicals and electronics, created a continually expanding range of new products, which, from packet soups to refrigerators and television, were made available at prices the mass of the population could afford with payment often deferred on credit terms.

The period from 1958 to 1973 saw the most rapid economic growth in French history. Its effects were cumulative. Per-capita income almost doubled between 1960 and 1975 and, significantly, it has been estimated that almost 60 per cent of this was due to technical innovation. Structural change in the economy occurred in response both to new opportunities and to growing competitive pressures. Adaptation was frequently difficult. One reaction to heightened competition was the growing size of enterprises, a response to financial as well as to technical pressures and encouraged by the state. Amongst the most spectacular have been the takeover of Citroën by Peugeot and the development of conglomerates like Péchiney–Ugine–Kuhlman in metal production and chemicals. The proportion of the industrial labour force employed in establishments with more than 500 workers (but excluding those with fewer than 10) rose from 37 per cent to 45 per cent between 1962 and 1974, to decline again to 38 per cent by 1982, due both to the decline of employment in such dinosaurs as steel and the motor industry and to the impact of automation on production processes and the more rapid rotation of stocks. Nevertheless the domination of economic activity by major financial and industrial holding companies like Peugeot, Rhône–Poulenc, BSN in foodstuffs, or Bouygues, the latter diversifying into petroleum, engineering, electric batteries, tourism, ships, newspapers and so on, appears to be a feature of modern capitalism, even if, on an international scale France has relatively few large enterprises. At the same time as small scale and artisanal production and retail outlets have declined in some sectors, specialisation or the provision of a variety of services has allowed others to prosper.

Table 7.1. *Structure of the active population (per cent)*

	1973	1985
Primary sector	10.9	7.5
Secondary sector	37.8	30.6
Tertiary sector	51.3	61.9

The impact of sustained growth upon the economic structures of the country, as well as the prevailing trends of structural change, are illustrated in table 7.1.

It reveals the growing importance and dynamism of the tertiary (service) sector reflecting a diversity of processes including urbanisation, the development of information technology and of financial services, and growing expenditure on health care and leisure. The figures also suggest that France (like Britain) is experiencing de-industrialisation because of the collapse of enterprises unable to compete in international markets, a trend which must cause grave concern. The development of the tertiary sector has taken various forms including personal services, from plumbers to lawyers; the public sector including teachers, post office workers and so on; transport and tourism; banking and assurance; advertising and the retail–wholesale systems. By the 1980s some 60 per cent of the active labour force worked within the tertiary sector, including some of the most highly rewarded and the most poorly paid. The 1960s, with the release of a pent-up consumer boom, saw the beginnings of the transformation of commerce and daily life with the development first of super- and then hypermarkets by enterprises like Carrefour, Radar and Euromarché and more specialised chains like FNAC in photographic equipment and books, Darty in household electrical goods, or the butchers, Bernard. All increasingly accessible to the growing numbers of motorists and all operating according to the same basic principles of low profit margins on each item, rapid rotation of stocks, bulk purchases and delayed payments to suppliers to allow the use of receipts for operations on the financial markets. In spite of restrictive legislation, in the 1960s in the Paris suburbs alone the number of supermarkets grew from 10 to 253, a development sufficient to create unsustainable competition for many small shopkeepers. Supermarkets accounted for 8 per cent of foodstuff sales in 1965 and 45 per cent by 1985. Yet many niches remained in which small businessmen survived by providing a personal service, guaranteed quality or by means of specialisation in the sale for example of sports goods or perfume even as the supermarkets' share of non-foodstuff sales has also risen from 12 per cent to 23 per cent. The spectacular modernisation of information technology and of banking is closely connected with and has greatly facilitated the growth of industrial and commercial activity.

Although in the twenty years after 1967 economic growth continued at a rate of 3.3 per cent per annum (Germany 2.8 per cent, Britain 2.6 per cent, Japan 5.3 per cent), a marked slowing became evident after the peak of 5.9 per cent in 1973, and in the 1980s growth rates averaged around 2 per cent. This slowing has been blamed by the more optimistic economists on the massive increases in energy costs which followed the oil crises of 1973 and 1979, and certainly the first of these marked the onset of a severe depression. France, like the other industrial economies had benefited substantially from low energy costs. In 1973 74.5 per cent of energy needs were supplied by imported oil. Inevitably the quadrupling of oil prices between September 1973 and January 1974 had a substantial impact on both the balance of payments and industrial costs – equivalent in 1973–4 to 4 per cent of national income. Furthermore the increased cost of petrol had a depressive effect by reducing demand for other products. By 1979–80 however the cost had been reduced to 2.6 per cent of national income as more efficient energy use and investment in nuclear power – which by 1987 produced 70 per cent of domestic electricity – eased dependence on imported energy. Instead of the temporary effects of higher energy costs, the pessimists have therefore focused on the structural problems caused by insufficient investment in new technologies and the maldistribution of resources induced by welfarism at a time when the rapid internationalisation of trade was intensifying competition. It seems clear that there would have been a recession in the early 1970s without the oil crisis, which however, substantially intensified the difficulties. The national statistical institute (INSEE) estimated that whereas labour productivity rose by 5.1 per cent per annum between 1953 and 1973 and 3.2 per cent between 1973 and 1979, the rate of increase fell to 2.4 per cent between 1979 and 1984 and explained this in terms both of the transfer of labour into low productivity parts of the service sector and inadequate investments in the training of labour and new capital equipment. Even so levels of capital investment have been sufficient to allow the continuous improvement of living standards, in contrast with previous periods of crisis in the 1930s. In spite of the pessimism, the sense of crisis found in so much of the contemporary literature, the economy continued to perform well by international standards.

Unlike in the 1930s world trade continued to expand. Where resort to protectionism caused a reduction in exports of 44 per cent between 1929 and 1935, between 1973 and 1979 they actually rose by 50 per cent. Furthermore the French share of world industrial exports rose from 7.9 per cent in 1973 to 8.6 per cent in 1978, so that the balance of payments, thrown into disequilibrium by the rise in oil prices, had been restored by 1978–79, on the eve of the second petrol crisis. In terms of both the export of goods and of services France overtook the United Kingdom during this decade. National income grew by an annual 3 per cent between 1973 and 1979 and the rise in real incomes was sufficient to ensure a continuing high level of demand for consumer products. The widespread pessimism which prevailed in spite of these successes was due to rising inflation which governments appeared unable to control, to the growth of unemployment and the disconcerting effect of a long period of relative stagnation. Unemployment, which had affected less than 3 per cent of the active population before 1973 rose rapidly and remained at 10.7 per cent in 1987, its impact concentrated on the young, unskilled and immigrants. The complex of causes rendered a solution difficult. These included the increasing numbers of young people entering the labour market, a problem which would eventually be eased as population aged, a trend which however brought problems of its own; by the adverse impact of the oil crisis on international demand for some products and especially industrial equipment; and rising wages costs which encouraged efforts to maintain profitability through capital investment to replace labour. Most seriously affected were the traditional staple industries of the north and east – steel, coal and textiles – which additionally faced the disruption of their markets by the use of alternative energy sources and materials. The regional policies designed in the 1960s to assist declining or underdeveloped areas and limit congestion in the Paris region were of limited effectiveness, providing in the main poorly paid part-time and unskilled employment, mostly for women, except where combined with substantial investment in infrastructure, in technical and scientific education and research, and in state-assisted projects as in Grenoble and Toulouse. Quite clearly some regions due to the availability of specialised labour, capital and entrepreneurial skills and efficient communications and to their attractiveness as markets are more suitable for economic development than others.

The other unique feature of the crisis was that it was accompanied by a return to high levels of inflation, rather than the deflation which economic theory and experience might have suggested. The annual rate had already risen from 3.3 per cent between 1965 and 1968 to 6.3 per cent in the period 1970–1973. In 1974 it rose to 15.2 per cent and remained at around 10–12 per cent for the remainder of the decade. Higher oil prices contributed only 2 per cent of this further increase. The major causes were wage rises due to skill shortages, growing company and state indebtedness, rising levels of bank credit in spite of high interest rates, the declining exchange value of the franc and the growing disequilibrium of the international financial system. It was becoming increasingly apparent that the state's ability to develop financial and economic policies independently of its main trading partners was limited. The French economy was too closely intertwined in a competitive international system. By 1987 79 per cent of exports went to economically advanced trading partners within the OECD and international trade accounted for 20 per cent of GDP. Faced with unprecedented problems which the Keynsian solutions previously favoured proved incapable of solving, governments adopted often contradictory policies. The Chirac government's use of credit restrictions in 1974 resulted in a deepening recession and was rapidly abandoned in favour of reflationary policies which only stimulated higher inflation. His successor, Barre, in 1976 first concentrated on the fight against inflation and subsequently on securing business profitability in order to encourage investment, but with limited success. The Socialist government elected in 1981 initially gave priority to the struggle against unemployment but the result of its nationalisations, anti-business rhetoric, costly social reforms and reflation was once again rising inflation, declining business confidence, a deterioration in the balance of payments and an enforced devaluation of the currency. The Mauroy government was forced, like its predecessors, into a reversal of policy, in this case deflationary efforts to reduce the rise of government expenditure, limit wage increases, restrict credit and to abandon interventionist policies in favour of market liberalisation. The successive efforts of both conservative and socialist governments to reflate the economy, most notably in 1975–76 and 1981–82, had essentially negative effects contributing to the rise in inflation and reduction in international competitiveness. The controls devised in the 1940s and 1950s no longer seemed appropriate. Failure however bred a widespread internal political consensus which recognised the need for caution and participation in the international trend towards deflationary financial policy and market-place deregulation which has been effective in reducing levels of inflation.

The depths of the recession were reached in 1981–82. Subsequently inflation fell and as the burden of company indebtedness declined and profitability and business confidence rose, so levels of investment slowly recovered, although subsequently GDP growth has rarely exceeded 1.5 per cent per annum. The discipline associated with membership of the European Monetary System has helped to moderate wage claims and limit inflation. France has been able to achieve a high degree of convergence with Germany and the Benelux countries. Certainly substantial problems remain, including a fragile balance of payments and the weakness of the franc in international currency markets. Unemployment – currently over 12 per cent – remains high, and its concentration amongst the young and ethnic minorities creates a potentially explosive situation in many disadvantaged urban centres. Particularly serious is the inadequate funding of research and development and the weaknesses of such key sectors as information technology and machine tools. The establishment of the single European market, its perceived opportunities and the heightened competition it will provoke, has been greeted with a mixture of eager anticipation and fear. In spite of privatisation France still possesses the most state-dominated economy in the EC. Its political leaders seem divided between the proponents of an interventionist strategy based on long-term investment by both state-owned and private financial institutions and the liberal advocates of further deregulation. However, on the need for massive state investment in infrastructure and education there is little disagreement. Moreover, in spite of its structural weaknesses the sustained growth of the 1980s has placed the French economy in a much stronger competitive position than its more erratic British counterpart, firmly establishing it, after the United States, Japan and Germany, as the World's fourth economic power.

SOCIETY

Such massive economic change involving increasingly rapid technological innovation most recently in electronics, information technology and robotics, was accompanied by the transformation of living standards, of mentalities and of social relationships, but also of course by continuities. At any single point in time the perceptions each generation possesses of society and events is greatly influenced by the experience of its formative years. The historian needs to set generation alongside class or place of origin as a basic determinant of attitude and behaviour. Of the three generations alive in the 1960s, the oldest had been formed by the experience of the First World War. Most had direct links with the rural world. Their children, born in the 1920s and '30s, and relatively few in number, had been marked by the experience of the second war and post-war austerity. This was nevertheless the generation which broke with tradition, with the 'eternal France'. Their children, those of the 'baby boom' were far more numerous, and had grown up in a world of plenty. These were the first children of the consumer society, their values profoundly different from those of either their parents or grand-parents. The 1960s were to be the 'years of rupture' (Borne). Economic growth facilitated both geographical and social mobility. The towns recovered their dynamism, and the exodus from the countryside accelerated. Traditional religious and moral values were questioned as part of a revolution in 'taste and expectations' (Rioux). The clearest indicators of the scale of change are the statistics on socio-professional structures, revealing as they do a rapid decline in the population employed in agriculture, stability in the number of industrial workers, growth in that of office workers, and a decline in the number of employers offset by a substantial growth in the professional and managerial categories, contributing to a strengthening of the middle classes.

An early sign of change was the rise in birth-rate evident from 1942, a change of mood in a period of acute crisis and difficult to explain.

Table 7.2. *Evolution of socio-professional groups 1954–1975*
(percentage of active population)

	1954	1962	1968	1975
Farmers	20.7	15.8	12	7.7
Agricultural labourers	6	4.3	2.9	1.8
Businessmen	12	10.6	9.6	8.7
Liberal professions and upper management	2.9	4	4.9	6.9
Middle management	5.8	7.8	9.9	13.8
Office workers	10.8	12.5	14.8	16.6
Workers	33.8	36.7	37.7	37
Others	8	8.3	8.3	7.5

Source: J.-L. Monneron and A. Rowley, *Les 25 ans qui ont transformé la France* (1986), p. 133.

This proved to be more substantial and sustained than the increase which had followed the previous war. The average rate of 21 per thousand for 1945–50 was the highest for fifty years, and although subsequently it fell, it remained at an average of 17 per thousand as late as 1966–73, encouraged by generous family allowances and a growing confidence in the future. Combined with falling mortality and rising life expectancy in all social groups, this resulted in the most rapid rate of natural demographic growth in French history, of 0.8 per cent per annum between 1946 and 1962. The presence of large numbers of young people, and a reduction in the age of retirement, placed a considerable burden on the relatively small active generation born in the inter-war period. The problem of the shortage of labour was to be eased by the eventual repatriation of over a million French citizens from North Africa, by the greater employment of women, by the movement from low-productivity agricultural to more productive urban employment and by large scale immigration from the poorer regions of Europe and from the former African colonies. The number of resident foreigners rose from 1.7 million in 1954 to 4.1 million by 1975 (6.5 per cent of the population). Population growth both reflected and stimulated economic expansion, eventually resulting in a substantial increase in the labour force, by 2.5 million between the census of 1962 and that of 1975. A new demographic phase however became evident from the 1970s resulting in a declining rate of reproduction. The size of the average family again declined. One result of this will be a renewed ageing of the population, especially as the 'baby boom' children reach retirement age towards the turn of the century, which will impose severe strains on the social welfare system. To a large degree the renewed popularity of the small family was a response to the development of a consumer society. Women, themselves developing a greater sense of personal autonomy, were also anxious to remain at work in order to improve family living standards. The development of more reliable methods of birth control made this easier. The influence of both the law and religion on sexual activity was increasingly marginalised. The 1975 law legalising abortion probably did nothing more than displace a widespread practice from the back-streets into the more sanitary conditions of the hospital. The growing popularity of cohabitation outside marriage, and of divorce were indicative of greater individual autonomy although the family remains the fundamental social unit.

To a substantial extent economic recovery after the war was at the expense of current consumption. The better living standards which many had expected following the defeat of Germany were slow to appear. Even the much needed improvements in the housing stock, made all the more urgent by neglect since the onset of depression in the 1930s, were postponed in the face of the more pressing investment needs of the basic industries. Although all political parties agreed on the priority given to increasing industrial production, the CNR had also committed itself to measures of social reform. These, together with immediate wage increases, awarded to compensate for a reduction in real wages of the order of 30–40 per cent during the war, were additionally important means of encouraging the productive effort. In a major statement of principle, the preamble to the 1946 Constitution recognised the right to social security. Decrees of 4 and 19 October 1945 substantially extended protection against sickness, old age and accidents at work. Steps were also taken to increase the rights of tenant farmers and, to the intense irritation of employers, to create enterprise committees as a means of involving workers in the management of their work-places. The state through the Plan, by means of direct intervention in the economy and through its guarantees of social welfare, had taken steps which represented a transition from a liberal to a mixed economic and social system. Yet whilst insisting upon these major changes, continuities should also be stressed. Measures like those establishing enterprise committees were in practice to be largely ineffective and governments anxious above all to increase production were unwilling to press radical initiatives. For much the same reason no effort was made to implement such measures in the CNR charter as the confiscation of black market profits or those made on contracts with the German occupiers. Although most conservative politicians and businessmen were maintaining a low profile and had little choice but to accept reform, their time would come again. Little had happened to alter the basically inegalitarian character of French society or to enlarge the small circle of key decision-makers.

In these circumstances widespread discontent was inevitable. Food supplies were inadequate. Queues were endless. Shortages were blamed on speculators and the greed of the rich. Real incomes were slow to recover. In spring 1947 wages were worth only 64 per cent of their 1938 level. Working hours were long – an average of 45 hours a week in 1948. At least unemployment was minimal, but inflation rapidly eroded the value of wage increases. Even when food supplies improved, consumer goods were in short supply. There were few rewards for considerable effort. Political agitation intensified unrest and the widespread sense of insecurity and injustice. The property-owning classes complained about what they saw as the privileged treatment of the workers, denounced rent controls, trade unions and wage increases. They were concerned about the impact of inflation on their incomes and worried about their future social status. Nevertheless many farmers, manufacturers, merchants and shopkeepers, operating in a sellers' market did very well, in contrast with wage earners who appear to have been consistently disadvantaged.

Much of the population continued to live in overcrowded and insanitary accommodation little changed since the nineteenth century. At its most extreme the shortage of housing was represented by the *bidonvilles*, the shanty towns found on the outskirts of many urban areas. Only gradually, from around 1954, was the housing stock increased and improved although many of the standardised, low-cost, high rise suburban estates built for factory and office workers in the 1960s were ill-conceived and poorly constructed and rapidly degenerated into new slums. Even so higher incomes and government subsidies ensured that standards of accommodation were considerably improved. By 1975 one family in two lived in recently constructed buildings. In 1954 more than one-third of households lacked running water. Only 17.5 per cent had a bathroom or shower. By 1975 70 per cent possessed these facilities. Central heating also spread rapidly with 19 per cent of households enjoying its benefits in 1962 and 67 per cent in 1982. Greater spaciousness and physical comfort was accompanied by changing life styles. The television replaced the dining table as the focus of family life. The improvement of housing was combined with efforts to modernise and rejuvenate urban centres. Thus Paris saw the removal of the meat market from the city centre at Les Halles to Rungis and its replacement by a subterranean shopping complex topped with a park. Efforts were also made from the 1960s to promote economic decentralisation and encourage regional development but inevitably with varying degrees of success.

The economic growth and rising labour productivity of the 1950s allowed a substantial rise in real incomes and in purchasing power. With the improvement in real incomes averaging around 6 per cent the following decade saw a veritable explosion of pent-up consumer demand and the diffusion of the four products, now increasingly purchased on credit, which symbolised the new age – the refrigerator (present in only 7.5 per cent of households in 1959); the washing machine (10 per cent); television (26 per cent); and the motor car (21 per cent), the number of which increased from 5 to 15 million between 1960 and 1975. To these would be added in the 1970s the telephone found in only 15 per cent of homes in 1968 and 74 per cent by 1982, a new means of communication to replace letter writing. Equally symbolic the proportion of incomes spent on food fell from 34 to 27 per cent during the 1960s whilst that spent on housing, health and leisure grew. The less well-off revealed a great determination to catch up with the prosperous middle classes and acquire consumer durables whilst the many heirs of peasants and small businessmen remained faithful to the dream of property ownership. Amongst forty-year-olds 50 per cent owned their accommodation in 1978 compared with only 20 per cent in 1955. By the 1970s too they were searching for a greater autonomy and expressing a preference for the little house with its own garden rather than the apartment. One of the paradoxes of the period was the greater uniformity in consumption combined with a multiplication of the opportunities to express individuality in terms of dress or culture. Whilst intellectuals and the wealthy expressed their contempt for the values of this consumer society, resenting the extension to the many of privileges previously reserved to the few, most of the population enjoyed the reality of a security and comfort they had previously only dreamt about. Nevertheless income disparities between and indeed within social groups remained substantial.

The development of a welfare state contributed to the reduction of perceived inequality. Social security was born with the decrees of 1945 and law of May 1946 which sought to improve the partial protection previously available against illness, invalidity, childbirth and old age and to extend it to all wage-earners and progressively to the entire population. At the same time and largely as a pro-natalist measure existing family allowances were substantially increased. In 1947 a national minimum wage was introduced (known since 1970 as the SMIC – *salaire minimum interprofessional de croissance*), although in practice governments in order to limit its inflationary impact on the wages of the low-paid have generally allowed its levels to lag behind those of wages in general. Assurance against unemployment was only generalised in the 1950s and in France as elsewhere its spiralling cost was to become a major problem as unemployment rose in the 1970s, leading in 1984 to restrictions on entitlement, particularly harsh in their consequences for the young and long-term unemployed. More ominously this situation also encouraged a revival of neo-liberal criticism of the welfare state.

Improvements in health care, seen most notably in the disappearance of the scourge of tuberculosis, and the possibility, through a combination of social security (reimbursing 80 per cent of the cost) and assurance, of virtually free access to medical care has substantially increased public expenditure. Growing longevity and rising numbers of old people have intensified this trend. The old, together with the handicapped, were for long neglected by a social security system concerned essentially with improving the situation of children and workers. Minimal pensions were extended to most of the population between 1946 and 1952, but as growing social mobility reduced familial solidarities it gradually became clear that more needed to be done. Thus increases in the real value of pensions have been combined with initiatives by municipalities and parishes and above all self-help to provide a wide range of assistance and entertainment and have significantly improved the situation of the older age groups.

In these various ways social security has played a crucial role in protecting family living standards. Its significance as a component of average household revenue has risen from 2.9 per cent in 1929, to 16.6 per cent in 1950, 25 per cent in 1970, and then largely under the impact of rising unemployment to 35.2 per cent in 1980. Funded by assurance, employer contributions and taxation, the system involves transfer payments from the better-off to the poorer members of society, and as such has inevitably suffered from considerable criticism, voiced in particular by special interest groups like doctors anxious to protect their independence and earnings, and by businessmen critical of a contributions system which adds to their costs. The better-off in their self-interested and indeed selfish condemnation of the so-called dependency culture tend to ignore the inequities of a taxation structure which, heavily based as it is on indirect taxes, imposes a major burden on the poor. They also forget the inherently conservative impact of a system which reduces discontent.

One major consequence of economic expansion combined with that of the educational system has been to increase the opportunities for geographical and social mobility. Between 1954 and 1962, 12 million people are calculated to have changed their commune of residence. In spite of substantial upward movement the acquisition by the less well-off of the educational qualifications necessary for mobility continued to be obstructed by both social and self-imposed handicaps as well as by the simple fact that even as the numbers of skilled, supervisory, managerial and professional positions expanded, there were none-theless definite limits. The space created for newcomers was inevitably restricted both by the levels of economic growth and the ability of the already relatively privileged to maintain their positions within the overlapping professional, status and wealth hierarchies. It would be the generation reaching maturity in the 1960s which would be in the best position to take advantage of the expansion of opportunity. Subsequent generations, disadvantaged by the slowing of growth and the enlarge-ment of the active labour force, needed to struggle harder to succeed. Around the turn of the century, as the 'baby-boomers' retire and a smaller generation reaches maturity, opportunities are again likely to expand. The answer to labour shortages in the past was to encourage immigration. Absorbing large numbers of people from different races and cultures however proved difficult, especially as unemployment rose in the 1970s, and it has become politically impossible to accept large-scale influxes from outside the European Community.

The educational system, besides training young people for productive activity, is also clearly a means of integrating them into the national society. The structure inherited in 1945 provided for obligatory primary instruction until fourteen. Secondary education was reserved for a small minority (about 200,000 at any one time). Most received a humanistic teaching in which the classics retained a dominant position. Only some 3 per cent of each age group took the final examination, the *baccalauréat*. The system largely reflected the prevailing social hierarchy with a fundamental segregation between the primary and secondary levels, and between the sexes. With the exception of a very small group of 'deserving' and often intellectually outstanding working-class and peasant children, secondary education was reserved for the middle classes. The dominance of the state was unchallenged, with a uniform curriculum designed to ensure the diffusion of a common culture and sense of civic virtue although, especially in the west, private Catholic schools were tolerated. Their continuing popularity amongst parents is based not only on the religious instruction they provide but on their reputation for firmer discipline and their 'snob' value. This educational system was increasingly criticised both for its élitism and neglect of scientific and technical instruction.

The arrival of the baby-boom generations, urbanisation and the commitment of post-war governments to extending the period of study to sixteen, as well as to increasing access to secondary education, created a pressing need for both an increase and a redistribution of resources. A substantial rise in demand should anyway have been anticipated. It had already affected nursery schools from 1949/50, primary education from 1951/52, and would hit the secondary schools in 1957/58 and finally higher education from 1964. However successive governments failed fully to appreciate that growing population and the modernisation of French society would result in substantial increases in participation rates and in the demand for secondary and higher education and their response was rarely adequate. The number of pupils attending secondary schools rose from around 1 million in 1950/51 to 5 million by 1979/80. Over one-third of these obtained the *baccalauréat* turning what had been the means by which a small minority qualified for entry into the élite into a mass qualification. The problems of expansion were enormous. Schools had to be constructed and equipped, teachers trained, and teaching programmes adapted to the needs of mass instruction. Reform followed reform, adding to the confusion, with the most far-reaching probably being the imposition of the comprehensive principle by Giscard d'Estaing's education minister René Haby in 1975. Access has been massively widened although élitism survives through the selection processes of particular prestigious *lycées* or private schools. Mathematics has long replaced the humanities as the chosen path to higher education. The powerful teaching unions, concerned overwhelmingly with the protection of their own vested interests, contributed little of any value to an increasingly bitter debate on the objectives and methods of education. Nevertheless, and in line with the development of less overtly authoritarian relationships in society as a whole, teaching methods changed. A new generation of teachers was concerned less with the transmission of knowledge and more with the development of the pupils curiosity and critical faculties. An idealistic pedagogy designed for enthusiastic and competent teachers and intelligent and highly motivated children has however frequently failed in practice, so that in the 1980s and '90s a search appears to be underway, and not only in France, for some sort of compromise between the desire to encourage pupil creativity and the return to a more structured and disciplined system of education.

Higher education too faced the problems of expansion with, by 1980, a ten-fold growth from the 100,000 students of 1950 and further massive expansion likely in the 1990s as governments make determined efforts to widen access. In this sphere, élitism has been preserved by the selection procedures of the most prestigious institutions of higher education, the *grandes écoles*, including the *Polytechnique* and the *Ecole nationale d'administration*, and recently of the more prestigious private business schools, which offer access to the most powerful and highly remunerated positions in the public service and private enterprise. This remains a basic characteristic of French élite formation and part of the explanation of the network of links established across the boundaries between the state and private sectors.

Have economic growth and social reform reduced social inequality? Certainly living standards have considerably improved, and social mobility increased, but the barriers crossed have been essentially those between the peasants and workers and the lower clerical and managerial grades. Access to the higher managerial and bureaucratic posts remains extremely restricted, and it is these groups which possess power. They include the directors and managers of major companies, senior civil servants, and well-known professionals in the medical and legal spheres, in the media, and certain pressure groups, and last if certainly not least, politicians. The relationship between wealth and power is extremely complex. Certainly a family based *patronat* has survived in such major enterprises as Michelin, Dassault or Schlumberger, but most large enterprises are run by managers and owned by a diverse group of individual or institutional shareholders. Whilst one should certainly avoid the mistake of thinking about social and political élites in monolithic terms, and pay careful attention to sometimes bitter personal, generational, professional and ideological rivalries, what this 'untidy reality' (V. Wright) adds up to is the existence of a group holding public and private power which is recruited primarily amongst the Parisian bourgeoisie and given a sense of unity by linkages based on shared social origins, education, intermarriage, acceptance of common norms of behaviour and of a Parisian location, and by shared goals including the effective management of a pluralistic society, a capitalistic economy and the safeguarding of the established social order. Greater upward mobility into an expanding and increasingly technocratic civil service and managerial class has not profoundly altered this situation. Success remains normally the result of accumulated effort, often spread over two or three generations, and its translation into wealth and cultural capital. The minority of newcomers succeed because of both ability and effort and their willingness to conform to established expectations. As so often in the past, in post-war France, old and new élites have coalesced.

Whatever the limits on social mobility, economic expansion has facilitated upward mobility on a substantial scale, creating a large middle class, as determined as ever to emphasise the social and cultural gulf which separates it from the working classes. These are the groups which have particularly benefited from the development of educational opportunity and of the welfare state. Although there has been a decline,

Table 7.3. *Middle-class professions*

	1954	1975	1982
Industrialists	86,000	61,600	71,300
Wholesale merchants	183,700	190,200	210,300
Artisans	734,700	535,344	573,800
Shopkeepers	1,274,000	921,000	869,600
Liberal professions	163,160	249,440	328,640

Source: D. Borne, *Histoire de la société française depuis 1945* (1988), p. 112.

in relative terms, in the numbers of business and professional people, the middle classes have tended to stabilise in recent years. Technological change and economic concentration have had their most marked adverse effects on artisans and shopkeepers, with their insecurity being translated into political terms through Poujadism in the 1950s and the *Front national* in the 1980s and '90s. Even so for many workers and immigrants a small business still represents the possibility of social promotion. New opportunities have also developed reflecting the growing complexity and tertiarisation of the economy and expansion of public services. The numbers of doctors and teachers and of managerial and technical staff in both public and private employment have grown considerably. Entry into these groups however clearly depends upon high educational qualifications.

In marked contrast the reduced significance of agriculture is evident from both its declining contribution to GNP and the fall in the share of agriculture in the total active population from 35 per cent to 6 per cent between 1945 and 1990, with another third to a half of the remaining one million farms expected to disappear with their ageing owners before the end of the century. The peasantry has virtually disappeared. The rural exodus, involving most notably the young and landless, together with government encouragement of restructuring, have facilitated an increase in the average size of farms. When combined with technical innovation and price supports this has resulted in substantial increases in farm incomes. Nevertheless with the exception of the large capitalist farms of the north and the Paris Basin, these remain relatively low. The improvement in communications and the enhanced awareness of the wider society and constant desire for better living standards has increased rural discontent and support for pressure group activity. Increasingly however the demand for higher guaranteed prices is coming into conflict with the desire of both the national government and the European Commission to reduce agricultural over-production. The Common Agricultural Policy which initially brought prosperity is now viewed in a less positive light. Moreover dependence on traditional social élites has only been replaced by subordination to the banks (especially the Crédit Agricole) which financed the technical revolution, and to the cooperative and processing companies to which most farmers are tied by long-term contracts. During the post-war decades the decline in rural population has been accompanied by the deterioration of public services as churches, schools, post offices and shops have closed due to lack of custom. Formerly vital social networks have withered. The purchase of holiday homes by outsiders has in many regions pushed house prices beyond the levels which local young couples can afford. The rate of migration has certainly slowed since the mid-1970s, suggesting that a new equilibrium between land and population is in the making. This must however remain fragile, particularly as the reduced size of the rural population and of its vote have made it more vulnerable politically, encouraging governments to give primacy to consumer demands for cheaper food. It will perhaps be through the growing ecological movement that the status of the farmer, as the guardian of the countryside, might be restored, but this would call once again for major changes in farming methods and in a way of life. In the meantime the sense of desperation evident in many rural communities is likely to provoke repeated disorderly protest.

A relatively homogeneous, even if politically divided, working class, symbolised by the miner and the steelworker or the more modern figure on the motor car assembly line, seemed to have emerged by the 1950s, although in fact it continued to be divided by skill levels and questions of status as well as by major wage differentials. These widened in the 1950s and early 1960s to reflect shortages of skilled labour. Opportunities for social promotion however remained extremely limited and workers shared a resentment of authoritarian management, of the petty tyranny and stop-watch mentality of managers and foremen. They seem to have been more aware of the threat posed to their living standards by inflation than of the gradual rise in their real incomes.

This 'class' was to be radically restructured from the 1960s with the emergence of new forms of manufacture and the decline of the old staple industries. These changes involving automation and the development of assembly work by unskilled labour, often immigrants in the motor industry and elsewhere including growing numbers of women, increased the threat of deskilling. In large factories mass-producing consumer goods as well as in the smaller enterprises of the clothing or building industries the aim of management was increasingly to take on a cheap and relatively undemanding labour force, whose members could easily be dismissed in case of recession and replaced when conditions improved. But flexibility and restructuring for the businessman represented increased insecurity for the worker. To add to this, widespread urban renewal has physically destroyed many formally vibrant – if appallingly housed – working-class communities. In contrast innovation in sectors of industry with a high proportion of skilled labour like aeronautics, chemicals or electronics has resulted in more stable, high-wage employment. The same was true of many small and medium size family enterprises in sectors like engineering. These diverse developments represented a greater fragmentation of the labour market, and of the working class, as working conditions and life styles grew more diverse. Whilst the better rewarded and workers in the public sector have been able to maintain the protection of trade union membership, other groups lacking effective representation have in effect been marginalised.

Workers have shared in the expansion of leisure time which is such a feature of contemporary society, both in terms of time gained from work and by means of the decline of traditional pursuits like Sunday church-going. For most of the population religion, whilst surviving as a formative cultural phenomenon, has declined to insignificance as a feature of daily life. The collapse of religious vocations in the 1950s and the resultant ageing and sharp decline in the number of priests are clear signs of a crisis and of an inability to combat secularisation, especially on such crucial moral questions as abortion and contraception and this in spite of the development of a less rigorist moral theology. A new Sunday, for a new society, and a mass culture emerged in the 1960s. The decade saw the emergence of a relatively classless 'pop' culture devoted to such idols as Johnny Hallyday and Sylvie Vartan. Television, gambling and sport have boomed, as has expenditure on holidays. In 1983 30 million people took at least one holiday. Social differences of course survive. Orchestral concerts, the opera, theatre, major exhibitions, and a range of specialised books and journals tend only to attract the growing number of relatively well educated and/or pretentious. The Socialist governments of the 1980s, like post-Liberation regimes, were to be disappointed in their dream of the democratisation of culture. Within the media politically committed newspapers appear to have given way to periodicals like the Figaro Magazine and to those targeted at particular groups of women, gardeners, motorists and so on. More threatening is the tendency for the various means of publicity, the press, cinema, and radio and television too following the privatisations of the 1980s, to fall under the control of a small number of powerful financial groups. This trend, inevitable in a free market, has potentially serious implications for the country's political life. Criticism of this consumerism has had little impact. Admittedly much of this criticism has been misplaced. Thus individualism and materialism, and the decline of religious practice, have not destroyed the family, the ultimate repository of moral values. In spite of divorce, family loyalties remain of central importance and are based on more affective and less authoritarian relationships.

Regardless of class, women have in general been more likely to find work outside the home, and for longer periods of their lives, in order to meet the growing material needs of their families. Single parent families are also far more numerous due to the increased prevalence of divorce and changed attitudes towards marriage. Women's status in law has changed. The provisions of the Napoleonic Code which subordinated them to their fathers or husbands were abrogated in 1965. Nevertheless, and in spite of such provisions as the 1975 law on equal pay, women remain in an inferior position. In employment they are still concentrated in particular professions. Thus women represented in 1975 97.6 per cent of secretaries, 83.9 per cent of nurses and 67.2 per cent of primary school teachers. In a male-dominated society the progressive feminisation of shop and clerical work as the tasks involved were simplified by new technologies, from the typewriter to the computer, is especially revealing. In the higher professional and managerial positions, although the situation has improved, male dominance remains overwhelming. Within the family an opinion poll conducted in 1983 revealed that one Frenchman in three believed that male authority ought to reign supreme, but even that was a considerable improvement on the one in two who adopted the same attitude when questioned in 1974. Marriage seems, slowly, to be becoming a more equal partnership, but with women still accepting more than their share of domestic responsibilities and thus remaining more home and family orientated than their male partners.

POLITICAL LIFE

The Fourth Republic

The Third Republic was finally declared dead by a large popular majority in a referendum on 21 October 1945. A Constituent Assembly with a mission to prepare a new constitution was elected on the same day. For the first time women were allowed to vote. This innovation had been accepted by the Chamber of Deputies on four occasions between the wars but blocked in the senate by Radicals afraid of clerical influence upon female voters, realistically enough perhaps until the 1980s. This election, conducted using a system of proportional representation, revealed an overwhelming shift to the left. Three-quarters of the electorate supported the parties most clearly identified with the Liberation, the Communists (*Parti Communiste Français* (PCF)), Socialists (*Section Française de l'Internationale Ouvrière* (SFIO)), and Christian Democrats (*Mouvement Républicain Populaire* (MRP)). However the divisions between these groups would soon become evident as they jockeyed for power. So too would the tensions between these elected politicians and General de Gaulle. His unique position as head of state was initially recognised by the assembly but on 20 January 1946, following a disagreement with ministers over the military budget, the General resigned, recognising that with the restoration of the party system his authority was increasingly likely to be challenged.

The surviving idealism of the resistance and the initially secure majority of the three parties committed to a cooperative *tripartisme*, together with suspicion of authoritarian government, ensured the rapid re-establishment of a parliamentary system, with a largely decorative presidency, although it does seem likely that much of the electorate, given the difficult circumstances in which the country found itself, would have welcomed a strong executive power. The initial proposals

Table 7.4. *Results of election to Constituent Assembly,*
21 October 1945

	Votes	Share (percentage of votes)	Seats
Communists	5,024,174	26.12	159
Socialists	4,491,152	23.35	146
Radicals, UDSR[a] and others	2,018,665	10.49	60
MRP	4,580,222	23.81	150
Conservatives, Independents and others	3,001,063	15.60	64
Abstentions	4,965,256	20.1[b]	

[a] Union démocratique et socialiste de la Résistance.
[b] Percentage of registered voters.

made by the assembly, and supported especially by the Socialists and Communists, provided for a unicameral system with an omnipotent Chamber of Deputies. This was surprisingly rejected in a referendum held on 5 May 1946, by 10.5 million votes to 9.4, largely it seems because of anxiety about the possible Communist dominance of such an assembly. During the campaign for the election of a second constituent assembly in June, the MRP which had called for rejection, significantly increased its support at the expense of the Socialists. It was clear that the parties of the left (Communists and Socialists) no longer commanded an absolute majority in the assembly. Although *tripartisme* survived, an alternative majority made up of the centre-left (MRP) and the re-emerging centre-right began to appear a real possibility, particularly with the return of de Gaulle to the political scene. In a speech made in Bayeux on 16 June 1946 he called for the establishment of a presidential regime, with a head of state independent of party, although responsible to parliament. However, on 13 October another referendum accepted the second Constituent Assembly's proposals for the establishment of a Fourth Republic with a bicameral assembly. Both its upper house and the president were to enjoy only very limited authority. Power would rest with the elected representatives in the Chamber of Deputies. The most disturbing features of this prolonged constitutional debate were the widespread public apathy

– born partly from disillusionment caused by economic hardship – together with the lack of interest and commitment shown by many leading political figures. Hardly an auspicious beginning.

Politically the Fourth Republic can be divided into four phases. First that of *tripartisme* with government based on a coalition of Socialists, Communists and Christian Democrats. This was a fruitful period of economic and social reform, brought to an end in May 1947, when, as a consequence of the emerging Cold War, the Communists were forced into opposition. They were replaced by a combination of Radicals and other centrists who helped constitute a Third Force opposed to both the Communists and the Gaullists on the right. Subsequently, after the 1951 elections, the predominant groups in government were to be Radicals and conservatives, until in 1956 a majority made up of Socialists and their allies was returned to try to cope with mounting financial problems and the colonial war in Algeria.

The desire of the three main political groups within the resistance to work together represented a commitment to implementing the reform measures included in the CNR charter. The strength of popular support for these parties had been made clear in the election of the Constituent Assembly in October 1945. Unity was however, and perhaps inevitably, short-lived. The defeat of the common enemy was followed by a reconstitution of political life, much along pre-war lines. Tension rapidly grew between the partners to this uneasy alliance. Distrust of the Communists was evident from the start. Events in Eastern Europe kindled considerable suspicion. The PCF's strong electoral showing raised the unappealing prospect, particularly for the Socialists, of serving as the junior partners in a communist-dominated coalition. Neither the Socialists nor the MRP would however accept the Communist leader Thorez as prime minister, whilst de Gaulle ensured that their representatives in the government were excluded from key ministries controlling the police and army. The initial willingness of the Communists to discount the revolutionary dreams of many of their supporters had reflected both Stalin's reluctance to challenge the western powers at a time when his main concern was to secure Soviet control over Eastern Europe, and the commitment of the French Communist leaders to reconstruction combined with their belief that a brilliant war record and considerable moral credit would ensure continued mass support. The prospect of assuming power, perhaps with Socialist collaboration must have seemed very real. At the end of 1946 the PCF with 800,000 members was the largest political party, well-organised, with an effective propaganda machine and a predominating influence within the trades unions.

In contrast the MRP had been founded in November 1944 as a means of reconciling the working classes with the Church and the Church with the Republic. The Catholic hierarchy, discredited by its close links with Vichy, was prepared to accept a more liberal politics as the price of preserving its influence over the new regime. Even in 1945–46 however the left-wing idealism of its founders was giving way before the more conservative outlook of many of its supporters. Many of these were simply refugees from more overtly conservative groups discredited by their association with Vichy's collaborationist policies. They viewed the MRP primarily as a bulwark against Marxism, so that more than ever political behaviour came to reflect the map of religious beliefs.

It was the emergence of the Cold War which increasingly determined the political situation within France. Initially most politicians, including the Communists, shared a determination to restore the country to its pre-war position as a leading military and imperial power. Coming to terms with being a second-rank state and with the loss of empire was always going to be difficult. The struggle for hegemony between the two super-powers together with the agonies of decolonisation made it all the more painful. De Gaulle's sensibilities had been greatly offended by the absence of an invitation to attend the great power discussions at Yalta and Potsdam in 1945. However dependence upon American aid made it difficult to adopt a tough, independent line. Concessions had to be made on such key issues as the creation of a centralized administration in West Germany, and on free access to the French market for American products. The US administration also made clear its growing unhappiness about the presence of Communists in the French government, with Acheson in February 1947 warning President Truman that a Communist takeover in France was a very real possibility. The Marshall Plan announced in June and providing for a massive programme of free aid (between April 1948 and January 1952 France received 2629 million dollars, of which 2122 million were non-repayable) was conceived of both as a way of providing markets for American goods by assisting European recovery, and as a means of

Table 7.5. *Results of National Assembly elections,*
10 November 1946

	Votes	Share (percentage of votes)	Seats
Communists	5,430,593	28.2	182
Socialists	3,433,901	17.8	102
Radicals, UDSR and others	2,136,152	11.1	69
MRP	4,988,609	25.9	173
Conservatives, Independents and others	3,072,743	15.9	76
Abstentions	5,504,913		

reducing the likelihood of unemployment and misery and thus of Communist-inspired political disorder. It was to be a major stage in the reinforcement of the Western alliance and indeed in the development of prosperity.

The elections to the National Assembly held on 10 November 1946 made it clear that a process of left-right polarisation was under way and that the left was in a minority. The tripartite alliance was riven by dissension, and a renewal of the governing coalition had become impossible. The efforts of a minority Socialist administration under Blum to control inflation and stimulate economic recovery were short-lived. The Socialists themselves were bitterly divided. At their July 1946 Congress they had elected Guy Mollet as party secretary on a platform, which whilst rejecting the Soviet model, reaffirmed the party's commitment to Marxist ideology, warned against close collaboration with the bourgeois parties and recommended closer links with the Communists. This was not however the moment. As the international situation deteriorated, the Communists, stung by Soviet criticism, denounced western imperialism and the Marshall Plan and all those, including the Socialists, who supported it. The brutal imposition of Soviet rule in Eastern Europe persuaded even most Socialists that Communism was a far greater danger than liberal, capitalistic democracy. Rumours of an imminent Communist coup led Ramadier, another Socialist, who had succeeded Blum in January 1947 with a government which now included Radicals and other representatives of the centre, to alert reliable military units. In this situation the dismissal of Communist ministers from the Ramadier government in May 1947 was inevitable. It was occasioned by Thorez's denunciation of wage and price controls and the refusal of the ministers concerned to vote credits for the war in Indochina. Tactically the PCF was determined to win the support of workers disappointed with the slowness of reform and of the improvement of living standards and resorting to strikes and violence in protest. At this stage however the eventual return of Communist ministers to government was certainly expected. This and such events as the Communist take-over in Prague which was welcomed by the PCF as the 'great victory of Czech democracy' helped to sustain an increasingly hysterical but also very understandable anti-communism. The French Communists in response, with considerable support amongst intellectuals as well as the working class, denounced American imperialism and the subservience of French governments.

Internal political tension grew all the more bitter as the fear of a global nuclear conflict reached its peak between 1948 and 1958 with events in Prague, the Berlin blockade and war in Korea. In 1949 the efforts of foreign minister Bidault and his British counterpart Bevin to secure American military support were rewarded with the establishment of NATO, as the prelude to an eventual and much resented rearmament of Western Germany. The Communist party developed as a party of permanent opposition. In a period of intense political debate and of engaged militancy, enjoying the prestige it and the Soviet Union had won in the liberation of Europe, the Party and its various organisations were able to create a dynamic counter culture and to offer a spiritual refuge to those members of an increasingly exhausted and demoralised working class still prepared to continue the struggle against low wages and social injustice. In spite of the ineffectiveness of its political and industrial tactics a quarter of the electorate voted for the Party in 1951. Subsequently support would, gradually, but almost continually, decline. Increasingly inward looking, concerned to preserve its Stalinist purity and to purge dissenters, the Party welcomed Soviet repression of the 1956 Hungarian revolt as yet another famous victory for Leninism. Although it was able to retain much of its working-class support, even when anti-communists split the trade union federation (the CGT) to form the CGT–FO (*Force Ouvrière*) in

Plate 52 Troops, employed by Socialist ministers as strike breakers in October 1947 and early 1948, guarding pitheads in the Saint-Etienne region

April 1948, the Party was unable to escape from its isolation. It became patently unable to come to terms with economic and social developments which resulted in the improvement of living standards. Moreover changes in the structure of the work force resulted in a continuous decline in the size and economic importance of its working class constituency which was becoming both more diverse and more fully integrated into the national society.

Ramadier's fragile coalition gave way in November 1947 to a government led by Schuman of the MRP, the composition of which marked a clear shift to the right. Within it even the Socialist Interior Minister, Jules Moch, was committed to repressive action against strikers and demonstrators. In the interests of 'Republican defence' he mobilised 60,000 riot police and troops against 15,000 miners during November and December. The Socialists, a party with a revolutionary ideology, were, however uncomfortably, to remain within a series of increasingly conservative 'Third Force', governments, all committed to the Atlantic alliance, to colonial wars, to the rejection of further

Table 7.6. *National Assembly elections, 17 June 1951*
(metropolitan France only)

	Votes	Share (percentage of votes)	Seats (including overseas)
Communists	4,910,547	25.67	101
Socialists	2,744,842	14.35	107
Radicals	1,887,583	9.87	95
MRP	2,369,778	12.39	96
Conservatives, Independents and others	2,656,995	13.88	108
Gaullists	4,125,492	21.56	120
Abstentions	4,859,968		

social reform and to the repression of the working-class movement. Although they brought down a whole series of governments on questions of economic and social reform between 1947 and 1951 they were unable to effectively combat the MRP's growing adherence to liberalism or the essential conservatism of a reviving Radical Party still led by such stalwarts of the Third Republic as Herriot and Daladier. As a result of this situation and of the internal differences it provoked, the Socialist Party was to lose much of its credibility. Membership collapsed from 280,000 in 1947 to 130,000 in 1951 and was increasingly confined to the old strongholds in the north and Midi. This weakening was clearly revealed by the results of the 1951 elections, and in spite of changes in the electoral system designed to disadvantage the critics of the regime on both left (Communists) and right (Gaullists). In future governments would be drawn from the centre-right, with only occasional Socialist participation.

The Cold War whilst it divided the left helped to restore the right, and, under the anti-communist banner, to ensure it mass support. It facilitated the return to political life of many former Vichy sympathisers. The fear of social revolution, which in the nineteenth century had led to the bloody massacres of 1848 and 1871, remained a potent political force. This was a theme which could be stressed by the Catholic MRP as well as by de Gaulle in founding his *Rassemblement du Peuple Français* (RPF) in April 1947. Apparently convinced that a global war against communism was close, the General called for the association of capital and labour within the free enterprise system, for the rejection of confrontational party politics, for a strong and independent France within the western alliance, and for firm and effective internal government. This declaration of war on the Fourth Republic appealed especially to the possessing classes but in a fashion reminiscent of Bonapartism it won adherents in all social groups. By the end of the year the movement had perhaps one million members, many of them attracted from the MRP. Such a dynamic organisation clearly posed a threat to the regime, but it proved impossible to sustain the commitment of the disparate groups which had looked on it as yet another new beginning. The years 1950–51 saw a substantial loss of enthusiasm and a collapse of membership.

The recovery of the right was nevertheless quite evident. The governments which emerged from the assembly elected in 1951, whilst supported by the MRP were essentially representative of the centre-right. This was clear from the policies of the 1952 Pinay administration which sought to promote economic liberalisation, to limit state expenditure and reduce taxation. These were policies well-suited to the times, helping to moderate and to sustain economic growth and to ease the transition from austerity to consumerism. In the shorter term however they could do little to reduce the budget deficit, caused in large part by colonial war in Indo-China, which might well have been avoided if the colonial lobby and military commanders on the spot had been prepared to respect the agreement reached in 1946 between the Communist leader Ho Chi Minh and de Gaulle's emissary Jean Sainteny. Another persistent problem was the unfavourable balance of payments. There was widespread popular discontent, amongst farmers due to falling agricultural prices, and more generally because of the impact of regressive tax structures and of inflation on incomes. Ministerial instability, with governments rarely lasting more than six months, added to the impression of chaos. Although in practice the establishment of a new government involved little more than a reshuffling of ministerial personnel, it was clear that political stability was impossible on the basis of the Assembly elected in 1951. There were too many fissures within as well as between parties. Governments could be suddenly overturned on all manner of issues.

Perhaps the last chance for the Fourth Republic came in the

Plate 53 The government of Pierre Mendès-France, 19 June 1954.
François Mitterrand is on his right

aftermath of the military disaster at Dien Bien Phu, when on 17 June
1954 Pierre Mendès-France, a severe critic of the political system and
proponent of strong, coherent and reforming government, became
prime minister with apparently broad parliamentary and public
support. His objectives were to negotiate a withdrawal from Indo-
China, and to accelerate the pace of economic and social modernisation. The new prime minister's energy and unwillingness to play
the usual political game and the radio broadcasts in which he seemed
to be appealing to the nation over the heads of the political
establishment, however, aroused considerable suspicion and nowhere
more than within the ranks of his own Radical party. In place of the
usual sharing of ministries between the governing parties Mendès-
France had moreover insisted upon the appointment of relatively
youthful and independent figures of proven competence including
François Mitterrand, representing the centre-left, to the Interior
Ministry and the left-gaullist Jacques Chaban-Delmas to Public Works,
to add to the experience of an Edgar Faure at Finance.

The most pressing problem, that of Indo-China was solved by an
armistice signed on 21 July which provided for partition along the
seventeenth parallel and the withdrawal of the French expeditionary
force. This had already lost some 92,000 men. Its leaders were to be left

with a deep sense of humiliation by the agreement. Blaming the politicians for their failure, they were determined to make no further concessions in what many of them saw as a crusade against international communism. The Assembly on 10 August also proved willing to grant Mendès-France special economic powers, and in spite of its short life the government was able to introduce a series of measures intended to improve the competitiveness of the French economy. These included agricultural price supports and cheap loans and assistance for industrial restructuring and training. Surprisingly little public interest was shown in a social policy which promised increased expenditure on housing and education. In contrast, the government's campaign against alcoholism drew venomous attacks from both the home distillers and the commercial alcohol lobby, much of it anti-semitic in character and intended to throw doubt on the patriotic credentials of a prime minister who seemed to prefer milk to more manly national beverages. Although initially opinion polls suggested that Mendès-France had secured the enthusiastic support of most of the population, this was to be short-lived. Mendès-France was attacked from the right for his supposed betrayal of empire. Doubt was thrown on his determination to defend vital French interests. The question of the European Defence Community and the implications for national sovereignty of the possible creation of a European army resulted in a bitter political debate indicative of deep divisions amongst government supporters. Mitterrand was actually accused of leaking defence secrets to the Communists, the victim of a secret service plot to discredit the government it was supposed to serve. On the left Mollet, the Socialist leader, was more concerned with preserving the unity of his own party than with supporting the government. In this context it was hardly surprising that Mendès-France's proposals for constitutional reform to strengthen the executive enjoyed limited parliamentary support, although it seems clear that there was a widespread public desire for the curtailment of an increasingly sterile political conflict. It was to be events in North Africa which led however to the final showdown. Certainly the government had reacted firmly to the outbreak of violence in Algeria in November 1954 and to the foundation of the *Front de Libération Nationale* (FLN). Mitterrand had unequivocally declared that Algeria would remain part of France and supported this with troop reinforcements and widespread arrests.

However Mendès-France's willingness to end the French protectorate over Tunisia and to improve the situation of Algerian Muslims had thrown doubt upon his commitment.

The final parliamentary defeat came on 5 February 1955 when conservatives fearful that they might lose from Mendès-France's modernisation programme were joined by MRP deputies who saw the possibility of reform in Algeria as a sign of weakness, and by the Communists, consistent opponents of any 'neo-capitalist' administration. The Radical Party itself was to be irremediably split. Edgar Faure challenged Mendès-France for the party leadership and was eventually able to form a centre-right government on 23 February, but even this master of political compromise was unable to survive a parliamentary debate on electoral reform on 29 November. On this occasion, rather than simply accept defeat Faure made use of some of the more complicated articles of the constitution to secure the dissolution of parliament before the end of its full term, the first time this had happened since 1877. The campaign which preceded the elections held on 2 January 1956 revealed growing political fragmentation. Mendès-France was able to form a *Front républicain* with support from the Socialists and from a diverse centre-left which included Mitterrand and members of the UDSR (*Union démocratique et socialiste de la Résistance*) as well as Chaban-Delmas and some Gaullists. Their inevitably vague programme supported a negotiated peace in Algeria and the continuation of economic modernisation and social reform at home. In an unpleasant campaign moderate conservatives were, with some reason, anxious about the prospect of being outflanked on the right by candidates of the Poujadist movement (after the name of its leader) the *Union de défense des commerçants et artisans*. This was supported especially by small businessmen and farmers from the economically under-developed centre and south-west, attracted by its opposition to modernisation. The party also enjoyed the support of an extreme right fighting the cause of French Algeria (*Algérie française*) and including such luminaries as the violent ex-paratrooper Le Pen. These groups shared a contempt for parliament, an extreme xenophobia, anti-semitism and a visceral anti-communism.

Once again the elections failed to provide a clear parliamentary majority. The Gaullists in particular, whether of the centre-left or

Table 7.7. *National Assembly elections, 2 January 1956*
(*metropolitan France*)

	Votes	Share (percentage of votes)	Seats (including overseas)
Communists	5,514,403	25.36	150
Socialists	3,247,431	14.93	95
Radicals, UDSR and others	3,227,484	14.84	91
MRP	2,366,321	10.88	83
Conservatives, Independents and others	3,259,782	14.99	95
Poujadists, extreme right	2,744,562	12.62	52
Gaullists	842,351	3.87	22
Abstentions	4,602,942		

-right, lost heavily. The President of the Republic, Coty, decided that the Socialist Mollet rather than Mendès-France stood the better chance of forming a government. This would in practice be based on a very uncertain centre-left parliamentary combination, constantly imperilled by the lack of party discipline and divisions between its constituent parts. Although the Mendès-France government is often represented as the last real opportunity to preserve the Fourth Republic by means of reform, the Mollet administration, in spite of the usual incensed opposition of conservatives to tax increases, was able to secure substantial improvements in welfare provisions for the aged and sick, as well as to increase funding for housing and regional aid. Ominously however the war in Algeria was beginning to absorb capital and manpower on a scale which seemed to threaten financial stability and economic growth. It also further embittered political life.

Mollet acted on the mistaken assumption that the FLN would settle for something less than full independence and that Europeans in Algeria would accept major reforms undermining their privileges. He was to be rapidly disabused. The revenge killings by French soldiers and civilians which had followed the FLN-inspired massacre of 123 European civilians in the Constantine region in August 1955 probably destroyed any lingering hope of a compromise based upon the integration of Algeria into France with full rights of citizenship for all its inhabitants. The limited political concessions actually made to the Moslem population, and often not implemented by the colonial administration, did little to counter the growing unwillingness of the majority population to tolerate social and racial inferiority. The mistakes of Indo-China were about to be repeated. Successive governments were to accept the self-interested advice of colonial administrators and military commanders, and to succumb to pressure from settler opinion and conservative politicians. In so doing they would play into the hands of extreme nationalists. Thus in the search for a military solution Mollet would find himself in the paradoxical position of increasingly being condemned by the left and winning support from the right. 'Pacification' now became a precondition for reform.

The army would enjoy considerable success. Its officers had developed a new sense of purpose as a result of their harsh experience in Indo-China. They believed they had a mission to integrate Algeria into the national community and to continue the crusade against the communist-inspired subversion which alone in their eyes prevented the achievement of this aim. Once again the officer corps, in assuming ever closer control over Algeria, could pose as the incarnation of France. Their patriotism was exceeded only by their arrogance and by their contempt for the politicians who they believed had betrayed them in the earlier war and might do so again. Some 400,000 men were eventually committed. General Massu's paratroopers fought and won the battle of Algiers against the FLN's urban networks. The construction of the electrified Morice line made it impossible for independence fighters to cross the frontier from their havens in Tunisia without suffering heavy casualties. The recruitment of Muslim auxiliaries revealed and reinforced divisions within the indigenous population at the same time as strengthening the French military position. Politically however the campaign was a disaster. In November 1956, in cooperation with Britain and Israel, France launched an attack on Nasser's Egypt, believed to be both the inspiration and armourer of Algerian insurgents. The bombing of the Tunisian village of Sakhiet in February 1958 and particularly the growing use of torture to obtain information added to the sense of international outrage. Within France itself the initial broad support for preserving French Algeria was dissipating. Criticism of government policy was voiced especially by Communists, by some Catholic activists and members of socialist youth groups like Michel Rocard and in leading newspapers like *Le Monde* and the weekly *L'Express*, although this was little enough in comparison with the pro-war sentiments of the mass circulation right-wing press and the government-controlled radio and television. Nevertheless public opinion, which had been relatively indifferent to the distant Indo-Chinese war fought mainly by regular and colonial troops, was much more concerned about a war waged in an area, nominally at least part of France, and which drew in rising numbers of young conscripts. A majority of the respondents to an opinion poll in autumn 1957 already doubted whether Algeria would remain French. The rise of opposition was based on moral and political objections and doubts as to whether the rising costs of the war in terms of men and money could be maintained, in spite of the willingness of the United States to absorb some of the material costs as part of the world-wide struggle against communism. The resignation of Mendès-France, Minister without Portfolio in the Mollet government, and the criticism voiced by Mitterrand, whilst remaining in office, were signs of a loss of confidence within the political élite itself.

The replacement of Mollet successively by the Radicals Bourgès-Manoury and Gaillard represented a reshuffling of ministries between Socialists, members of the MRP and Radicals and the absence of new initiatives towards Algeria or the escalating financial problems caused by the war. In May 1958 however the Socialists finally decided that coalitions with parties of the right in efforts to solve the Algerian problem were leading nowhere. Their withdrawal made the formation of a government all the more difficult. After almost a month President Coty called on Pflimlin of the MRP to form an administration. The real significance of this was that he had previously called for negotiations with the FLN. His appointment was greeted by demonstrations in Paris and an open rejection of the government's authority by civilians and the army in Algeria. The final crisis of the regime had arrived.

In Algeria, European extremists had called for resistance, and on this occasion received support from senior military commanders. On 13 May a Committee of Public Safety, amongst whose members was General Massu, assumed power. Pflimlin, in response, took an apparently tough line, calling on all parties to join him in the defence of the Republic. In a parliamentary vote of confidence he obtained the support of 274 deputies, but a significant 129 rejected his policy. The

Socialists at least were prepared to re-enter the government. The prime minister was however clearly unwilling to risk civil war in an effort to assert his authority. His desire for a compromise encouraged the rebel generals, as did the manoeuvres of leading Gaullists like Chaban-Delmas and Debré. On 15 May General Salan the commander-in-chief in Algeria was heard to shout *Vive de Gaulle* to crowds gathered in front of the Government-General building in Algiers. Later that day de Gaulle himself announced that he was prepared to reassume power, a move which the government failed to condemn.

Civil war remained a real possibility, with generals in Algeria planning parachute drops in the Paris region to link up with potentially rebellious troops already there, and de Gaulle saying nothing to discourage this planned military coup. As the days passed it became more and more evident that the authority of the government was disintegrating, with ministers paralysed by fear of provoking a civil war in which their staunchest supporters would be the despised Communists, and with Pflimlin, his deputy Mollet and even President Coty all in touch with de Gaulle. Corsica was taken over by the rebels on 24–25 May, without resistance. On 27 May de Gaulle, with complete contempt for the constitution, announced that he intended to form a government and Pflimlin, aware of his growing isolation, and anxious to avoid conflict, resigned. The alternatives, as they appeared to President Coty, were now military dictatorship or the inauguration of de Gaulle. He preferred the latter, and de Gaulle was duly invited to become the last prime minister of the Fourth Republic. Although he had refused to condemn the military *putchistes* and had clearly manipulated the crisis to his own advantage in the hope of being called upon once more as the saviour of his country, the General's promise to respect republican institutions at least seemed to offer escape from the crisis without total humiliation.

On 1 June de Gaulle appeared before the National Assembly and was granted emergency powers for six months. Some 329 deputies supported this and 224, including the Communists and half the Socialists, opposed. De Gaulle's administration reflected the widespread desire for compromise. The situation seemed to demand a government of national unity. It included leading parliamentary figures from all parties save the Communist, with most notably his predecessor Pflimlin, together with Pinay at Finance. Reassuringly it included few committed Gaullists. One of its first tasks was to prepare a new constitution and bring down the curtain on the Fourth Republic. In this, as opinion polls and the referendum of 28 September would reveal de Gaulle, as the 'saviour' of the nation once before, enjoyed the support of most of the population. People were impatient with the seeming incompetence, the constant squabbling, and the indecisiveness of the parliamentary regime, and anxious for the restoration of the authority of the state.

Yet it would be unwise to condemn the defunct regime out of hand. A system of government based, like that of the Third Republic, on rapidly shifting alliances within a class of political notables and election by proportional representation was inherently unstable. Governments with impermanent majorities were not best suited to dealing with the problems of reconstruction, the rapid expansion of the state's responsibilities, with colonial wars, repeated financial crises, and the social tension caused by unequal access to the rewards of economic growth. However in contrast with the Third Republic, when the state had appeared as the helpless spectator of economic and social change, the result was no longer stalemate. Economic and social forces, and in particular the internationalisation of economic activity resulting from American predominance and the moves towards European integration were too strong. Moreover guidance and continuity had been provided by an increasingly self-confident and assertive bureaucracy. In this respect, one of the regime's weaknesses, the disassociation between political and administrative and economic power, had facilitated reconstruction, the establishment of a welfare state, and inaugurated an unprecedented period of sustained economic growth and improvement in the standard of living. In many respects the regime had revealed a firmer grasp of the economic and political realities than had British governments of the same period. Thus alongside the ill-advised efforts to hang on to empire, major moves had also been taken towards Franco–German reconciliation and greater European unity within the OEEC (1948), the Council of Europe and NATO (1949), the European Coal and Steel Community (1951) and finally with the signing of the Treaty of Rome in 1957.

The Fifth Republic

The style of political authority and the structures of political institutions were to undergo major changes. De Gaulle's objective remained that stated in the 1946 Bayeux speech, that is, whilst preserving a parliamentary system, to reinforce the power of the President of the Republic and his ability to secure the common interest against the particularism of political parties, trades unions, business and other private interests. Another urgent priority was to bring the Algerian war to an end, and with it the continual drain on French manpower and money. These objectives were to be the means of achieving a greater end, the modernisation of the French economy and society, and of its defences, in order to establish internal unity and order, and to restore the country to its rightful place amongst the great powers. De Gaulle's frequent references to the eternal values of France thus concealed a determination to adapt to the realities of a rapidly changing world.

The new constitution was prepared by a Committee of experts and one of ministers chaired by de Gaulle's henchman Debré and including such eminent representatives of the old regime as Pflimlin and Mollet. The result very much reflected the general's views. It provided for a President who would select his prime minister and assume responsibility for the conduct of government. His position was reinforced by the right to appeal to the nation through referenda, the old Bonapartist tactic and with results so unpredictable as to be rarely resorted to; he had the right to dissolve the National Assembly, a useful means of putting pressure on its members; and to assume emergency powers. Governments remained responsible to the National Assembly and could be forced to resign by a vote of no confidence, although this would now require the support of an absolute majority of deputies and to make this all the more difficult to achieve, abstentions would be counted as rejections of the censure motion. The assembly was to be further weakened by restrictions on the rights of deputies to ask questions or to seek to amend legislation, a reduction in the length of its sessions and in its overall legislative responsibilities. This represented a very deliberate weakening of parliament, and a determination to transfer authority to the executive power. In future it was intended that, as in Britain, parliament would be able to influence government but not to control it. Moreover the many ambiguities contained in the constitutional document were to be resolved by de Gaulle himself during a long period of office lasting until April 1969,. The development of presidential authority would be assisted by the failure of deputies to develop the potential powers of parliament and their tolerance of abuses. Published on 4 September the new constitution was accepted by almost 80 per cent of those who voted in a referendum held on 28 September. The parties of the right were strongly in favour, those of the left divided. The main opposition came from the Communists, together with prominent but isolated figures like Mendès-France and Mitterrand.

A new electoral system for legislative elections was introduced by decree. Its inbuilt unfairness can be seen from the fact that a successful candidate from the right would need to gain 20,000 votes, a Socialist 79,000 and a Communist 380,000. In the elections which followed on 23 and 30 November 1958 major changes in voting behaviour were nevertheless evident with massive gains for the Gaullists and other conservatives, united in the *Union pour la Nouvelle République* *(UNR)*, whilst the left lost heavily because of its confused or hostile attitudes towards de Gaulle. Some 70 per cent of the deputies elected were supporters of de Gaulle. This was also to be an assembly very much made up of newcomers. Only around one-quarter of the new deputies had sat in the previous parliament. Such prominent opponents of the new regime as Mendès-France and Mitterrand had been defeated.

In the presidential election held on 21 December, 78.5 per cent of the local councillors and deputies who made up the electoral college (80,000 people in all) supported de Gaulle. On 10 January 1959 the general asked Debré, a committed Gaullist, and also passionate advocate of the retention of French control over Algeria, to form a government. It soon became clear that de Gaulle intended to define his own spheres of action and regarded ministers, including the prime minister, as very much his subordinates. Unwillingness to accept this role meant certain and rapid dismissal with a tendency for technocrats to replace the more independent political figures. Ministers might enjoy devolved power, but certainly not autonomy. The strict separation of powers which made membership of parliament incompatible with ministerial office, sought to ensure, if with only limited success, that ministers were deprived of an independent power

Table 7.8. *National Assembly elections, 23 and 30 November 1958*
(metropolitan France)

	Percentage of first ballot votes	Seats after two ballots	Percentage of seats
Communists	18.9	10 (including overseas 10)	2.1
Socialists	15.7	40 (including overseas 47)	8.6
Radicals and others	8.2	37 (including overseas 40)	8.0
MRP	10.8	55 (including overseas 64)	11.8
Gaullists	20.3	196 (including overseas 206)	42.2
Conservatives, Independents and others	24.2	127 (including overseas 129)	27.3
Others		81 overseas deputies	

base. Moreover the position of the president was to be further reinforced following the referendum of September 1962 which decided in favour of election by universal suffrage. This would enhance the legitimacy of the holder of presidential office. Clearly too, following the near success of an assassination attempt by *Algérie française* extremists at Petit-Clamart on 22 August, de Gaulle wished to provide the means by which his successor might acquire sufficient prestige, as the elect of the people, to continue to provide strong leadership. Hostile commentators represented this as a major assault on the republican tradition, reminding their readers that the last president elected by universal suffrage had been Louis-Napoléon Bonaparte and his success had been followed by a dictatorship. De Gaulle's response to parliamentary opposition to these proposals, which was strong enough to bring down the Pompidou government, was to dissolve the assembly and hold a referendum on the question (28 October), followed by elections to a new assembly (18 and 25 November). In both votes he was successful, with his UNR gaining record levels of support for a French political party, although neither victory was as overwhelming as he might have wished. The centre was crushed, but the left achieved a respectable showing in what was in effect a developing process of

Table 7.9. Results of referendum of 28 October 1962

		Percentage
Registered voters	27,582,113	
Abstentions	6,280,297	22.7
Spoiled ballots	559,758	2.0
Yes	12,809,363	61.7
No	7,932,695	38.2

Table 7.10. National Assembly elections, 18 and 25 November 1962

	First ballot votes	Percentage of votes	Seats after two ballots
Communists	3,992,431	21.7	41
Socialists	2,319,662	12.6	66
Radicals and others	1,384,498	7.5	42
MRP	1,635,452	8.9	38
Gaullists and others	5,847,403	31.9	233
Conservatives, Independents and others	2,540,615	14.3	52

political polarisation. These successes saw the completion of the work of constitutional reform which created the presidential system of the Fifth Republic. The process of institutional change and the more gradual development of constitutional conventions, were to create a new political culture. Perhaps de Gaulle's greatest achievement, during what was to be an extremely constructive period of government, was to be the creation of a political system acceptable to almost the entire population. For the first time since the Revolution there was a general consensus in favour of republican institutions.

The political system which emerged after 1958 was clearly presidential. De Gaulle in particular reserved for himself the spheres of defence and foreign policy and the Algerian question. The prime minister, whatever his constitutional position, was in practice very much the president's man. Ministers were executants, drawn increasingly from the bureaucracy and replaceable at will, rather than from a parliament which was treated in disdainful fashion as good for debate but incapable of decision-taking. The replacement of the faithful Debré with Pompidou in April 1962 was symptomatic of the General's assertiveness, as was the immediate reappointment of the latter in October after a parliamentary motion of no-confidence had forced him to resign.

Another major trend, evident from elections, was the beginning of a process of 'bipolarisation', a political restructuring, in which the various parties tended to coalesce into Gaullist and opposition groups with the parties of the centre like the Radicals and MRP largely absorbed into the presidential coalition. This process of adjustment to new institutions was largely forced on politicians by an electoral system which required alliances for success. The development of a dominant, if still heterogeneous, conservative coalition – in marked contrast with the Third and Fourth Republics – demanded a comparable drive towards unity on the left. So too did de Gaulle's own, seemingly contradictory, role as a party leader determined to secure a parliamentary majority for his UNR and its allies. He thus recognised that even a president elected by universal suffrage depended on the institutionalised support of a political party during his lengthy (seven year) period of office. Another factor promoting bipolarisation was of course the presidential system which focused attention on the need to support the personalities capable of capturing that key office in a final ballot which allowed for only two candidates. From the point of view of the voter the reduction in competition between parties whilst reducing freedom of choice has at least provided more clearly defined alternatives.

De Gaulle's return to power corresponded with, and he sought to encourage, an acceleration of the processes of industrialisation, urbanisation and secularisation. These developments were accompanied by a waning of some traditionally divisive constitutional and cultural issues, as they gave way to an absorbing concern with economic betterment. In this situation, whatever the rhetoric of national unity, his was essentially government from the right, its economic and social policies acceptable to a broad coalition of centrist and conservative opinion. Additionally, for as long as de Gaulle himself remained head of state, the regime benefited from the unique status of the former leader of Free France. The great advantage the

Gaullist state would provide was the political stability essential to continued modernisation. First however the last great legacy of colonialism had to be eliminated.

Concerted rebellion by Moslems in Algeria in protest against the European ascendancy had begun on 1 November 1954 and was to lead in July 1962, after great bloodshed and numerous atrocities on both sides, to French withdrawal. It was the army's distrust of the political leadership which had led to de Gaulle's return. It was to be the General's own apparent betrayal of the cause of *Algérie française* which was to lead many of these same soldiers into a second attempted coup in April 1961. In practice de Gaulle's policy was essentially pragmatic. It evolved from a basic desire to maintain close ties between France and Algeria and a commitment to a combination of continued military repression with social and political reform to a reluctant acceptance (possibly by as early as September 1959) that 'self determination' for Algeria was unavoidable. Disengagement had come to be seen not only as the vital means of avoiding the wastage of material and human resources essential for the modernisation of France, (although the economic costs were probably exaggerated at the time), but also as necessary to bring to an end a sustained crisis which had brought the army into politics and continued to threaten political stability, and which because of much-publicised atrocities threatened the country's international moral standing. The referendum of 8 January 1961 made it clear that a large majority of war-weary voters agreed (75.2 per cent). Those who voted against de Gaulle's proposals included the Communists who with typically false logic strongly favoured independence for Algeria but opposed the government on principle, as well as the extreme right which wanted to impose a military solution whatever the cost. The murderous campaign subsequently waged in both France and Algeria by rebel officers and civilians failed to change government policy, only widening the already enormous gulf between the two communities in Algeria and ensuring that there would be no place in an independent Algeria for its million European residents or for the Moslem auxiliaries of the French army, 150,000 of whom with their families were forced to join the exodus of Europeans. Shamefully many more were abandoned to a gruesome fate.

In foreign policy too the advent of de Gaulle meant not only a change

Plate 54 General de Gaulle speaks to the nation on television, 23 April 1961. Condemning the military putsch in Algeria he concluded with the appeal: 'Français, Françaises, aidez moi'

of perspective but a greater determination to secure what were believed to be vital national interests. In May 1962 the General declared his opposition to closer integration within the developing European Community, favouring instead cooperation within a much looser

Plate 55 Reconciliation and the construction of a new Europe.
General de Gaulle with Chancellor Adenauer during his visit to
West Germany in September 1962

'Europe of the Nations'. He assumed that the nation-state was, and
would remain, the fundamental reality in international affairs. France
increasingly distanced itself from the Western Alliance and particularly
American foreign policy, finally withdrawing from the NATO command structure in March 1966. Whilst recognising the continued
importance of American nuclear protection, de Gaulle's regime poured
much greater resources than had previous governments into the
development of an independent nuclear force. This would safeguard
France from nuclear blackmail by Russia or any other state in situations
in which the United States might not be willing to risk all-out nuclear
war to protect one of its allies. Suspicion of American intentions was
one reason for de Gaulle's refusal to agree to British membership of the
European Community. The British it was assumed would too closely
represent American interests. In contrast Franco–German reconciliation was energetically pursued by both the French president and the
West German chancellor, Adenauer. The development of a broad
popular consensus in support of these policies provided an important
political underpinning for governments of the right throughout the

A L'AUBE DU MARCHÉ COMMUN
VENDRE EST AUSSI IMPORTANT QUE PRODUIRE

IPEAC INSTITUT POUR LA PROMOTION ÉCONOMIQUE PAR L'ACTION COMMERCIALE

Plate 56 The establishment of the Common Market by the Treaty of Rome signed on 25 March 1957 and taking effect from 1 January 1958 provided both an opportunity and a challenge to French enterprises. This poster by Savignac encourages industrial modernisation to ensure competitiveness

following decades. France appeared to have been restored to its 'true' position as a major power. The reality, in spite of efforts to secure a rapprochment with the Soviet Union, was a continued anti-communist commitment and dependence on the Western Alliance particularly evident during such moments of heightened international tension as the Czech crisis of August 1968.

Enhanced military strength was of course closely dependent upon economic modernisation. While the foundations had already been laid, economic growth and restructuring were to continue at an accelerating pace. This was greatly facilitated by the political stability combined with greater governmental financial rigour and a more effective anti-inflationary policy which characterised the de Gaulle presidency. The progressive opening of frontiers within the EEC reflected the deliberate

Table 7.11. *National Assembly Elections, 5 and 12 March 1967*

	First ballot votes	Share (percentage of votes)	Seats after second ballot
Communists	5,039,032	22.51	73
FGDS	4,231,173	18.90	121
Centre démocrate	3,153,367	14.09	41
UDR (Gaullists) and allies	8,608,959	38.45	244

intention of forcing French enterprises to become internationally competitive. They were assisted by massive subsidies and tax incentives and the rapid growth (especially before 1975) of both the West European and World economies. Economic growth additionally facilitated the improvement of living standards, with per capita incomes rising by an annual average of 4.5 per cent between 1959 and 1973. The regime certainly took much of the credit for this greater prosperity. Widespread discontent nevertheless persisted. In part this was because rising aspirations made gross inequalities in the distribution of wealth all the harder to bear, in part because government policies designed to limit the inflationary consequences of continuous growth led to the neglect of social investment in housing, schools and hospitals and to wage controls, periodic rises in unemployment and greater insecurity. The revival of political opposition was one symptom of a sense of malaise, made all the greater by the patent inability of a weak and fragmented trades union movement to influence events.

The emergence of the Fifth Republic had created a potentially disastrous situation for the left. In the 1958 elections only 10 Communists, 44 Socialists and 33 Radical deputies had been returned. The Communists set out on what was to be a prolonged, though for long concealed, decline. The Socialists, like the Radicals, remained closely associated in the public mind with the failures of the Fourth Republic. Moreover cooperation between these parties was made all the more unlikely by the Communist's rigidly Stalinist and pro-Soviet stance. The 1962 legislative elections, with de Gaulle enjoying the credit for the solution of the Algerian affair, only reinforced this picture of apparently terminal decline. Increasingly however, as the 1960s progressed, the left took a stand against the excessive 'personal' power of the president and social injustice. The presidential elections of December 1965 when de Gaulle failed to win an overall majority in the first round and was forced into a humiliating run-off with Mitterrand (finally obtaining 55.2 per cent of the votes cast), and the legislative elections in March 1967 revealed a growing audience for its point of view.

The improved showing of the opposition was due to the more cooperative spirit of the Communists and the emergence of a credible alternative to de Gaulle in the person of Mitterrand. He had succeeded in persuading the mainstream Socialists and various splinter groups as well as the Radicals to collaborate in a new *Fédération de la gauche démocrate et socialiste* (FGDS). His longer-term strategy would be to alter the political balance on the left, and by reducing the Communists to a clearly subordinate position broaden the opposition's electoral appeal.

The widespread and so utterly unexpected disorders of 1968 were to provide further proof of discontent. All manner of smouldering resentments were suddenly able to surface, against authoritarianism in the family as well as in government and in the workplace; against élitism in society and its manifestations in secondary and higher education; against overcrowded and inadequately resourced teaching facilities; against inequality, injustice and the insecurity bred by rapid social change. The movement began in March at the Nanterre campus on the outskirts of Paris, with student protest about both the shortcomings of the educational system and the workings of the international capitalist order whose fundamental immorality seemed to have been made clear by American policy in Vietnam. This was engineered by small and normally marginal groups of Trotskyists, Anarchists and Maoists. It spread because of the ineptitude of the university administration and police brutality. The night of 10–11 May saw the first barricades and rioting in the centre of the capital. Subsequently demonstrations spread into the provinces. There were massive strikes and factory occupations involving 10 million workers and the loss of 150 million workdays. Together these helped to create, especially amongst the young, gathering in the faculties, theatres, cafés

Plate 57 Police chasing demonstrators, 6 May 1968

and streets of Paris, the euphoric sense of a new beginning. A government taken completely by surprise and which now improvised a programme based on the vague project of *participation* by students and employees in decision-taking and offers of wage increases was largely ignored. So too was Mitterrand's declaration that it was necessary to

Plate 58 A Gaullist demonstration in the Champs-Elysées, 30 May 1968 (50,000 were expected, 300–400,000 turned up)

establish a provisional government under Mendès-France. His further
announcement that he would become a candidate for the presidency
seemed to many to be redolent of the worst kind of political
opportunism. To student demonstrators all this manoeuvering
amongst the old political élite was irrelevant.

These events showed up some of the disadvantages of an excessively
centralised political system, dependent on decision-making by an
ageing head of state, and virtually incapable of rapid response to an
unexpected crisis. They revealed a widespread loss of confidence in
existing institutions. France appeared to be on the verge of another
revolution, almost nineteenth-century in its characteristics. Yet this
was not to be. De Gaulle recovered from what seems to have been an
initial loss of confidence and through a mixture of concessions and
repression regained the initiative. With the benefit of hindsight this
seems not to have been a difficult task. The government was greatly
assisted by the lack of unity amongst its critics. Trades union leaders
had limited objectives such as securing improvements in wages and
working conditions and were anxious to control and restrain protest.
This was in marked contrast with those denounced by the Communist
leader, Georges Marchais, as 'counterfeit revolutionaries': the more
utopian student leaders and members of extreme left splinter groups,
inspired by the flood of words and the sheer theatricality of events.
There was however no organisation willing or able to take the final
step and attempt to seize power. The decision of the Communist Party,
the major organised force on the left, to remain within the bounds of
legality and avoid a possible bloodbath was especially significant as
was the government's own determination to avoid the escalation of
violence so typical of the revolutions of the previous century. In a
broadcast on 30 May de Gaulle announced the dissolution of the
National Assembly and called for action to defend the Republic against
the threat of anarchy and communism. A massive and carefully
orchestrated Gaullist demonstration along the Champs-Elysées lent
weight to his demand. In the elections which followed on 23 and 30
June the regime, fighting on a law and order platform, was able to go
a long way to restoring its legitimacy. The 'silent majority' most
certainly did not want a revolution. The old values remained vibrant.
The extreme left was isolated. A gradual return to work occurred and
with it the renewed marginalisation of revolutionary protest.

Table 7.12. *National Assembly elections, 23 and 30 June 1968*

	First ballot votes	Share (percentage of votes)	Seats after second ballot
Communists	4,435,357	20.03	34
FGDS	3,654,003	16.50	57
Centre (PDM)	2,290,165	10.34	33
UDR (Gaullist)	9,663,605	43.65	293
Independent Republicans	917,533	4.14	61

Above all the election result revealed the strength of political conservatism. To a large degree it was an instinctive reaction based on fear of social revolution. In spite of this victory, it was nevertheless clear that the events of May had considerably weakened the authority of de Gaulle. Only prime minister Pompidou, who had seemed better able to cope with the crisis, emerged with his reputation enhanced. His subsequent dismissal appeared as a petty-minded attempt by the General to remove a former dependant transformed by events into a potential successor. This was also the moment de Gaulle chose to renew his search for a 'third way' between capitalism and communism as a means of re-launching the regime. He presented for the electorate's approval a series of proposals designed to enhance participation. These would have resulted in greater worker involvement in enterprise management and in a limited decentralisation of government by means of regional devolution. This would however have been balanced by a reduction in the powers of the senate which had served as a frequent sounding board for opposition. The proposals were a major misjudgement. They attracted little public interest. Such eminent representatives of the conservative majority as Valéry Giscard d'Estaing, embittered at being used as a scapegoat for unpopular measures and then dismissed from the Finance Ministry in 1966, called for rejection, and even more decisively Pompidou announced that he would be a candidate at the next presidential elections, an act which assured conservatives that a dependable successor to de Gaulle stood in the wings. On hearing that 53 per cent of those voting had rejected his proposals de Gaulle resigned, as he had promised in case of defeat. He returned to private life and died 18 months later on 9 November 1970.

The demise of its leader might have been expected to have caused major problems for the Gaullist party, which possessed little in the way of a programme and had owed its unity to loyalty to the General, together with a desire to share in the spoils of office. Pompidou, the son of a socialist schoolteacher from the impoverished Cantal who had reached the top through the *Ecole Normale Supérieure* and the banking world, had been virtually unknown to the public when de Gaulle had thrust him into the office of prime minister. He had however proved his ability as a political leader in the following six years and it had been his emergence as heir apparent in 1968 which had led de Gaulle to remove him from office. He was the obvious presidential candidate for the right in June 1969 and, assisted by the evident disarray of the left, he was elected with a substantial majority (58.21 per cent of votes) against the centrist Poher. Significantly though much of the popular support which de Gaulle had enjoyed had melted away, leaving him much more dependent on the loyalty of traditional conservatives.

This would not however result in the re-establishment of the political situation prior to de Gaulle's return. Pompidou was determined to exercise his constitutional powers to the full and possessed all the status of a president elected by universal suffrage. This, and the willingness of the various political parties to continue to adapt to the constitution created between 1958 and 1962, resulted in the 'normalisation' of a system which in its origins had owed so much to the 'charismatic' leadership of de Gaulle.

For organised political support Pompidou depended particularly on the gaullist UNR, a group built initially very much on the mystique of the liberation and on claims to be above the traditional party conflict, but which had rapidly taken on the attributes of a party of the right. As the party in power it had attracted support from other, non-gaullist groups from the centre and right of the political spectrum, and most notably the *Républicains-Indépendants* led by Giscard d'Estaing. For the first time in France, a powerful federation of the right had been created, united by the desire to retain power and face the threat posed by the slow recovery of the parties of the left. It was not without its internal divisions, both personal and institutional. Jacques Chaban-Delmas, appointed prime minister, had managed to combine both an

Table 7.13. *National Assembly elections, 4 and 11 March 1973*

	First ballot votes	Share (percentage of votes)	Seats after second ballot
Communists	5,084,824	21.40	73
Socialists and allies	4,919,426	20.71	102
Réformateurs (Centre)	3,048,520	12.88	34
UDR and allies	9,009,432	37.32	183
Independent Republicans			55

impeccable record of loyalty to de Gaulle with an image of respect for parliament. He was however to become increasingly unacceptable to Pompidou as he attempted to enhance the authority of his own office at the expense of that of the president. In doing this he was able to appeal to the resentment amongst gaullists of a president who had played no part in the heroic days of their movement during the resistance, in the RPF after the war, or in 1958. Chaban, influenced by the Christian trades unionism of a Jacques Delors was also anxious to improve relations between government, employers and labour and to improve material conditions by such measures as increasing the minimum wage. Although the reforms actually introduced were essentially cosmetic, his talk of a 'contractual politics' and of the need to create a 'new society' profoundly irritated Pompidou. In 1972 he was replaced with Pierre Messmer, clearly the president's man, whose selection represented a restatement of the presidential character of the regime and of its commitment to financial orthodoxy and economic growth. With elections due in 1973 conservatives rallied to the government and gained a surprisingly comfortable victory.

This was the reward for the restoration of social order in 1968 and for the success of economic policies designed to combat inflation, balance the budget, restore business confidence and encourage continued economic modernisation. For Pompidou this was the means of securing his place in history. As part of this policy of encouraging growth he also tolerated some of the uglier physical manifestations of

Plate 59 Paris in the year 2000? The urban landscape transformed
by the construction, on an unprecedented scale, of new offices and
apartments

property development and continued to commit vast funds to such
prestige projects as Concorde, the European Airbus, the creation of
the immense steelworks at Fos, near Marseilles, and to the ultimately
far more fruitful programme of investment in telecommunications.
These policies were to a large degree a continuation of those
inaugurated by de Gaulle. The same was to be true in foreign policy,
although Pompidou's greater commitment to the European Com-

munity was to allow its enlargement by means of the admission of Britain, Ireland and Denmark in 1972. At the same time he sought to ease the strains of modernisation, and to protect the conservative vote through guaranteed prices for farmers and restraints on supermarket development in the interests of small shopkeepers.

Pompidou had enjoyed considerable success in the difficult task of following de Gaulle. At the end of 1973 however he was to face new problems, caused by the sudden, fourfold, increase in the price of oil as a result of the Arab–Israeli war and the onset of a major international crisis. By February 1974 inflation had risen to 15.6 per cent, whilst the rate of economic growth was halved (to a still not inconsiderable 3 per cent). The balance of trade deteriorated sharply as the cost of oil imports increased. Unemployment rose rapidly, and so too did social tension and the general feeling of malaise. In a period when strong government was necessary the president was increasingly incapacitated by illness and was to die of leukemia on 2 April 1974.

In the electoral campaign which followed, conservatives had to choose between the candidatures of Chaban-Delmas and Giscard d'Estaing. The former's apparent strength as the nominee of the gaullist UDR was undermined by the desertion of a group of ambitious gaullist notables, led by Jacques Chirac, concerned about Chaban's interest in social reform. Chaban was forced to withdraw after the first ballot, his popular support further dented by indifferent television performances compared with either Mitterrand, the candidate of the left, or the Independent Republican leader, Giscard. As a result the conservative candidate for the second ballot was to be a non-gaullist, indicative of a shift in the balance of power within the conservative coalition and of a return to a more straightforward left – right competition for power. Giscard's victory (with 13,396,203 or 50.8 per cent of the votes cast) meant that, for the first time during the Fifth Republic, the president was not to be the leader of the largest party in parliament, a factor bound to cause problems of political management. On the other hand the continuing revival of the left with Mitterrand obtaining 12,971,604 (49.19 per cent) votes, would impose a certain sense of unity and willingness to compromise on conservative politicians.

The new president was an extremely well-connected member of the traditional social élite and a product of the *Ecole Nationale d'Admini-*

stration and *Polytechnique*. Like his predecessors he was committed to economic and social modernisation and to the preservation of social order, to 'change without risk'. The objective was to create an 'advanced liberal society'. Initially this involved important libertarian reforms in an effort to update the law so that it conformed better to a changing morality. The age of consent and of voting were reduced to 18 (law of 5 July 1974), abortion was legalised (17 January 1975), and divorce procedures simplified (11 July) and chemists were authorised to sell contraceptives (11 July 1975). Social security provisions were also made more generous and efforts made to improve access to secondary education (loi Haby 11 July 1975). Giscard also made an attempt to desacralise the office of president. He spoke on television in an informal, relaxed manner in marked contrast to the almost regal style he later developed. In spite of efforts to conciliate gaullists by the appointment of Chirac as prime minister, Giscard's early legislative programme caused considerable disquiet and tension within the conservative coalition. This certainly imposed limits on the course of reform. Most conservatives were unwilling to support proposals to reinforce workers rights against their employers or to increase the taxation of capital gains as a means of easing the burden which the predominance of indirect taxation imposed on the poor. Tension between the president and his prime minister grew over these matters and the former's unwillingness to accept a reflationary economic policy. Almost inevitably too there was disagreement over the balance of authority between them. Chirac eventually resigned on 25 August 1976 and was replaced by Raymond Barre, a professional economist.

Giscard had previously served as a very orthodox finance minister. His cautious economic policy was probably the only sensible response to the problems caused by the oil crisis. His essential objectives were the restoration of business confidence through the reduction of government expenditure and of the balance of payments deficit. Economic liberalisation, the reduction of government intervention in the economy, and reliance on market forces to restore international competitiveness were to be the keynotes. The conditions were to be created for a return to 'normal', that is to rapid economic growth. This, rather than the reduction of unemployment, which reached 1.3 million by the end of 1978, was to assume first priority. Indeed unemployment was a useful means of containing wage inflation. The

Table 7.14. *National Assembly elections, 12 and 19 March 1978*

	First ballot votes	Share (percentage of votes)	Seats after second ballot
Communists	5,791,125	20.61	86
Socialists	6,403,265	22.79	114
UDF	6,712,244	23.89	137
RPR	6,416,288	22.84	154

government's austerity programme which included increases in social security contributions and a price and wage freeze was hardly popular but it did contribute to stabilising inflation although at a high level (9 per cent in 1977).

The divisions within the conservative majority were to become increasingly apparent as Chirac effectively reorganised the gaullists into a more aggressively populist *Rassemblement pour la République* (RPR), a mechanism for assisting his own presidential ambitions. He further increased the pressure by standing for election to the newly created office of mayor of Paris on 25 March 1977 and defeating Giscard's own hand-picked candidate. The president's response was to organise the groups of non-gaullist conservatives into an *Union pour la démocratie française* (UDF) in the hope of widening his appeal in the centre, to political moderates. In the short-term, in spite of recurrent tensions, self-interest and an unwillingness to risk the loss of power ensured that a broad conservative alliance survived and was implemented for the second ballot in the legislative elections of March 1978, when once again a conservative victory was greatly assisted by the revival of internecine conflict on the left.

In the remaining years of his presidency Giscard turned more towards international affairs, with positive effect only in European matters where a joint Franco–German initiative led to the election of the European parliament by universal suffrage. This was in spite of gaullist distaste for any reinforcement of the principle of supra-nationality. Otherwise French 'mediation' in the increasingly tense relationship between the superpowers was clearly ignored. Indeed growing domestic problems inevitably reduced the government's international prestige. The second oil crisis brought a further tripling of prices in 1979–80, renewed balance of payments difficulties, and increased inflation (11.8 per cent in 1978, 13.4 per cent in 1979). Unemployment rose to 1.6 million in 1979 affecting some 10 per cent of the active population but with a much greater impact on the unskilled, the young, women and immigrants and in regions like the Nord-Pas-de-Calais where traditional heavy industry and textiles were in decline.

The general sense of disquiet and of insecurity was intensified by the threat of terrorism exemplified by the explosion at the synagogue in the rue Copernic. According to an *Institut français d'opinion publique* (IFOP) poll in September 1979 only 26 per cent of respondents were satisfied with the president's performance. Criticism was further stimulated by the strange affair of the 'Emperor's' diamonds, the gift made to Giscard by the unsavoury Bokassa, ruler of the Central African Republic. This and his growing hauteur, in marked contrast with his earlier efforts to democratise the presidency, increasingly made Giscard a figure of fun. Even so opinion polls throughout 1980 continued to suggest that he would beat any likely left-wing challenger in the 1981 presidential election. In spite of the economic 'crisis' most of the population was continuing to enjoy a very real prosperity.

Nevertheless the slow recovery of the left from the profound divisions and weakness of the early years of the Fifth Republic did pose a growing threat to conservative dominance. Serious efforts to establish an alliance had begun in 1964 on the initiative of the Communist Party, then the largest group on the left and anxious to escape from its political isolation. This had borne fruit in the candidature of Mitterrand in the 1965 presidential election. Further progress had been hindered by the events of 1968 and the splintering of the decrepit socialist party, the SFIO. It took the disastrous showing of the left in the 1969 presidential elections when both its candidates were eliminated in the first ballot, to stimulate a renewed effort. In this the creation of a new *Parti Socialiste* in July 1969 made little initial difference. Only after the election of Mitterrand, a man committed to the 'union of the left', as its first secretary at the Epinay congress in June 1971, did new initiatives become possible. These led to agreement on a common programme with the Communists on 7 June 1972. The partnership was however never going to be an easy one. The leaders of both parties were determined to assume the predominant role whilst at the same time preserving the autonomy of their own organisations. Even so the results of the March 1973 legislative elections seemed to confirm the value of the alliance. Although the performance of the left had improved only in comparison with its abysmal showing in 1969, the Socialists had managed to arrest their electoral decline and had attracted almost as great a share of the popular vote as the Communists.

In spite of the misgivings this caused them, the Communists agreed to support Mitterrand's candidature in the presidential election in May 1974 and made a major contribution to his creditable result. From the end of the year however Party spokesmen and particularly its secretary-general, Marchais, anxious about the growing Socialist challenge to Communist pre-eminence on the left, made increasingly frequent attacks on their erstwhile allies. Finally in September 1977, denouncing their partner's moderation and willingness to engage in class collaboration, the Communists renounced the union. Certainly there were still substantial ideological differences between an increasingly pragmatic Socialist party, and a Communist Party committed to state socialism on the Soviet model. Yet this change of tactics and the mutual recriminations which followed made little practical sense at a time when opinion polls had suggested that the left stood a good chance of achieving a majority in the March 1978 legislative elections. The twists and turns of Communist party policy reflected a growing fear of permanent decline in what had so recently been the strongest French political party. Already, from 28 per cent of the first ballot vote in 1946, and an average of 26 per cent throughout the Fourth Republic, its share of the vote had fallen to 20 per cent by 1978. This would continue with the subsequent collapse of electoral support to 16 per cent in 1981 and to 9.8 per cent in 1986 (fewer even than the *Front National*). Electoral decline has been accompanied by a loss of membership, declining militant activity, the falling circulation of its press, widespread demoralisation and its growing marginalisation even in the 'red-belt' towns of the Paris region. It would in any case have been difficult to resist a complex of mutually reinforcing pressures and particularly changes in social structure involving the decline of the traditional working class with its distinctive sub-culture; a lack of interest amongst young voters in Soviet style communism; and more effective competition from the Socialists. The inability of the Communist leadership to develop a coherent and sustained response to the crisis compounded the damage. This weakening of the Communist Party and the rise of a moderate Socialist alternative would however combine to de-radicalise the left and to make it more electable.

More immediately the effect of the Communists' abandonment of the electoral alliance in 1978 was only too clear. The left did well in the first ballot and even strengthened its position in the run-off, but it failed to achieve an overall majority. This was largely because of the unwillingness of many of those who voted Socialist in the first round to support Communists in the second, an outcome which led to a further deterioration in relations between the two parties. The left revealed once again that it found it even more difficult than the right to respond to the bipolarising tendencies set in play by the political system of the Fifth Republic. These divisions were if anything reinforced during the lengthy campaign which preceded the 1981 presidential elections. The Communists were seemingly preoccupied with destroying the chances of a Socialist victory and presented Marchais as their own candidate. The Socialists themselves were initially divided between the supporters of Rocard and those of another Mitterrand candidature. Fortunately for the left this was offset by dissension on the right where the RPR and its candidate Chirac constantly criticised the policy of a government in which it was represented and went so far as to delay the 1980 budget.

The surprise of the first ballot was the continued collapse of the Communist vote, forcing Marchais to desist in favour of Mitterrand. This failure weakened the validity of a major conservative criticism of Mitterrand, namely that his election would let the Communists in. Moreover the left maintained better electoral discipline, in comparison with Gaullist leaders who were less than enthusiastic in encouraging their supporters to vote for Giscard. Chirac, disappointed by his elimination in the first ballot, peevishly called on each to vote 'according to his conscience', leading the political commentator Raymond Aron to observe bitterly that 'it's not so much that the left won as the right committed suicide'. Giscard himself would accuse Chirac of 'premeditated treachery'.

Mitterrand's carefully planned campaign presented him as *la force tranquille*, the guardian of established values as well as the proponent of sensible and moderate reform. This was in marked contrast with the aggressive approach favoured by Marchais and Chirac and the studied ambiguities of Giscard. The policies he presented were substantially

Plate 60 Presidential elections, 5 May 1981. Valéry Giscard d'Estaing and François Mitterrand engage in a televised debate

Plate 61 Mitterrand's appeal as *la force tranquille*, making use of a calm rural background, combines both the promise of change with reassurance. Poster by Séguéla

less radical than the official programme of the Socialist Party. His victory, with 15,708,262 (51.76 per cent) of the votes cast, was nevertheless due especially to support from a left made up of the proponents of social reform. It reflected growing concern about unemployment and the threat to living standards for which the incumbent government was inevitably blamed. He was victorious in sixty-five of the ninety-six departments, and made unexpected progress in Catholic areas of the east and west, traditionally hostile to the left, as well as strengthening his position in the industrial north, the Paris region, Midi and Burgundy. Sociologically he did particularly well amongst manual and white-collar workers and the lower managerial groups. New voting patterns were beginning to emerge to reflect socio-economic change and the decline of both the Catholic and Communist subcultures. The electorate was becoming more fluid. In any event, the politician who had first gained eminence as a resistance activist, who had been a leading light of the discredited Fourth Republic, a man dismissed by conservatives as 'the eternal loser', and even accused on the left of seeking the leadership of the *Parti Socialiste* out of opportunism rather than any deep sense of commitment, had come back to prove his political skill as a critic of conservative governments and as the leader of a rejuvenated Socialist Party. Finally, at the third attempt, he had achieved his goal of securing election to the presidency. The new head of state was to be determined, in spite of his earlier criticisms of the regime, to exercise his presidential powers to the full. A reflective individual, concerned like de Gaulle with his place in history, he was equally determined to secure France's status amongst the great powers and, in order to ensure this, to continue with the process of economic and social modernisation. Additionally however he was motivated by a humanitarian commitment to greater social justice and equity,

As he had promised if successful, Mitterrand immediately dissolved the National Assembly in an attempt to secure a parliamentary majority committed to his support. The election, held in June 1981 marked a profound shift in the balance of power. In large part this was due to the abstention of large numbers of habitual conservative voters discouraged both by the election of a Socialist president and by the disarray of the right. It was not only the right which suffered. The effective working of the political system seemed to demand that the

Table 7.15. *National Assembly elections, 14 and 21 June 1982*

	First ballot votes	Share (percentage of votes)	Seats after second ballot	Share (percentage of votes)
Communists	4,003,025	16.13	44	9.0
Socialists	9,387,380	38.02	285	58.0
Union pour une nouvelle majorité (RPR and UDF)	10,649,476	42.9		
RPR			88	17.9
UDF			62	12.6

president and parliamentary majority be drawn from the same political milieu. As a result the Communist Party lost over half its seats, leaving the Socialists with an absolute majority.

The Socialists celebrated their presidential victory, in a fashion which revealed a strong sense of history, with a massive demonstration on the Place de la Bastille and a ceremony at the Panthéon in which the new president placed roses on the tombs of Jaurès, the humanitarian socialist assassinated by an extreme nationalist in 1914; of Jean Moulin, the Resistance martyr; and of Victor Schoelcher, a democratic–socialist opponent of Napoleon III. In power for the first time during the Fifth Republic, the left was in euphoric mood. A great sense of expectancy had been created based on the radical programme of the Socialist Party with its condemnation of the capitalist system, rather than the more cautious proposals presented by Mitterrand during his campaign. This was further encouraged by the appointment to the premiership of Pierre Mauroy, history teacher, trades unionist and youth worker, representing the old working-class bastions of the north, and by other equally symbolic measures including a concession to ecologists and peasants with the abandonment of the controversial plan for the extension of the military training area at Larzac; an increase of 10 per cent in the legal minimum wage; increased family allowances; and a project to create an immediate 55,000 public sector jobs. This heralded an unprecedented programme of reforms, influenced by Keynsian economics and the commitment to welfare spending. The success of these policies would however depend to a very large degree on prevailing economic and political circumstances. Politically the government enjoyed the advantage of a substantial parliamentary majority, and economically the stabilisation achieved by Barre provided a certain leeway but this would be offset by the impact of prolonged international recession.

The government itself was made up of thirty-six Socialists drawn, as in any party, from the various competing internal factions and including such luminaries as Delors at Economy and Finance, Defferre (Interior), and Savary (Education); and two left-radicals; but it was the presence of four Communists which attracted the most comment, both at home and abroad. Their uneasy participation in government, for the first time since 1947, represented a reward for electoral support and on their part an attempt to reverse their party's declining popularity, although their obviously subordinate position made this a dangerous tactic. They were indeed to enjoy little influence, whilst the alarm bells which rang in Washington were soon stilled by Mitterrand's obvious desire to improve cooperation with the western allies.

The economic and social policy the Socialist government now sought to introduce was a complicated package. Some of it was inherited from the Popular Front and criticised by Michel Rocard for its archaism. It additionally included a commitment, similar to that of its conservative predecessors, to the on-going programme of modernisation and more clearly than ever before to the integration of the European market. It was assumed that all classes would benefit from enhanced prosperity. However measures were also taken to secure greater social equity by means not only of an increase in the minimum wage and in welfare payments but through fiscal reform including a wealth tax. This essentially symbolic measure affected only the *gros*, the 1 per cent of households whose fortunes exceeded 3 million francs, but together with the rhetoric of attacks on the wealthy it damaged business confidence and, as in 1936, provoked a flight of capital. So too did efforts by the Minister of Labour, Auroux, to improve workers' collective rights at the expense of the employers' disciplinary powers. This seemed to the *patronat* to represent an assault upon its prerogatives. There was also grave concern about the impact on costs of the reduction in the working week (to thirty-nine hours) and the granting of a fifth week of paid holidays. These were measures which the government hoped would both improve the quality of life and, along with early retirement and re-training, contribute to the reduction of unemployment. The main thrust of government policy was however directed towards reflating the economy. Unemployment was to be reduced by means of increased public spending and the easier availability of credit. These policies were to be facilitated by the nationalisation of most of the remaining private banks to ensure that they would in future support the state's overall economic strategy, and compensate for the apparent timidity of private and institutional investors. Other targets for state ownership were the major steel companies, all on the verge of bankruptcy, and more significantly manufacturing companies strategically placed in such sectors as aeronautics, electronics, chemicals, and information technology. These were to serve as growth poles, whose development would stimulate the entire economy. As a result the state's share of industrial turnover was to increase from 16 to 30 per cent, whilst the public sector would in future employ 24.7 per cent of industrial workers instead of 11 per cent. It was assumed that government control over a much larger proportion of economic activity than was the norm in the other advanced economies would permit the development of a coherent investment programme. It was further assumed that increased investment and industrial restructuring would soak up unemployment and place French industry in a good position to take advantage of the expansion of the international economy so confidently, and incorrectly, predicted by the economic forecasters of the OECD. These were policies which horrified the business and financial world and the wealthy in general, and which generated almost unprecedented verbal violence.

In practice they had surprisingly little impact on levels of unemployment. The primary effect of these efforts to stimulate demand was increased imports, a deteriorating balance of payments and rapidly rising inflation. Although not as damaging as Chirac's reflation in 1975, the attempt to reflate the French economy at a time when most of her international competitors were persuing deflationary policies inevitably reduced the competitiveness of French enterprises. It led to three devaluations of the franc in the space of eighteen months and revealed the narrow limits to national autonomy imposed by international economic constraints. It leant credibility to the accusation that the Socialists had been ruled by their hearts and not by their heads.

Above all the inflationary spiral which had been created forced the government to re-assess its policies.

In a major turn-around an initial wages and prices freeze (July–November 1982) was followed by deliberate wage restraint in the public sector, whilst the private sector was able to take advantage of the fear of unemployment and the chronic weakness of the unions. Increased taxation and a squeeze on welfare expenditure reduced the government's budget deficit. High interest rates restricted consumer expenditure. Automatic wage indexation was ended to assist the fight against inflation, a measure the right had not dared to introduce. The wisdom of nationalisation was also questioned. Whatever the good intentions, it had clearly reduced the commercial freedom and competitiveness of major companies like Thomson, Pechiney, or Rhône–Poulenc, as well as resulting in the waste of resources poured into the declining coal and steel industries. It had become clear that only the encouragement of business initiative would secure a return to the high rates of growth which might effectively reduce unemployment. The strategy of the Fabius government which succeeded that of Mauroy, who resigned on 17 July 1984, would be to encourage profitability as the means to finance investment rather than directing state funds into a limited number of 'key' sectors. In 1984 substantial reductions in capacity were to be imposed on the coal, steel and ship-building industries. Both public and private companies were encouraged to shed labour in the interests of profitability. It was coming to be recognised that, with rapid technological change and structural adaptation in the economy, higher levels of unemployment than had previously been regarded as acceptable were likely to remain a permanent feature of the French as of other western economies. One likely consequence of such policies was the establishment of a wider gulf between the majority of the population which continued to enjoy rising living standards, and a substantial minority, an 'underclass', made up of the unskilled and those on low pay as well as the unemployed, the approximately 29 per cent of all families officially classified as 'poor', who in spite of the welfare system would live in relative poverty.

Fabius, an upper-middle class product of the *Ecole nationale d'Administration*, and a social democrat, was both the symbol and agent of a major policy shift. His objectives were to promote economic recovery and to reconstruct the government's image in time for the 1986 elections. The change was much resented by the left-wing of the Socialist Party, by trades unionists and by the Communists, who finally resigned from a government in which they had felt increasingly uncomfortable. Most Socialists seem however to have accepted, and with surprising ease, that there were limits to what the state could achieve in terms of social reform. They participated in the general shift of opinion in favour of liberalism, concealing the truth from themselves perhaps with Mauroy's assurance that the new policy was only a temporary adjustment. The reversal of policy nevertheless had profoundly negative effects on the government's popularity. Other policy decisions were intensifying the loss of confidence. Thus Savary's effort to make concessions to the old left-wing dream of creating a single secular educational system, whilst at the same time not really damaging the denominational schools, predictably satisfied none of the interested parties. Hostile agitation culminated in a demonstration by as many as a million people, on 24 June 1984, in support of the (since 1959 heavily subsidised by the state) independence of Catholic schools and the freedom of choice of the middle-class supporters of an exclusive, élitist education. The same minister had already been persuaded to exempt the *grandes écoles*, so important in the formation of the French élite, from supposedly egalitarian reforms of higher education. Subsequently the teachers, who made up about 58 per cent of Socialist deputies, and who are as conservative on educational questions as they are radical in politics, secured in Chevènement, Savary's replacement, a minister committed to adapting education to the needs of a changing world by means of the restoration of standards. The core curriculum, emphasis on science and technology, but also on basic literacy, numeracy and national history, the concern with measurable results rather than individual fulfilment, are features of the educational reforms proposed by French Socialist as well as British Conservative governments.

In contrast the law on decentralisation (3 March 1982), pushed through by Defferre, did mark a major shift away from the centralising traditions of the French state. It promised to revive local democracy and at the same time to serve the interests of a Socialist party well entrenched at local level, (although in fact it failed to prevent the sweeping victories of the right in the local elections of 1983 and 1985).

It provided the twenty-two planning regions established in 1972 with elected assemblies with considerable powers, particularly over economic planning. At the same time executive authority at departmental level was transferred from the prefect to the president of the elected department council (*conseil général*), made responsible especially for health, social services and roads. The planning powers of the communes were also increased. This was an attempt to make local government both more democratic and accountable, as well as more efficient. It has benefited the larger towns in particular, allowing economically depressed centres like Saint-Etienne to develop the social and cultural facilities necessary to attract investors, but at the cost of a burdensome indebtedness. Decentralisation will not become effective overnight. The problems of overlapping responsibilities have to be solved, and the passive resistance of those civil servants and local notables who resent the threat to their status and authority have to be overcome. It will take time for the rules of the political game to change and for intervention in decision-making by local associations to take effect, and even then local élites will doubtless remain unrepresentative of their constituents. Moreover dependence on the financial support of the central state and upon its technical services continues to obstruct the achievement of real autonomy, as does the all-pervasive control from Paris of the means of communication, and particularly the media, and of financial and economic decision-making. Nevertheless something has been done to reinforce the sensitivity of central government and private institutions to local needs.

The challenge to vested interests and especially the twists and turns of economic policy were inevitably damaging to Mitterrand's popularity. Many of those who had turned to him in hope of change were alienated. The results of the municipal elections in spring 1983 and of the European elections in June 1984 were decidedly unfavourable. According to an IFOP poll in November only 26 per cent of the electorate were satisfied with Mitterrand's performance. This gave renewed heart to the conservatives, who had at first been absolutely stunned and then alarmed by their unexpected loss of power in 1981. They had faced considerable difficulty in making their opposition effective. There were now three competing parties on the right with elections confirming the rise of the *Front National* especially in cities with large immigrant populations. It campaigned on the

Plate 62 Dependence on immigrant labour to sustain economic growth: typically accommodated in low-cost housing as here at Gennevilliers. Their presence has resulted in serious social problems and has been a key factor in the rise of the racist *Front National*

issues of rising crime and the threat to personal security, and by means of an ugly racialism blamed this and high unemployment on North African immigrants. Its appeal was to all those disillusioned with the existing parties. Its militants included members of previously marginalised extreme right-wing groups, including monarchists, former supporters of Vichy and of *Algérie française*, anti-semites and Catholic fundamentalists. It possessed an eloquent and energetic leader in Le Pen. Moreover the *Front* was lent credibility by media attention and the contorted efforts of Chirac, Giscard and Barre to avoid condemning out of hand a party which might turn out to be a useful electoral ally. Only in the spring of 1985, as if alarmed by the growing challenge from the extreme right and appreciating that more votes might be gained from an anti-racist stance, did conservative leaders seek to isolate the *Front National*, whilst at the same time seeking to steal its clothes by adopting the substance of its position on law and order. The conservative challenge to the government was also weakened by persistent feuding between and within the Giscardian UDF and Chirac's RPR due both to personal animosities and differences of emphasis in policy. The UDF tended to lay stress both on individual freedoms and the state's responsibility as a guarantor of social justice, the RPR to be populist and authoritarian in the Bonapartist tradition. Raymond Barre in the meantime attacked both. The right was thus unable to commit itself to a single leader and potential presidential candidate, although the balance in terms of popular support certainly moved in favour of Chirac whose more combative style assured him a higher public profile. Giscard's defeat in the presidential election and loss of patronage power had significantly weakened the UDF, which moreover lacked the basic organisational strength of the RPR. Nevertheless, and in spite of their bitter rivalry, self-interest promoted an alliance and the publication of a joint programme for the 1986 legislative elections. This promised the privatisation of nationalised companies, reductions in government expenditure and tax cuts which would unleash 'individual initiative in economic, social and cultural life'. In all it represented a reaffirmation of nineteenth-century liberalism's commitment to possessive individualism.

Whatever the problems of the right, it was clear in the run-up to the 1986 legislative elections that the Socialists were in a very weak position. In an effort to minimise the effects of declining electoral support, Mitterrand brought forward the extremely controversial proposal to change the electoral system which had figured in his 1981 electoral programme. Single member constituencies were to be replaced by a form of proportional representation on a departmental basis. The danger was that this return to the electoral system of the Fourth Republic might promote the re-establishment of the unstable multi-party system which had characterised that regime and in particular help legitimise and promote the fortunes of the *Front National*. This too appears to have been part of Mitterrand's calculation, presuming as he did that it would result in a loss of votes for the other conservative

Table 7.16. *National Assembly elections, 16 March 1986*

	Votes	Share (percentage of votes)	Seats
Communists	2,663,259	9.7	35
Socialists	8,688,034	31.6	215
RPR–UDF	11,506,618	42.1	
UDF			129
RPR			145
Front national	2,701,701	9.8	35

parties and contribute to the fragmentation of right-wing representation in parliament. The main themes of the campaign were unemployment and security against criminals and terrorists. More than ever the style was American, with the conservatives in particular using the latest marketing techniques. The results confirmed Mitterrand's astuteness.

Whilst the Socialists' somewhat lack-lustre attempt to stress the successes of their economic policy, particularly after the abandonment of reflation in 1982, was not entirely successful, the obvious divisions between conservative leaders reduced the credibility of their campaign. The UDF and RPR together gained an absolute parliamentary majority of only two. The Socialists and their allies remained the largest single group in the new parliament. However their surprising ability to retain some of their earlier gains, most notably in the west, could hardly conceal the severity of their defeat. Both the extremes, the Communists and the *Front National*, improved their position, with the latter gaining representation for the first time.

It was a situation in which the president, as an arbitrator, was left with considerable room for manoeuvre, although he felt constitutionally obliged to call on Chirac, as the leader of the largest party in the conservative alliance, to serve as prime minister. This created an unprecedented situation in the Fifth Republic, with the president and his prime minister drawn from different and contending political constellations. Giscard, during his presidency, had considered the possibility of an opposition majority in parliament, and had concluded that as elected president he would have to remain in office and at the same time accept the legislative programme of the left. Now hypothesis had turned into reality but with a conservative parliamentary majority cohabiting with a socialist president. Where would authority rest?

It took some time for the situation to become clearer, but by the autumn of 1986 an uneasy line of demarcation had emerged with Mitterrand assuming a prominent role in the spheres of international relations and defence, as indeed the constitution suggested he should. A broad policy consensus in these areas anyway reduced the possibility of conflict. There was only limited disagreement over the continuation of such basic tenets of Gaullist foreign policy as the maintenance of an assertive French presence on the world stage, backed by an independent nuclear deterrent. As well as reversing their previous hostility to this policy of *grandeur*, the Socialists also made evident their commitment to strengthening the European Community, partly to provide the continuing stimulus to modernisation and in recognition of the weakness of individual European states in an intensely competitive international economy, partly as a means of containing the single most powerful European power – Germany. An active role in international affairs had the advantage of allowing Mitterrand to remain constantly in the public eye. Furthermore he did not hesitate to give advice – public and private – on a whole range of domestic matters, and by refusing to sign administrative decrees could delay their implementation. In effect Mitterrand was beginning to refine a pose he had already begun to adopt towards the end of the period of socialist government, that of the president above party politics. Although Chirac, as leader of the parliamentary majority, was clearly the dominant partner he was handicapped by the unexpected recovery in the President's popularity, and by the public's obvious desire that 'cohabitation' should work and that a destabilising political crisis must at all costs be avoided. With their eyes set on the presidential elections due in 1988 neither Chirac nor Mitterrand were prepared to risk accepting responsibility for the failure of cohabitation.

Chirac had quickly established a government dominated by representatives of his own party, usually politicians with previous ministerial experience. To many commentators this re-establishment of the right in office seemed like a return to normal. Influenced by prevailing liberal intellectual fashion, Chirac was however determined to break with the authoritarian, statist past of gaullism. He proceeded with widespread privatisation and deregulation, although this was not to include traditional public sector monopolies like gas, electricity and telecommunications or strategic industries like aerospace. Disagreement on these matters was to be only one of the causes of friction within the government and conservative majority. Others were to include the perennial problem of financing the social security system, the reform of labour legislation to favour employers, the rewriting of the nationality laws to discriminate against immigrants, and the correct response to the Soviet leader Gorbachev's disarmament proposals. Chirac was also unlucky. The implementation of privatisation was hindered by the international stockmarket collapse in October 1987, although by then some 400,000 workers had already been transferred to the private sector. The almost inevitable student protest against higher education reform at the end of 1986 and strikes in the public services additionally created an impression of weakness. Moreover the government failed to produce the magical solution to the country's economic problems which many of its supporters seemed to expect. Indeed the main economic indicators – growth rates, budget deficit, inflation, unemployment, the balance of trade and international competitiveness – all seemed, by the end of 1987, to suggest failure. The decline in the government's popularity was closely linked to this. Opposition criticism was indeed rather muted with the Socialists suffering a crisis of confidence and paralysed both by Mitterrand's determination to make cohabitation work and their reliance upon his standing as the vehicle for a return to power. At its 1987 Congress the Party's various factions were at least able to agree on the need to present it as united, pragmatic and moderate.

During the April–May 1988 presidential campaign Mitterrand continued to distance himself from the Socialist Party and to broaden his appeal. The dominant theme of his campaign was national unity – *La France Unie*. His programme was vague but reassuring on such questions as the welfare state, and the commitment to continued economic modernisation and assistance to companies to prepare for the Single European Market in 1992. By 1988 the Socialists had clearly accepted the 'enterprise' culture. Mitterrand could also present himself as the guardian of democracy and of a pluralistic society against the threats posed by the Chirac government's heavy-handed emphasis on 'law and order' and the posturings of the extreme right. In the end the only surprise was the size of his second ballot majority. Chirac had been placed on the defensive by the need to defend a mixed record in office. The promise of further privatisation and what easily appeared to be tax cuts for the rich had limited appeal. Moreover, for the first ballot, Chirac had to devote a considerable effort to defeating his right-wing rivals, Barre and Le Pen. Whilst he could not afford to alienate their supporters upon whose votes he would depend in the run-off against Mitterrand, it was also clear that adopting a gentle approach towards the *Front National* might result in the defection of conservatives committed to democracy and a multi-racial society. Support for Barre was based upon his reputation for economic competence. His experience whilst prime minister of continuous denigration by Chirac had however created a sense of bitter personal animosity between the two men. Before the campaign Barre had seemed likely to become the leading conservative candidate but a lacklustre campaign, partly due to his unwillingness to employ the professional public relations experts who now seem essential to success, had cost him this position. The support which might have come from the UDF was restrained by Giscard's resentment of Barre's eminence. Increasingly a vote for Barre began to appear pointless. Chirac offered much the same policy, and in Mitterrand France already possessed a reassuring elder statesman. On the first ballot Barre gained 16.5 per cent of the vote compared with Chirac's 19.9 per cent. The sensation was Le Pen's 14.4 per cent, the votes of almost four and a half million people. On the major issues of immigration and law and order, he had set the agenda.

With Barre and Le Pen eliminated Chirac abandoned the quiet, statesmanlike pose he had previously adopted and threw his considerable energy into confrontation, using terms like 'mediocre, incompetant, unfit for public office' to describe the incumbent president. But even the theatricality of the closing days of the campaign, with the securing of the release of hostages in Beirut and a bloody assault on Kanak nationalists in the Pacific territory of New Caledonia, failed to attract sufficient support. Mitterrand secured 54.01 per cent of the vote, drawn particularly from the ranks of the unemployed, industrial workers, public employees and the young, with much less support amongst farmers, small businessmen, upper management, the elderly and practising Catholics. Although politically his supporters were a mixed bag from left and centre, polarisation between left and right was still evident. The nomination of Michel Rocard as prime

Table 7.17. *National Assembly election results, June 1988*

	Share of votes (in %)	Number of seats	Share of seats (in %)
Communists	11.3	27	4.7
Socialists	37.5	278	48.2
UDF	19.5	130	22.5
RPR	19.2	128	22.2
Other right-wingers	2.9	13	2.2
Front national	9.7	0[a]	

[a] One subsequent by-election victory.

minister on 9 May 1988 was followed by the dissolution of the National Assembly and an attempt to secure the election of a supportive Socialist majority. The results were disappointing with large-scale abstentions and a renewed sense of unity in the face of adversity on the right. This could not conceal Chirac's own failure, reflected in the shifting balance between the parties of the right, together with the appearance of a reconstituted centre, the UDC, made up of forty-one deputies alienated from the radical neo-liberalism of the right and reassured by the collapse of the Communists and the moderation of the Socialists. These would prove willing to consider an alliance with the left. Thus although the Socialists lacked an absolute majority in parliament their position in government was secured by this emergent centre-left together with the fact that they could only be defeated by the combined vote of the opposition including the Communists. The party's own internal discipline, which belied its past record of factionalism was to prove another key factor.

Significantly, in forming a government Michel Rocard looked towards the centre rather than towards the Communists for allies, although in local and regional politics bad-tempered cooperation between the two parties of the left remained the norm. The right was undoubtedly demoralised by this renewed exclusion from power which had seemed so unlikely as recently as mid-1987. It faced important strategic questions on such matters as whether the RPR and UDF should fuse to form a single liberal–conservative party, somewhat on the British model, and on what their attitude to the *Front National* should be. Criticism was voiced by left-wing Gaullists like Philippe Séguin of a leadership which they claimed had moved too far to the right. Bitter disagreements both within and between the parties of the right have left these matters largely unresolved. This should not however lead us to underestimate the strength of the right and particularly of the RPR which with its deputies, regional and municipal councillors and efficient mass organisation and determination to regain power remains a potent force. The UDF, although far more fragmented, and seemingly under permanent threat of dissolution, retains the allegiance of a substantial group of deputies. Together the two main parties of the right share a commitment to essential conservative values and the support of a powerful complex of pressure group and media forces. As they began the long haul to the 1993 legislative and 1995 presidential elections the joker in the pack remained the continued ability of the *Front national*, in spite of its poor showing in the 1988 legislative elections, to attract voters who would otherwise largely support the other parties of the right.

The choice by Mitterrand of a political rival, Rocard, as prime minister, might seem rather surprising, but as the leader of just one faction within the Socialist party Rocard remained dependent upon the President. Mitterrand also continued to distance himself from day-to-day matters of government and allowed his prime minster considerable autonomy in domestic matters, whilst again establishing his own mastery of defence, foreign and European affairs. This division of labour eased the problem of relationships between the two. Rocard having proved his competence was probably fortunate to be pushed into resignation in May 1991, following the successful conclusion of the Gulf War and just as economic growth slowed. To succeed him Mitterrand appointed Edith Cresson as France's first female prime minister, presumably in the hope that her outspokenness and robust socialist outlook would give new impetus to a rather lack-lusture administration and divert attention from both the economic slowdown and rumours of political corruption. Lacking strong factional backing within the Socialist Party she was also particularly dependent on the president, and was quickly nicknamed 'Edith At-my-feet' by the satirical television programme *The Bébétte Show*. Cresson's outspokenness proved to be a disaster. Her government was plagued by damaging public sector strikes, and her interventionist and protectionist conception of 'Fortress Europe' proved unacceptable to most of her colleagues. The presence in government of political heavyweights like her eventual successor (in April 1992) the liberal finance minister Pierre Bérégovoy imposed a severe limit on her authority.

In economic policy the lessons of the early 1980s did not need to be relearnt. The discipline of the international market seemed inescapable. Internal reforms were as a result very modest during this second term of Socialist government. The fight against inflation was given priority. The European dimension also assumed a greater prominence as part of the struggle to maintain economic competitiveness, but also as France sought reassurance against the impact of a German unity which would inevitably reduce its international status. This stimulated efforts to improve education and increase investment in research and development. Moreover, and in marked contrast with the attitude of the British government, the French have supported the 'social dimension' of the single-market project. Nevertheless reports which revealed that the average annual growth in real wages between 1983 and 1988 was virtually nil, as well as the widening gulf between rich and poor, caused considerable concern amongst those Socialist militants who believed that they should be aiming at more than becoming a party of government dedicated to the development of a 'tempered capitalism' (Rocard). Scandals caused by illicit political funding and outright corruption added to the sense of demoralisation.

The 1993 general elections brought disaster. The representation of the Socialists and their allies was reduced from 282 deputies to 67 and that of the Communists from 27 to 25, whilst on the right the UDF had 206 deputies instead of 129, and the RPR 242 in place of 127. Taking account of independents, 83% of the seats in the National Assembly were filled by conservatives. In spite of the lip service paid to gender equality the new parliament was characterised by the lowest rate of female representation in the European Union (5%). The Socialists' share of the vote, at 14.5%, was the worst since the party's foundation in 1971. Rocard, harassed by Mitterrand's allies, felt bound to resign as leader and the party seemed doomed to the electoral wilderness. Nevertheless the result was less a declaration of support for the right than a vote against a President and government which the electorate felt had let them down. Mitterrand entered a further period of quite amicable cohabitation with a prime minister, Balladur, a typically suave product of Sciences Po and ENA, drawn from the RPR, who very soon emerged as a rival to, rather than a dependent of, Chirac, its leader. Blaming his Socialist predecessors for the parlous state of government finances Balladur introduced an austerity budget with overall tax increases and reductions in spending on health care. His air of apparent self-satisfaction soon led to his being portrayed in the satirical press as 'His Sufficiency', a be-wigged and powdered Louis XVI carried by lackeys in a sedan chair. He was, even so, able to build on the public impression of competence he had previously created as finance minister and gain a generally good press through substantial tax concessions to the wealthy and his ability to make cohabitation work. Although suffering from the prostate cancer which would ultimately cause his death (on 8 January 1996), and seriously damaged by revelations about his youthful right-wing leanings and Vichy past, as well as the shady financial dealings of some of his closest associates, the President remained determined to oversee defence and foreign policy and quite capable of taking advantage of divisions amongst conservatives.

This is probably the place to offer an interim judgement of the Mitterrand years. In spite of his earlier tirades against de Gaulle, and his condemnation of the system of presidential government the general had inaugurated, as 'a permanent coup d'état', Mitterrand made full use of the extensive powers which came to him, and resisted proposed constitutional reforms which might have weakened his authority. A president elected on a mandate for change, he rapidly and almost instinctively appreciated that politics is, or at least ought to be, the art of the possible. The Socialist experiment of 1981/83 was a failure, but Mitterrand at least quickly recognised the fact. Preserving international economic competitiveness in the era of globalisation seemed to require de-regulation and the reduction of state expenditure. The dramatic policy reversals which followed might have appeared unavoidable but the cost in terms of disappointed expectations and shattered ideals has been heavy. Throughout the western world neo-liberalism has reigned supreme, whilst the parties of the left have failed to offer credible intellectual and practical alternatives. Mitterrand did nothing more nor less than share in this overwhelming failure, his margins for manoeuvre strictly limited by economic and political circumstances and by the need to react to, rather than to shape events. During his long political life

Mitterrand seemed to have flirted with a wide variety of political credoes. As a result he has been severely criticised for an apparent lack of integrity. There can certainly be no doubting his intense personal ambition, nor his determination to leave his mark on history. Towards the end of his second term in office his public image had become almost monarchical, that of a Machiavellian prince. In an interview with the historian François Bédarida just forty-eight hours before handing over power to Chirac Mitterrand claimed, however, that his socialist convictions were unchanged. He had wanted to transform the relationships between the rich and powerful and the mass of the population but circumstances had rendered this impossible. He similarly spoke passionately about what had become the major objective of his second term, that of greater European unity as a means of securing the future of France in a world of competing regional power blocs as well as of containing the threat of German dominance within Europe.

Persistence pays. In May 1995 Jacques Chirac finally achieved his long-standing ambition of securing presidential office. In a characteristically energetic campaign he presented himself as a strong leader, offering 'profound changes' and a 'break with the past'. For the first ballot he promised to reduce taxes and the government deficit. For the second ballot, once Balladur his rather uninspiring rival on the right had been eliminated, Chirac launched a populist appeal, focusing on the familiar right-wing issues of crime and immigration whilst seeking to outflank his Socialist opponent Jospin by concentrating on the issues of unemployment and poverty and the need to increase spending on education and welfare. He even called for wage increases to boost economic growth. This was not so much a political programme as an attempt to bribe the electorate, and it worked. Chirac, although suffering from a certain lack of credibility, gained 52.6% of the second ballot votes (15,766,658) including a majority of the under-35s and 40% of blue-collar workers. Jospin, selected by the Socialists only after the former President of the European Commission, Jacques Delors, had finally decided against standing (December 1994), at least had the advantage of not being too closely associated with Mitterrand and the accusations of sleaze and lack of principle which had darkened the dying President's last years in office. He presented an imaginative programme with promises of a reduction in working hours, taxes on 'speculative' capital movements and on polluting industries, as well as a reduction in the presidential term to five years, although he too affirmed a commitment to European monetary union and the consequent need to reduce the budget deficit and defend the value of the franc. In the circumstances and considering the Socialists' feeble performance in the 1994 European elections (with only 14.5% of the vote) his 47.4% share (14,191,019 votes) was quite an achievement, a reward for his apparent straightforwardness and effective oratory. It was clear that traditional right–left voting patterns had survived the new president's efforts to pose as a man above parties.

Once in power Chirac immediately adopted a more relaxed style in comparison with the stately grandeur of his predecessor, abandoning the presidential fleet of jets and the motorcades with their escorts of police motorcyclists and blaring sirens. Of much greater potential significance for the practice of government was a promise of longer parliamentary sessions and efforts to facilitate the more effective scrutiny of government activities, developments running counter to both the authoritarian personality of the new president and the traditions of his office. The promise of less *dirigiste* government also ran counter to the opportunities presented to the right through its current control of the presidency, of the National Assembly, of 20 of the 22 regional councils and four-fifths of the 96 departments. The appointment by the President of Alain Juppé as his prime minister – yet another cultured and rather distant technocrat educated at the ENA – appeared to promise competence and continuity. In reality, the almost immediate collapse in the new government's popularity was to be the inevitable result of the President's inability to deliver rapidly, if at all, on the many, often contradictory, promises made during his electoral campaign. Less than six months after taking office Chirac dismissed thirteen ministers in a desperate effort to counter unpopularity brought on by broken promises, sleaze and international reactions to the folly of a resumption of nuclear testing in the Pacific. The introduction of measures designed to reduce government spending by decree rather than through parliament and with virtually no preparation of public opinion was redolent of the worst practices of an autocratic presidential system. Unfortunately for them, and for the democratic process, the faction-riven Socialists appeared to be equally incapable of inspiring the electorate. These difficulties, whilst indicative of governmental incompetence, can also be taken to illustrate the severity of the problems it, and indeed most European governments, currently face. These include the need to reconcile the burgeoning costs of unemployment and health care with reductions in government spending in order to meet the criteria for European monetary union established in 1991 by the Maastricht Treaty. To which might be added the constant pressure to maintain economic competitiveness and to preserve the nation's international status.

In 1995 France remained the world's fourth economic power, with a record balance of payments surplus (of 85 billion francs). However, this position can be maintained only on the basis of high levels of capital investment, rising productivity and the reduction of costs. Economists and employers point at labour market rigidities reinforced by the minimum wage and high social security costs as well as the highest rates of taxation in the developed world (41.1% of GDP at the end of 1994, 47.5% by 1996), together with budget deficits and the high cost of borrowing as the major obstacles. Unfortunately the measures proposed to remove these constraints have had the effect of threatening the living standards of much of the population and increasing the numbers of jobless. Unemployment, which according to the official figures stood at 12.5% of the workforce in August 1996 and with perhaps 25% of the under-twenty-fives without work, has proved to be resistant to a variety of both inflationary and deflationary government polices over the past two decades. The employment situation seems likely to deteriorate further as a result of the actual or proposed restructuring of the public sector through the privatisation of enterprise like the Thompson electronics groups, of France Télécom and Air France, together with reductions in the size of the civil service and of state enterprises like the heavily subsidised railways. The ending of the Cold War has allowed substantial reductions in defence expenditure but with adverse consequences both for naval dockyards and for the armaments industry so important to French exports. Together with accelerating technological innovation and heightened international competition these policies have encouraged mergers and 'downsizing' across the industrial and service sectors of the economy. The result has been continuing job losses, the growth of part-time and short-term employment, spreading insecurity and growing poverty and inequality with around five million people living in impoverished conditions and suffering from a sense of deprivation exacerbated, all too frequently, by recourse to drugs and alcohol. These difficulties are at their most extreme on the high-rise housing estates built in the 1950s–60s to eliminate the slums and which have become the scene for clashes between racial groups, attacks on the police and a seemingly irreversible rising tide of crime.

Solving these problems has been rendered all the more difficult by the second major difficulty, the need to reduce government expenditure to enhance French economic competitiveness and to satisfy the Maastricht criteria for membership of the European monetary union. The budget deficit needed to be reduced from 6% to 3% of GDP by January 1999. Achieving this, rather than reducing unemployment, rapidly became the government's new 'priority of priorities' although, unsurprisingly the change of emphasis was heralded as the most effective means of cutting unemployment in the long term as reduced government borrowing led to falling interest rates, and this in turn stimulated investment and job creation. The obvious target for conservative politicians influenced by neo-liberal economics is the welfare state especially as the indebtedness of the social security system in 1995 was held to account for two-thirds of the budget deficit. High unemployment has substantially increased outgoings whilst simultaneously reducing tax income. Health service expenditure alone accounted for 9.1% of GDP (Britain 6.6%). Its rising costs can be explained by the ageing of the population, the impact of AIDS, the recrudescence of diseases associated with poverty and the impact of accelerating social change on stress levels, as well as the development of a more costly medical technology. There is also however considerable wastage with patients able to see doctors as frequently as they wish and little control over the forms of treatment they receive. Rationalisation is planned to result in greater parliamentary control over policy and spending within a health system currently controlled by the employers and unions, as well as higher charges for users. Reform will be obstructed by patients, doctors and health service workers, the latter anxious to protect job security, early retirement and generous pensions. The government's overall room for manoeuvre is clearly limited by such political constraints and will be resisted by a wide range of vested-interest groups including not only the beleaguered health workers but also teachers and civil servants protesting about wage freezes and deteriorating conditions of employment in the public sector, as well as farmers and industrial workers including key groups within the transport sector, all of whom have taken to the streets to manifest their sense of grievance. This widespread discontent and protest threatens economic disruption and has serious political implications. These can be seen in the growth of Euro-scepticism induced by the desire both to protect national sovereignty as well as to avoid the social cost of reductions in welfare spending. Rising social tension and frequent protest also serve to remind ministers of the approach of the 1998 general elections and the pressing political need to cut taxes. As if to illustrate the difficulty, on 4 October 1996, whilst affirming that the social security system was the 'last rampart against what could be a dramatic decline of civilisation', Chirac felt bound to add that its deficit, and particularly that of the public health service, had become 'unbearable'. It is hardly surprising if these conflicting pressures have resulted in government policies which appear contradictory and often simply incoherent. For all these reasons the financial markets, which constantly need to be appeased, remain sceptical about the ability of France to meet the Maastricht criteria, although the reduction in the government deficit might well be achieved (briefly) by means of a financial sleight of hand possibly involving one-off transfers from the France Télécom pension fund and the unemployment benefit fund, together with the sympathetic understanding of France's European partners. The achievement of monetary union is still held to be crucial to the preservation of the Franco–German partnership and the binding of German economic, demographic and potential military power into the European Union, which is at the heart of French foreign policy.

France clearly faces major problems in preserving its prosperity, its social cohesion, and its place in the world. The neo-liberal answer to structural change in the global economy has involved business rationalisation, privatisation of state assets, increased labour market flexibility and the reduction of non-wage (i.e. welfare) costs. Social legislation has been seen as an obstacle to the free working of the market. Accelerating technological change – information technology, robotics, biotechnology – has resulted in substantial gains in productivity and in national income and wealth, but at the same time in growing unemployment, insecurity, poverty and inequality, in a social divide between those with marketable skills and the unskilled, impoverished and excluded. The provision of assistance to the unemployed has increased government expenditure whilst tax receipts have fallen, reinforcing the pressure to reduce the cost of other forms of state aid. This is the new 'realism' so effectively promoted by international organisations like the OECD, by the European Commission and the newly independent Bank of France. As the Socialists found in 1981, the financial markets can be expected to punish severely any government that steps out of line. Since then the massive and unregulated growth in the volume of largely speculative financial transactions, as the potential of information technology has been more fully realised, has reinforced this threat.

The *Etat-Providence* is thus under attack. The European social model developed after 1945, the product of a century of struggle, has three main characteristics – the substantial role of the state in economic regulation and social protection; the institutionalised representation of employees at the level of the enterprise; and collective negotiation. This post-war compromise is threatened by a coalition of conservative politicians and business interests encouraged by the weakness of the trades unions and the parties of the left. They enjoy the support of mass media owned or dependent for their advertising revenue on major conglomerates like Alcatel-Alsthom (*L'Express, Le Point*) or Bouygues, and within which a small number of journalists/media personalities play a key role in 'informing' the public. The potential for profit is enormous. Substantial tax concessions – personal and corporate – have been presented as the essential means of relaunching the economy. In the meantime the burden of taxation has been shifted more and more onto the lower paid by the increasing use of indirect taxes to raise revenue. Furthermore, privatisation has offered state assets at attractive prices. The replacement of social assistance by private assurance will also be extremely lucrative. Symbolically it represents the growing commercialisation of every aspect of life.

Is there any alternative? Put another way, is this American model one which a civilised country should want to emulate? The collective guarantees of health and security established after 1945 ought to be defended on moral grounds and in the interests of democracy, or else out of self-interest in order to limit the growth of poverty and its companions crime, social tension and conflict. There is substantial scope for the provision of socially useful employment with a decent wage in such areas as health care and education which the market will never provide. A degree of market regulation needs to be reimposed to offset the insecurity caused by commercialisation and globalisation. The experience of the Socialist government in 1981 however makes it clear that no single state can hope to resist the pressures of the market. Paradoxically, therefore, it is through the extension and strengthening of the European Union and of its social as well as economic dimensions, through the partial loss of national sovereignty within the European community, that French institutions and a national identity can be best preserved.

Although there is a broad consensus which accepts that the nation's future lies within the European Union, traditional nationalistic concerns continue to be voiced. Defence remains a contentious issue. Chirac's decision in 1995 to resume nuclear testing, and his apparent indifference to critical international reactions, is evidence of a continued determination to assert the primary interests of national sovereignty. However, the financial strains imposed by the effort to maintain an independent nuclear deterrent were clear from the inability to provide an adequate modern conventional force for the 1991 Gulf War. The ending of the Cold War will not entirely remove the nuclear threat but ought to allow for some scaling down of the deterrent forces. The revolution in defence thinking which has resulted in the phased abolition of another sacred cow – conscription – will facilitate the creation of a more mobile professional intervention force. The hesitant moves towards a European foreign and defence policy also offer hope of eventual relief. Additionally of course they symbolise the threat to cherished ideals of patriotism and national sovereignty, and it would be unwise to discount entirely the possibility of a xenophobic backlash against moves towards European union, particularly whilst there are politicians like Le Pen and Philippe de Villiers on the extreme right, Séguin amongst the neo-Gaullists, or even Chevènement on the Jacobin left, willing to appeal to the historical myths of *grandeur*. It needs to be borne in mind that only 51% of voters were willing to accept ratification of the Maastricht Treaty.

In spite of the prosperity enjoyed by most of the population, a dangerous sense of malaise currently prevails. The government is criticised continually for its inability to solve the problems of agriculture, to prevent the rise in unemployment, to cope with the financial difficulties of the welfare system, to curb the rise in crime and guard against repeated acts of terrorism – for the widespread rise in insecurity which is blamed all too often on immigrants. That these are problems shared by every European government, regardless of its political complexion, makes no difference. The perceived failure to deal with them intensifies an almost instinctive distrust of politicians' motives and competence. A growing confusion between, and corruption of, public and business life has been exposed. Too many politicians at both local and national levels, including a former defence minister (Léotard) and minister for trade and industry (Madelin), have been accused of receiving funds for personal or party use from major companies like the Générale des Eaux anxious to gain lucrative contracts. The fact that prime minister Juppé and some of his relatives were found to be living at subsidised rents in luxury flats owned by the Paris city council was certainly not illegal, but again revealed the arrogance of those in power. Such behaviour is one result of the determination of a social élite, united by social origins, wealth, and education in a small number of *grands écoles*, to preserve its privileges and, whilst attacking the recipients of welfare payments, to benefit enormously themselves from reductions in the higher rates of personal and corporate tax and extremely well rewarded employment. Of course such behaviour is hardly new, but the scale of corruption in public life, involving both conservative and socialist politicians, is disturbing. It appears to be the product of the growing cost of elections, the decentralisation measures which gave planning powers to the mayors of most communes, intense business competition for contracts and the process of *pantouflage* through which civil servants have traditionally moved into closely related private sector employment. This cosy world, made up of an élite of directors of major companies, senior civil servants and leading politicians, has been upset by the determination of examining magistrates, encouraged by the successes of their Italian colleagues, to root out corruption. In the past ministers and civil servants repeatedly intervened to protect friends and allies from prosecution. For the moment at least, the President and Minister of Justice, concerned about the impact of covering-up on public opinion, have been unable to prevent a series of damaging investigations.

The results have fuelled the public's growing contempt for politicians perceived to be corrupt and incompetent, as well as a dangerous sense of alienation from the political system with its constant internecine squabbles and the jockeying for position by leaders with presidential ambitions. Public interest in politics, measured in terms of membership of political parties or of movements like the ecologists or feminists, or of trades unions, or even by newspaper readership, has clearly declined. 31% of the electorate, and especially the young and unemployed, abstained in the 1993 general election. Intellectuals, disillusioned by the discrediting of Marxism, have deserted the left leaving it bereft of new ideas. The blurring of ideological differences and the shared liberal consensus on so many economic and social issues, together with the collapse of communism, leaves street demonstrations or support for the extreme right as the only means available to many people of protesting against a system which appears to be letting them down. Opinion polls suggest that over 30% of the electorate approve of Le Pen's views on immigration, law and order, and the defence of 'traditional values'. The June 1996 municipal elections left the three southern towns of Toulon, Marignane and Orange under National Front control, whilst Le Pen himself gained a record 15% in the first round of the presidential elections on a populist and clearly discriminatory platform of 'national preference' which promised to give priority in housing, employment and welfare to 'nationals', ignoring the citizenship rights of the great majority of Muslims and calling for the repatriation of three million immigrants. At a time when the younger generations of French Muslims are increasingly vociferous as a result of high unemployment and the tense situation in Algeria, the widespread rejection of multiculturalism and the demand for the assimilation of Muslims into the French 'mainstream' through the secular education system seem likely to exacerbate ethnic tensions.

In spite of these serious problems it seems probable that the system of presidential government built upon the ruins of the Fourth Republic will survive and with it the basic commitment to 'republican order', to a liberal-democratic political structure, and a fundamentally capitalistic, market-oriented economic system. Short of a major international crisis, and there are potential causes aplenty, it seems likely that the French economy will continue to adapt to the opportunities and challenges of both the single European market and wider globalisation. This certainly will not be without difficulty in intensely competitive markets. Nevertheless, most of the population seem destined to enjoy growing prosperity. They will retain a strong sense of national identity within the European Union, reminded of the political and cultural achievements of the past as well as those of the Mitterrand presidency by such massive projects as the renovation of the Louvre and Tuileries palaces and the construction of the Opéra de la Bastille, the Grande Arche and the new Bibliothèque nationale. There remains considerable potential for internal conflict over unequal access to political power, to educational and employment opportunities, and to wealth, whilst the hideous tensions caused by racial and cultural differences retain their potency. Every social system is subject to stress which might be intensified by unpredictable pressures. Suffice it to conclude that France is at least well prepared to meet the unpredictable.

A SHORT GUIDE TO FURTHER READING

Unless stated the place of publication is either London or Paris.

GENERAL

Asselain, J.-C., *Histoire économique de la France du XVIIIe siècle à nos jours*, 2 vols. 1984.
Bergeron, L., *Paris. Genèse d'un paysage.* 1989.
Braudel, F., *L'identité de la France.* 3 vols. 1986.
Braudel, F. and Labrousse, E., *Histoire économique et sociale de la France.* 4 vols. 1970–79.
Clout, H. D. (ed.), *Themes in the historical geography of France.* 1977.
Duby, G. (ed.), *Histoire de la France urbaine.* 5 vols. 1976.
Duby, G. and Wallon, A. (eds.), *Histoire de la France rurale.* 4 vols. 1976.
Dupâquier, J. (ed.), *Histoire de la population française.* 4 vols. 1988.
Gildea, R., *The past in French history.* 1994.
Harouel, J.-L. et al., *Histoire des institutions de l'époque franque à la Révolution.* 1987.
Jones, C., *The Cambridge illustrated history of France.* Cambridge 1994.
Le Goff, J. (ed.), *L'état et les pouvoirs.* 1989.
Lequin, Y., *Histoire des français. XIX–XXe siècles.* 3 vols. 1984.
McMillan, J., *Twentieth century France: Politics and society 1898–1991.* 1992.
Moulin, A., *Peasantry and society in France since 1789.* 1991.
Planhol, X. de, *An historical geography of France.* Cambridge 1994.
Price, R., *An economic history of modern France, c. 1730–1914.* 1981.
Revel, J. (ed.), *L'espace français.* 1989.
Rosanvallon, P., *L'état en France de 1789 à nos jours.* 1993.
Tilly, C., *The contentious French: four centuries of popular struggle.* 1986.
Zeldin, T., *France 1848–1945.* 2 vols. Oxford 1972–77.

Readers of English might also usefully refer to the following journals: *French History. French Historical Studies*, and *Modern and Contemporary France.*

THE MIDDLE AGES

Allmand, C., *The Hundred Years War.* 1987.

Allmand, C. (ed.), *Power, culture and religion, c.1350–c.1550.* 1989.

Baldwin, J.W., *The government of Philip Augustus. Foundations of French royal power in the middle ages.* 1986.

Cazelles, R., *Société politique, noblesse et couronne sous Jean le bon et Charles V.* Geneva 1982.

Derville, A., *L'économie française au moyen âge.* 1995.

Duby, G., *France in the middle ages 987–1460.* 1991.

Dunbabin, J., *France in the making 843–1180.* 1985.

Hallam, E. H., *Capetian France.* 1980.

James, E., *The origins of France, from Clovis to the Capetians, 500–1000.* 1982.

Kaeuper, R. W., *War, justice and public order: England and France in the later middle ages.* 1988.

Le Goff, J., *Medieval civilization.* 1988.

Le Goff, J., *Saint Louis.* 1996.

Lemarignier, J.-F., *Le gouvernement royal aux premiers temps capétiens (987–1108).* 1965.

Lemarignier, J.-F., *La France médiévale. Institutions et société.* 1970.

Lewis, P., *France at the end of the middle ages.* 1968.

Mollat, M., *Gènese médiévale de la France moderne.* 1970.

Rials, S. (ed.), *Le miracle capétien, 987–1789.* 1987.

Werner, K. F., *Les origines (avant l'an mil).* 1984.

EARLY MODERN FRANCE

Baker, K., *The political culture of the old regime.* 1987.

Barret-Kriegel, F., *Les chemins de l'état.* 1986.

Behrens, B., *The ancien regime.* 1967.

Beik, W., *Absolutism and society in seventeenth-century France. State, power, and provincial aristocracy in Langeudoc.* 1985.

Bergin, J., *The rise of Richelieu.* 1991.

Bluche, F., *Louis XIV.* 1990.

Bonney, R., *The king's debts. Finance and politics in France, 1598–1661.* 1981.

Bonney, R., *Society and government in France under Richelieu and Mazarin, 1624–61.* 1988.

Bosher, J., *French finances, 1770–95. From business to bureaucracy.* 1970.

Briggs, R. M., *Communities of belief: cultural and social tensions in early modern France.* 1988.

Campbell, P. R., *The ancien regime in France.* 1988.

Chaussinand-Nogaret, G., *Une histoire des élites.* 1975.

Collins, J., *The state in early modern France.* Cambridge 1995.

Davis, N. Z., *Society and culture in early modern France.* 1965.

Dessert, D., *Argent, pouvoir et société au Grand Siècle.* 1984

Egret, J., *Louis XV et l'opposition parlementaire. 1715–74.* 1970.

Goubert, P., *L'ancien régime.* 2 vols. 1969–70.

Goubert, P. and Roche, D., *Les français et l'ancien régime.* 2 vols. 1984.

Greengrass, M., *France in the age of Henri IV: the struggle for stability.* 1995.

Gruder, V. R., *The royal provincial intendants. A governing elite in eighteenth-century France.* 1978.

Hardman, J., *French politics, 1774–89.* 1995.

Hayden, J. M., *France and the Estates General of 1614.* 1974.

Hickey, D., *The coming of French absolutism. The struggle for tax reform in the province of Dauphiné, 1540–1640.* 1986.

Holt, M. P., *The French wars of religion, 1562–1629.* Cambridge 1995.

Hufton, O., *The poor in eighteenth-century France.* Oxford 1974.

Kaplan, S. L., *Bread and political economy in the reign of Louis XV.* 2 vols. The Hague 1976.

Knecht, R., *Francis I.* 1982.

Knecht, R., *The French wars of religion, 1559–98.* 1989.

Le Roy Ladurie, E., *The royal French state, 1460–1610.* Oxford 1994.

Le Roy Ladurie, E., *L'ancien régime. 1987.*

Lloyd, H. A., *The state, France and the sixteenth century.* 1983.

Major, R., *From Renaissance monarchy to absolute monarchy.* 1995.

Mandrou, R., *Introduction à la France moderne, Essai de psychologie historique. 1500–1640.* 1961.

Mettam, R., *Power and faction in Louis XIV's France.* 1988.

Parker, D., *Class and state in ancien régime France.* 1996.

Potter, D., *War and government in the French provinces: Picardy, 1470–1560.* Cambridge 1993.

Ranum, O., *The Fronde, a French revolution, 1648–52.* 1993.

Riley, J. C., *The Seven Years War and the old regime in France.* 1986.

Roche, D., *La France des lumières.* 1995.

Shennan, J., *Louis XIV.* 1986.

Stone, B., *The French parlements and the crisis of the old regime.* N. Carolina 1989.

Sutherland, N. M., *Princes, politics, and religion, 1547–89,* 1984.

REVOLUTIONARY AND NAPOLEONIC FRANCE

Bergeron, L., *France under Napoleon.* Cambridge 1981.

Berthaud, J.-P., *The army of the French Revolution: from citizen soldiers to instruments of power.* 1988.

Berthaud, J.-P., *Le Consulat et l'Empire, 1799–1815.* 1988.

Cobb, R. C., *The police and the people.* Oxford 1970.

Blanning, T. C. W., *The origins of the French revolutionary wars*. 1986.

Doyle, W., *The origins of the French Revolution*. Oxford 1988.

Doyle, W., *The Oxford history of the French Revolution*. 1989.

Dupuy, R. (ed.), *Les resistances à la Révolution*. 1987.

Egret, J., *La pré-révolution française (1787–88)*. 1962.

Forrest, A., *Conscripts and deserters. The army and French society during the Revolution and Empire*. 1989.

Forrest, A., *The Revolution in provincial France: Aquitaine, 1789–99*. Oxford 1996.

Furet, F., *Revolutionary France, 1770–1880*. Oxford 1992.

Godechot, J., *Les institutions de la France sous la Révolution et l'Empire*. 3rd edn, 1985.

Jones, P. M., *The peasantry in the French Revolution*. 1988.

Jones, P. M., *Reform and revolution in France. The politics of transition, 1774–91*. Cambridge 1996.

Lefebvre, G., *The coming of the French Revolution*. 1947.

Lewis, G., *The French Revolution. Rethinking the debate*. 1993.

Lewis, G. and Lucas, C. (eds.), *Beyond the Terror. Essays in French regional and social history*. 1983.

Lucas, C. (ed.), *The political culture of the French Revolution*. 1988.

Lyons, M., *Napoleon Bonaparte and the legacy of the French Revolution*. 1994.

Sutherland, D., *France 1789–1815. Revolution and counter-revolution*. 1985.

Tulard, J., *Napoleon. The myth of the saviour*. 1984.

Vovelle, M., *The fall of the French monarchy*. 1984.

Woloch, I., *The new regime. Transformation of the French civic order, 1789–1820*. 1994.

THE NINETEENTH CENTURY

Agulhon, M., *The republican experiment, 1848–52*. Cambridge 1983.

Agulhon, M., *La République 1882–1987*. 1988.

Anderson, R., *France 1870–1914*. 1977.

Audoin-Rouzeau, S., 1870. *La France dans la guerre*. 1989.

Becker, J.-J. and Audoin-Rouzeau, S., *La France, la nation, la guerre; 1850–1920*. 1996.

Caron, F., *La France des patriotes de 1851 à 1918*. 1985.

Charle, C., *A social history of France in the nineteenth century*. Oxford 1994.

Clout, H., *The land of France 1815–1914*. 1983.

Collingham, H. A. C., *The July Monarchy 1830–48*. 1988.

Edwards, S., *The Paris Commune*. 1971.

Fortesque, W., *Revolution and counter-revolution in France 1815–52*. 1988.

Girard, L., *Napoléon III*. 1986.

Jardin, A. and Tudesq, A. J., *Restoration and reaction 1815–48*. Cambridge 1983.

Magraw, R., *France 1815–1914. The bourgeois century*. 1983.

Mayeur, A. J. and Réberioux, M., *The Third Republic from its origins to the Great War 1871–1914*. Cambridge 1982.
McMillan, J. F., *Napoleon III*. 1990.
McPhee, P., *A social history of France 1780–1880*. 1992.
Merriman, J. (ed.), *French cities in the nineteenth century*. 1982.
Pilbeam, P., *The French Revolution of 1830*. 1991.
Pinkney, D., *La Révolution de 1830 en France*. 1988.
Plessis, A., *The rise and fall of the Second Empire*. Cambridge 1983.
Price, R., *The French Second Republic. A social history*. 1972.
Price, R., *The modernization of rural France*. 1983.
Price, R., *A social history of nineteenth-century France*. 1987.
Price, R., *Napoléon III and the Second Empire*. 1997.
Smith, W. H. C., *Second Empire and Commune*. 1985.
Tombs, R., *France 1814–1914*. 1996
Weber, E., *Peasants into Frenchmen*. 1977.

A TIME OF CRISIS, 1914–45

Adamthwaite, A., *Grandeur and misery: France's bid for power in Europe, 1914–40*. 1995.
Azéma, J.-P., *From Munich to the Liberation, 1938–44*. Cambridge 1988.
Azéma, J. P., *1940, l'année terrible*. 1990.
Azéma, J.-P. and Bédarida, F. (eds.), *La France des années noires*. 2 vols. 1993.
Becker, J.-J., *The Great War and the French people*. 1985.
Becker, J.-J., *La France en guerre 1914–18*. 1988.
Bernard, P. and Dubief, H., *The decline of the Third Republic*. Cambridge 1988.
Bernstein, S., *La France des années 30*. 1988.
Burrin, P., *Living with defeat. France under the German occupation 1940–44*. 1996.
Crémieux-Brilhac, J.-F., *Les français de l'an 40*. 2 vols. 1990.
Durand, Y., *La France dans la 2e guerre mondiale*. 1989.
Dreyfus, F.-G., *Histoire de Vichy*. 1990.
Jackson, J., *The Popular Front in France*. 1988.
Kedward, H. R., *Occupied France. Collaboration and resistance 1940–44*. 1985.
Laborie, P., *L'opinion française sous Vichy*. 1990.
Mayeur, J.-M., *La vie politique sous la 3e République. 1870–1940*. 1984.
Paxton, R. O., *Vichy France*. 1972.
Vinen, R., *France, 1934–70*. 1996.

RECONSTRUCTION AND RENEWAL, 1945–97

Becker, J.-J., *Histoire politique de la France depuis 1945*. 1988.
Bernstein, S., *The Republic of de Gaulle*. 1994.

Birnbaum, N., *Les sommets de l'état. Essai sur l'élite du pouvoir en France.* 1977.

Bloch-Lainé, F. and Bouvier, J., *La France restaurée 1944–54.* 1986.

Borne, D., *Histoire de la société française depuis 1945.* 1988.

Chapsal, J., *La vie politique sous la Ve République.* 1984.

Cole, A., *François Mitterrand: a study in political leadership.* 1994.

Eck, J.-F., *Histoire de l'économie française depuis 1945.* 1988.

Favier, P. and Roland, M., *La décennie Mitterrand: les ruptures (1981–84).* 1990.

Gildea, R., *France since 1945.* Oxford 1996.

Giles, F., *The locust years: the story of the Fourth French Republic.* 1991.

Jackson, J., *Charles de Gaulle.* 1990.

Lacouture, J., *De Gaulle.* 3 vols. 1984–86.

Larkin, M., *France since the Popular Front.* 1988.

Mendras, H. and Cole, A., *Social change in modern France: towards a cultural anthropology of the Fifth Republic.* Cambridge 1991.

Pinchemel, P., *France. A geographical, social and economic survey.* 1987.

Shennan, A., *Rethinking France.* 1989.

Tuppen, J., *France under recession.* 1988.

Tuppen, J., *Chirac's France, 1986–88.* 1991.

Rioux, J.-P., *The Fourth Republic, 1944–58.* Cambridge 1987.

Wright, V. *The government and politics of France.* 3rd edn 1992.

INDEX